Hypnotic Alteration of
Sensory, Perceptual and
Psychophysiological Processes

Milton H. Erickson, MD
(1901–1980)

Ernest L. Rossi, PhD

Hypnotic Alteration of Sensory, Perceptual and Psychophysiological Processes

by MILTON H. ERICKSON

The Collected Papers of
Milton H. Erickson on Hypnosis
Volume II

Edited by Ernest L. Rossi

IRVINGTON PUBLISHERS, INC., New York

Library of Congress Cataloging in Publication Data

Erickson, Milton H.
Hypnotic alteration of sensory, perceptual, and
psychophysiological processes

(The collected papers of Milton H. Erickson on
hypnosis; v. 2)
Bibliography: p.
1. Hypnotism. 2. Perception. 3. Hypnotism—
Physiological effect. 4. Hypnotism—Research.
I. Rossi, Ernest Lawrence. II. Title.
RC495.E714 vol. 2.   616.8′916′208s   [616.8′916′208]
ISBN 0-8290-0543-9   79-15940

Printed in the United States of America

Foreword

This series of Milton Erickson's papers contains a fascinating array of original contributions related to every phase of hypnotic theory and practice. The papers contain stores of invaluable data that can be productively mined by researchers and clinicians for treasures useful in hypothetical structuring and experiment, as well as catalyzing psychotherapy. Dr. Erickson is perhaps the most creative and imaginative contemporary worker in the area of hypnosis and his inspired writings in this series rank among the enduring classics in the field.

Lewis R. Wolberg, M.D.
Clinical Professor of Psychiatry,
New York University School of Medicine

Emeritus Dean, Postgraduate Center
for Mental Health

Acknowledgments

The Editor wishes to acknowledge the assistance and suggestions of many colleagues and members of the American Society of Clinical Hypnosis in the preparation of these volumes. In particular: Marian Moore, Robert Pearson, Florence Sharp, and Andre Weitzenhoffer. Significant editorial and organizational skills have been contributed by Margaret Ryan.

The following journals and publishers have generously permitted the republication of papers in these volumes:

American Journal of Clinical Hypnosis, American Journal of Psychiatry, American Medical Association, American Psychiatric Association, American Psychological Association, Appleton-Century-Crofts, *Archives of Neurology and Psychiatry, British Journal of Medical Psychology, Bulletin of the Georgetown University Medical Center, Diseases of the Nervous System,* Encyclopedia Britannica, Family Process, Harper and Row, Paul B. Hoeber, Inc., *Journal of Abnormal and Social Psychology, Journal of Clinical and Experimental Hypnosis, Journal of Experimental Psychology, Journal of General Psychology, Journal of Genetic Psychology, Journal of Nervous and Mental Disease, Journal of the American Society of Psychosomatic Dentistry and Medicine,* Journal Press, Julian Press, Macmillan Company, Medical Clinics of North America, Merck, Sharp and Dohme, *Perceptual and Motor Skills,* Physicians Postgraduate Press, *Psychiatry, Psychoanalytic Quarterly, Psychosomatic Medicine,* W. B. Saunders Company, Springer Verlag, William Alanson White Psychiatric Foundation, Williams and Wilkins, and Woodrow Press.

Contents

Editor's Preface

These four volumes of Milton H. Erickson's selected papers have been collected for clinicians and researchers who wish to explore in depth the work of one of the most seminal minds in the history of hypnosis and psychotherapy. When Erickson began publishing his studies in the early 1930s, hypnosis was in a curious position: most investigators agreed that hypnosis had played a central role in the early studies of psychopathology and our first efforts at psychotherapy, but the authoritative approaches associated with its use were supplanted on the one hand by the seemingly more sophisticated approaches of the psychoanalytic schools, and on the other hand by experimental psychology.

The situation might have continued in just this manner, with hypnosis regarded as nothing more significant than a colorful curiosity in our therapeutic past. Into this situation, however, came the accident that was Milton H. Erickson. He was an accident of nature born with a number of congenital sensory-perceptual problems that led him to experience the world in ways so different that his acute mind could survive only by realizing at a very early age the relativity of our human frames of reference. To these early problems was added the rare medical tragedy of being stricken by two different strains of polio at the ages of 17 and 51. His efforts to rehabilitate himself led to a personal rediscovery of many classical hypnotic phenomena and how they could be utilized therapeutically.

Erickson's experimental and therapeutic explorations with the hypnotic modality span more than 50 years. His successful rejuvenation of the entire field may be attributed to his development of the nonauthoritarian, indirect approaches to suggestion wherein subjects learn how to experience hypnotic phenomena and how to utilize their own potentials to solve problems in their own way. The contents of these five volumes can be best understood as working papers on a journey of discovery. There is little that is fixed, final, or permanently validated about them. Most of these papers are heuristics that can stimulate the mind of the reader and evoke the awe of discovery, the potentials for which are unlimited in the dimension of human consciousness.

The problem of how to present these papers in the best order could have been solved in many ways. A simple chronological order seemed unsatisfactory because the record of much of Erickson's earliest work was published only at a later date. Many papers dealing with the same theme which should obviously be grouped together were published in different phases of his career. Because of this the editor decided to make a balanced presentation wherein each volume identifies a major area of exploration with appropriate sections wherein the papers are presented in an approximation of chronological order.

Each of the first four volumes of this series contains a number of unpublished papers selected by the editor from several boxes of manuscripts entrusted to him by Erickson for this purpose. A companion volume, in preparation, will contain only previously unpublished lectures and hypnotic demonstrations by Erickson throughout his career. Many of these exist in various forms of neglect and deterioration all over the world wherever he gave his numerous presentations. The editor is currently assembling as many of these as can be accurately transcribed and reviewing them with Erickson for his elucidating commentaries. So subtle are his approaches that even a detailed study of his demonstrations often leaves the investigator without a full understanding of what Erickson is doing. Because of this the editor would like to take the occasion of the publication of these four volumes to make an appeal to whomever is in possession of previously unpublished records of Erickson's work to make them available to us for possible inclusion in this companion volume. It is only through such cooperation that we can all grow together.

Ernest L. Rossi

I. Visual Processes

The experimental studies of this volume constitute some of Erickson's most careful and incisive work in hypnotic research. So subtle and numerous are the problems in this area that it is difficult for different investigators to replicate each other's work. The first two papers of this section are examples of this. The first paper, "The hypnotic induction of hallucinatory color vision followed by pseudonegative afterimages," introduces an ingenious experimental paradigm whereby Erickson is able to explore the genuineness of hallucinatory color vision. Hibler's failure to replicate these findings is then discussed in the second paper as a "demonstration of how misleading and unreliable experimental results can be when their results are based upon the completion of an experimental procedure without due regard or provision for the nature and character of the phenomena under investigation . . . ." Erickson belives that much of the failure of replication in experimental work is due to the superficial and inadequate trance states that many investigators are willing to use.

In experimental work extra care must be given to the character of the hypnotic state. Erickson typically gave his subjects an average of eight hours of trance training and carefully assessed the genuineness of their hypnotic responsiveness by evoking varieties of deep hypnotic phenomena, ranging from stuporous states to somnambulism. In addition, he was always careful to permit his experimental subjects to deepen their trance for at least 15 to 30 minutes before undertaking any serious experimental work. He found empirically that this amount of time was required even by the best trained hypnotic subjects before they could undergo the requisite neuro- and psychophysiological changes for deep trance phenomena to become manifest. A more rapid induction of trance could lead to compliance by well-trained subjects that gave the appearance of deep trance experience, but such trances invariably had an admixture of conscious intentionality along with the more genuine, hypnotic manifestations of involuntary and autonomous behavior.

The importance of indirect suggestion and hypnotic amnesia for associations relevant to the behavior being investigated is also made startlingly clear by these papers. Direct suggestions frequently give the subject in deep trance an impossible task. As Erickson describes it in his next paper, "The induction of color blindness by a technique of hypnotic suggestion," if we directly tell the subject *what to see* and *what not to see*, it paradoxically implies that *all must be seen.* It requires that *seeing all* must be present on some level, and this could interfere with the phenomena of *not seeing* under investigation.

A careful study and "reading between the lines" of many of Erickson's papers reveals his preoccupation with the problem of differentiating between genuine hypnotic phenomena and the hypnotic subject's wish to please the investigator. In the next paper of this section, "An experimental investigation of the hypnotic subject's apparent ability to become unaware of stimuli," he states, "Indeed, it is axiomatic that subjects in an experimental situation in which they know what is expected of them tend to behave in accord with the experimental demands." Because of this he turns in this paper and in much of his research thereafter to the "naturalistic," or what has been called "field observations," method for an unobtrusive exploration of hypnotic phenomena instead of the traditionally open experimental laboratory approach, wherein the subject might sense the object of investigation and then voluntarily attempt to help the experimenter obtain certain results. It wasn't until a generation later that these biases of the experimental situation became generally known and appreciated as a popular issue by many psychological investigators.

This naturalistic approach is continued in the next paper, "The development of an acute obsessional hysterical state in a normal hypnotic subject," where Erickson presents a remarkably clear demonstration of the incredibly arduous and complex demands that may be placed upon the investigator who hopes to facilitate the experience of complex hypnotic phenomena. This paper presents a paradigm for hypnotic work that allows time for the successive development of *a deep trance state,* a *stuporous trance state,* and finally a *somnambulistic state.* Only in this and one earlier paper (see the first paper of the next section on hypnotic deafness) does he describe how they are related and the suggestions he uses to build them up step by step. This is followed by a further description of at least nine stage in the progressive presentation of suggestions that make it possible to experience a phenomenon as complex as hypnotic blindness. Even with these elaborate preparations, however, his overeager subjects fail to experiece hypnotic blindness on their first trials.

Most investigators would call their efforts to an end at this point and fall back on the cliché that most subjects really cannot experience such complex hypnotic phenomena. Many researchers and most texts on hypnosis declare it as a basic fact that only a small proportion of the general public (16 to 20 percent) can experience deep hypnotic phenomena. But this is a basic fact only for those who make relatively superficial efforts at the induction of hypnosis and usually offer only a standardized and narrow range of direct suggestions. To the best of this editor's knowledge, there is no one other than Erickson in the entire history of hypnosis who has made such extensive efforts to understand an individual subject's own frames of reference and particular motivations and then ingeniously utilize these to facilitate profound hypnotic experiences. The eventual, startling, frightening success of Erickson's subject in her experience of hypnotic blindness reveals the type of highly personal psychodynamics that may be involved in this work. Most subjects certainly would not want to undergo such a painful experience, and most investigators probably lack the perspicacity and persistence to facilitate it. The fact that it *can* be done, however, is very important for our understanding of hypnosis as well as our understanding of psychodynamics in general. (See Volume 3 of this series for Erickson's demonstrations of psychodynamics.)

The approaches carefully described in this paper can serve as a model and inspiration for other workers, particularly younger workers in our field. All of us can expect much failure as we struggle to develop the understanding and skills required. Erickson had about 30 years of extensive personal and professional experience with hypnosis as a background for his work in this paper. As we continue to learn more about the particulars of facilitating altered states and deep trance phenomena, however, we can certainly expect that a shorter training period will be required. We can expect that such training will lead to a new generation of clinicians and researchers with more heightened sensitivity and performance skills in the realm of human communication and relating.

1. The Hypnotic Induction of Hallucinatory Color Vision Followed by Pseudonegative Afterimages

Milton H. Erickson and Elizabeth M. Erickson

Previous experimentation on the induction by hypnosis of various hallucinatory phenomena suggested the possibility of inducing hallucinatory color vision. Accordingly, an experiment was devised involving the hallucination of the colors red, green, yellow, and blue in response to direct hypnotic suggestion, followed by the spontaneous hallucination by the subjects of the complement of each of these colors in a fashion comparable to the development of negative after-images.

The experiment was conducted on five university freshmen, selected from among commerce and engineering students, all of whom had been used repeatedly for hypnotic work but not in connection with the hallucination of colors. In addition, they had been trained over a long period of time to develop exceedingly deep hypnotic trances, and for this experiment from 30-45 minutes of continuous suggestion was given after a trance had been induced to insure a consistently profound hypnotic trance.

PROCEDURE

The procedure employed was comprised of the following steps:

1. The administration in the waking state of a word association test containing a hundred words, among which were "red," "green," "yellow," "blue," and "bright."

2. The induction of a profound somnambulistic trance and the administration of a second word association test, also containing a hundred words, some of which were common to the first list, and among which in a different order were the same critical words.

3. The giving of the following instructions while the subject continued in the deep hypnotic trance:

Reprinted with permission from *Journal of Experimental Psychology*, 1938, 22, 581-588.

> I am going to show you, one at a time, sheets of colored paper. Each sheet is entirely of one solid color, and this color will be very bright. All of the sheets will be colored, but no two successive sheets will be of the same color. I will name the color of the first sheet, and you will name the color of the next sheet, and we will continue in this alternate fashion. As I name the color of the first sheet, you will look at it carefully until you see it plainly and clearly, just exactly as I have described it. Nod your head as soon as you see it plainly, and I will then put it out of sight in the left-hand drawer of the desk and take a new one from the right-hand drawer. As I show you this next sheet, you are to look at it carefully and tell me what color it is. It, too, will be of a single bright color, but a color different from the one I named. After you have named the color of your sheet, it will then be my turn to name the color of the next sheet; then your turn will come.

These instructions were repeated several times to insure full comprehension.

4. The exhibition, one at a time, of 16 sheets of plain white typing paper. Of these, eight alternate sheets were described by the experimenter in the following order as "red," "yellow," "green," "blue," "green," "yellow," "red," and "blue," the adjective "bright" being added each time, while the subject was called upon to identify the eight intervening sheets as of some one bright color other than that just named by the experimenter.

5. The exhibition, as a control measure against the development of strong associative values between the complementary colors, of brightly hued red, yellow, blue, and green sheets of paper. These sheets were presented in pairs, with each color paired with itself and with each of the other three colors, making a total of 16 pairings exhibited in random order. As these pairs were presented, the subject named the colors aloud.

6. The repetition of Step 4 followed by questioning of the subjects concerning the color intensity of the various sheets. Such questioning had been avoided previously because of the possible effect of suggestion.

7. The administration of the first word-association test while the subject was still in the trance state.

8. The administration of the second word-association test after awakening the subject.

9. Questioning concerning the definition of complementary colors, and the hazarding of guesses by the subjects when the definition of complementary colors had been given by the experimenter.

RESULTS

1. The preliminary word-association test disclosed no direct association of the various color with their complements.

2. The exhibition for about one or two minutes each of the eight alternate sheets of white paper disclosed four of the five subjects as being fully capable of "hallucinating" in every instance the color specified by the experimenter. The fifth subject invariably saw only a white sheet of paper. Extensive hypnotic suggestion did not alter this behavior. Nevertheless, the entire experiment was performed on this subject.

3. The four subjects who hallucinated the specified color invariably declared the succeeding sheet to be of the appropriate complementary color. There were no failures, except those of the fifth subject.

4. The name of the control pairs of colored-sheets was done correctly by all five subjects.

5. The repetition of the experimental procedure yielded results identical with those first obtained.

6. Questioning of the subjects concerning the color intensity of the various sheets exhibited to them elicited the information that the sheets described by the experimenter were brightly hued but that the sheets described by them were "softer," "duller" and "nowhere near so bright."

7. The word-association test immediately after the experimental procedure, with the subjects in the trance state, yielded a total of nine instances of color associations: red-brown; red-pink; yellow-orange; yellow-tan; yellow-green; blue-red; blue-purplish; yellow-blue; red-green. One of the two associations of complementary colors was given by the fifth subject.

8. The word-association test given after awakening the subjects yielded only two color associations, neither of which was of complementary colors.

9. The post-experimental questioning of the subjects disclosed them to be unable to define or to name complementary colors when asked directly. When a definition had been given them and they were asked to hazard guesses, their tendency was to contrast light and dark colors, such as pink and brown.

To sum up: Of the five hypnotized subjects employed, one failed completely to meet the test situation. The remaining four, in response to appropriate hypnotic suggestions, hallucinated as red, blue, green, or yellow the alternate sheets of white paper exhibited to them and invariably described the intervening white sheets as of the complementary color appropriate to the hallucinated color of the preceding sheet. The results obtained from the control procedures indicate clearly that the experimental findings derived directly from the procedure employed.

COMMENT

The general limitations of these findings coupled with the present inadequate understanding of color vision preclude any attempt at a theoretical elaboration of the results in relation to color vision and limit discussion to tentative suggestion of the processes by which these may have been achieved.

An immediate consideration is that of the role of the hypnosis employed. Although the hypnotic state constituted an integral part of the procedure, its role may safely be described as only one of providing a setting favorable to the performance of the experiment. Unquestionably, the experiment could be repeated in the waking state, but probably with less ease and effectiveness. Hence, in any analysis of the results, the question of hypnosis as such may properly be disregarded.

The next question concerns the character of the stimuli given to the subject. Obviously, the retinal stimulation by white paper did not enter directly into the situation except as a part of the experimental setting, although indirectly it may have had definite, though remote, significance. As for color stimuli, these were wholly auditory in character and were so given as to derive any significance entirely from the subject's experiential past. Hence, a definite statement may be made that the responses elicited arose primarily from activity of central processes, and that the entire problem thus becomes essentially one of central, rather than peripheral, processes and activities.

Two possible interpretations of the findings may be suggested. The first of these refers to purely psychological or associational processes. The experiencing of a color is ordinarily succeeded by a negative after-image. In consequence of this sequence of psychophysiological processes, there is established a direct association between their experiential aspects. Hence, stimuli serving to arouse directly the experintial values of a color would presumably serve to a somewhat lesser extent to arouse the experiential values of the associated negative after-image.

Since no actual color stimuli were given, and since each of the four subjects who entered into the experimental situation showed no failures for any of the 16 test instances, the assumption may be warranted that there is a direct associational bond between the experiential values of a color and its complement sufficiently strong to permit its evocation by purely psychological stimuli.

While this explanation constitutes a possible interpretation of the experimental findings, it is unquestionably far too simple. A second interpretation may be suggested: The inadequancies of our present understanding of color vision preclude more than a statement of possible factors.

First is the effect of the instruction to *see*. This instruction in itself, even if the subject had his eyes closed, would constitute an actual stimulus serving to arouse into activity various psychophysiological processes preliminary to vision and upon which visual activity could be based. But since the subjects actually did receive visual stimulation, though neutral in character so far as color vision was concerned, there was some actual visual activity, with a consequent augmentation of the psychophysiological processes involved in vision previously aroused by the nature of the situation.

The suggestion to see a specific color would serve to establish a certain "mental set," leading to the various preliminary psychophysiological processes upon which could be based the initition of the actual activity of color vision, and which would be derived from the psychophysiological activities based upon past learning. Thus, the specifying of a definite color, while constituting a purely psychological stimulus, would stimulate various mental processes intimately related to the psychophysiological activity of vision already in progress, and these, in turn, would serve to reinforce each other.

Additionally, the naming of a specific color would stimulate into activity various mental processes related to the experiential values of the chosen color, and these processes would also serve to augment the activity of the other processes already aroused.

Hence, although no visual color stimulus had been given, there would be active various psychophysiological and experimental processes, all of which would be intimately associated with each other and ordinarily contingent upon color stimulation of a particular character.

The character of the suggestions to see the specified color was also such as to create a state of tension in the subject compelling a response but limiting the possibility of a response strictly to the subject's own concept of color. Therefore, his response could derive only from his own experiential associations and learned activities. From this state of tension, with its limitations, there could derive a process of control and direction of the various psychophysiological processes in activity leading to the color-vision response normally contingent upon such processes.

Thus, in place of an actual color stimulus, there would be the interaction of these various processes, each serving to initiate further and more complete activity comparable to that of the actual processes of color vision, with the entire process culminating in an actual psychological response of color, the validity of which was clearly indicated by the ensuing subjective response of the complementary color.

When the subjects had made their response to the various psychophysiological processes aroused in them by the presentation of the stimulus sheet described as colored by the experimenter, there followed the withdrawal of this sheet and the presentation of a second sheet which they were to describe as colored. This withdrawal and replacement of sheets constituted an actual stimulus for the cessation of the psychophysiological activity in progress, thereby initiating directly the readjustive activities consequent upon the cessation of psycho- and neurophysiological activity. Since the subjects invariably described the second sheet of each pair as of the correct complementary color, the assumption is warranted that readjustive processes and activities did occur and that these corresponded in character and degree to those consequent upon actual color vision, and were sufficiently diverse and strong as to permit a subjective response comparable to that deriving from a negative afterimage.

CONCLUSION

Emphasis must be placed entirely upon the factual findings rather than upon the attempted interpretations. The essential consideration of the experiment is that the hallucination of various colors was sufficiently valid subjectively to permit a spontaneous and invariable hallucination of complementary colors in the form of negative afterimages.

Unquestionably, associational and neuro- and psychophysiological processes entered into the production of the phenomena, but not necessarily as has been suggested. Further development of the understanding of color vision is requisite for any adequate interpretation of the experimental findings; hence their significance must be restricted to their evidential values in relation to the importance of cortical processes in color vision.

2. Discussion: Critical Comments On Hibler's Presentation Of His Work On Negative Afterimages Of Hypnotically Induced Hallucinated Colors

Elizabeth M. Erickson

In the June 1938 issue of this Journal Erickson and Erickson (1938) presented experimental findings demonstrating that, by use of an adequate hypnotic technique, subjects could hallucinate colors which were invariably followed by the appropriate negative afterimage. These subjects were shown to be naive concerning the theory and nature of afterimages by both word-association tests and extensive questioning.

In the July 1940 issue of this Journal Francis W. Hibler (1940) reports similarly directed work which purports to contradict the work of Erickson and Erickson, and submits the following theoretical position: "Since hallucinated colors definitely do not have the properties of actual colors, and since no evidence of the existence of the hallucination was discovered except a mere verbal agreement with the hypnotizer, hypnotic hallucinations are probably verbal in nature rather than sensory or a function of the central nervous system."

It is the purpose of this paper to demonstrate that Hibler's negative results derived not from the inability of a hypnotic subject to obtain true hallucinations meeting every subjective criterion of reality, but rather, from the inadequate hypnotic technique that was employed; that Hibler's results can be dismissed as complaisant cooperation on the part of inadequately hypnotized, inadequately instructed subjects, sophisticated as to the subject matter of the experiments; that the findings of Erickson and Erickson's earlier experiment as to the validity of the hallucinations and the spontaneity of the negative afterimages have not been contradicted; and that Hibler's work does not constitute an experimental checking of their findings.

The first criticism to be made of Hibler's experiment concerns his selection of subjects. Of four subjects, three were sophisticated concerning afterimages; the fourth had faulty knowledge, believing that in the experimental setup for

Reprinted with permission from the *Journal of Experimental Psychology*, August, 1941, *29,164-170.*

negative afterimages, positive ones would appear. As will be shown later, such sophistication on the part of the subjects seriously militates against the reliability of the experimental results and precludes their adequate evaluation.

The second general criticism which may be made is that Hibler invoked his hypnotic trances too rapidly, although he notes that Erickson suggests a trance induction of at least 15 to 30 minutes. Hibler admits that the "exact importance of the time element is certainly worthy of further research"; yet he spent only a total of eight minutes, five in verbal trance suggestion, three in which the subject simply waited, in order to induce his hypnotic trance. In this short time he proposed to produce sufficiently profound dissociation to permit such difficult phenomena as valid visual hallucinations and possible neuro- and psychophysiological changes; and, in such a trace, to test accurately the ability of the subject to demonstrate these phenomena. My co-worker, in his extensive experience as evidenced in work involving similar phenomena, and possible physiological changes by hypnotic suggestion (Erickson, 1938a, 1938b, 1939d; Huston et al., 1934), has come to the conclusion that superficially a subject, especially a trained subject, can within a period of a few seconds manifest the appearance of a deep trance, and can easily meet all the usual criteria of the hypnotic trance. However, to establish a state adequate for serious experimental work, and so far removed from the normal waking state that hallucinations can exhibit all qualities of reality, requires that the subject be given at least 15 to 30 minutes to permit the development of possible neuro- and psychophysiological changes and to adjust himself.

Hibler does not seem to realize that the appearance of hypnotic phenomena and the meeting of the usual trance criteria have to do only with the manifestations of a simple trance and not with highly complex phenomena to be developed out of that trance state. To establish a hypnotic trance state adequate for the induction of significant alterations of customary processes of behavior requires a period of time directly proportional to the complexity of the alterations desired. A parallel might be drawn in relation to the depth and stability of the state of physiological sleep immediately upon falling asleep and at later intervals during the course of that sleep. Hibler desired profound alterations in behavior processes, yet made no provision for the temporal requirements for such developments.

To proceed to the specific experimental setup, it should first be noted that Hibler's preliminary control series consisted of a test to check the extent of the subject's knowledge of afterimages. It consisted of questioning the subject as to his opinion of what would appear following fixation on each of the primary colors. This test may be objected to on the grounds that it possibly served to inform the subject that the experiment to follow would concern afterimages, of which he did have knowledge. Erickson and Erickson's subjects had no such preliminary hints, all investigation previous to the actual test work being concealed in the form of word-association tests, and questioning being resorted to only after the experimental work had been finished.

After this preliminary series, Hibler proceeded to his tests of trance hallucinations. His apparatus setup, consisting of a Dockeray tachistoscope using two blank gray cards so presented that the subject did not need to shift his ocular fixation, is excellent. The first card was always described to the subject as having on it a disc of one of the primary colors; then he was asked to describe what he observed on the second card.

Three of the four subjects consistently described discs of a color appropriate to the negative afterimage of the primary color named. The fourth subject equally consistently described discs of the same color as the primary color named. All results were in accord with the subjects' previously expressed expectations.

Now these results may be explained in three different ways:

1. Hypnotic subjects are capable not of actual hallucinations but only of complaisant cooperation. This is the point of view to which Hibler inclines.

2. The hypnotic subjects all obtained actual hallucinations. Three subjects obtained actual negative afterimages from their hallucinations. The fourth subject's hallucinations, as is so often the case, were slow to appear and develop. They had just started with the first card and attained full development with the second.

Inasmuch as the fourth subject expected afterimages of a positive nature, this explanation is unlikely to be true. Nevertheless it must be considered. Had subjects been chosen who were completely naive as to the theory and nature of afterimages, this difficulty could not have arisen.

3. Hypnotic subjects in a deep trance may or may not be capable of actual hallucinations. However, hypnotic subjects in a light trance, given a visual test in which they expect a definite result, may not experience visual hallucinations when so instructed, but may, at a level of verbalized agreement, give the expected answer.

Any one of the explanations is possible. The third we hold to be the most acceptable.

Hibler's next series is to be criticized not only in its interpretation, but also from the point of view of the specific instructions given to the subject.

Hibler's purpose was to test the subject for the afterimages in "the waking state, without knowledge of the hallucinated color stimulus," to a color hallucinated in the trance state. Therefore he desired to have his subjects in a trance state while the original color was hallucinated and awake when the afterimage, if any, developed. He attempted to do this by giving the following suggestions while the subject fixated the hallucinated color disc:

"'Now I am going to wake you to the count of three. When I say *three*, you will be wide awake, feeling fine in every way. While you are awakening, your eyes will remain glued on the dot on the card in front of you, and you will not remember anything that happened while you were asleep. Ready, one-two-three. What do you see?' (Experimenter removed card with hallucinated color between count of one and two.)"

Now, using the same experimental setup and suggestions, but using real rather than hallucinated color discs, each subject had reported the appropriate negative afterimage in every case, showing that the awakening from trance alone does not disrupt the actual development of a real afterimage. In using real rather than hallucinated cards, the experimenter was depending upon a reality situation totally independent of the hypnotic state. Memory of having seen the real card does not enter into the development of a negative afterimage. Thus he could be shown the real card in the trance state, awakened with no memory of having seen it, and yet, in the ordinary course of events, experience the negative afterimage.

But when hallucinated colors were used in this series, no afterimage appeared in any case. Analysis of the suggestion given shows that the subjects had been told to hold themselves in readiness to awaken. Now this suggestion in itself served to arouse the subject from the hypnotic trance to a certain extent, putting him into a ready-to-awaken or an altered trance state, more akin to the waking than to the deep trance state. Essentially the subject has been asked to hallucinate in the trance state, is then asked to awaken, and thus to abolish the trance state, and yet at the same time to continue his trance activities. The experimental data obtained from subjects in this borderline state relates to the realities to be expected after awakening, not to the activities of the trance, which have been abruptly and unintentionally abolished. Thus Hibler requests certain responses and then inhibits them by changing the total situation upon which those responses depend. Yet Hibler gives as "the only possible interpretation that if an afterimage of any sort is experienced in the trance state as the result of an hallucinated color, it must be very different from that experienced from the presentation of an actual color stimulus."

Hibler's final series was much more complicated. It assumes the following (p. 55): "If the subject actually experiences red, it should make no difference if that red is superimposed over blue, or is on a gray card."

This primary assumption is certainly disputable. An hallucination in the usual sense is without doubt superimposed upon a background of reality. The subject does not see the hallucinated red disc all by itself with the rest of the visual field a neutral haze; he sees it in the appropriate opening in the tachistoscope. If that opening in the tachistoscope is occupied by a blank gray card, his task—to hallucinate a red disc on it—is relatively easy. But if it is occupied by a gray card on which there is already a blue disc, the difficulty of his task is increased many fold; it now becomes that of seeing a distinct object, the blue disc, as one totally different, a red one; and this transformation is to have absolute validity.

Now how does Hibler propose to suggest to his subject that this extemely difficult task be accomplished? He gives the following suggestion:

"You see this disc. What color is it? (Pointing to the red disc.) That's right. Now this disc (blue) is exactly the same as this one (red). It is the same in every way, the same hue, brightness, and saturation. It is the *same* color. Now take this card in your hand and describe this disc to me. (Subject takes blue disc and describes it as red, giving size and shade as a rule.) That's right, now remember, this (blue) is the same as this (red) until I tell you differently."

Before commenting on these specific suggestions, it is necessary to emphasize the care which must be taken with the wording of hypnotic suggestions. It is of extreme importance in giving hypnotic suggestions, particularly in what is intended to be a closely controlled experimental situation, to be certain that the meaning of every word the experimenter says has been carefully evaluated, especially for its most literal sense, so that the subject is not led astray by the superficial meanings of the words employed, but, rather comprehends the actual significance of the instructions.

In experimental work with waking subjects this extreme care is not ordinarily so necessary. For example, a subject was given an examination which necessitated filling out a questionnaire concerning her age, nativity, and education. One question ran "Where born: City _____, State _____." In the waking state the subject unhesitatingly filled in the name of the city and state. The same subject in the hypnotic state wrote 'Yes' in each blank. This is not a chance example, but rather one typical of numerous comparable instances.

Similarly, a subject was shown a tray containing a number of objects for a few moments and asked what he saw. In the waking state it made no difference which of these two forms of the question was used:

"Will you please tell me everything you saw on the tray."

"Please tell me everything you saw on the tray."

Yet, when hypnotized, the same subject usually answered simply "yes" to the first form of the question and quietly awaited further instructions, but would give the expected type of answer to the second form.

In addition to this literalness the hypnotized subject often responds to cues which the waking subject would not notice or would ignore as accidental or insignificant. One needs only to see a subject in a deep trance state to realize and be impressed by the fact that the subject can, upon observing a slight gesture, an intonation, a change in wording on the part of the hypnotist—which may even have been unwittingly made—unhesitatingly carry out the suggestion implied by it.

To return now to Hibler's suggestions, the final sentence, "That's right, now remember, this (blue) is the same as this (red) until I tell you differently," distinctly told the subjects that the change of color was to be one of understood agreement only and thus effectively destroyed any force which the preceding suggestions might have had. It is not sufficient to have the subject agree only—rather, the subject must perform the infinitely harder task of experiencing, and the acceptance of Hibler's suggestions did not imply an acting upon them but only an abidance by them. To show the inadequacy and self-contradictory character of any such suggestions, one might parallel them as follows: "You see this watch. It is a gift to you. It is to be all yours, your very own permanently yours, *until I tell you differently.*"

But even without this final nullification the suggestions in themselves are far too simple, brief, and casual to cause such a marked effect as was desired.

Adequate suggestions should have been similar to the following, with sufficient time allowed for full comprehension of and full response to each suggestion and a variation from one subject to the next to insure individual understanding on the same significances:

"You see this disc. What color is it? (Red). I want you to see it plainly and clearly and to continue to see this red disc plainly and clearly. Now I want you to see this other disc. What color is it? (Blue). Now I want you to look at it carefully and steadily because slowly, gradually, sooner or later it will lose its present color and will acquire a new, different, and equally bright color. And as you keep looking, you will begin to note its changing; you will become increasingly aware of the change, and at first, as you note the change, this disc becomes increasingly neutral in appearance. Then, after it becomes neutral, it will acquire a new and bright and familiar color, and as you begin to wonder what this color may be, you will begin to note that this disc is rapidly becoming red, even as red as the first disc; and as you look at it you see and feel and know the redness, just as you see and feel and know the redness of the first disc, and so now you will continue to see either of these red discs at any time necessary, seeing them both clearly, fully, and readily."

The purpose of the suggestions is to induce an experiential response, not a tacit agreement. This is difficult; it requires a subject in a deep trance; it requires repeated suggestions making the desired change in color through small gradations. The color is first faded to neutral because that is a change more acceptable to the subject, in keeping with his general past experience, such as scotopic vision. The experiential values of the first red disc are emphasized, and finally of the two red discs, and after the change is made, no word is spoken which suggests or even hints of pretense or of any difference between the two. Then and only then can we expect genuine responses.

Hibler's results are exactly as would be expected: when results were reported in the waking state (the "hypnotic" work having been done in a state preparatory to awakening), all afterimages were of the real rather than the suggested color; when results were reported in the trance state, two subjects reported the results they expected to get from the suggested color (positive on the part of one, negative on the part of the other), while two reported the afterimages of the real rather than the suggested color. In other words all these results can be readily explained on the assumption of mere verbal cooperation on the part of the subjects, and failure to induce experiential responses.

In Erickson and Erickson's study the subjects, so far as could be determined by association tests and extensive questioning afterward, and from their selection from the classes of commerce and engineering freshmen, were naive concerning the nature of complementary colors. Well-trained subjects were used, a period of 30 to 45 minutes of trance induction was allowed to insure profound trances and experiential responses rather than verbalized agreement. The use of alternate sheets of white paper, described as all being colored, the subject and the experimenter to name the color of the alternate sheets, prevented the subjects from even realizing that the test concerned afterimages, or (since they were found to know nothing of afterimages) of a white sheet of paper seen after looking at a colored one. Of five subjects, one failed completely to meet the test situation apparently for the reason that he could not hallucinate colors. The other four invariably described the intervening white sheets as of the complementary color appropriate to the hallucinated color of the preceding sheet. Hibler's carefully set-up apparatus gives the superficial impression of greater accuracy than the simple sheets of white paper; yet careful evaluation showed that his extreme control of experimental conditions concerned everything but the actual essentials.

Hibler's experiment proved only that an inadequately hypnotized subject who knows about afterimages sees the appropriate afterimages in what he realizes to be an afterimage set-up; that subjects instructed to hallucinate colors in a semi-waking state do not experience afterimages of those colors; and that subjects instructed to regard and treat one color as another, knowing about afterimages, may or may not carry the cooperation so far as to report the afterimage they assume to be correct.

Hence Erickson and Erickson's earlier experiment, not having been repeated or even checked in any detail by Hibler's, must still be considered to be accurate, and its final conclusion to stand: that the hallucination of various colors by hypnotic subjects can be sufficiently valid subjectively to permit a spontaneous and invariable hallucination of complementary colors somewhat in the form of negative afterimages.

The real contribution of Hibler's experiment to hypnotic investigative work is its demonstration of how misleading and unreliable experimental results can be when their acceptance is based upon the completion of an experimental procedure without due regard or provision for the nature and character of the phenomena under investigation by that procedure.

3. The Induction of Color Blindness By A Technique of Hypnotic Suggestion

Milton H. Erickson

Previous work on the induction by hypnotic techniques of deafness (Erickson, 1938a,b) and of hallucinatory color vision with pseudo negative afterimages (Erickson and Erickson, 1938) suggested the possibility of effecting other alterations of sensory functioning by hypnosis. Accordingly, an experiment was devised for the hypnotic induction of color blindness in subjects having normal color vision. Slected as a measure of color vision was the Ishihara *Color Blindness Test,* since it consists of plates of colored dots so arranged as to outline various numerals, the perception of which is directly dependent upon and limited to the actual degree of color discrimination present.

A. EXPERIMENTAL PROCEDURE

Preliminary work soon disclosed that induced color blindness constituted so complex a phenomenon that a satisfactory and effective technique of suggestion would necessarily be more extensive and comprehensive than the simple, direct type of hypnotic suggestion usually employed in hypnotic experimentation. Accordingly, a number of well-trained subjects were utilized solely for the purpose of developing a technique of suggestion adequate for the experimental project. These subjects, selected at random from among those available, underwent various clinical procedures leading to the development of what finally seemed to be a satisfactory experimental technique. They were then dismissed, because of possible sophistication, as unsuitable for the actual experiment, and new subjects, unacquainted with any of the steps of the experimental procedure, were employed.

A total of six new subjects, four female and two male, were used, of whom two were nurses, two occupational therapists, one a medical student, and the other a hospital attendant. All were of normal or superior intelligence and were capable hypnotic subjects. None had had any previous acquaintance with the Ishihara Test, and for experimental reasons no preliminary test was made of their color vision. The occupational therapists, however, were found afterward

Reprinted with permission from *The Journal of General Psychology,* 1939, *29,* 61-89.

to be acquainted with a wool-sorting test for color vision.

The experimental sessions were held in the midafternoon of bright, sunny days in a room well lighted by the sun but free from glare. The plates were exhibited in a vertical position on a frame supporting them at the level of the subject's eyes and at a distance of approximately 28 inches.

To acquaint the subject fully with the nature of the proposed task, cards similar to the test plates but bearing numerals cut from a calendar were presented under test conditions, and the subject was required to read them aloud. Instruction was then given to read any other similar cards in a like fashion, without straining the eyes or staring hard, and with mention made promptly of any difficulty or uncertainty in reading.

To preclude the possibility of cues being given unconsciously to the subjects by the experimenter, two additional control measures were of service. The first of these was the experimenter's own state of color blindness, which precluded his identification of the plates. The second measure lay in shuffling the cards face down and then labeling them on the back with a distinguishing letter. In presenting the cards the subject was not permitted to see the distinguishing letter, and with the exception of Plates 14, 15, and 16, which are read as having winding pathways, care was taken by the experimenter to avoid seeing the face of the card. The plates were relabeled for each experimental session to prevent any accidental association by the experimenter between a reply and a distinguishing letter.

The suggestions of the various types of color blindness were made in the order given in Table 1.

The actual experimental method evolved varied slightly in details from subject to subject, depending upon the order of suggestion of total, red, green, and red-green blindness. The essential steps in the procedure, however, may be summarized briefly as follows:

1. The slow, gradual induction of a profound somnambulistic hypnotic trance.

2. The induction by slow degrees of a state of "hypnotic blindness," this blindness to persist throughout the trance and posthypnotically.

3. The awakening of the subject in this suggested blind state to permit the spontaneous development of affective distress and anxiety over the subjective visual loss.

TABLE 1

Subject	Session 1	Session 2	Session 3	Session 4
A	Total	Red	Green	Red-green
B	Red-green	Green	Red	Total
C	Total	Red-Green	Red	Green
D	Green	Red	Red-green	Total
E	Total	Green	Red	Red-green
F	Red	Green	Red-green	Total

4.   The induction of a second trance during which the blindness was reinforced as a preliminary measure to the next step.

5.   The explanation to the subjects that it was now proposed to alter this blindness by "restoring" vision in part, yet leaving a "limited" blindness which would preclude the seeing of a certain color or colors. All objects would be seen clearly, but the chosen color itself, which was directly specified, would not and could not be seen. Instead, while all objects might be seen, certain of them would appear in a new and unfamiliar guise, their appearance being one of a totally neutral color tone.

6.   The induction of a profound amnesia, to ensue at once and to persist indefinitely, for the chosen critical color or colors which had been specified. In addition, there were given vague general instructions serving to effect an inclusion in the amnesia of all connotations and associations for that color, thereby rendering the name of the color either a nonsense syllable or a totally unfamiliar word.

7.   The slow gradual "restoration" of vision accompanied by the giving of elaborate detailed suggestions. These were to the effect that soon everything would be clearly visible and yet vision would be incomplete. This incompleteness would derive from changes effected in the visual capacity by the induced blindness. These changes would cause things to be altered in hue, and while colors would seem to be normally bright and vivid, there would be more neutral tones. These neutral tones would serve to alter materially the appearance of familiar objects, and this alteration would be of such character as to be indefinable. No mention was made in this step of the chosen color, since presumably that had become a nonsense syllable for the subject. Neither was mention made up to this point, either directly or indirectly, of the Ishihara Test.

8.   The administration, with the subject in the deep trance, of the Ishihara Test, exhibiting the cards in a different order for each session, with the exception of the sample card, which was consistently shown first. This was followed by the administration of the test in a posthypnotic somnambulistic state, with the subject still under the influence of the hypnotic suggestion and with the shuffling of the cards including the sample card.

9.   The repetition in separate experimental sessions, usually several days or a week apart, of the foregoing procedure for each suggested variety of color blindness.

10.   The separate administration of the test by an associate and by the experimenter at later dates with the subject in the normal waking state and in the simple trance state.

11.   An attempt to induce the subjects in the waking state to see figures other than those read previously in the normal waking state. Care was exercised to keep the conditions of exhibition of the cards standard so far as light, position, and angle of vision were concerned.

In giving the test, all 16 plates were used, and a total of 13 separate administrations of the test were made for each subject, only eight of which were actually experimental in character. Of these eight, four were made during the deep trance states and the remainder during the succeeding posthypnotic somnambulistic states. Hence there were two administrations of the test for each experimental session. Of the five control administrations made subsequent to the experimental work with the subjects in the normal waking and in the simple trance states, two were given by the experimenter, and these were repeated by an associate. The fifth control, actually requiring several administrations of the test, was the one in which an effort was made to force or to induce the subjects to see other or additional figures in the plates, or to fail to see those actually there.

B. EXPERIMENTAL FINDINGS

1. Results on Control Tests

The control examinations disclosed normal color vision for all six subjects. However, Subject *B* consistently read 71 for Plate 5, which is usually read as 74 by the normal, as 21 by the red-green blind, and with difficulty if at all by the totally color blind. No other evidences of color blindness were detected for this subject. Otherwise the reading of the plates by all the subjects was strictly in accord with the criteria of the test for normal color vision.

In the final control administration of the test, the subjects were asked to be certain of their previous readings of the plates. When each reading had been confirmed, instruction was given to the effect that the plates would be shown again. This time they were told that, if the plates were scrutinized with great care, it would be possible to see *different numerals, additional numerals,* or even to *see the plates as having no numerals,* and they were admonished to exercise much effort to read the plates in an entirely new fashion. These instructions were repeated upon the exhibition of each plate.

Upon presentation of the first plate, two of the subjects consciously inverted 12, reading it as 71, and it was necessary to correct this error of understanding.

Plate 2 was read by three of the subjects as either 8 or 3 with the explanation that the numeral could be a 3 if one chose "to ignore part of the 8."

Plate 3 was consistently read as 6, the normal response, although several of the subjects explained that if they studied it, they could get slight changes in the form of the 6. None saw the 5 as such.

Plate 4 was read by two subjects as a possible 8, tracing the 5 and part of the 2 to form the numeral 8. However, they did see the 5, which is the normal reading, but did not distinguish the 2 as a separate numeral.

Plate 5 was read consistently by Subject *B* as 71; he explained that parts of the number seemed to be slightly obscured, but he could not define these parts. Three of the subjects explained that one might direct attention to one or the other of the two figures and thus read only a single numeral. Except for Subject

B, all subjects gave the normal reading.

Plates 6, 7, 8, and 9 were vainly scrutinized for additional figures. None of the subjects seemed to realize the possibility of seeing these plates as having no numerals.

Plates 10 and 11 were declared by most of the subjects as having fragmentary lines wich could be construed as forming various numerals or letters of imperfect outline. Three of the subjects outlined vaguely and inaccurately the numeral 5 for Plate 10, and a fourth subject repeatedly experienced fleeting glimpses of the 5. Two subjects outlined the numeral 2 on Plate 11 but declared it to be "practically invisible"; two others succeeded in outlining it inaccurately, explaining, "If you look hard enough, you get a feeling that maybe there is a 2 there"; the remaining two declared that there was no numeral.

On Plates 12 and 13, reports similar to those given in relation to Plate 5 were obtained. In addition, four of the subjects explained that the numeral 6 on Plate 12 and the numeral 2 on Plate 13 could be the figures most easily overlooked by redirection of attention.

On Plate 14, the normal response was given, although four subjects could see, in addition, fragmentary parts of the other line.

On Plate 15, all subjects saw the normal line.

On Plate 16, all of the subjects succeeded in seeing fragmentary parts of the line usually seen by the red-green blind, but in addition, false lines.

As an additional measure, the subjects were shown the cards briefly illuminated by red, blue, green, and yellow lights separately. Much astonishment was manifested by the subjects when they discovered that figures hitherto unseen by them could actually be made visible on the cards. The test was then repeated under standard conditions after shuffling the cards. Despite their sophistication by the exhibition of the cards under colored lights, the subjects were unable to do more than confirm their previous normal responses. However, they were more confident in their statements about additional numerals.

Essentially, this control procedure disclosed that, while the subjects could be induced to see more on the card than was usually perceived, *the process was essentially one of addition to the normal perception or direct subtraction from it* without there being any change or substitution or alteration of perceptual values. Hence, these findings may be summarized by the statement that, even under pressure to read the plates in a new or different fashion, the subjects continued to read them in the previous normal fashion, and the slight evidence obtained in some instances of an ability to detect other possible readings disclosed the subjects as unable to attach a clear perceptual validity to the new readings.

2. Results on Experimental Tests

Since the responses obtained for the trance state and for the posthypnotic somnambulistic state were essentially identical, no differentiation will be made between them. Occasionally a subject would be slightly more certain of his readings in one state than in the other, but there was no reliable difference. The test responses for the various types of suggested color blindness, because of their diversity and multiplicity, will be presented in the form of tables,[1] from which Plate 1, actually a sample plate, is omitted since it was consistently read correctly in all sessions by each subject. In addition, the rating of each response, as determined by the criteria of the test, is included in the appropriate tables. In assigning these score values, those instances permitting two possible interpretations of color vision defect are given a rating signifying the less color blind condition, while those instances permitting several possible interpretations are listed as doubtful or as undifferentiated. While this arbitrary method of interpreting these responses may introduce an error, it is one of conservatism, hence serves to emphasize the clearly positive results.

Table 2 shows the distribution of possible responses for the various test plates, and indicates those responses indicative respectively of normal color vision and of defective color vision. As may be readily seen, 10 normal responses are possible, three do not permit differentiation between normal color vision and total color blindness, and two do not permit differentiation between normal color vision and red-green blindness. The other possible responses are those indicative of color vision defects.

Tables 3-6 [2]show the individual responses of each subject to the various test plates, together with the rating of the responses according to the test criteria.

A summary of the individual test responses according to their rating for the four types of suggested color blindness may be found in Table 7. Comparison of this table with Table 2 permits a ready appreciation of the extent and character of the color vision changes induced in each of the subjects.

A further summary of the results may be found in Table 8, showing the

[1]In compiling each of these tables, various abbreviations have been used. For the convenience of the reader, these may be listed as follows:

N—normal.
R—red blind.
G—green blind.
RG—red-green blind.
T—totally color blind.
O—plate described as blank.
N/T—either normal or totally color blind.
5?—numeral read uncertainly and with difficulty.
2/6?—first digit read easily, second with difficulty.
5, 6—both numerals seen equally well.
?—numeral seen vaguely but not clearly defined. In column headed, "Plate Explanation," it signifies, "Read with difficulty if at all."
Inc.—incomplete.
Comp.—complete.
Resp.—response.
Rat.—rating.
D—doubtful.

[2]Tables 3 through 8 will be found following page 32.

TABLE 2
DISTRIBUTION OF POSSIBLE RESPONSES ACCORDING TO PLATES

Plate No.	Normal color vision responses				Defective color vision responses		
	N	N/T	N/RG	T	RG	R	G
2	1			1	1		
3	1			1	1		
4	1			1	1		
5	1			1	1		
6	1			1			
7	1			1			
8	1			1			
9	1			1			
10		1			1		
11		1			1		
12			1			1	1
13			1			1	1
14	1			1	1		
15	1			1			
16		1			1		
Totals	10	3	2	10	8	2	2
Comparative totals for 6 subjects	60	18	12	60	48	12	12

distribution of test responses in accordance with the significance of the test plates and in relation to the various types of color blindness suggested.

C. SUMMARY OF RESULTS

The results of this experiment were similar in character for all six subjects and may be summarized as follows:

1. Normal color vision was disclosed to be consistently present in ordinary waking and hypnotic states.

2. Control procedures directed to the purpose of enabling the subjects to detect test plate numerals indicative of color vision deficiencies failed. Despite these procedures, the subjects continued to see the numerals indicative of normal color vision.

3. The hypnotic suggestion of various types of color blindness was found to induce consistent deficiencies in color vision comparable in degree and character to those found in actual color blindness.

4. The extent of the induced color vision defect for the various types of suggested color blindness was progressively greater in the following order: green, red, red-green, and total color blindness. The proportion of normal color

vision responses out of a possible 60 were, respectively, for the suggested green, red, red-green, and total color blindness, 30, 17, 6 and 4, and the number of definitely color blind responses not possible ordinarily for the subjects were, respectively, 44, 54, 84, and 73 (the lower numerical value of this last figure is a function of the test itself and derives from its significant limitations for total color blindness).

D. COMMENT

1. General Considerations

Before commenting on the experimental results, mention will be made of the subjective reactions manifested during and after each experimental session. These reactions were essentially the same in character for all subjects though not always of the same degree from subject to subject or from session to session. They may be summarized as complaints of extreme fatigue, muscular stiffness, and severe headaches following each experimental session. Frequently during the experiment it became necessary to allow a rest period between the trance and the posthypnotic states, during which the subjects merely rested quietly in the hypnotic sleep. There were, however, no observable manifestations of these symptoms during trance states other than the verbal complaints which were elicited only upon direct inquiry. In the waking state, complaints were offered spontaneously. After each session all of the subjects were most curious to know what sort of strenuous physical exercise they had been given in the trance which could account for their general muscular stiffness, intense fatigue, and throbbing headaches. These reactions are suggestive of profound neurophysiological responses to the hypnotic suggestions.

Another preliminary consideration is the type or character of the hypnotic trance used, since in all probability the slowly induced, exceedingly profound trances employed in this experiment contributed greatly to the results obtained. In regard to the hypnotic training of these subjects, an average of eight hours was spent in the initial training procedures for each subject. This time was devoted entirely to the task of teaching them to sleep soundly and stuporously and to develop profound somnambulistic states. *Not until this had been done was any attempt made to induce other hypnotic phenomena or to use the subjects for investigatory purposes.*

In the author's experience, it is only by such laborious measures that there can be secured a sound, psychologically consistent and effective hypnotic trance of a character permitting the acceptance and execution of complicated and difficult suggestions. The ordinary deep trance, rapidly induced, with the subject given direct and emphatic suggestions, does not permit the gradual and effective development of what may be called the "mental set" which is requisite for the execution of complicated behavior free from the influence of waking patterns of response. Once adequately trained, the subject can be hypnotized quickly and deeply, but a slow induction extending over 15 to 30 minutes is desirable for difficult experimental work. Apparently, the element of time is an important factor in securing a neuropsychological state which will permit the subject to accept and act upon a suggestion freely and completely and without inhibitions and limitations deriving from customary waking habits and patterns of behavior.

The speculation may be offered that the deep trance and the lapse of time permit a quiescence or a general state of mental inertia to develop, so that when a hypnotic suggestion is given, it serves only to arouse those mental processes immediately involved, and is acted upon free, in large part, from the conditioning or controlling influences that would be imposed upon it by the activation of various inhibiting mental processes or response patterns derived from other and past experiences. In this way, apparently, the hypnotic task can be approached by the subject as a new experience uninfluenced by past experiences and their derivatives.

Concerning the rationale of the varied hypnotic instructions given to the experimental subjects, certain explanations are warranted to clarify their extent and character.

In this regard, as was discovered early in the preliminary clinical experimentation, direct suggestions of color blindness were ineffectual since they were at absolute variance with the subject's intellectual grasp of reality and thus in utter conflict with the established products of past learning and experience. In addition, such direct suggestions required the subject to differentiate between *what was to be seen* and *what was not to be seen,* a differentiation possible only if *all were seen.* These two serious obstacles resulted either in a failure to accept suggestions, or, if they were accepted, in a negation of seeing which did not constitute color blindness.

Hence, the problem became one of circumventing these difficulties. This could be done, presumably, by creating a psychological situation which would permit an approximation of an actual state of color blindness, in which intellectual conflicts could not arise about the existence or nonexistence of colors, and in which full vision could obtain without a need either to differentiate between colors or to avoid seeing colors.

Accordingly, the solution of this problem was attempted by first suggesting total blindness, intellectually an entirely conceivable state, and causing to develop in the subject a strong, unpleasant affective reaction. This, in turn, would lead to a ready acceptance of any suggestion affording relief from the emotional distress arising from the subjective blindness. There followed a restoration of vision with the relief from the emotional distress of subjective blindness made indirectly and unnoticeably conditional upon the acceptance of direct suggestions of color blindness. Thus, any critical intellectual tendencies would be held completely in abeyance by inner forces deriving from the emotional needs of the subject, these affective needs compelling the subject to accept color blindness suggestions in full as the only means of securing affective comfort. Hence, there could develop neither the occasion nor any need to bring about an adjustment between the critical faculties and the suggestions of color blindness, since the subject's primary purpose and object became the seeking of affective satisfactions and not the consideration of an intellectual problem. Thus, the color blindness suggestions became possessed of legitimate and essential values for the subject, enforcing their acceptance.

Having secured the acceptance of the suggestions of color blindness as an integral part of the satisfaction of significant affective needs, the next step lay in the development of a mental state approximating that of the color blind person to whom colors are nonexistent as perceptions, require no differentiation from each other, and have no direct associations or connotations. To develop this mental state, an extensive amnesia was suggested for the chosen color or colors together with all color associations and connotations. Such an amnesia is, in itself, entirely acceptable to the critical intelligence, and it serves to effect a complete, although indirect, disregard of or lack of response to the specified color, permitting the same behavior or lack of behavior as would derive from absolute color blindness. By this measure, presumably, all perceptual values would become inactive and hence lost, without there being any need for a negation of seeing or an avoidance of seeing. This constitutes, essentially, a situation comparable to that obtaining in the color blind. The color stimulus of the plates is present, but it arouses no responsive activity because of the indirect blocking of the capacity for response through the loss of perceptual qualities effected by the amnesia. This loss of perceptual values may be taken psychophysiologically as constituting a raising of the sensory threshold to the critical color.

In consequence of the failure of capacity for response to the stimuli emanating from the critical color, the subjects respond as if there existed no such color, and the character and nature of their responses are determined by those stimuli which do possess perceptual values. Particularly favorable to the possibility of this type of responsive behavior is the intrinsic nature of the Ishihara Test, which causes any alteration of its stimulatory values to be reflected indirectly by an adequate and different response, precluding an indirect sensing of any deficiency or incompleteness.

In illustration of these assumptions concerning the loss of perceptual and conceptual values, the following findings made on one of the subjects employed in the preliminary clinical experimentation may be cited. Red blindness had been suggested to him, and, as a means of distracting his attention from the problem in hand, he was asked, by chance, to count aloud various objects, beginning with his fingers. There followed a bewildering experience for both the experimenter and the subject, since the latter, in counting his fingers, totalled them as 11, although he declared that there were and could be only 10. Closer attention disclosed that he consistently omitted the "3" in his counting. More than an hour was spent letting the subject try to solve this problem of 11 fingers by count, 10 by knowledge, 6 on each hand by count, 5 by knowledge, 10 when counted by twos and 11 when counted singly. Repeatedly he narrowed the problem down to "2 fingers plus 2 fingers equals 4 fingers, which brings you to the index finger, but when you count them singly, you come only to the middle finger," and he would then start fresh in his reasoning.

Finally, he was told to abandon this "puzzle" and was given reading and number cancellation tests. The word "three" was regarded as a misprint of the word "tree" or as a nonsense syllable which he would pronounce correctly, and the numeral "3" was either misread as an 8, where the type style permitted, or was regarded as a nonsense character.

Extensive questioning and investigation disclosed other and innumerable losses of the conceptual values of 3 and its derivatives.

Return was then made to the original problem of red blindness. He was found to be red-blind, his responses being almost identical on the Ishihara Test with those of Subject F for the same suggested blindness. Plate 2, however, was read as an "incomplete 8, or part of a B."

Hypnotic suggestions were then given, restoring the conceptual significances of "3." Readministration of the Ishihara Test disclosed normal color vision. Further experimental investigation disclosed an absolute interdependence between red color vision and the conceptual significations of "3" of such character that suggestion directed to one would affect both.

Subsequent inquiry elicited the following significant explanation:

> The number 3 is red to me. I can't see a 3 or even think of it without thinking or seeing or feeling red. There's a lot of words that are colored to me. Ideas, feelings, too! I can't explain it. It's always been that way with me.

This accidental finding led to rapid progress in the development of an experimental procedure. The inclusion in the experimental technique of suggestions affecting conceptual values was found to enable induction of color blindness in subjects previously resistant, and repeated clinical experimentation with the preliminary group of subjects led finally to the acceptance of the procedure described above.

2.   Comments on Experimental Findings

In discussion of the acutal experimental results, one of the first considerations is the character of the findings. Study of the data, both control and experimental, indicates definitely that the findings are attributable directly to the experimental measures employed and do not reflect incidental or chance factors. It discloses further that, while both positive and negative results were obtained, the significance of the negative findings is confined to an indication of the incompleteness with which the experimental object was attained, and does not constitute a contradiction or indicate an inherent limitation of the experimental methods and objectives. As for the positive results, these are clearly definite and unequivocal in character and show that the demands of the experimental situation were actually met in accord with the measures employed. Visual perceptions, ordinarily possible only to the color blind and demonstrated as impossible under ordinary conditions to the subjects, were elicited repeatedly from each of the subjects under the experimental conditions. This fact constitutes the primary and significant finding of the experiment.

The intrinsic nature of the Ishihara Test is such that it permits a variety of possible responses for each test instance, but without affording any opportunity for a deliberate, purposeful selection of responses. Each of the possible responses is adequate and complete in itself, meets fully the demands placed upon the subject for a response, and carries its own significance. Also, any combination of the possible responses that may be given by the subject bears a positive meaning peculiar to such a combination. Furthermore, this variety of responses depends upon the existence within the subject of certain absolute conditions, with most of the responses possible only if the subject fulfills those requisite conditions. Yet, throughout the experiment, responses were elicited consistently and repeatedly of a character possible only if the absolute requirements of the test were met adequately by the subjects. Since such responses were obtained repeatedly from all of the subjects, and since these responses varied appropriately in accordance with the theoretical demands of each experimental situation, the findings may be regarded as clearly similar or comparable to those obtainable in various conditions of defective color vision.

The next problem concerns the possible mechanisms or psychological processes by which the experimental findings were obtained. This requires consideration of the nature of the experimental procedure, the character of the stimuli employed, the character of the responses obtained, and the associated and underlying psychological conditions entering into those results.

As has been indicated above, the hypnotic measures employed undoubtedly played a significant, though indirect, rôle through an inhibition of various mental processes and activities which ordinarily would interfere with the performance of the suggested task. This inhibition, restriction, or limitation of various activities related entirely to conceptual and perceptual values of a chosen color or colors, but left the subject free to respond to the stimulatory values deriving from other colors or from the lack or absence of color values, or from other indirect stimulatory values such as brightness.

To illustrate from the experiment, the suggestion of red blindness effected an inhibition of all responses to redness, but left the subject free to respond to brightness, blueness, etc. Hence, in looking at a test plate weighted with red values, the retinal stimulation deriving from the redness could not lead to perceptual or conceptual response in the subject with suggested red-blindness, because of the inhibitions in force, while the other stimulatory values would lead freely to responsive activity. Thus, the visual image obtained would be dominated by those stimuli actually secondary physically to the redness, and they alone would serve to give a meaning to what was seen. In other words, there occurred a relative raising of the red thresholds.

Concerning the character of the stimuli, little can be said, since regardless of the hypnotic suggestions and induced mental states, color stimulation of the retina did occur and the subjects did possess normal color vision. However, the assumption is warranted that in normal color vision, the visual image is the result of various fusion processes involving all retinal stimuli, and hence that the normal person receives the same stimuli as does the color blind, but in addition, other stimuli which actually dominate the entire situation and determine the nature and the character of the response. But in the hypnotically color blind, apparently, despite the complete retinal stimulation, only certain stimuli served to arouse responsive activity, with the consequence that the responses aroused were limited in character though adequate for the total stiatuion.

As stated above, the responses obtained were both positive and negative for color blindness, with those positive clearly indicative of definite alterations of color vision perception, while those negative suggesting an inadequacy of the experimental method. Particularly is this suggested by the variations of response to a single test plate from one state to another of suggested color blindness, as shown in the tables of the individual responses and in Table 7. Responses elicited in one state of suggested color blindness did not necessarily develop in another state, although there was a marked trend toward a persistence and increase of color blind responses directly proportional to the extensiveness of the color blindness suggested. This variation of responses for different states of color blindness indicates that the responses were a direct, if not a complete, function of the suggested condition. This is best illustrated in Table 8, which shows one red-blind and one green-blind response for green blindness, eight red-blind responses for red blindness, eight red-blind and two green-blind responses for red-green blindness, and four red-blind and five green-blind responses for total color blindness.

Also in this connection, study of the distribution of responses by subjects in connection with Table 1 does not indicate, so far as can be determined, any practice effect accruing in consequence of the order of suggestion of color vision defects.

Concerning the associated and underlying psychological conditions entering into the results, consideration must be given to the changed mental perspectives afforded by both the amnesia suggested and the loss of color values. All of the female subjects manifested discomfort and even distress over their dresses, which they declared were not their own. The examining room, acutally familiar to them, was described as similar to the experimenter's "regular office," but "much different in many ways" and totally unfamiliar to them, and they were observed to build up an orientation for the examining room by checking their observations with their memory of the "regular office." Their entire behavior reflected the reactions of a new experience. Their reaction to the test plates may be summarized in the following quotation from one of the subjects:

> This is the fourth time I've been here, and each time you've shown me a pack of cards, twice each time. But the next time I come, it's a different pack. You see, there's a No. 12 (Plate I) in every pack, and I keep watching for it to see if it is the same card that you slip from one pack to the next, but each time it's a different card even though the number is the same. I wonder just how many of those cards you're going to have.

Obviously, the personal situation for each of the subjects constituted a new and unfamiliar experience to which they could respond adequately but without utilizing certain associations, memories, and learned responses. Questioning of the subjects in the experimental situations could not be done because of the possibility of disturbing established conditions, and postexperimental questioning was postponed until it was clear that no further work would be done, thus precluding more than a retrospective account. However, a general statement is warranted that the experimental experience was entered into as a totally new experience, and the extent and effects of this can only be speculated upon in the light of general clinical understandings.

While discussion has been offered of various psychological aspects of the experimental findings, the problems remain of their interpretation in terms of how they were elicited and of the actual neuro- and psychophysiological process entering into their production. Much of the discussion above may be taken to indicate that psychological processes and mechanisms constituted the primary factors, and the illustrative case of synaesthesia tends to confirm this possibility. The probability is, however, that these psychological considerations constituted no more than a favorable setting in which various neuro- and psychophysiological processes could be aroused into activity by indirect forces, and that these resulting activities constituted the primary factors in the manifestation of limited color vision. Hence, any satisfactory interpretation of the experimental findings must be based primarily upon the elucidation of the underlying neural activities.

That such an elucidation, however necessary and important, can be made is questionable. The exceedingly complex character of the experimental procedure, the complicated intrinsic nature of the color vision test plates, the limited number of subjects, and the irregularity, despite their general consistency, of the individual findings all serve to make difficult and uncertain any attempt at interpretation. In addition, the present limited knowledge of the functions of color vision and the neuro- and psychophysiological processes entering into it, the uncertainties regarding the respective rôles of peripheral and central activities, and the lack of understanding of the nature of color vision, except in general terms, also serve to preclude an interpretation of the experimental findings in terms of neural activites.

However, one general interpretation in the form of the conclusion is warranted, namely, that the findings demonstrate clearly that cortical processes and activities can play a highly significant role in color vision and can effect results similar if not identical with those based primarily upon peripheral activity and conditions.

E. CONCLUSIONS

The conclusions warranted by the experimental findings on these six subjects may be listed briefly as follows:

1. Color blindness—red, green, red-green, and total in character—as determined by the Ishihara *Color Blindness Test,* was hypnotically induced in subjects known to have normal color vision and who were found to be unable under ordinary conditions, either spontaneously or responsively, to meet the test criteria for defective color vision.
2. No conclusion can be offered concerning the psychological mechanisms and the neuro- and psychophysiological processes involved in the production of the suggested color blindness.
3. The significance of the findings lies in their evidential values concerning the importance of cortical processes in color vision.

F. SUMMARY

An experimental hypnotic technique was devised involving the suggestion separately of red, green, red-green, and total color blindness, each accompanied by an amnesia for all conceptual significations of the critical color or colors. Six persons having normal color vision were subjected to this experimental procedure, and administration of the Ishihara *Color Blindness Test* disclosed them to have developed definite alterations in color vision comparable in degree and character with actual color blindness. Application of control measures disclosed the subjects to be unable to duplicate or even to approach, under ordinary conditions, their experimental behavior. Comment is made upon the rationale of the experimental procedure, the psychological processes and mechanisms entering into the production of the results, and emphasis is placed upon the need for more adequate knowledge of the neuro- and psychophysiological processes involved in color vision before an interpretation is made of the experimental findings. A final conclusion is offered that cortical processes and activities, as evidenced by these experimental findings, have a definite though undefined significance in the problem of color vision.

TABLE 3
INDIVIDUAL RESPONSES FOR SUGGESTED GREEN BLINDNESS

Plate No.	Plate explanation	Subject A Resp.	Rat.	Subject B Resp.	Rat.	Subject C Resp.	Rat.	Subject D Resp.	Rat.	Subject E Resp.	Rat.	Subject F Resp.	Rat.
2.	N—8 RG—3 T—?	8?	N	8?	N	3?	D	8?	N	8	N	3	RG
3.	N—6 RG—5 T—?	5	RG	6?	N	5/6	N	6/3	N	6?	N	5/6?	N
4.	N—5 RG—2 T—?	2?	RG	2	RG	5/2	N	0	T	2	RG	2	RG
5.	N—74 RG—21 T—?	?/1	D	0	T	24	D	0	T	2/?	RG	2/4?	D
6.	N—2 T—?	0	T	2?	N	2?	N	0	T	2?	N	0	T
7.	N—6 T—?	0	T	6?	N	6?	N	6?	N	0	T	0	T
8.	N—5 T—?	0	T	0	T	5?	N	0	T	5?	N	0	T

TABLE 3 (continued)

Plate No.	Plate explanation	Subject A Resp.	Subject A Rat.	Subject B Resp.	Subject B Rat.	Subject C Resp.	Subject C Rat.	Subject D Resp.	Subject D Rat.	Subject E Resp.	Subject E Rat.	Subject F Resp.	Subject F Rat.
9.	N—7 T—?	O	T	O	T	7?	N	O	T	7?	N	O	T
10.	N—? T—? RG—5	?	D	5	RG	O	N/T	5	RG	5?	RG	5	RG
11.	N—? T—? RG—2	2?	D	2	RG	O	N/T	2	RG	2?	D	2	RG
12.	N Inc. RG 26 Comp. R—6 Comp. G—2	2	G	2/6?	D	2/6?	D	26?	N	26?	N	2/6?	D
13.	N Inc. RG 42 Comp. R—2 Comp. G—4	2	R	4/2?	D	4/2?	D	42?	N	42?	N	42?	N
14.	N—red line RG—blue line T—?	N	N	RG	RG	RG	RG	RG	RG	RG	RG	RG	RG
15.	N—follows line T—?	N?	N	N?	N	N?	N	N?	N	O	T	O	T
16.	N—? T—? RG—follows line	RG?	RG	RG?	RG	RG?	RG	RG?	RG	O	N/T	O	N/T

TABLE 4

INDIVIDUAL RESPONSES FOR SUGGESTED RED BLINDNESS

Plate No.	Plate explanation	Subject A Resp.	Rat.	Subject B Resp.	Rat.	Subject C Resp.	Rat.	Subject D Resp.	Rat.	Subject E Resp.	Rat.	Subject F Resp.	Rat.
2.	N—8 RG—3 T—?	3	RG	3	RG	8,3?	N	0	T	3	RG	?	D
3.	N—6 RG—5 T—?	5	RG	"Zero"	D	5,6?	N	3?	D	5	RG	6	N
4.	N—5 RG—2 T—?	2	RG	2	RG	2	RG	5?	N	2?	D	2	RG
5.	N—7+ RG—21 T—?	0	T	71?	N	2+	D	7/4?	N	2?	D	2/4?	D
6.	N—2 T—?	0	T	?	D	0	T	2?	N	0	T	0	T
7.	N—6 T—?	0	T	0	T	0	T	3?	D	0	T	0	T
8.	N—5 T—?	5	N	5?	N	5?	N	5?	T	5?	N	5?	N

TABLE 4 (*continued*)

Plate No.	Plate explanation	Subject A Resp.	Subject A Rat.	Subject B Resp.	Subject B Rat.	Subject C Resp.	Subject C Rat.	Subject D Resp.	Subject D Rat.	Subject E Resp.	Subject E Rat.	Subject F Resp.	Subject F Rat.
9.	N—7 T—?	O	T	?	D	?	D	O	T	7?	N	7?	N
10.	N—? T—? RG—5	O	N/T	5	RG	5?	D	O	N/T	5	RG	5	RG
11.	N—? T—? RG—2	2	RG	2	RG	2?	D	2	RG	2	RG	2	RG
12.	N Inc. RG $\{$ 26 Comp. R—6 Comp. G—2	6	R	6	R	2/6?	D	6	R	6	R	6	R
13.	N Inc. RG $\{$ 42 Comp. R—2 Comp. G—+	O	T	42?	D	4/2?	D	2	R	2	R	2	R
14.	N—red line RG—blue line T—?	O	T	RG	RG	N	N	RG?	RG	RG?	RG	RG?	RG
15.	N—follows line T—?	O	T	O	T	N?	N	O	T	N?	T	N?	N
16.	N—? T—? RG—follows line RG?	RG?	RG	RG	RG	RG?	RG	RG?	RG	RG?	RG	O	N/T

TABLE 5
INDIVIDUAL RESPONSES FOR SUGGESTED RED-GREEN BLINDNESS

Plate No.	Plate explanation	Subject A		Subject B		Subject C		Subject D		Subject E		Subject F	
		Resp.	Rat.	Resp.	Rat.	Resp.	Rat.	Resp.	Rat.	Resp.	Rat.	Resp.	Rat.
2.	N—8 RG—3 T—?	3	RG	3	RG	0	T	3	RG	0	T	3	RG
3.	N—6 RG—5 T—?	5?	N	0	T	5	RG	0	. T	5	RG	5?	N
4.	N—5 RG—2 T—?	2	RG	2	RG	0	T	0	T	2	RG	0	T
5.	N—7+ RG—21 T—?	2	RG	24?	N	1	RG	21	RG	2	RG	0	T
6.	N—2 T—?	0	T	0	T	0	T	0	T	0	T	0	T
7.	N—6 T—?	0	T	0	T	0	T	0	T	0	T	0	T
8.	N—5 T—?	0	T	0	T	0	T	0	T	0	T	0	T

TABLE 5 (*continued*)

No. Plate	explanation Plate	Subject A Resp.	Subject A Rat.	Subject B Resp.	Subject B Rat.	Subject C Resp.	Subject C Rat.	Subject D Resp.	Subject D Rat.	Subject E Resp.	Subject E Rat.	Subject F Resp.	Subject F Rat.
9.	N—7 T—?	O	T	O	T	O	T	O	T	O	T	O	T
10.	N—? T—? RG—5	5	RG	O	T	O	T	5	RG	5	RG	5	RG
11.	N—? T—? RG—2	2	RG	2	RG	2	RG	2	RG	2	RG	2	RG
12.	N Inc. RG { 26 Comp. R—6 Comp. G—2	6	R	O	T	6	R	6	R	2	G	6	R
13.	N Inc. RG { +2 Comp. R—2 Comp. G—+	2	R	O	T	2	R	2	R	+	G	2	R
14.	N—red line RG—blue line T—?	RG?	RG	RG?	RG	RG	RG	RG	RG	RG	RG	RG?	RG
15.	N—follows line T—?	O	T	O	T	O	T	O	T	O	T	O	T
16.	N—? T—? RG—follows line RG?	RG	N	RG	RG	RG?	N	RG	RG	RG	RG	RG?	N

TABLE 6
INDIVIDUAL RESPONSES FOR SUGGESTED TOTAL COLOR BLINDNESS

Plate No.	Plate explanation	Subject A		Subject B		Subject C		Subject D		Subject E		Subject F	
		Resp.	Rat.	Resp.	Rat.	Resp.	Rat.	Resp.	Rat.	Resp.	Rat.	Resp.	Rat.
2.	N—8 RG—3 T—?	O	T	O	T	O	T	O	T	O	T	O	T
3.	N—6 RG—5 T—?	5?	N	O	T	O	T	O	T	O	T	5?	N
4.	N—5 RG—2 T—?	O	T	2?	N	O	T	O	T	2?	N	?	D
5.	N—74 RG—21 T—?	2?	RG	O	T	1?	RG	O	T	O	T	2?	RG
6.	N—2 T—?	O	T	O	T	O	T	O	T	O	T	O	T
7.	N—6 T—?	O	T	O	T	O	T	O	T	O	T	O	T
8.	N—5 T—?	O	T	O	T	O	T	O	T	O	T	O	T

TABLE 6 (continued)

Plate No.	Plate explanation	Subject A Resp.	Subject A Rat.	Subject B Resp.	Subject B Rat.	Subject C Resp.	Subject C Rat.	Subject D Resp.	Subject D Rat.	Subject E Resp.	Subject E Rat.	Subject F Resp.	Subject F Rat.
9.	N—7 T—?	O	T	O	T	O	T	O	T	O	T	O	T
10.	N—? T—? RG—5	5?	RG	O		NT O	N/T	5?	RG	5?	RG	5?	RG
11.	N—? T—? RG—2	O	N/T	O		NT 2	RG	O	N/T	O	N/T	O	N/T
12.	N Inc. RG } 26 Comp. G—? Comp. G—2	2?	G	O	T	2?	G	2?	G	6?	R	O	T
13.	N Inc. RG +2 Comp. R—2 Comp. G—+	1?	D	4?	G	4?	G	2?	R	2?	R	2?	R
14.	N—red line RG—blue line T—?	?	T	RG-?	T	RG RG-?	RG	?	T	?	T	RG-?	RG
15.	N—follows line T—?	O	I	O	T	O	T	O	T	O	T	O	T
16.	N—? T—? RG—follows line ?	?	N/T	RG-?	N/T	RG RG-?	RG	?	N/T	?	N/T	?	N/T

TABLE 7
Distribution of Responses by Plates

Plate No.	Suggested green blindness					Suggested red blindness					Suggested red-green blindness					Suggested total color blindness				
	N	T	RG	R or G	D or N/T	N	T	RG	R or G	D or N/T	N	T	RG	R or G	D or N/T	N	T	RG	R or G	D or N/T
2	2		1		1D	1	1	3		1D		2	4				6			
3	5		1			2		2		2D	2	2	2			2	4			
4	1	1	4			1		4		1D	2	3	3			2	3			1D
5	2				3D	2	1			3D	1	1	4				3	3		
6	3		3					5		1D			6				6			
7	3		3										6				6			
8	2		4										6				6			
9	2		4							2D			6				6			
10			4		1N/T 1D					2N/T 1D		2	4					4		2N/T
11			3		1N/T 2D			5		1D			6					1		5N/T
12	2			1G	3D				5R	1D		1		1G 4R			2		3G 1R	
13	3			1R	2D				3R	2D		1		1G 4R					2G 3R	1D
14	1		5										6				3	3		
15	4		2					4		1N/T			6				6			
16			4		2N/T					1D			3				2	2		4N/T
Total	30	19	23	1G 1R	4N/T 12D	17	20	26	8R	3N/T 16D	6	42	32	2G 8R		4	51	13	5G 4R	11N/T 2D

TABLE 8
Distribution of Responses According to Plate Significance

Plate analysis	No. of instances	Suggested green blindness					Suggested red blindness					Suggested red-green blindness					Suggested total color blindness				
		N	T	RG	R or G	D or N/T	N	T	RG	R or G	D or N/T	N	T	RG	R or G	D or N/T	N	T	RG	R or G	D or N/T
Differentiating N and T (Plates 6, 7, 8, 9, 15)	30	14	16				10	16			4D		30					30			
Differentiating N, T and RG (Plates 2, 3, 4, 5, 14)	30	11	3	12		4D	7	3	13		7D	3	8	19			4	19	6		1D
Differentiating N and T from RG (Plates 10, 11, 16)	18			11		4N/T 3D			13		3N/T 2D	3	2	13					7		11N/T
Differentiating N and Inc. RG from Complete R and from Complete G (Plates 12, 13)	12	5			1R 1G	5D		1		8R	3D		2		8R 2G			2		4R 5G	1D
Totals		30	19	23	1R 1G	12D 4N/T	17	20	26	8R	16D 3N/T	6	42	32	8R 2G		4	51	13	4R 5G	2D 11N/T

4. An Experimental Investigation Of The Hypnotic Subjects Apparent Ability To Become Unaware Of Stimuli

Milton H. Erickson

The experimental study of the unresponsiveness of deeply hypnotized subjects to stimuli ordinarily effective and, conversely, their responsiveness to suggested but not real stimuli is a most difficult problem. Aside from the complexity of such phenomena, the subjects' necessary awareness and understanding of what they are or are not to do in such experimentation raises the important question: In what part are the experimental results to be attributed to actual experiential process of behavior within the subject, and in what part are they indicative only of the subject's full cooperation in manifesting that type of behavior proper only to the actual achievement of the suggested task?

For example, a cooperative subect who accepts the hypnotic task of becoming unaware of the presence of a third person may presumably become actually unaware of that third person, or despite an awareness, may behave in strict accordance with a lack of such awareness. Thus, in one instance his behavior seemingly is that of no response, and, in the other, that of successfully inhibited responses. But this is an oversimplification of the problem. Hence, for lack of more definitive language, examples of comparable behavior from common experience will be cited for their pertinency and because they illustrate various important considerations for an adequate understanding of this total problem.

The first of these relates to a man reading a book who may falsely believe himself to be alone. While so absorbed, he may respond to a gentle touch as if it were an itch and react adequately to this understanding of the stimulation by scratching behavior. His responsiveness to the stimulus in no way destroys or alters his unawareness of the presence of another person. Or he may behave as if annoyed by a fly, thus recognizing the external character of the stimulation but still making a mistaken response to it. Such stimulation may be repeated until its persistent recurrence compels another type of response. If this new response leads to an awareness of the presence of another, the startle or fright reaction may be regarded as an outward culmination of the experiential process of developing that awareness.

Reprinted with permission from *The Journal of General Psychology,* 1944, *31*, 191-212.

A second example is that of the tired mother who sleeps soundly despite disturbing noises. Nevertheless, at the slightest cry from her baby she rouses at once. Thus, in relation to certain types of stimuli she is unusually alert despite her unresponsiveness to other and even similar stimuli.

A third example is that of the ability of jute mill workers and boiler factory employees to carry on conversations in relatively normal tones of voice despite the shop din. The newcomer in such a situation, as personal experience has repeatedly disclosed, is often unable to hear clearly even loud shouting. With experience, however, one can learn to disregard the disturbing noises and to carry on conversations without undue effort and strain.

Discussion of these examples is difficult. Not only does their complexity present serious obstacles to investigative study, but any awareness by the subjects of an experimental approach to such behavior would alter completely the situation for them and militate against reliable and informative findings. Thus, one cannot determine how subjects would behave when they mistakenly believe they are alone if they know that they are mistaken in that belief. Nor can subjects' lowered thresholds for certain stimuli be tested satisfactorily as such if they expect to be tested for alertness to those special stimuli. Indeed, it is axiomatic that subjects in an experimental situation in which they know what is expected of them tend to behave in accord with the experimental demands. In such a situation any findings made are the result of both the experimental procedure and the subjects' readiness to yield such findings.

Hence a naturalistic as opposed to a frank experimental laboratory approach is essential to a study of various psychological phenomena. Especially is this true in relation to many hypnotic phenomena wherein a subject's mere readiness to behave in a certain way may yield the same outward objective findings as would result from actual experimental processes of behavior. All the more so is the naturalistic approach indicated when the introduction of experimental methods or any awareness that behavior is being systematically studied may lead the subjects to cooperate for the purposes of giving the "scientific" results apparently desired.

In this account it is proposed to report the procedures and results obtained in investigating certain hypnotic phenomena often described categorically as "selective sensory anaesthesias." In all probability, such a descriptive term is not necessarily applicable since, as one subject aptly declared, "It is not a question of being unaware of stimuli but, rather, a giving of all attention to certain stimuli or to certain aspects of a stimulus complex without other stimuli entering into the situation." The pertinency of this statement is readily appreciated in relation to the first example from common experience cited above.

The investigative procedure used in this study was a combination of both the naturalistic and the direct experimental approaches carried out in an informal social setting. So far as the subject was concerned, the purposes to be served were obvious and understandable and only related to the social situation, and full cooperation was readily given. However, the subject did not know that the apparent purposes were only secondary to unrealized and actually experimental objectives. Indeed, in the second account the experimenter himself did not realize that a second behavioral development was taking place until the results disclosed the fact, following which there was a simple utilization of the spontaneous developments.

In both accounts the experimental objective was the investigation of the hypnotic subject's ability to become unresponsive or unawarare, at both visual and auditory levels, of the presence of selected persons at a social gathering. In the first report the subject was given full instructions to become unaware of a certain person, and after these suggestions had been repeated adequately and what was considered a sufficient amount of time had elapsed, they were intentionally made inclusive of a second person. So far as the subject was concerned, the object in mind was a demonstration for a social group of his unawareness of the presence of those two people. The actual experimental purpose was to contrast his behavior in response to each of those persons and to determine if the element of time itself played a significant role in the effectiveness with which he performed his task.

In the second report the original purpose was merely a demonstration in a social situation of somnambulistic behavior. Fortunately a chance incident so altered the demonstration situation that, contrary to all suggestions given to the subject, an unexpected demonstration was given of "selective deafness" and "selective blindness."

As a necessary preliminary to the presentation of these reports, a short discussion will be offered of a serious misconception of hypnosis frequently encountered even among those who have had extensive experience. This misconception, briefly stated, is that hypnosis in some particular, undefined fashion necessarily deprives subjects of their natural abilities for responsive, self-expressive, and aggressive behavior, and limits and restricts them to the role of purely passive and receptive instruments of the hypnosis.

The fact that receptiveness and passivity can be used to induce those processes of behavior that result in a trance state does not signify that they constitute essential criteria of the trance condition itself. Rather, there should be recognition of the fact that the general tendency of the hypnotic subject to be passive and receptive is simply expressive of the suggestibility of the hypnotic subject, hence a direct result of the suggestions employed to induce hypnosis and not a function of the hypnotic state.

Neverthelesss, the mistaken assumption is often made that hypnotic subjects must display the same passive receptive behavior when in a trance that they displayed in the process of going into the trance. The fact that the hypnotic subject's psychological state of awareness has been altered constitutes no logical barrier to any form of self-expressive behavior within the general frame of reference, and experience discloses that, in addition to their usual abilities, hypnotic subjects are often capable of behavior ordinarily impossible for them.

In the following experiments utilization has been made of the ability of hypnotic subjects to behave in full accord with their natural capacities. This was accomplished by a training procedure of first hypnotizing them deeply by a prolonged laborious technique that did not demand immediate results. Then situations were devised in which the subjects had ample time and opportunity to discover and to develop their abilities to respond to the demands made of them with as little interference from the hypnotist as possible. After such preliminary training in hypnosis, experiments like the following can be conducted with relative ease.

In accord with the informal social situation in which they were conducted, both experiments will be reported in narrative form to permit greater comprehensiveness.

EXPERIMENT NO. I

During the course of a demonstration of hypnotic phenomena before a medically trained group the question of "negative hallucinations," that is, the inability to perceive actual stimuli, was raised privately to the hypnotist. After some discussion out of the subject's hearing concerning the validity of such phenomena, it was decided to conduct an experiment for the group in the form of a simple demonstration.

Accordingly, the subject was deeply hypnotized and a somnambulistic state induced. She was instructed to look about the room carefully and to become fully aware of those present. After she had scrutinized everyone carefully and identified them by name, she was told that shortly she would discover that Dr. A had left. Indeed, it was emphasized that soon she would realize that she had been mistaken in thinking that A had been present. Finally, she was told that she would really know that A had originally intended to be present but that he had failed to arrive. This fact, it was explained, would account for her original impression that he had been present. These instructions were systematically repeated in various forms with increasing emphasis upon her full realization that A had not been there and that in all probability he would not be able to appear.

In the meanwhile, acting upon instruction, A withdrew quietly and unobtrusively into the background, where he remained out of range of the subject's vision.

When it seemed that the subject understood fully the suggestions given to her, she was kept busy with various attention-absorbing tasks for about 20 minutes. She was then reminded in a casual fashion that A had originally intended to be present but that he had been unable to come and would probably not be able to attend at all. When she nodded in agreement, the original series of suggestions was repeated, but this time in connection with Dr. B. When this second series had been fully impressed upon her, she was again given attention-absorbing tasks for two or three minutes while B, even as had A, remained quietly in the background. Then the same casual general reminder previously made in relation to A was repeated in connection with B.

Thus, approximately 25 minutes and 5 minutes elapsed from the giving of the suggestions relating respectively to A and to B.

Thereupon her attention was directed to the group and she was asked to identify those present. This she did readily, omitting, however, both A and B. The group was then told quietly to challenge her statements and to break down her exclusion of those two gentlemen.

Very shortly it became apparent that there was a marked difference in her behavior in relation to A and B. She was apparently completely unaware of A's presence and entirely at ease in offering the false explanation that had been given her, nor did she show any evidence that his absence could be regarded as a debatable issue. In no way did she disclose any awareness of his presence.

In relation to B, however, her behavior was decidedly different. There were definite avoidance responses, evidences of confusion and blocking, and she seemed to be uncertain about the situation although emphatic in her assertion that B was not present. It was noted that, when told to look in his direction, there was a marked tendency to glance aside, or in looking slowly about the room, to skip B by a quick glance past him. None of this behavior was apparent in relation to A.

Upon a signal both A and B joined in the general conversation. To A's voice no response of any sort could be detected by the group. To B's voice many partial responses were made, such as a slight involuntary turn of her head, puzzled looks, a spontaneous statement that she thought she heard someone speaking, and that she felt uncomfortable, that is, as if all were not right. She resisted successfully the efforts of the group to break down her expressed conviction that B was not there, but her behavior was suggestive of resistance to the development of an awareness, or of an inhibition of responses.

In connection with A, however, she displayed no need to resist since, for her, he simply was not there. In other words there seemed to be neither responses nor need to inhibit responses.

After about 10 minutes of such investigation the subject was again busied with various attention-absorbing tasks for 15 or 20 minutes. Then again the group was told to investigate the situation.

This time there was found to be no difference in her behavior in relation to both A and B. So far as could be determined, she made no response of any sort to their presence. There was no avoidance behavior, no uncertainty, and no evidence of mental strain. She readily recalled the previous questioning and related that at that time she had had an uncomfortable feeling that B might have arrived without her awareness and that this feeling had made her uneasy about the questioning and uncertain in her replies. She also recalled having thought that she had heard his voice, but she attributed this to her general state of confusion caused by her conviction that he was not there and a feeling that he might be secretly present.

When A and B joined in the questioning and discussion, none of the previous partial responses to B's voice were made. Her behavior was as if they were actually absent.

Upon signals both A and B lifted her arm and shook hands with her. She became aware of this at once, looked down at her hand each time with an expression of amusement and interest. Questioned by the group about this, she explained with simple earnestness that in all probability she had been given some posthypnotic cue which had caused her unconsciously to respond as if she were shaking hands with someone. Her only uncertainty was whether or not there had been an actual movement of her hand or just an hallucinatory experience.

Promptly both A and B shook her hand again, and she explained that it was a genuine motor and visual experience even though the tactile sensations were hallucinatory, since there was nothing touching her hand. In responding to the questions of the group, she made no effort to look around the body of either A or B but seemed to be looking through them. Questioning by the group elicited her understanding that a nodding of my head, actually a signal to A and B, was a signal for her to undergo some planned hypnotic experience, which she had now discovered to be the hallucination of shaking hands with someone.

(As a parenthetical insert in elaboration of this point, an account may be given of results obtained from a number of other subjects. Instructed to remember carefully that a member of the audience was sitting in a certain chair, the subject would thereafter continue to see that person in the specified chair despite a change of position. The subject, however, would readily detect the alteration in the location of that person's voice resulting from the change of position. Usually the subject responds to this situation by scrutinizing the chair and the source of the voice alternately. Several outcomes are possible. The subject may rationalize the altered location of the voice as an inexplicable phenomenon with a failure to see the person in the new position and with a substitution of a memory image for the actual person. Or the subject may discover that there has been a change of seat and will call the hypnotist's attention to the matter so that further instruction may be given. A third and not infrequent development for the subject is to discover the person sitting in both places and become confused as to which is the real person. In subjects trained in psychology or psychiatry this becomes an interesting phenomenon to observe. The usual procedure followed by subjects is to suggest to themselves that the person is to make some movement or to perform some act. The visual image does, and the real person does not. Occasionally the subject merely studies the two figures to see which one tends to fade and blur, and this is recognized as the visual image.)

The subject was instructed to perform aloud simple sums in addition, the numbers to be suggested by the members of the group. After a dozen such additions had been rapidly called to her, both A and B separately called numbers to her. No response of any sort could be detected. She merely sat quietly and expectantly, waiting for those members of the group who were present for her to call problems for her. Several repetitions of this failed to elicit responses to

A and *B*. Nor did the measure of having *A* and *B* call the same and other numbers in unison with the others serve to confuse her. Apparently she was selectively deaf to both of them.

Advantage was taken of a telephone call to tell her that both *A* and *B* would arrive in exactly five minutes, and her attention was directed to a clock. In about five minutes she was observed to turn her head toward the door and to go through the behavior of watching somebody enter the room. Close observation of her eyeballs disclosed her to be watching apparently hallucinated figures entering the room and to be glancing over the available chairs. She was observed to go through the process of letting one select the chair where *A* was really sitting and the other select the chair where *B* was sitting. She greeted them courteously and then her eye movements disclosed her to be watching them sit down in the selected chairs. Thereafter, both were fully present for her.

(A second digression is necessary in this regard. Approximately 50 persons, most of whom had seen this type of hypnotic behavior but who had not been hypnotized, have been asked to duplicate it in detail or to perform a comparable act. One simple procedure easily described is as follows: The unhypnotized experimental subjects are instructed to behave as if a selected third person actually present is not present, and after they feel confident of their ability in this pretense, they are instructed to hallucinate or fantasy a picture of that person hanging on the wall. The unhypnotized subject goes through a mental process of hanging a fantasied picture with regard for good spacing on a wall usually remote from the third person. There is a definite quality of avoidance of the real object in his behavior.

The hypnotized subject, however, given the same task, hangs the hallucinatory picture on the wall in close proximity to the person presumably absent and with a disregard for proper spacing. Usually the hypnotic subject recognizes that the picture should be hung elsewhere with regard to proper arrangement but explains that for some inexplicable reason it seems best to put the picture where he has placed it, actually in proximity to the supposedly absent person. Thus, in contrast to the unhypnotized subject, a utilization of the real object rather than an avoidance response is made.)

Subsequently the subject was questioned under hypnosis about these experiences. She explained that, in relation to *A*, she had been convinced at first that he was present. This had been followed by a state of mental confusion and uncertainty about his presence. Shortly this confusion had resolved itself into a realization that *A* was not present but that she had only expected him to be there. While these ideas were developing, she had recalled identifying someone as *A* and this had caused her some feeling of embarrassment and made her hope that no offense had been taken. This feeling of emotional distress had made her wish that the author would proceed with whatever plans he might have.

Then, when suggestions were given her about *B*, a similar train of events began to develop, but while she was still confused and uncertain about him, the group began to question her. This had added to her confusion and uncertainty and had made her most uncomfortable, a fact she had labored to conceal. The questioning about *A* she had not been able to understand since it seemed to be out of place and without basis, since she was certain no one could know about her previous misunderstandings.

Following the interlude in which she had been asked to read aloud, this general confusion about *B* and her vague impressions of having heard his voice disappeared, and she found herself at a loss to understand the purposes of the group in questioning her further. Not until the "hallucinatory" handshaking occurred did she realize that a hypnotic demonstration was occurring. With that understanding she had developed a mild passive interest in the situation and had tried to meet whatever demands were made upon her as adequately as possible, since this understanding explained fully her previous states of confusion.

No effort was made to correct these misinterpretations of the total situation. Rather, it was left open on the possibility of future experimental developments.

Summary

This account may be summarized best by itemizing in chronological order the experimental developments.

1. A deeply hypnotized subject in a somnambulistic trance was instructed to become unaware of the presence of a selected person.
2. After proper suggestions to this end a period of 10 minutes was allowed to elapse as a measure of permitting the subject to develop that "mental set" or the neuro- and psychophysiological processes necessary to such a state of unawareness.
3. The subject was instructed as previously to become unaware of a second person.
4. A period of time considered too brief for the development of a mental set was allowed to elapse.
5. Tests were made for behavioral responses in relation to the two selected persons.
6. The subject showed no responses to the first person but made many partial responses and avoidance reactions in relation to the second person.
7. A sufficient period of time was allowed to elapse for the development of the proper mental set in relation to the second person.
8. Testing disclosed the subject to be equally unresponsive to and unaware of both persons at visual and auditory levels.
9. Tactile stimulation by the selected two persons was misinterpreted as hallucinatory experiences possibly deriving from posthypnotic cues.
10. The subject hallucinated the arrival of the selected persons and reestablished contact with them.
11. Subsequent questioning of the subject under hypnosis disclosed a persistence of an understanding of the total situation in full accord with the hyp-

notic suggestions and not in accord with the actual facts.

EXPERIMENT NO. II

Before a group of associates in the author's office a well-trained subject was hypnotized deeply and given instructions to develop the somnambulistic state. Additionally, he was told that upon the development of this somnambulistic state he was to establish full contact with the group and to act in every detail of his behavior as if he were actually wide awake. Thus, by his behavior, conversation, and participation in group activities he was to convince everybody that he was unquestionably wide awake and not in a hypnotic trance. However, he was told that, when questioned directly as to whether or not he was in the trance, he was to reply honestly, readily, and directly.

After these suggestions had been repeated several times to insure his full understanding, and after he had been given about 20 minutes while he was sleeping deeply in which to mull them over and to develop what may conveniently be called the mental set essential to their performance, he was told to proceed with his task.

The subject responded by lifting his head, yawning, stretching, and remarking that he felt rather sleepy, that apparently it was up to him to be a bit more lively.

This subject had a very charming personality, was a pleasing conversationalist, alert, responsive, and possessed of good wit and high intelligence. Immediately one of the group asked him if he was asleep, to which the subject replied:

> Yes, I'm very much asleep, sound asleep in a trance state, but you'll never be able to detect it. In fact, you're going to have a hard time proving in your own mind that I am asleep, but if you wish you can ask Dr. Erickson or you can ask me, and we will both tell you the truth, which is that I am in a deep hypnotic trance. Would you like to talk to me and find out how a hypnotized subject can talk and act even though asleep?

For about an hour the subject kept the group busy asking questions or responding to questions put to him, and the range of conversation was very wide. Books were discussed, the typewriter in the office was used by the subject upon request, jokes were told, and the subject's alertness and responsiveness to everything occurring in the office was repeatedly demonstrated by him. Nevertheless, at every straightforward question about his status, the subject replied with the simple factual statement that he was in a trance, and, to the experienced hypnotist, there were many indirect evidences of this fact. Usually when this question was asked of him, after making his straightforward reply, the subject would make his questioner the butt of jesting remarks. At the end of an hour a medically trained colleague, Dr. C, who had had no experience with hypnosis, stepped into the office, remarking that he had heard the sound of laughter and conversation and he wanted to know if a hypnotic demonstration was taking place. The subject responded at once by asking C if it seemed to him that anybody appeared to be hypnotized. C answered in the negative, but added that he hoped he might have the chance to see hypnosis. To this the subject replied with the ambiguous statement that his best opportunity was to observe what was going on, since the afternoon's plans called for nothing more than the present activities. Following this the subject and C engaged in a casual conversation on various items and shortly C left. The group then continued as they had before. Presently a second visitor, Dr. D., entered the office. This doctor more or less regularly dropped in on Saturday afternoons, a fact well known to the subject, and hence he was not a totally unexpected visitor. As he entered the room and noted the group, he promptly asked if the author were demonstrating hypnosis. An affirmative reply was given, and the subject suggested, since he knew D very well, that look over the group and see if he could tell who might be a good hypnotic subject. D promptly replied that he knew the subject himself was well trained and that two others in the group had also been hypnotic subjects, and therefore it might be any one of the three or for that matter someone else in the group. One of the others then spoke up and asked the visitor if he thought anybody in the room was in a hypnotic trance. Since D had done some hypnosis himself and had often seen some of the author's subjects in somnambulistic trances, he glanced carefully about the room, sizing up each individual present, verbalizing comments as he scrutinized them and carrying on a casual conversation, asking general questions about how long the group had been gathered in the room, what work they had been engaged in during the morning and similar items. Finally he remarked that if he were pressed to venture a guess, he would select the subject as the most likely choice for the afternoon's work and that he felt that this choice of possible subjects was probably in a somnambulistic state at the actual moment. Immediately the subject asked him to justify his guess. D's explanation was that there were certain rigidities in the subject's movements, a loss of associated movements, some lag between his speech and his gestures and head movements and a marked pupillary dilation. He also explained that the subject moved his arms and walked very much as if he were in a trance state. As D made these remarks, the subject slowly flushed, turned to the author apologetically, and expressed his regret that he had failed to obey instructions completely. Then turning to D, he confirmed D's guess and admitted that he was in a somnambulistic state. The subject was comforted about having betrayed himself by the author's pointing out that D's own experience had enabled him to recognize certain evidences of the trance state ordinarily overlooked.

After a brief chat D left and the group then busied itself with attempts to detect alterations in the subject's motor behavior. The two other subjects soon demonstrated an ability to single out some of these behavioral alterations, but the rest of the group experienced difficulty. Furthermore, as this investigation continued, the subject became increasingly successful in simulating the motor behavior of a person fully awake. Eventually he succeeded in interesting the group in a general conversation, and this was allowed to drift along ordinary social channels.

Unexpectedly a third visitor, Dr. $E.$, from out of town and whom the subject did not know, dropped in for a brief visit while on his way to Detroit. This arrival was totally unexpected by the author. Hence it differed markedly from the visits of C and D, inasmuch as they constituted something entirely within the usual course of events. For this reason their visits could be regarded as legitimate extensions of the total office situation. The visit by E belonged to another and totally different category of events and could not be expected to occur. It was entirely outside the range of the situation the subject had been asked to meet. As this visitor approached the office door, which had been left open, his arrival was noted and he was immediately signalled to be quiet and to wait outside the door and to keep out of visual range of the others present. Watching for opportunities when the subject was engaged in discussing matters with one or another of the group, the author displayed to all except the subject a sheet of paper on which was written, "Ignore our new visitor, do not disclose any awareness of his presence." When all of the group had been warned and the subject's attention was distracted, the visitor was signalled to enter the room. He did so quietly and took his seat on the edge of the group. The subject was allowed to finish the discussion in which he was engaged with one of the group and then he was asked to review the course of the afternoon's events, the seeming purpose being to summarize them for the benefit of the group.

Promptly and adequately he reviewed the entire course of the demonstration. During this discourse he was asked repeatedly to point out where the various members of the group had been sitting at different times. When he came to the time of the entrance of C, he pointed out how C had stood beside the secretary's desk alongside of which was now sitting E. He was asked why C had remained standing when the secretary's chair was available, but he explained that C had undoubtedly been busy and did not want to stay long enough to take a seat. He then continued his discussion up to the point of arrival of D. He flushed as he recounted D's recognition of his hypnotic behavior, and among other things, related that D had sat in the chair where E was then sitting. He was asked if he were sure that the chair had remained constantly in one position throughout the entire time. He declared this doubtful since it was a swivel chair and since D had swung around repeatedly as he talked to the various members of the group. At no time did he become aware of the presence of E. When the subject had completed his summarization, it was suggested that the group continue as previously.

When the subject's attention was taken up by a discussion with one of the group, E was signalled to join in the conversation. He did so readily, timing his remarks to coincide with those of another speaker. The subject replied readily to the other members of the group and did not seem to hear E or to be confused by the simultaneity of two utterances. This continued for some time but soon resulted in the group hesitating and faltering in their utterances when E spoke. This distressed the subject, and he began scrutinizing the various members of the group. Shortly he asked the author if there were something wrong. When asked his reason for this question, he replied that the others seemed to be ill at ease and uncertain in their behavior, that they turned their heads unexpectedly and then would halt the movement, that they did not seem to be acting normally. E promptly asked the subject what that might mean, but apparently the subject did not hear this question. The subject was assured that everything was all right, that he need not be concerned about the group since everything was going along satisfactorily *and that no matter what occurred it would all be of interest. Also, it was suggested that he might be interested to discover what the situation was.* (The generality of these and other instructions and statements was intentional, the purpose being to give the subject free opportunity to become aware of E. Furthermore, it was expected that he would do so, since it was not realized how completely the subject had limited himself to the expected situation and thus excluded from awareness any unusual developments).

After still further conversation with the group, the subject turned again and stated that he had figured out the situation. The explanation he offered was in full accord with what he had seen at a previous hypnotic demonstration, and it was as follows: While his attention had been distracted, advantage had been taken of such an opportunity to induce somnambulistic states in all those present. He explained that repeatedly various members of the group would start to say something and then falter and hesitate, that they kept turning their heads and moving about in an uncertain way as if they were not quite certain what to do. This behavior, he added, was similar to that he had seen at other demonstrations when subjects had been induced to experience active hallucinations. He was asked if he were convinced of his explanation. Scrutinizing the group closely, he admitted that he did not see the usual evidences of the trance state, but that he could not conceive of any other explanation which would account for their peculiar behavior. After thinking still further on the matter he volunteered as a second possible explanation, that secret instructions to the group to act in this way might have been given without inducing a trance state, but he declared that he did not see how they could carry on such pretenses so effectively.

Here the question may be raised why the subject offered such a rationalization when he knew that he was in a trance state and hence that his state of awareness might be limited. The answer to this probably lies in the misleading effects of his previous experiences and in the fact that the total experimental situation compelled him to believe that he was fully aware of everything. Thus there was no recourse for him except to offer an explanation in terms of established understandings and not in terms of unfamiliar and unexpected possibilities.

The subject was asked if he were willing to continue with his task of behaving as if he were wide awake and giving no evidence that he was in the trance state.

He again expressed his willingness, whereupon he was told to continue but to take care that his general behavior in no way betrayed that he was in a trance state, although he was still, upon direct inquiry, to admit that he was hypnotized. The subject asked earnestly and worriedly if he were disclosing his hypnotic state by his general behavior, but was promptly reassured by the general statement that whatever happened would unquestionably be most desirable. Care was taken in this instance as well as all others not to limit or to restrict the subject's possible responses. Rather, reassurances and instructions were worded generally so that the subject was at liberty to make any response for which the occasion arose, and similarly all instructions were given in general terms to permit a spontaneous development of the situation.

Shortly he became interested in a conversation with a member of the group, and at once a signal was quietly given to E, who stepped over and lifted the subject's arm.

(To digress: Ordinarily there are two usual reactions to this type of maneuver. Either the subject may remain totally unaware of what has occurred and continue in his behavior without alteration except for the substitution of memory images of tactile and visual images to permit him to feel and see his hand and arm in the original position. If the enforced hand movements serve to disrupt his general posture and become too forceful, he tends to experience discomfort as if originating in the shoulder. From this point on he may proceed to discover the actual change in position of his arm, sometimes with and sometimes without an awareness of the person manipulating the arm.

Or he may immediately detect the arm movement, become puzzled, and proceed to attribute it to hypnotic suggestion or to determine the actual state of affairs, depending upon the nature of the experimental situation. In the present situation the subject was obligated to be aware of all motor behavior, hence his immediate response.)

The subject became aware at once that something was happening to his hand and arm. He flushed, glanced at the author in a somewhat frightened and guilty fashion, attempted to replace his hand in his lap, and then tried to resist the handshaking forced upon him. The silent, interested scrutiny of the entire group distressed him, and he explained in a worried fashion that he knew he should not display unusual motor behavior indicative of the trance state but that something had happened which he could not control and which he could not explain or understand.

In speaking and in glancing at the members of the group, he made no effort to look around E nor did he seem to be aware that E kept stepping in front of him to block his line of vision.

Urged to describe what was happening, he explained that it seemed as if somebody were manipulating his hand—that the texture of the skin and strength of the grip that he seemed to sense made him feel that some man whom he could not see was present and shaking hands with him. Instead of being given any reply he was asked if he were not, in utter violation of instructions, betraying by his general behavior that he was in a trance state. The subject flushed anew, and his face again became expressive of guilt. He protested earnestly that he was doing the best that he could, but the situation had become inexplicable to him and he did not understand what was happening unless the author had, in some indirect way, given him special cues or hypnotic suggestions for which he had an amnesia.

While the subject waited for some reassuring or comforting answer, the author turned aside, greeted E, and proceeded to introduce him formally to the entire group one by one. The subject watched this performance, apparently heard the remarks made and the replies of the group, but he gave no indication of hearing E's acknowledgments. Finally, stepping over to the subject, the author introduced E by saying with a rising inflection of the voice, "And this is Dr. E." The subject merely repeated the words as if they carried no meaning and stared blankly, making no response to E's courteous acknowledgment of the introduction. Thereupon E clapped him jovially on the back. This caused the subject to whirl quickly in a startled fashion and to look about behind him. Seeing nobody, he stepped backward and leaned with his back against the bookcase as if protecting himself from further assault.

No further attention was paid to him for some minutes, and the entire group entered into a conversation with E. While they were so engaged, the subject was observed to study his hand, to move his shoulders as if to feel again the clap on the back, and then to study the behavior of the group and to repeat in a puzzled fashion the acknowledgments of the introductions made by the members of the group.

After some minutes of such intense study, with much puzzled looking at the author and at the group, the subject finally offered the explanation that everybody was acting as if someone else were present and that he himself had had tactile sensations such as would be experienced from actual contact with a person. He asked if this state of affairs was some sort of an experiment intended to induce him to hallucinate the presence of someone or if there were actually some person present unknown to him as the result of his being in a trance. He reasoned that this latter possibility was not readily tenable, since he had become aware at once of the arrivals of C and D and that, therefore, the present situation was best explained as a result of indirect hypnotic cues and suggestions given to him, supplemented by careful and secret instructions to the group regarding their behavior. This, he declared, was quite likely, since the afternoon session had been greatly prolonged, had dragged slowly at times, and furthermore the group at times had acted uncertain in their behavior, as if they did not know just what to do next. Even as he was making these remarks, E interrupted to explain that he now had to leave, made the appropriate remarks, and took his departure. The subject completed his remarks without noticing the intentional interruption by E, and seemed amused as he watched everybody apparently shaking hands with the empty air and saying good-bye. When, however, E stepped over and shook hands with him, he appeared at first bewildered and amused and satisfied. He declared that he was right in his guess, explained that the elaborate shaking of hands was nothing more than a beautiful build-up of indirect suggestions to induce him to do the same thing, and he expressed his pleasure in noting how adequately he had unwittingly responded.

Following E's departure a general conversation was resumed, and after the lapse of half an hour the subject was awakened and thanked for his services. He was astonished to note the time and said that he hoped that whatever he had done during the course of the afternoon had proved satisfactory. Of this he was fully assured.

The next day and on several later occasions, indirect remarks were made to evoke associations that might disclose some recollections of his trance experiences. These elicited no positive results of any sort.

Subsequently he was hypnotized and asked to recall the events of that afternoon. This he did adequately, except that he disclosed no awareness that there had been a third visitor, even though he recounted fully the seemingly inexplicable developments that had taken place.

Still later, in a deep trance, he was asked to do some crystal gazing and by this means to describe everything that had happened that afternoon in its correct chronological order. This he did adequately and in much fuller detail than he had previously recounted it verbally, but again there was the same awareness of the presence of E.

During the process of the crystal gazing he hallucinated the remarks of the group and was much impressed by what he described as the excellence of the performance of the group in acting as if someone else were present. He called attention repeatedly to the faltering and hesitation the group showed in speaking, as if someone else had started to speak at the same time. He also commented freely on the tendency of the group, as he visualized them in the crystal, to turn their heads and to speak as if they were addressing someone who was not present.

No attempt was made to give him a true understanding. He was thanked for his careful work in crystal gazing and asked if he were satisfied with everything. When he stated simply that he was, the matter was dropped with the hope that sometime later there might be other informative developments. However, to date, the subject remains, so far as can be determined, amnesic in the waking state for the events of that afternoon. In the trance state there is still a persistence of his original understandings.

Summary

The experimental developments may be summarized by itemizing them in chronological order.
1. For purposes of a group demonstration in the author's office a deeply hypnotized subject was instructed to develop a somnambulistic state and in this

state to simulate, as completely as possible, ordinary waking behavior but to state upon direct questioning whether or not he was in a trance.

2. After a lapse of sufficient time to permit the subject to develop what was considered an adequate mental set for this task he was told to proceed.

3. The subject appeared to awaken and participated readily and capably in group activities, impressing everyone with his state of ordinary wakefulness. Direct questions elicited the acknowledgment that he was hypnotized.

4. The subject became aware at once of the separate, unplanned, and unanticipated arrivals of two persons well known to him and who were frequent office visitors.

5. From one of these visitors, who had had no experience with hypnosis but who was well aware of the subject's hypnotic work, the subject successfully concealed his trance state.

6. The second visitor, like the first, was fully aware of the general facts about the subject and was, in addition, experienced in hypnosis. After careful study of the entire group this visitor recognized the subject's somnambulistic state and substantiated this discovery by pointing out significant characteristic hypnotic alterations of behavior.

7. After the departure of this visitor the subject, apologetic because of his failure to perform his task satisfactorily and aided by the more critical observations of the group, made renewed efforts to simulate more effectively ordinary waking behavior.

8. There arrived, unexpectedly, an out-of-town visitor whom the subject did not know, who could not be considered a legitimate extension of the office situation, and who was introduced unobtrusively into the general situation when the subject's attention was otherwise directed.

9. The subject remained consistently unaware of and unresponsive to this visitor at both auditory and visual levels despite his full contact with the situation in other regards.

10. The altered behavior of the group in relation to this visitor was readily observed by the subject but was not understood by him, and he offered various rationalizations in explanation of it. These were in accord with his previous hypnotic experiences and his apparent immediate limitations of awareness.

11. Physical manipulation of the subject by this visitor evoked general manifestations in accord with his hypnotic condition. This caused the subject to develop startle and fright reactions and led him to express guilt feelings because he found himself uncontrollably violating instructions to behave as if wide awake.

12. Further instruction to behave fully as if wide awake did not enable the subject to become aware of the visitor, although the group increasingly manifested involuntary reactions to the visitor's presence.

13. The subject finally resolved his inability to understand the situation as it had developed for him by misinterpreting it as a planned and systematic use

of indirect suggestions by the entire group to elicit involuntary hypnotic responses from him.

14. Subsequent questioning of the subject in the waking state disclosed an apparent amnesia for all trance events.

15. Inquiry under hypnosis elicited a ready verbal account of everything except an awareness of the third visitor.

16. Crystal gazing by the subject resulted in a full detailed account, but without the discovery of the presence of the third visitor. No effort was made to correct the subject's understanding of the total situation.

CONCLUDING REMARKS

Definitive conclusions cannot be drawn from two reports of behavior as complex as that which these subjects displayed. Nevertheless, the statement is warranted that the results obtained are not an atypical, highly individualistic phenomenon, and that similar behavior may reasonably be expected, but not necessarily be easily obtained, from other subjects under comparable conditions.

Neither can there be any extensive discussion of the possible nature and significances of these experimental results, since they constitute an initial study of a most difficult problem, an understanding of which can be reached only by repeated successful studies variously controlled and yielding informative negative or positive results. However, it is to be noted that these experimental findings, so expressive of an altered state of awareness not ordinarily conceivable, are in accord with the findings made in other experimental hypnotic studies of induced deafness, color blindness, "regression states," amnesia, aphasia, anaesthesia and, posthypnotic states (Erickson, 1938a & b; 1939a,b,c,d; 1941; 1943a,b,c; Erickson & Brickner, 1942; Erickson & Erickson, 1938 & 1941; Erickson & Kubie, 1941). Additionally, they are comparable in some degree to those common spontaneous limited restrictions of awareness seen in states of intense concentration, abstraction, and reverie or in the failure to perceive something obvious because of a state of expectation of someting quite different.

Certain general considerations, already mentioned in the introduction, may be reemphasized. The first of these, stated briefly, concerns the investigative possibilities of this type of experimental procedure for certain complex psychological phenomena, as contrasted to rigidly controlled experimental procedures which cannot provide for unexpected spontaneous developments extending beyond the devised experimental situation. Often such unanticipated behavioral developments constitute the more significant findings and are of primary importance in the experimental study of complex and involved phenomena. When such behavior has been elicited, there is then an opportunity to devise rigidly controlled experimental conditions by which to define it in terms of a known situation, instead of attempting the difficult problem of trying initially to define the precise conditions under which presumably possible behavior might appear.

The second consideration relates to the variety of spontaneous volitional activities by deeply hypnotized subjects. These two reports disclose the capacity of hypnotized subjects to respond adequately to a given situation without being restricted or limited to the passively responsive behavior so often regarded as a criterion of the trance state. In other words, there seems to be no valid reason to expect hypnotized subjects to lose their capacities for spontaneous, expressive, and capable behavior or to expect them to become simply instruments of the hypnotist. Rather, the subjects may more properly be expected to behave adequately within the situation that is established for them, and hence, even as these subjects did, to function as capably in the trance state as in the waking state.

The third consideration is the possible importance of neuro- and psychophysiological processes in eliciting extremely complex hypnotic behavior. It is hardly reasonable to expect a hypnotized subject, upon a snap of the fingers or the utterance of a simple command, to develop at once significant, complex, and persistent changes in behavioral functioning. Rather, it is to be expected that time and effort are required to permit a development of any profound alterations in behavior. Such alteration must presumably arise from neuro- and psychophysiological changes and processes within the subject, which are basic to behavioral manifestations, and not from the simple experience of hearing a command spoken by the hypnotist. One needs only to take into consideration the marked neuro- and psychophysiological differences between the behavior of the hypnotized subject in an ordinary trance state and that of the unhypnotized subject to realize that still further developments in hypnotic behavior may be dependent upon additional and extensive changes in the neurological and the psychological functioning of the individual. In brief, these two reports indicate that complex hypnotic behavior is not a superficial phenomenon elicited readily by simple commands, but rather, that it is based upon significant processes of behavioral functioning within the subject which are fundamental to outward manifestations and that it constitutes an experiential process for the subject.

5. The Development of an Acute Limited Obsessional Hysterical State in a Normal Hypnotic Subject

Milton H. Erickson

In any experimental hypnotic work, however well-planned, there are always the questions of what results will be secured, how they will become manifest, what will constitute adequate procedures, and what the experiment will mean in the experiential life of the subject. The following experiment is reported for the illustrations it offers of these interrelated problems.

The subject of this experiment was generally regarded as a normal, well-adjusted, highly intelligent 25-year-old woman engaged in completing her work for a doctorate in psychology. During a 15-months' period she had often been used as a hypnotic subject for both experimental and demonstration purposes. Additionally, she had often critically and interestedly observed hypnotic experimentation done with other subjects, sometimes contributing both suggestions and assistance.

Among the experimental procedures she had witnessed had been the induction of hypnotic deafness, blindness, and color blindness, but these trance phenomena had never been induced in her. Nevertheless, while in deep trance and somnambulistic states she customarily manifested an apparently total unawareness of auditory, visual, and tactile stimuli which did not actually belong to the hypnotic situation itself. Thus she had demonstrated repeatedly the development of at least a marked decrease in perceptual activity at those sensory levels, a fact of which she was unaware.

In observing the hypnotic experimentation with other subjects, she had been particularly interested in the effect of hypnotic suggestion upon sensory behavior. This interest, she had explained at length, derived from her study in that field. She had frankly expressed doubts about the genuineness of such phenomena induced experimentally in the other subjects and had often asked permission to make her own tests of the results obtained. After a critical examination and

Read in part at the 4th annual meeting of the Society for Clinical and Experimental Hypnosis, New York Academy of Sciences, Sept. 26, 1953; and in part at the 1st Annual meeting of the Southern Calif. Psychiatric Society, Los Angeles, Calif., Nov. 14, 1953; reprinted with permission from *The Journal of Clinical & Experimental Hypnosis,* January, 1954, 2, 27-41.

testing of several subjects showing variously deafness, blindness, color blindness, and anaesthesia, she became unwillingly convinced of the validity of the phenomena. However, she reacted personally by declaring emphatically that, regardless of what could be accomplished at those sensory levels with other subjects, such altered states could not possibly be developed in her.

After some discussion of this topic she conceded that anaesthesia might be induced in her, but she rationalized this concession by explaining that it would derive only from a full direction of her attention to other things so that the perception of tactile stimuli would be precluded. Thus, she argued, a state of unawareness similar in effect to anaesthesia could be made to exist, but it would be abolished upon refocussing of attention. When she was asked to permit the induction of hypnotic anaestheisa in her hand, she consented readily. Contrary to her expectation, she found that the focussing of attention played no role in the development or the continuance of either a state of anaesthesia or of analgesia. This discovery she finally rationalized by trying to relate those conditions logically to the deliberate seeking of relief from a headache by going to the cinema and also to the difficulty ordinarily experienced in sensing the odor of one's own breath or the tactile stimuli deriving from one's own clothing.

After some further general discussion the topic was dropped. It was evident that her opinions and beliefs were unchanged, although she was puzzled.

Several months later she evinced a renewal of her interest in the hypnotic modification of sensory behavior, especially hypnotic blindness. She explained that the reality of that experience for other subjects, and the outcome of her own test procedures on those subjects had continued to interest her greatly and had made her desirous of undergoing the same experience as a definite subjective experience. She explained further that she believed that hypnotic blindness must be something quite other than it appeared to be and that her purpose was to discover subjectively what that other condition might be, since objective test procedures yielded no informative results. To this end she suggested that she be hypnotized and hypnotic blindness be induced, but even as she made this request, she declared emphatically that she was confident such a condition could not be induced in her. Nevertheless, she wished the attempt to be made, since the effort itself might serve to give her a better understanding of the condition.

Her offer was immediately accepted, but the stipulation was made that the method of procedure was to be determined entirely by the hypnotist. To this she readily agreed.

As a preliminary measure she was hypnotized deeply and questioned carefully for her general beliefs, attitudes, and purposes. These were found to agree with those expressed in the waking state. Nevertheless, despite her skepticism it was felt that her offer was sincere.

Accordingly, she was told to think over the entire matter at both a conscious and an unconscious level for several days. If she found that her interest continued and that she really felt that she wished to experience hypnotic blindness, she could then return for the specific purpose of undergoing the experiment. Following this she was awakened and given essentially the same instructions.

A few days later she returned, reaffirmed her desires, and was given a definite appointment.

She appeared promptly at the set time, seemed dubious about the possibilities but definitely hopeful that an adequate technique of suggestion had been worked out in the meanwhile.

Upon being hypnotized and questioned again, she was found to persist in her waking attitudes and beliefs.

Since otherwise the general situation seemed favorable, the experiment was initiated.

Because of her firmly fixed attitude of disbelief and skepticism, a prolonged and exceedingly tedious technique of suggestion had been devised. This, for convenience, may be divided into three separate but actually overlapping steps:

1. *The development of a deep trance state.* Approximately 20 minutes were spent in giving her instructions to sleep deeply, soundly, continuously, and more and more profoundly. This was done to insure a deep trance rigidly established by long continuance so that it might not easily be disturbed or disrupted.

2. *The development of a stuporous trance state.* Approximately 20 minutes were spent in suggesting a profoundly stuporous state, of stuporous absorption in "just sleeping without interests, desires, feeling," and "thinking, sensing, feeling nothing but a stuporous, lethargic sleep in a timeless, endless way." The purpose of this was to establish firmly an extremely passive, receptive, yielding mental state and attitude.

3. *The development of a somnambulistic state.* Approximately 15 minutes more were spent suggesting that the subject, now in a profound stuporous trance, remain so but at the same time recover slowly and gradually her ability to think, to move, to feel, and to respond as if she were awake but only to that exact degree required by whatever instructions she might be given. Thus she was permitted to become passively responsive, but only within the hypnotic situation.

In such a state the subject presents very much the behavior of a person heavily drugged but not yet fully in the narcotized state and has been so described by subjects who have experienced both conditions.

With the development of this passively responsive and receptive somnambulistic state, new series of suggestions were given. These were directed toward:

(1) The development of an increasingly intense desire and hope to experience hypnotic blindness.

(2) The progressive growth of a full expectation of experiencing such a condition *sooner or later.*

(3) The progressive realization of the actual and immediately impending possibility of that condition.

(4) The development of an intention to resist for some time the self-discovery of the blindness and a concomitant ever-growing realization that such a discovery could neither be resisted nor indefinitely postponed.

(5) The development of a full intention of concealing from the hypnotist as

long as possible the condition of blindness.

(6) The progressive development of an intense, impatient, overwhelming desire to experience all the subjective aspects of the blindness.

(7) The sudden unexpected and growing realization that blindness had already started to develop, probably first by blurring and uncertainty of vision, then possibly by a concentric narrowing of the field of vision, then finally by a blotting out of a capacity to see outlines, and then the occurrence of blankness.

(8) The development, as this course of events occurred, of strong but mixed emotions of satisfaction and fear, impatience and hesitation, and finally of completely helpless acceptance of the fact of blindness.

(9) The development of a feeling of reckless determination to plunge into the subjective aspect of the existing blindness, with the understanding that all emotional reactions were to be capitalized by experiencing everything in full.

The subject's general reactions and responses to these varied, overlapping, and repetitiously given suggestions were in harmony with those elicited from other subjects who had developed hypnotic blindness successfully. As the procedure continued, every indication of her behavior suggested the effectiveness of the hypnotic instructions. However, when in accord with the instructions to plunge into the subjective aspects of the experience, she slowly, hesitantly, and somewhat fearfully opened her eyes, her immediate reaction was one of intensely bitter disappointment. She explained at once that she still could see even though she had been fully convinced of the effectiveness of the suggestions and had genuinely expected that she really would be blind.

To reassure her a long, plausible explanation was given to the effect that becoming hypnotically blind required practice and repeated effort, that it was essentially a matter of trial-and-error learning, that she had already accomplished much by fully expecting complete success at her first trial, and that she could now confidently expect blindness to develop with further effort and trials. These reassurances were readily accpeted. Ordinarily such a measure of explanation and reassurance is highly effective as a suggestion technique.

Thereupon the entire procedure of suggestion was repeated again and again with variations and reemphasis directed to a blurring of vision, a concentric narrowing of the visual field, etc., until the subject seemed to have developed a satisfactory state of blindness. However, it was soon learned that in her over-eagerness to experience the condition she was actually deceiving herself into thinking that she had developed hypnotic blindness.

A systematic effort was made to capitalize upon this manifestation and to transform it into an effective hypnotic blindness, but it soon became apparent that this could not be done.

Also, after still further effort and modification of technique it became equally apparent that hypnotic blindness could not be induced in the subject by any ordinarily satisfactory technique.

Thereupon a full explanation of the situation was given to the subject. Her self-deception was easily corrected, since it was decidedly superficial in character, and she expressed a feeling of inexplicable relief that it had not been accepted as valid. The subject reacted to the experimental failure with intense disappointment both in the trance and the waking state. She asked for a critical appraisal by the hypnotist of her own attitude and behavior so that she might correct anything possible. She apologized for having caused the hypnotist so many hours of futile labor, but followed this was a request that he persevere in his efforts, since it seemed to her that the experimental objectives were of sufficient value to warrant further effort. She in turn was asked for advice and suggestions in regard to technique, but she declared she was content to rely wholly upon the hypnotist.

Accordingly she was assured that the task would be continued and that the next few days would be spent working out an entirely new and adequate technique of suggestion. She was asked earnestly, as a measure of making this reassurance impressive, for full permission to use any measure of suggestion, however drastic, that gave promise of success. Not only did she give unqualified consent but she demanded that the hypnotist regard the total problem merely as an experimental project and not as a matter involving personal considerations.

This course of experimental developments suggested a need for a review of the total situation to determine the current status and the possibilities for future experimentation. Of primary interest in this review were various items of fact and the subject's inconsistencies, contradictions and unusual behavior reactions and attitudes. These may be listed briefly in the order of their manifestation:

1. Her extensive passive and active background of hypnotic experience and her unexpected manifestation of distrust of certain trance phenomena.

2. Her unwilling acceptance of her own experimental proof of the validity of certain trance developments in other subjects.

3. Her acceptance of the reality of subjective sensory trance experiences for other subjects but rejection of the possibility of a similar personal experience.

4. Her ready consent to the induction of hypnotic analgesia and anaesthesia and her apparent need for rationalizations of those experiences.

5. Her persistence in her quest after the passage of several months, despite her doubts, disbeliefs, and general ambivalences.

6. Her selection of blindness from among several hypnotically altered sensory states, even though she felt that objective test procedures for such a condition were not informative.

7. Her insistent request that she be made hypnotically blind, coupled with the immediate declaration of the futility of any such attempt.

8. Her rationalization that she was not interested in blindness but rather in the effort to induce such a state, and the coupling of this statement with the declaration that she desired the subjective experience of blindness itself.

9. Her readiness and hopefulness in submitting to hypnosis for a specific purpose, despite her skepticism and doubt about the outcome.

10. Her submissiveness and receptiveness to hypnotic suggestion, and her failure to respond to an ordinarily satisfactory technique.

11. Her reaction of intense disappointment to failure, her effort at self-deception, and her sense of relief at the detection of that self-deception.

12. Her marked aggressive insistence upon further work, coupled with her ready consent to submit to any drastic measure.

13. Her demand that the entire project be regarded as an *objective procedure not involving any personal considerations.*

Reflection on these various items in her behavior suggested that she was not primarily interested in the experience of hypnotic blindness. Rather, it seemed much more probable that she had an intense unrecognized fear of blindness and that she was really attempting, through the guise of an intellectual interest in an experiment, to serve other and unconscious goals and purposes of her own.

Hence it seemed that the experimental task more probably was not simply the induction of hypnotic blindness but rather the much more difficult and extensive task of meeting unrecognized and unconscious personality needs. Obviously the subject was seeking more than could be readily understood in terms of the actual experimental project, and yet she was apparently compelled to make that search entirely in such terms. Consideration of these possibilities suggested that the total situation presented a unique opportunity for another type of experimentation, namely, investigative research through the measure of developing in her an acute reactive mental disturbance.

Hence, under the pretense of continuing the original experiment, a new project was formulated. This was to be an attempt, within a limited controlled laboratory situation, to develop in the subject an acute hysterical obsessional compulsive mental state which would be accompanied by hypnotic blindness and which would parallel or resemble the obsessive compulsive hysterical mental disturbances encountered in psychiatric practice.

To accomplish this it was reasoned that, against the background of her tremendous interest in the experience and the sense of failure and disappointment arising from the original experiment, a deliberate, systematic suggestion of obsessive compulsive ideation, affects, and behavior would lead to the development of an acute laboratory neurosis which would resemble an actual neurotic disturbance. In brief, the project was to determine experimentally whether or not a carefully chosen set of circumstances, ideas, emotional reactions, and psychological stimuli could be employed directly, intentionally, and in accord with a predetermined plan to cause a psychoneurotic state of a recognizable psychiatric type, and which could be understandable in terms of the actual stimulation given to the patient. Thus an experimental procedure, parallel in kind to that employed in laboratory medicine, was planned in relation to a psychiatric problem.

In accord with this new project another technique of procedure was devised. This was based upon the following three considerations:

(1) A crude, inaccurate statement of the James-Lange theory of emotions, i.e., "first you run away from the bear and then you become afraid."

(2) The commonly experienced tendency to meet with the mishap one strives

too hard to avoid, i.e. the bicyclist, overly intent on avoiding a stone, actually strikes it.

(3) The implying and giving of absolute reality to something by the measure of developing an intense resistance to that something, the principle being that one cannot resist that which is nonexistent.

The first step in the development of adequate hypnotic suggestions for the proposed new experimental project was the determination of the actual form, pattern, or structure of the suggestions to be used. To this end the hospital wards were visited by the writer and extensive verbatim records were made of the compulsive utterances, obsessive ideation, and repetitious pleadings and self-reassurances of a number of mental patients. These records were then systematically paraphrased so that, while the general structure and succession of utterances remained unchanged, their content had been transformed by the paraphrasing into that of the hypnotic suggestions taken from the original technique. Thus a definite form or pattern was developed into which the hypnotic suggestions were fitted, so that they could all be given to the subject in the form of compulsive obsessive repetitious ideas.

Interspersed with the actual suggestions were paraphrases of the pleading utterances and self-reassurances of agitated obsessional patients. These were so worded as to be applicable to the subject in her immediate situation.

Additionally, accounts of various incidents relating to blindness—most of them fabrications, two actually taken from her own past experiences—were woven into the series of suggestions to give further weight of ideational content.

These two instances had been related to the hypnotist by the subject's roommate, and both were highly traumatic. The first centered around the development of blindness in a pet kitten of her childhood, its subsequent sickness, and an accident that had crushed and mangled it. The result had been a persistent phobia for cats unless fully grown and black in color.

The second traumatic instance was the relatively recent actual blindness in a close friend as a result of an automobile accident. The subject had been tremendously distressed by this occurrence.

Although she knew that the hypnotist had some general awareness of these two unhappy events, and she had been urged by her roommate to discuss them with the hypnotist, she had not done so.

In this way there was prepared a long, repetitious, discursive, interwoven monologue of morbid ideas, hypnotic suggestions, pleading utterances, reference to trauma, and self-reassurances, all in the form of compulsive obsessive ideation and utterances. This was directed to the intentional development of an acute obsessional state in the subject which could culminate in hypnotic blindness.

In presenting this material to the subject every effort was to be made to secure, in any form and order, the following types of response and behavior:

1. A compulsive need, while her eyes were closed in the trance state, to make groping, uncertain, uneasy movements, and now and then to walk gropingly

and unwillingly, experiencing all the while intense emotional distress as she tried blindly to find her way and to identify by tactile sensations the objects with which she came in contact.

2. A constantly increasing need to depend upon and to secure from the hypnotist reassurances in addition to those she found compelled to utter to herself.

3. An obsessive, constantly recurring fear that she would timidly and fearfully grope her way about and collide blindly and painfully with various objects and be helplessly unable to avoid doing so over and over as she continued to be unable to see.

4. An obsessive compulsive need to assure and reassure herself that she would not and could not become hypnotically blind, that the concept of hypnotic blindness was in itself absurd, unreasonable, and could not possibly hold any meaning for her.

5. An intense desire to prove over and over that she really could see if only she could open her eyes, and an intense resolve that she would resist strenuously, frantically, the slightest diminution of her vision.

6. And finally, an intense fear of and a morbid fascination with the thought that she was really hypnotically blind. This fact she would resist discovering as long as possible, and she would find herself compelled to grope blindly about, pretending to see and trying to believe that she could see.

Upon the subject's return for further work she was hypnotized deeply, and the original technique of suggestions was emphatically disparaged and discredited by the hypnotist while the subject was asked repeatedly to agree with all the various condemnatory remarks. This she readily did. Additionally, and always out of context, apparently irrelevant statements were made repeatedly to the effect that *if ever she did develop hypnotic blindness, it would happen quickly and unexpectedly*. Each of these statements was always coupled with an easily accepted disparaging remark about the original technique to which she was asked to agree, but without opportunity to make reply in relation to the idea of the development of sudden blindness.

Next she was told that hypnotic blindness would actually hold for her many unpleasant and even fearful emotional significances, and as she continued to think on the topic, she would find those unpleasant emotions increasing in number even though she would not be able to identify them. These, it was explained, would be simply troublesome but unformed and unidentified affects of a distressing character. Yet, if she really had something to gain from the experience, her intellectual curiosity would continue to grow despite, and probably because of, these unpleasant emotional reactions until she found herself "practically obsessed and morbidly fascinated by the whole idea."

After these various suggestions had been repeated sufficiently to insure her adequate understanding of them, she was awakened from the trance and the procedure repeated, this time in the guise of a conversational explanation of what she could reasonably expect to happen in relation to the proposed experimentation. She was then dismissed with instructions to return in a few days and to report upon the course of development within herself.

Instead of letting her return voluntarily, she was deliberately sought out several days later in another connection. Advantage of this was taken to rehypnotize her and question her. She related that the suggestions given her had been unpleasantly effective. This had distressed her but at the same time it had amused her, and this feeling of amusement had augmented her curiosity greatly and had made her all the more intent upon continuing with the experiment.

Immediately the suggestion was offered that she continue to sleep more and more deeply until she was as deeply asleep as she had been in the first experimental situation. While she was thus going into a deep trance, she was told to think about the proposed experiment continuously. Approximately 15 minutes were spent in giving reiterative suggestions to secure a trance state similar to that originally employed.

When a suitable trance state seemed to be sufficiently established, and since her behavior disclosed no unfavorable reaction, the planned series of suggestions was begun. At first this was done slowly, gently, persuasively, and then with progressively greater urgency and insistence. As this course of action continued, some of the planned suggestions had to be modified slightly or temporarily postponed, while others had to be given new emphasis in accord with the subject's immediate reaction to them, but these changes were all essentially minor and did not alter the original plan.

As this procedure continued, the subject became increasingly restless. Repeatedly she would start to rise and then slump back into her chair as if trying to retreat or withdraw from the situation only to become again more and more responsive to the various suggestions and to act upon them. Also, as the suggestions continued, the subject was variously induced to:

(1) Perform unwillingly but compulsively various groping movements, including walking, to experience a conviction that she was going to make a certain movement and then to find that she was unwillingly, confirming the truth of that conviction.

(2) Reassure herself over and over that nothing was going to happen, that she was really not afraid, that she was confident that she could resist all suggestions, that if she could not, at least she could resist discovering that she was hypnotically blind.

(3) And to cast futilely about in her mind for any possible means by which to resist and to postpone the discovery of the blindness, and also to try helplessly to think exclusively about other things.

As the subject became more and more seriously distressed, agitated, compulsive and obsessional in her behavior, a new measure was employed. This consisted of suggesting in an almost triumphant manner that she could defeat and actually overthrow the whole project of compelling her to experience hypnotic blindness by deliberately and defensively resorting to her old familiar childhood trick of rolling back her eyeballs so that only the whites of her eyes would be visible. Thus she could honestly believe and demonstrate that she could not see for only physical reasons.

The subject seized upon this suggestion at once, rolled back her eyeballs, raised her lids, and began groping her way about. Immediately the suggestion was offered that she would now lose control of her ocular muscles, that they would become cataleptic, and she would not be able to roll her eyes down again nor would she ever be able to do so until she was ready and willing to face the fact of her blindness. Thus a dilemma was created, either alternative of which signified an inability to see, hence blindness.

The ocular catalepsy developed at once. She was encouraged to try to overcome it, to rub her eyes, and to strain to regain muscular control. Along with these suggestions she was reminded of her interests in the subjective aspects of her hypnotic blindness, and she was urged to try to discount, disparage, and deny that interest, to insist that she was more interested in moving her eyes, *that it was not a question any longer of seeing,* but simply a question of moving her eyeballs.

As the subject became increasingly distressed by this new problem, she was told that no matter how distressed she now felt, everything would eventually turn out satisfactorily and that soon, very soon, she would discover suddenly and unexpectedly, without any warning at all, that she was blind. This discovery, it was explained, would be made at a moment in which she would have no opportunity to resist, to reassure herself, even to think, that within a moment's time she would be plunged directly and deliberately into the middle of the subjective experience of hypnotic blindness. Until that moment, however, she was to rest quietly, to sleep deeply. As she obeyed, and before she had time to puzzle out the meaning of these remarks, she was told abruptly, emphatically, to awaken.

She reacted with a start and a frightened cry, tried to plead that she be allowed to sleep longer, but rapid, insistent commands to awaken compelled her to obey. In this way a waking state with altered visual behavior as a post-trance phenomenon could be secured.

As she began awakening, she cried, protested that she did not want to open her eyes, that she was afraid she was going to open her eyes. She gave evidence of intense conflict and of deep emotional panic, with much compulsive activity centering about her eyes. She held them shut very tightly, yet seemed to be straining to open them, and her eyeballs could be seen rolling rapidly back and forth and up and down underneath her lids. Frequently she would press her hands to her eyes and then tremblingly withdraw them. Finally she stiffened in her chair, thrust her arms stiffly outward, and a rigid, strained, fearful expression appeared on her face. Her eyes slowly opened, but with a blank, unseeing expression. There followed a rapid succession of closing and opening them, of rubbing them, of strained, peering behavior, of crying, and of inarticulate vocalizations of intense fear and panic, with incoherent denials and self-reassurances.

At first it was not possible to attract her attention. She seemed to be entirely absorbed in distressing emotional reactions. After trying vainly, because of her frantic disorganized behavior, for about 20 minutes to get into contact with her, it was noted that she was becoming greatly exhausted. Accordingly, as a measure of keeping control over the situation, a posthypnotic cue which had often been used in the past to induce a hypnotic trance was given. She responded by falling immediately into a deep trance with her eyes shut. She was promptly told to rest quietly for some time, and then, when she felt herself ready and willing to do so, she was again to awaken and to reexperience the same subjective state.

After some minutes she was again awakened in an urgent, commanding fashion. There occurred a repetition of the previous disturbed emotional behavior, similar to that of an acute hysterical panic state. Again it was not possible to establish conversational contact with her, but after some 15 minutes the severity of her panic lessened somewhat and she began to make piteous, repetitious appeals for restoration of vision and for reassurances. At first she seemed unable to grasp the meaning of replies given her. Slowly, however, she came to be able to listen attentively to what was said and to seem to understand fully. With considerable difficulty the explanation was given her that her blindness was under control, that it would be continued only so long as it served a legitimate purpose. With even more difficulty her own experimental objective was explained to her. She seemed to have forgotten entirely her personal interests and to be unable to understand what was being said. As progress was finally made in this direction, her general fright and distress decreased and her original interest in the subjective aspects of hypnotic blindness revived slowly. However, there would recur from time to time sudden outbursts of panic and intense fright with excited, disorganized activity which would slowly yield to careful reassurance.

Approximately half an hour was spent in letting her investigate her state of blindness, which she did in a rather futile, spasmodic fashion by groping and peering behavior. She finally declared, when the suggestion was offered that she test her vision, that the making of visual tests was absurd since, ''blind people don't test themselves to see if they are blind. You just know you are blind, and that is all the farther you can go on that proposition.'' As she uttered this declaration, she developed another severe panic and required extensive reassurance.

When it was proposed that the hypnotist test her vision, she declared such a measure to be as absurd as her own efforts but expressed entire willingness. Accordingly she was asked to face the hypnotist, and a rapid conversation on topics of interest to her was begun. She made no motor response to a sudden interruption of the conversation by the hypnotist's sudden turning to stare in an intent, puzzled fashion across the room. Nor did she make any of the involuntary reflex movements so natural as, for example, when an object within the visual range is accidentally knocked over, and a variety of other indirect test procedures which would result in involuntary reflex motor response. However, she did show violent startle reactions and fright to any noise occasioned.

When it was proposed to test her eyes with a flashlight, she was much interested in her normal pupillary response, and she experienced the flash of light as a "hardening sensation" of her eyeballs. When subjects deceive themselves about visual alteration, the response is one of ignoring the situation completely. No satisfactorily explanation of this "hardening" could be secured. Later she was engaged in conversation from across the room and a pocket mirror was used surreptitiously to flash a beam of sunlight in her eyes. There was no withdrawal reaction, but she immediately announced that she felt the "hardening sensation" in her eyes and was much distressed, since she knew that the flashlight could not have been used from where the hypnotist was speaking. There followed then a severe hysterical panic, since she felt certain that something must be happening to her eyes.

A chance incident of note occurred while she was speaking when the hypnotist unthinkingly crossed quietly the room to a position behind her, and in picking up an object made an audible noise. To this she reacted with a violent startle reaction, demanded of the hypnotist, as if he had not moved, to tell what had happened, who had entered the room, and she began to cry. When a full explanation was given her, she demanded that the hypnotist be more careful, that her nerves were all on edge, that she could scarcely maintain her composure, and that, while she was willing to continue in the present state as long as was necessary, she was becoming increasingly frightened and worried. She begged that things be done speedily, and then broke down into piteous sobbing.

When finally she was quieted, the question was raised that she might be interested in recalling how she had reacted to the suggestions given to her in the trance state, and it was suggested that she recollect her trance experience and give an account of it. To this she agreed with some enthusiasm, but immediately as she made the effort, she became extremely distressed emotionally. It soon became apparent that she could not perform this task. She did, however, succeed in explaining that, as the series of suggestions had been given her, she had felt herself caught up in a welter of confusing and incomplete ideas and emotions that had swept her helplessly along.

Finally the question of restoring her vision was raised. She was asked for her opinions and wishes in this matter. After some thinking she replied that the suddenness and unexpectedness of the blindness had been so unpleasant that she felt that it would probably be better to restore her vision by slow degrees. This could be done, she thought, by letting her become aware visually of the first one object and then another. After thinking this matter over, her permission was asked to proceed with the task in a manner that might be interesting. To this the subject agreed readily.

Professing a need to think matters over, the hypnotist stepped out of the range of her vision, merely as a precaution, and secretly removed his black right shoe, replacing it with a brown left one. He then returned to a position about six feet in front of her and had her lean forward and direct her eyes, as closely as possible, to a certain spot on the floor. At this point he placed his left foot on which he was wearing the black shoe, while the other foot remained concealed behind a piece of furniture. Slowly and systematically suggestions were given her to the effect that sooner or later she would begin to see a blurred object which would become progressively clearer in outline until she would finally begin to see his shoe. This she was to identify and describe. After much suggestion she began to see a shoe, at first very dimly and then increasingly plainly, until she was able to identify it as a black left shoe. When this much had been achieved, the right foot was placed alongside of the left, and she was instructed to see the *other* shoe. Similar suggestions were given, but without effect. After extensive suggestion far beyond the degree that had been necessary to induce a seeing of the left foot, the subject became greatly alarmed and expressed fears that the hypnotist was failing in his efforts to restore her vision completely, and another violent panic reaction ensued. Much reassurance had to be given her before it subsided. After continued emphatic and urgent instruction to see *another shoe* alongside the first, she finally began to respond to this suggestion. However, when that shoe began to be sufficiently clear in outline for her to recognize it as a second left shoe and of a brown color, she became much alarmed and distressed. She was convinced that she was not really seeing either of those shoes, that she was merely hallucinating them, and there was no realization that she might be undergoing an unexpected test. Instead, another serious hysterical state developed.

Much effort was required to regain contact with her and to reassure her emotionally without betraying the actual test situation. This was finally achieved by impressing upon her the desirability of determining, purely as an intellectual task, whether or not the shoes as seen were both hallucinatory or if only one were hallucinatory, and which one that might be. When she became engaged in this task, the subject found herself unable to make any differentiation in the reality values of the two shoes and finally requested the hypnotist to walk about if he were wearing the shoes or to move them, explaining that the movement of the shoes, if the hypnotist were really wearing them, might be of value. Before the room had been crossed in response to her request, the subject broke into a relieved smile and grasped the circumstances fully, since the hypnotist's familiar right-sided limp betrayed the situation to her. With this discovery, her feeling of terror about the mismated shoes disappeared, and she dismissed the possibility of hallucinations. Much relieved and more confident, the subject continued with the task of recovering her vision, asking that she be permitted to pursue that task without any further aid by suggestion or frightening manipulations on the part of the hypnotist. Approximately 15 minutes were spent by her in enlarging her visual field to include socks, trousers, chair, and finally everything within her normal visual range.

Upon restoration of her vision she demonstrated a tremendous visual hunger, eyeing intently first one object and then another as she verbalized a feeling of immense relief. Finally she was rehypnotized, told to review the entire experience from beginning to end, and to remember fully all the details of the entire experience, subjective and objective, especially the emotional components. Following this review she was to prepare herself to discuss freely any of the items that might be of a troublesome or distressing character. After she had been allowed to remain in the trance state for what seemed to be a sufficient period of time to permit an adequate mental review of the experience, she was awakened with instructions to talk freely and readily with the hypnotist about the entire procedure.

Upon awakening, the subject sat quietly and thoughtfully for some time and then remarked that the entire experience had been decidedly painful, frightening, and remarkably fatiguing, but that her general reaction was one of satisfaction such as is experienced after successfully completing a hard, difficult task. However, details of the experience, she declared, were vague and unclear. As for the validity of hypnotic blindness, she had no doubts, and she expressed amazement that other subjects had been able to accept it with so little distress as they had shown.

When she was questioned about the possibility of relating or writing out in detail a full recollection of the entire thing, she expressed doubts, explaining that she was very much of the opinion that any such effort on her part would lead to a revivification of the intense emotional reactions she had experienced. This, she declared, would preclude her from giving a description in adequate detail. Furthermore, most of the experience had been largely a matter of emotions, distressing fears, and a feeling of utter helplessness. An effort to persuade her to make the attempt caused immediate emotional distress that threatened to become a panic state even in her present waking state.

However, she did declare again that she now had no doubt about the reality of hypnotic blindness, that the only problem confronting her in that regard was how such a phenomenon could occur. Additionally, she declared that she felt herself to be in a position to understand better the intensity of the reactions of psychotic patients to hallucinations. Her uncertainty about the reality of the mismated shoes had been most terrifying to her, and even more so had been the sight of those two shoes walking by themselves until she had grasped the situation.

Some weeks later this subject requested a repetition of the experiment, declaring that she wished to learn if she "could take it comfortably." Immediately upon going into a deep trance, she readily and easily developed hypnotic blindness without any more emotional distress than that signified by her prompt and spontaneous declaration of confidence that the hypnotist could control it thoroughly. Nor was any elaborate technique of suggestion necessary.

Subsequently, both upon her spontaneous offer and the hypnotist's request, she volunteered for experimental and demonstration hypnotic work, including hypnotic blindness.

Several years later she was met by chance and, after some reminiscing, inquiry was made about her recollections of the experiment. She recalled the experimental aspects vividly and without distress. She stated that to date she had no understanding of how there could be hypnotic blindness, but that there was no doubt in her mind of its validity.

After further desultory conversation she was asked about her cat phobia. Somewhat amazed by the inquiry, she recalled it and described it as belonging only to her childhood, something she had forgotten about "long ago."

Inquiry about her blinded friend puzzled her also, but she related the story in a matter-of-fact manner and added that she had once thought of discussing it with the hypnotist but that for some unknown reason it had lost the distressing emotional significance it once held for her.

GENERAL COMMENT

It seems obvious that the experimental subject had two objectives in mind. One was the experiential satisfaction of definitely intellectual desires related to her educational background. The other, unrecognized and unconscious, concerned the seeking of a subjective understanding of at least two traumatic experiences which had made a deep impression upon her.

Her willingness to submit to "drastic" measures and to endure the painful developments of the experimental procedure signified the intensity of her unconscious needs.

The description of the experimental results as the induction of an experimental neurosis in a normal person is both right and wrong. It is right because an acute neurotic disturbance of a definite pattern was secured in accord with a preestablished plan of procedure.

It is wrong only in that underlying circumscribed neurotic affects became a part of and were added to the experimental results. However, these neurotic components in no way vitiated the experiment as such. Rather they were dispersed as a result of the experimental neurosis. This is a finding previously reported (Erickson, 1935, 1943c, 1944).

Finally, this experiment has been reported in detail to present an account of hypnotic experimental technique and to portray the meaningfulness of language in eliciting hypnotic phenomena and the possibility of consequently satisfying personality needs of the hypnotized subject.

6. Observations Concerning Alterations in Hypnosis of Visual Perceptions

Elizabeth M. Erickson

A study was published in the *Journal of Abnormal and Social Psychology,* 1939, Vol. 34, pp. 114-117, by Loyd W. Rowland, Ph.D., then of the University of Tulsa, Oklahoma, entitled "Will Hypnotized Persons Try to Harm Themselves or Others?" In this study Rowland recounted his experiments into what he considered the possibility of a hypnotized subject being induced to perform harmful or objectionable acts through deception and persuasion.

These two experiments were devised as follows: The one consisted of asking deeply hypnotized subjects to pick up a rattlesnake, variously described to them as a rubber hose and as a snake, lying in a box the front of which was made of "invisible glass," presenting the impression of being open; the second consisted of asking the subject to throw a fluid, which had been demonstrated to him as being a strong acid, at the experimenter's face, which was protected by a pane of "invisible glass." Four hypnotized subjects were used in the first experiment, and three complied with the request. Two subjects were used in the second, and both did as instructed.

Controls were 42 subjects in a waking state. None of them could be induced to perform the acts.

Dr. Rowland concludes that the subjects acted against their better judgment because of their trust and confidence in the hypnotist: He calls for a reexamination of the question of the possible misuse of hypnosis. The experiment has become well known and is frequently alluded to in the literature, often being cited as proof that subjects will perform harmful and dangerous acts.

This is a question which arises repeatedly in the study of hypnosis, and many experimenters have presented results of experiments of great ingenuity in which both falsified and genuine situations are presented to subsjects to see if acts against themselves or others can be induced, with results which have been variously interpreted. In no case has a completely acceptable procedure been devised to which critics have not been able to point out flaws in technique or alternative interpretations of the results.

It has been shown repeatedly, and should be obvious from ordinary everyday

Reprinted with permission from *The American Journal of Clinical Hypnosis,* October, 1962, *5,* 131-134.

experience, that one person can influence another, without resort to hypnosis, to commit antisocial acts, both directly and through deception. Whether hypnosis may be an element of accentuation or may ever be an element essential to such deception or persuasion is something else again. This is actually the central question raised in Paul Reiter's book, *Antisocial or Criminal Acts and Hypnosis* (1958), and the role played by hypnosis as such in this case is indeed most debatable.

A person can also deceive or trick another into performing a dangerous act which the subject does not realize is harmful, and the fact that the subjects are in a hypnotic trance may make them more accepting of the trickery, or it may, on the contrary, cause them to increase their defenses and become more dubious and cautious. This is the essential question frequently raised by Dr. George Estabrooks' speculations in various publications, e.g., *Death in the Mind* (with Richard Lockridge, 1947), and *Hypnotism* (1943), and it is a question which he actually answers with speculations only.

One person may also deceive or trick another into attempting an act which is actually perfectly safe and harmless but which the subject cannot possibly regard as being in a protected situation without danger to anyone. This, in essence, is what Rowland purported to have done, and this is the point which is frequently cited as having been proved by his study; or at least, of having been strongly indicated by the evidence of the results. In point of actual fact the situation *was* a protected and safe one. If the subjects were aware of this in any way, the study proves only that subjects will carry out seemingly adverse acts in a known protected situation, which is a well-known fact in itself. If they were actually completely and definitely unaware of the protection, as Dr. Rowland believed, then indeed the study may be regarded as evidence that they can be induced to perform unsafe acts.

It may be argued that because the experiments were performed in a laboratory setting and because the experimenters were respected as responsible citizens, the subjects therefore would inevitably infer the presence of protection. This possibility was meant to be eliminated by the use of the waking controls. Whether this was an adequate control is debatable, since one might argue that the subjects might also infer that the experimenter expected waking subjects to accept more responsibility for their actions and might hence provide protection only under hypnotic conditions.

But even if one accepts the validity of the performance in a laboratory setting, the possibility arises of the actual detection of the protection afforded to the subjects in a hypnotic trance, although they were unaware of it in a waking state. The investigation of this possibility and the control of it were lacking in Rowland's work, and if there is evidence that the detection of the protection is definitely more likely in a hypnotic state, then the experiments proved nothing one way or the other concerning a subject's willingness to perform an act harmful in reality.

The following account is presented as an indication of evidence of the definite possibility of a hypnotic subject's ability to be aware of a visual perception in the trance state which was not appreciated as such in the waking state. It is presented as a first-person account, as written out by her shortly after the experience. The subject has had a great deal of experience in developing hypnotic states, both autohypnosis and heterohypnosis.

SUBJECT'S ACCOUNT

I walked by the show window—a window at viewing height (about four feet above the ground level) of the New York store which sells the product of an outstanding manufacturer of fine glass. The window is made of curved "invisible glass." In the show case of the window are several beautiful glass objects, and the interior of the store is also visible. The window is about four feet long and two feet high. From the sidewalk there is a perfect illusion of no glass barrier at all. Standing very close and giving attention, one can see a few flecks of dust on the glass, and realizes that if they had been floating in midair, they would not, of course, be stationary, as they are. Also, where the end of the glass fits into the wall, one can see the joining place. But the glass as such is not visible.

I began thinking of Rowland's well-known experiments, in which he found that hypnotized subjects were willing to throw acid on the experimenter, and to attempt to pick up a live rattlesnake through an "invisible glass" barrier. The control was that of using the same experimental subjects and setups for both the trance and waking states, as well as using additional nonhypnotized subjects. Universal refusal and the development of emotional agitation resulted. I realized that the joint where the glass joined the frame would undoubtedly be concealed, but I wondered about dust control in Rowland's experiment. Perhaps the subjects, in a state of hypnotic concentration and emotional calm, might be more likely to see a few specks of dust, and this alone might be enough to cause them to infer the presence of a barrier and to have confidence in that inference.

Two days later I decided to look at the window again. I walked over to the store and looked at it closely, again becoming immediately aware of motionless dust specks. On impulse I decided to develop an autohypnotic state. I did not expect to observe any difference whatsoever. I do not believe my visual acuity is increased in any way by hypnosis. I took my time and developed a good deep trance state. To my utter amazement the "invisible glass" became as visible as an ordinary window pane. I could not believe it. I thought I had made some kind of mistake. So I stood there for 15 to 20 minutes, experimenting in every way I could think of. I went in and out of a hypnotic state, focussing my eyes successively on the glass itself, the objects in the window, and the interior of the store. In every case, when I was in a hypnotic trance the glass became immediately visible. When I was awake, it was not. I tried to analyze what this visibility consisted of, and could not decide. It did not seem to me to be reflections. All I can say is that there was simply an alteration of appearance. Objects near the glass seemed to be equally clear in both states, but in a hypnotic state there was a very slight blurring of the objects at the back of the store. This was the only specific change I could detect, but this does not describe the difference adequately. Essentially the difference was simply that of the general experience of looking through a closed window having a clean pane of good-quality glass, and the experience of looking through a wide-open window.

On a third occasion, some months later, I repeated my observations in the company of a companion who had had much experience in the study of hypnotic perception. His own findings were that in his waking state changes in visual focussing to include the area of the window itself, the area immediately behind the window, the interior of the store, and the back of the store did not affect for him the invisibility of the glass nor the illusion that the area was empty of any barrier. His waking experience was entirely similar to mine.

DISCUSSION

This experiment is by no means a controlled one. But neither should Rowland's and similar experiments be considered "controlled," unless the subjects are first tested with several containers in random arrangements, some with "invisible glass" panels and some without. The subjects should be observed without their knowledge; or the arrangement of the boxes should not be known to the observer, this to prevent unconscious cues which are now being increasingly recognized as important experimental variables. Perhaps both precautions could be taken. The subjects should be tested in both waking and trance states, to see whether or not they could pick out the glass-in boxes on a better-than-chance average.

If the experience of this specific subject proves to be a valid one, and her interpretation correct, a possible explanation might lie in spontaneous vascular and other changes in the eye during the trance state, such as those observed by Strosberg and Vics, described in "Physiologic changes in the eye during hypnosis" (*American Journal of Clinical Hypnosis*, 1962, 4, 264–267).

It is hoped that well-controlled experimentation in the field of sensory discrimination and of perception in hypnotized subjects will clarify this and other problems as yet unsolved. In the meantime the conclusion that Rowland's experimentation demonstrated the willingness of hypnotized subjects to expose themselves or others to harm, even in a laboratory setting and with the responsibility shifted to the experimenter, should be reevaluated. If the subjects were aware of the presence of the glass in the hypnotized state, whether or not that awareness was consciously known to them, then the experiments demonstrated only that awareness and nothing more. It is unfortunate that Rowland did not control a most important possible variable in his experiment. Instead, he merely assumed that there would be no alteration of visual experience from the waking to the trance state such as occurred in the above report.

SPECIAL COMMENT

The absence of the waking-state phobic response to rattlesnakes by the hypnotized subjects is a striking phenomenon which, being merely described but not being specifically mentioned or investigated as a significant observation meriting investigation, has been obscured and overlooked in the discussions of Rowland's experimentation and the conclusions that have been drawn from it. In a personal communication Dr. Rowland described as "a horrible sight—the subject reaching for that mighty diamondback rattlesnake right up to and touching the invisible glass a few short inches from the head of the snake with the lashing tongue, inflated head pouches, rattles vibrating until they were blurred." This marked personal reaction was shared by many of his waking subjects, and the reaction of others was even more intense. A graphic description is given of the shuddering near-hysteria evoked by the mere sight of the snakes, and of the calm detachment of the hypnotized subject. Yet this striking and interesting difference of behavior on the part of the hypnotized subject, with the many experimental and therapeutic possibilities which are implied by it, was overlooked at the time and has not been investigated.

7. Further Observations on Hypnotic Alteration of Visual Perception

Elizabeth M. Erickson

Since having the experience given in detail in *Observations Concerning Alterations in Hypnosis of Visual Perception* (The American Journal of Clinical Hypnosis, October 1962, *5*, 131–134), I have wondered from time to time what was the nature of the actual difference between the visual perceptions of "invisible glass" in the waking state and in the trance state.

"Invisible glass" is a term for panes of a high-quality glass, very clear and almost flawless, which are curved at an arc which is calculated mathematically so that reflections are eliminated. The appearance to the observer is that of an open space rather than a window.

Nearly five years after the original experience, while walking down Michigan Avenue in Chicago, I happened to pass a jewelry store which had two display windows with this type of glass. The windows were somewhat smaller than the window of the previous experience, but the illusion of open spaces was equally striking aided by the absence of window frames with the glass set directly in the building wall, thus intensifying the illusion of an open place in the wall.

I decided to see if again I could perceive the glass in the trance state with the same lack of conscious intention or effort and with the same immediate facility. I stood there and developed a trance state, and the glass at once became visible. I awakened and the glass vanished.

I decided to attempt to analyze these experiences further. Again I had neither expectations of nor belief in any improvement in visual acuity.

I noted again that minute specks of dust, stationary of course, were clearly visible on the glass when one focussed on them. There were also what appeared to be very slight reflections at the extreme edges of the glass where it joined the wall, and also a very small streak which was probably cleaning compound incompletely wiped off. These items of experience were equally visible in the trance state and in the waking state when one looked for them, but the perception of them differed. In the trance state they were separate items of experience; in the waking state they were very unimportant details in the entire overall experience.

Reprinted with permission from *The American Journal of Clinical Hypnosis,* January, 1966, *8*, 187–188.

This comprehension started me on a train of reasoning which, I believe, explains how the glass becomes "visible" in the hypnotic state.

Everyone who has assisted with editorial work becomes familiar with what is called "proofreader's error." This is the type of perception which leads one to read and reread manuscript, galley and page proof, and finally to approve the material as absolutely error free, only to note, when the material is in print, that there are conspicuous, possibly even ludicrous errors, omissions, or transpositions of letters. The error-free portions previous and following, plus the expectation of what should reasonably be between them, lead one to "see" the material in a correct but nonexistent state.

Similarly, the lack of ordinary reflections, scratches, and distortions in the invisible glass leads one in the waking state to be unaware of the visibility of the minute dust particles and of the logical consequences of their presence. But the hypnotized subject perceives these same particles as a separate visual experience and does not make the overall percept of the entire visual field. Thus the area in which these minute but perceivable visual stimuli are located, regarded as a separate unit, becomes "visible."

Related to this is the well-known literalness of the hypnotic subject's responses in performing other tasks. In the trance state the subject *looks at* the window as one experience and *looks through* it as a second experience. In looking *at* the window the dust specks and any streakings lead to the perception of the glass as a visual experience. In the waking state long experience in looking *through* a window with a disregard of dust specks, streakings, and the actual flaws of ordinary glass, conditions the waking person not to see the glass. Hence this conditioning, enhanced by the flawlessness and almost perfect lack of reflections, leads to the illusion of the "invisibility" of the glass.

In this connection one can bring to mind the housewife's technique of washing one side of a window pane with vertical strokes and the other side with horizontal strokes to enable her to "see if the glass is clean." A chance interrogation of professional window cleaners in the Empire State Building made years ago and repeated more recently at the O'Hare Airport in Chicago yielded identical results. The inquiry of "How do you really know if the window is clean?" elicited from both sets of window washers the reply, "You have to look at the window in a special way. If you don't, you will look right through it and you won't see the dirt you missed."

The comparison with "proofreader's error" leads to the logical corollary as to whether or not proofreading might not be much more efficient in the trance state. Regrettably, so far as I myself am concerned, I conclude that this would not be feasible. The slowing down which seems to be an inevitable accompaniment of the trance for me would lead to such an increase in the time required for the task that any increased accuracy would not be worthwhile.

8. An Investigation of Optokinetic Nystagmus

Milton H. Erickson

Optokinetic nystagmus was discussed at a diagnostic conference as a possible aid in differentiating between "hysterical" blindness, "malingered" blindness, and the deliberate deceit sometimes practiced by patients commonly designated as psychopathic personalities.

All discussants agreed that the normal person could not inhibit optokinetic nystagmus even when apprised of its nature and coached on how to suppress it. This conclusion was confirmed later by systematic testing by various investigators, all of whom rigorously excluded hypnosis as a variable in the test procedures. A revolving screen designed to induce optokinetic nystagmus was employed as the test apparatus.

Normal hypnotic subjects were then tested under controlled conditions in both waking and trance states. Optokinetic nystagmus readily developed in both states of awareness. When the subjects were instructed in the trance state to develop hypnotic blindness, a slow diminution and a total disappearance of the nystagmus occurred, usually within five minutes. Given the same instructions in the waking state, the subjects slowly developed a spontaneous trance and then manifested blindness and a loss of nystagmus.

When they were asked in the trance state to develop negative visual hallucinations—that is, to see only empty space instead of the reality objects present or to develop positive visual hallucinations, that is, to see objects other than those actually present—optokinetic nystagmus consistently disappeared. Regression, which would imply a different environmental surrounding, invariably abolished the nystagmus which would return immediately upon the reorientation of the subject to the current situation.

Two of the normal subjects available were medical students who commuted daily by train to attend classes. In the somnambulistic state they were asked to hallucinate themselves on the morning train in the company of the author and his colleague and to carry on a casual group conversation. As they responded to these instructions, the author directed attention to the fenceposts, trees, bushes, etc., along the immediate right-of-way. Both students showed an optokinetic

---

Reprinted with permission from *The American Journal of Clinical Hypnosis,* 1962, *4,* 181—183.

nystagmus as they looked out upon the hallucinated scene. Shortly one of them showed a diminution and then a cessation of the nystagmus. Upon the author's puzzled inquiry concerning what had happened, that student succinctly named the first scheduled stop of the train. Immediately, the other student, still showing nystagmus, looked around, remarked, "I hadn't noticed," and immediately lost his nystagmus. Shortly each student showed a return of the nystagmus and a diminution and cessation of it when the author casually commented upon the immediately impending arrival at the next station. Throughout the rest of the hallucinated train ride, without further intervention by the author, the students continued to show optokinetic nystagmus and its diminution, cessation, and renewal in accord with the actual train schedule. There was no unison in their performance in that subjectively they "traveled" at different rates of speed so that one could be experiencing a station stop while the other was still traveling between stations. (This same experiment was subsequently repeated with similar results before a medical school class without any preorientation as a measure of instructing the students in the validity of subjective experience.)

Four patients, not all at the same time since they were not simultaneously available, manifesting hysterical blindness were tested for optokinetic nystagmus. Two showed none, but it was noted that they both showed marked muscular tension and rigidity both in the test situation and all examination situations. One of the remaining two patients showed a beginning nystagmus, complained at once of a sudden severe headache, and showed no more nystagmus. The fourth patient was uncooperative and resistive, but the general impression was formed that had she been willing to look in the direction of the revolving screen, nystagmus would probably have developed.

Later the first two patients were tested after successful psychotherapy. Both showed normal optokinetic nystagmus in a test situation and the disappearance of it when hypnotically regressed to the period of their hysterical blindness, but prompt recurrence of it when reoriented to the current situation.

Two patients classified as psychopathic personalities, one a man, the other an adolescent girl, were asked to "put on a good act of faked total blindness" in the laboratory for the deception of a staff member they both disliked. Both, because of their innate aggressiveness, agreed readily, and the experiments were conducted separately but with essentially identical results.

The procedure was as follows: Each patient was brought into the laboratory by the author and several colleagues, and they were engaged in a casual conversation directing their attention to another colleague sitting on the opposite side of the room laboriously watching the revolving screen and seemingly trying to make careful notations. Each patient was noted by all observers to develop optokinetic nystagmus as they curiously watched the revolving screen. The seating arrangement had been devised to prevent the patient from seeing any nystagmus in the eyes of the others present.

When adequate observations had been made, the selected staff member was summoned by a secret signal. He entered the room silently out of the patient's visual range while the patient was looking at the rotating screen and manifesting nystagmus. By prearrangement the staff member made known his presence by a scoffing remark about the patient, whose immediate response was one of immediate "freezing" of body mobility, including a loss of optokinetic nystagmus, although the patient continued to "look" in the direction of the revolving screen. A prepared explanation was offered to the staff member about the patient's sudden development of blindness, to which the staff member replied with disparaging comments although he approached the patient and waved his hands back and forth as if testing the patient's vision. Then, quietly, out of the visual range of the patient, he left the room. Both patients reacted the same. Their rigid, frozen, unseeing behavior continued. The observers spoke freely to the patients, and they replied readily, but the only spontaneous freedom of movement for the patients seemed to be that of speech, and both patients made critical remarks about the staff member. Indirect tests were made for hypnotic phenomena. None was noted. When informed that the staff member had left the room, both patients "unfroze," and nystagmus returned. A casual conversation was initiated about the figures on the revolving screen. Again the staff member, upon the secret signal, reentered the room from another entrance well within the patient's visual field for both the screen and the doorway. Again both patients manifested the same remarkably inhibited behavior and again they did not seem to note the staff member's departure, this time by the doorway within the visual field. When told he had departed, their bodies seemed to relax or to become less tense, and the nystagmus recurred.

Later, efforts were made by the author and others to hypnotize these patients, but no hypnotic responses could be obtained. Both, however, boastfully volunteered "to fake a trance." Their offers were accepted, but experienced observers discredited their performances as mistaken efforts at simulation of hypnotic behavior.

SUMMARY

This study indicates that optokinetic nystagmus can be a function of subjective perception of reality in normal persons and in patients with personality or character disorders. It also indicates that optokinetic nystagmus is not reliable for use in differential diagnosis of visual alterations of psychogenic origin.

9. Acquired Control of Pupillary Responses

Milton H. Erickson

An eight-year-old girl with a marked visual defect in one eye and a strabismus of that eye was under the care of an ophthalmologist. He had prescribed various eye exercises and the wearing of an eye-patch over the stronger eye to correct the suppression of vision in the weak eye. The girl performed her exercises faithfully, sitting in front of a mirror so that she could see what she was doing. During the course of therapy she became much interested in her pupils and soon discovered the pupillary responses to bright and dimmed lights. Since she was an excellent somnambulistic hypnotic subject and had had extensive experience with suggested visual hallucinations, some of which she intentionally remembered subsequent to arousal from the trance state, she became greatly interested in watching her eyes while "I thought different things." The wearing of the eye-patch was "thought about," and she watched the pupils of her eyes as she did this "thinking." She would "think about" bright lights, semidarkness, and visual hallucinations close to her eyes and far off in the distance. She became markedly aware of the difference in the visual acuity between her eyes, and she would hallucinate an eye-patch over her eye. She learned to dilate and to contract her pupils at will. Then she became interested in unilateral pupillary responses. This, she explained, was harder to learn, therefore more interesting. To accomplish this she "imagined" wearing an eye-patch and seeing with only the weaker eye. Then, undoubtedly aided by the learnings effected by the suppression of the vision in the weaker eye, she "imagined" seeing with only the normal eye while she "stopped looking" with the weaker eye. This uniocular effort of hers may also have been aided by a possible central fusion defect, which the ophthalmologist had suggested as distinctly a possibility during his first studies of her vision. In furthering uniocular behavior the girl had called upon her hypnotic experience to hallucinate a patch over one eye and a bright light in front of the other. There were variations of this, such as "imagining looking at something close by with one eye and at something else far away with the other," an item of behavior highly suggestive of the accomplishment of students who learn to

Reprinted with permission from *The American Journal of Clinical Hypnosis,* January, 1965, 7, 207—208.

look through a microscope with one eye while using the other in reading or sketching.

When it came time for a reexamination of her eyes, she sat demurely in the chair while the ophthalmologist proceeded with the task. After an initial look at both eyes, he made a careful study of the right eye, making notations of pupillary size and of other findings. Then he turned to her left eye and was startled to see the pupil widely dilated. He glanced hurriedly at the right eye and then made an intense, searching examination of the left eye, carefully recording his findings including pupillary measurements. Then he leaned back in his chair to study and compare the separate data he had noted. Much puzzled, he glanced reflectively at her eyes and was again startled, this time because both pupils were equally widely dilated. He promptly reexamined the right eye, discovering nothing new except the dilation of the pupil. Again he studied his notations and again looked up to find that the right pupil was still dilated but that the left was markedly contracted.

His facial expression of astonishment and bewilderment was too much for the little girl, and she burst into giggles, declaring, "I did that." "But you can't, nobody can," was his reply. "Oh yes I can, you just watch." Thereupon she demonstrated bilateral and unilateral pupillary behavior, doing so in accord with specific requests from him. She explained to him, "All you have to do is look in a mirror and see your pupils and then you imagine you are in a trance and then you imagine looking at different things. You can look at different things that you imagine with one eye and at something else with the other, like looking at a bright light with one eye and the clouds in the sky when it's almost dark with the other, and you can look at things far off and right close by. You can imagine a patch over one eye and just seeing with the other. You can imagine all kinds of different things to look at in different kinds of ways with each eye."

Years later, at a seminar on hypnosis where she was present, this matter of pupillary control was mentioned. Several physicians challenged the possibility. Upon their request she obligingly demonstrated. At the time of the writing of this paper she was asked to read it for possible alterations or additions. When she finished, she remarked, "I haven't done that for years. I wonder if I can do it now." She began reminiscing about the framed mirror into which she had gazed, the overhead light she had used, the window beside which she had sat, and as she did so she demonstrated a retention of her original skill. She also added the comment that she could still, as she remembered doing previously, feel the contraction of the pupil, although the dilation as such was not felt. She could not explain better than to say, "You just feel something happening to that eye, but you cannot name the sensation."

COMMENT

At first thought one would not think this sort of pupillary control possible, until reflection brings to mind the ease with which a conditioned response can be induced by a related light-sound stimulus, the evocation of the pupillary response by the sound stimulus alone, and then a reconditioning of the pupillary response to a related sound-tactile stimulus with the pupillary response then being elicited by the tactile stimulus alone, etc.

Also, undoubtedly important is the fact that many hypnotic subjects manifest altered pupillary behavior in the trance state. Most frequently this is a dilation of the pupils particularly in the somnambulistic state and the pupillary size changes when visual hallucinations are suggested at various distances. There are also pupillary changes that accompany suggestions of fear and anger states, and of the experience of pain. Also pertinent is the fact that this young girl was later discovered to be remarkably competent in developing autohypnotic trances to obliterate pain, disturbing sounds when studying, and to establish hyperacousia when background noises interfered with her normal hearing.

In brief summary, the report indicates that pupillary responses ordinarily regarded as reflexes not accessible to voluntary control are, in fact, subject to intentional control.

II. Auditory Processes

The first two papers of this section present the results of Erickson's pioneering experimental and clinical studies on hypnotic deafness. The first of these presents Erickson's first published description of the hypnotic training of his subjects through the three stages of deep trance, stuporous trance, and somnambulistic trance described in the previous section. The progressive series of nine stages of suggestions for hypnotic deafness parallels that of his approach to hypnotic blindness (in his 1954 paper on "The development of an acute limited obsessional hysterical state in a normal subject" presented in the previous section). This parallelism suggests that this very carefully graduated series of suggestions can serve as a paradigm for the hypnotic alteration of any sensory-perceptual modality (including pain).

Of the 100 normal college students originally selected as subjects for these two papers, only 30 developed the profound trances required for this type of study, and of these only six were able to experience apparent total deafness; 14 showed various degrees of impairment; and 10 showed no form of deafness. Perhaps the most interesting aspect of this initial study is the variations of hearing impairments which were manifested. The impairments of spatial localization and time relationships, selective deafness, hallucinatory phenomena, and associated sensory and motor disturbances that accompanied hearing loss, all present fascinating insights into the interdependence of many mental functions associated with audition.

The second paper, Erickson's "Experimental findings with a conditioned response technique," utilized two of the six subjects who experienced apparent total deafness in the previous study. This paper has important bearing on the question of precisely what is meant by the experience of "apparent hypnotic deafness." Even today many investigators believe that hypnotic alterations of sensory-perceptual and cognitive functions mean only that hypnotic subjects, in their desire to please the experimenter, *act as if* they do not see, hear, or remember. According to this view the actual sensory-perceptual functions of vision and hearing, for example, remain unimpaired: Hypnotic suggestion serves only to make subjects act as if they do not see or hear by inhibiting their verbal responsiveness to these sensory-perceptual functions.

Erickson's technique of using a conditioned response to study the nature of a hypnotic alteration of sensory-perceptual functioning provided an interesting approach that attempted to bypass the complaisance of hypnotic subjects. He is again dealing with the basic issue of differentiating between the nature of genuine hypnotic phenomena and the hypnotic subject's wish to please the investigator. He found: "The experimental findings with the conditioned response technique indicate that, in addition to failure of response, there was an actual failure to receive stimuli sufficiently either to establish the neurological process of conditioning or to activate such a process already established. . . . The experimental findings warrant the conclusion that, in addition to being unconscious of a sound, there was an actual change in the capacity to utilize sound stimuli, if not an actual incapacity to receive them." This together with other characteristics of his subjects' responses enabled him to summarize, ". . . that the induction of a state of hypnotic deafness results in significant and extensive psychological and neurophysiological changes in auditory functioning comparable in degree and character with those arising from organic deafness."

The other two papers in this section, "Chemo-anesthesia in relation to hearing and memory" and "A field investigation by hypnosis of sound loci in human behavior," continue to provide details about the interdependence of and interrelationship between sensory-perceptual processes as well as many cognitive and physiological functions. The sound loci paper describes some of the important scientific and field observations that took place as early as 1929, which were crucial in helping Erickson understand the significance of minimal sensory cues in affecting human behavior and the means of utilizing them in what he would later describe as the naturalistic and indirect approaches to evoking hypnotic phenomena. Together with the chemo-anesthesia paper it sets the stage for an understanding of Erickson's studies of psychophysiological processes and psychosomatic phenomena, which are presented in the next section.

10. A Study of Clinical and Experimental Findings on Hypnotic Deafness: I. Clinical Experimentation and Findings

Milton H. Erickson

The induction of a state of apparent deafness in a normal hypnotic subject constitutes a familiar but little tested psychological phenomenon. Significant questions centering about this manifestation concern first of all its comparability with organic deafness and secondly the nature of the processes entering into it production, whether as an actual or only as an apparent condition, together with the systematic problems that arise in distinguishing between "apparent" and "actual." To investigate these questions extensive clinical studies were conducted over a period of years on normal hypnotic subjects, and these in turn were followed by an experimental study, to be reported in Section II of this paper. The clinical investigations were directed chiefly to the question of the validity of the phenomenon, utilizing for this purpose various clinical tests and measures of hearing and, particularly, careful observation of the subjects' behavior. Emphasis was placed upon the latter, since it was felt that the clinical behavior and the subjective reactions might prove suggestive of various psychological processes and forces entering into the condition.

SELECTION AND TRAINING OF SUBJECTS

Initially, more than 100 normal college students of both sexes, all of whom had been trained as hypnotic subjects, were used to develop a special technique to induce a psychologically consistent deep hypnotic trance. From this number approximately 70 were selected as sufficiently capable hypnotic subjects to be used for the induction of the more stuporous trance and the profound somnambulistic state, as contrasted to ordinary deep hypnotic sleep, which were considered necessary for reliable experimental results. From this group 30 were selected as especially capable of developing such profound trances, and these were then employed for this study.

The rationale for such a high degree of selection may be stated as follows:

Reprinted with permission from *The Journal of General Psychology* 1938, *19*, 127—150.

Past experience had demonstrated repeatedly that a deep trance, characterized by catalepsy, automatism, hypersuggestibility, and profound amnesia, often permits the subject to retain a definite capacity to react in a spontaneous volitional manner apart from the demands of the hypnotic situation and in keeping with waking patterns of behavior. Thus in such trance states behavior may actually consist of a mixture of responses to the immediate hypnotic situation and responses deriving from ordinary waking behavior. Since the contemplated experimental work necessitated the overthrow and negation of ingrained patterns of normal response and behavior, and since the study was concerned with the character of the manifestations rather than with the frequency with which they could be induced, it was considered essential to secure subjects capable of responding fully and completely to the difficult hypnotic suggestions to be given. Such subjects would be those whose responses could be limited to the immediate stimuli of the hypnotic situation uninfluenced by their usual associative and habitual modes of reaction, and who would not feel a need to continue in contact in some way with waking reality, thus eliminating sources of error arising from faulty, incomplete, or superficial trances.

The actual details of the technique employed are too extensive and laborious to be reported in full. Essentially the procedure consisted of the induction of a deep trance, followed by a deep hypnotic stupor and succeeded in turn by a profound somnambulistic state. Thus, after the first selection had been made to secure subjects capable of deep trances, attention was directed to the induction of stuporous trance states. A slow, systematic technique of graduated suggestions was employed. On the average, two hours of systematic suggestion for susceptible subjects were given before they were considered to have reached a sufficiently stuporous state, which closely resembled a profound catatonic stupor.

The next step in training was the teaching of the subjects to become somnambulistic without lessening the degree of their hypnosis. Usually the procedure with deeply hypnotized subjects is to suggest that they open their eyes and act as if they were awake. Long experience on the part of the experimenter and his colleagues has shown, however, that in somnambulistic states thus crudely suggested critical observation can detect a definite mixture of normal waking and hypnotic behavior leading to unsatisfactory findings and to a more or less ready disorganization of the somnambulism as a state in itself.

To avoid such difficulties and uncertainties, a special technique of suggestion was devised by which subjects in the stuporous trance could slowly and gradually adjust themselves to the demands of the somnambulistic trance. Usually an hour or more was spent in systematic suggestion, building up the somnambulistic state so that all behavior manifested was actually in response to the immediate hypnotic situation, with no need on the part of the subjects to bring into the situation their usual responses to a normal waking situation. Essentially this training was directed to a complete inhibition of all spontaneous activity, while giving entire freedom for all responsive activity. The final step in the preliminary training was the repetition of the entire process over and over again at irregular intervals during a period of a week or more, until it was possible to secure the stuporous trance and the somnambulistic state within 10 minutes.

When this preliminary training had been satisfactorily completed, measures were taken to prepare subjects for the investigative work, of which they were entirely in ignorance. The steps in this procedure were:

1. A clear, concise, emphatic statement that it was proposed "to hypnotize" the subject into a "state of absolute deafness."
2. The statement that, as this was done, hypnotic suggestions would be given which would cause slight difficulty, and then more and more difficulty, in hearing until finally all sounds, including the hypnotist's voice, "would fade into nothingness."
3. The statement that, as all sounds faded away, subjects would receive a sharp slap on the shoulder which would cause "the utter silence of absolute deafness," and that *ever afterward whenever they were in a deep trance,* merely a blow on the shoulder would produce "instant and absolute deafness."
4. The statement that the deafness would persist *unchanged and complete* until their right wrist was squeezed, or until they were informed definitely in some way to recover their hearing, whereupon their hearing would return "instantly and completely."
5. The induction of a state of amnesia for all commands and instructions, the amnesia to be present continuously for all future trance, posthypnotic, and waking states.

These instructions were given slowly, emphatically and impressively, and were repeated many times to insure full comprehension and acceptance.

Upon the completion of this preparation the following series of suggestions was given slowly, repetitiously, and insistently, progressing gradually from one type to the next as each subject seemed to accept them:

1. Realization that deafness *could* be achieved.
2. That it *would* be achieved.
3. That it was an absolute reality of the *future*.
4. That it was an *impending actuality* of the moment.
5. That the subjects were now *preparing to become* totally deaf.
6. That they were *now prepared* and ready.
7. That they were now *awaiting the total deafness* to ensue upon suggestion.
8. That they were now *getting* deaf, that sounds *were fading out,* that the silence was *getting deeper,* that it was *harder and harder* to hear, that they *felt* themselves *growing* more and more deaf.
9. Finally, they were given a rapid series of loud, emphatic, and absolute instructions to become deaf, totally deaf, with the experimenter's voice

gradually fading out as these instructions were concluded.

The cessation of the verbal suggestions culminated in the prearranged physical stimulus. A few moments of rest were allowed, and then, as a reinforcement, pressure was applied to the shoulder, at first gently and then with increasing force, until each subject's facial expression indicated discomfort, whereupon the pressure was slowly released. After a few moments some simple clinical tests were made, followed by restoration of hearing in accordance with the established physical stimulus. After another short rest repetitions were made of the whole procedure, gradually decreasing the verbal aspects until the physical stimulus alone proved sufficient. The time required to induce the first deaf state ranged from 20 to 40 minutes, an interval indicated by previous experience with other hypnotic subjects as requisite to achieve the mental set permitting a consistent, reliable state of deafness to develop.

CLINICAL FINDINGS

The clinical findings made were obtained by (a) direct observation of the subject's behavior by the experimenter and his assistants; (b) subjective reports obtained either at the time or subsequently by written or oral inquiry depending upon the subject's state of hearing; and (c) the execution of various procedures by the subject.

The clinical findings varied in number, kind, character, and combination from subject to subject, precluding classification by subject groups and making necessary classification according to general types of reaction, the various items of which will now be illustrated and discussed.

1. General Hypnotic Responses

Although the 30 subjects selected were capable of developing the usual deep hypnotic trance characterized by the phenomena cited above, approximately one-third, to be referred to as Group A, failed to develop the stuporous trance. A second third, Group B, went into the stuporous state but failed to develop the desired profound somnambulistic state. The remainder, Group C, developed both the stupor and the profound somnambulistic states, and it is of significance that these were the subjects who showed the more marked changes in the experimental situation. However, Groups A and B, who manifested the lesser degree of auditory impairment, did develop somnambulistic states of the apparently more superficial character usually employed in hypnotic work. Also, regardless of the apparent depth of the trances, the entire battery of hearing tests was administered to all subjects whenever possible. Of the total of 30 subjects, 10 were eliminated entirely by the tests as showing no form of deafness, six were found to be apparently totally deaf, and 14 showed various degrees of impairment of hearing.

2. Impairment of Auditory Functioning

a. Fluctuation of Auditory Threshold. (a) Progressive increase in deafness. This type of reaction was found consistently among the subjects in Groups *A* and *B* and also, to a much less extent, in Group *C*. The typical fluctuation of the auditory threshold resulting in progressive increase in deafness was as follows: Certain subjects claimed to be able to hear all sounds but explained that the sounds were changed in character by being faint and distant. In conversation, they seemed to experience a considerable degree of difficulty in distinguishing words spoken in a normal tone of voice. This difficulty, however, could be lessened by raising the voice. Soon this raising of the voice would prove to be insufficient, and they would explain that the experimenter again seemed to be "mumbling," although his voice had been maintained at a constant level. Elevating the voice still more would again enable the subject to hear more clearly, but each time this was done, as the conversation was prolonged, the subject would experience increasing difficulty in hearing clearly, and he would explain that the experimenter's voice was slowly becoming a mere "mumble." Furthermore, it was discovered that a conversation conducted in a tone of voice sufficiently loud to be audible in the same loud tone of voice, would be described by the subject as indistinct "mumbling." Also, it was learned that the "faint sounds" reported heard at the onset of the deafness tended to drop out as the subject became increasingly deaf to the experimenter's voice, and a subjective report of "complete silence" could be obtained.

To investigate further, the subject was blindfolded so that he could not watch lip movements. A long series of remarks was made to him in an increasingly loud tone of voice. Suddenly the remarks were interrupted, and silence was maintained for a minute or two, following which the remarks were continued in the same loud tone. However, a period of one to two minutes would elapse before the subject became aware of the resumption of the speech, which he would describe then as a "mumbling." Also, while still blindfolded, if a series of ,narks were addressed to him in an increasingly loud tone of voice, and th(.1 the voice was suddenly dropped to a normal level without interruption of speech, the subject would remain unaware of the continuance of the remarks until after one to two r nutes. Then again he would begin to hear vaguely and indistinctly, and inquir y would disclose his assumption that the experimenter had remained silent for a while. Continued investigation disclosed that this indistinct hearing would persist about a half-minute and would then fade out. After another one to two minutes of continued speech, he would again hear indistinctly for a brief interval, and this manifestation, highly suggestive of a process of summation of stimuli, could be continued indefinitely.

(b) Progressive decrease in deafness. Certain other subjects manifested an opposite reaction. They would disclaim any ability to hear, and their general behavior confirmed this contention. Nevertheless, if a series of remarks was addressed to them, they would, after about a minute's delay, gradually begin to hear faintly and then more and more distinctly until the experimenter's normal tone of voice became fully audible to them.

Cessation of speech for a minute or two followed by a resumption would again meet with complete deafness, which would slowly decrease in degree after a minute or two until the subject could again hear plainly. Continued repetition of the process slowly reduced the period of apparently complete deafness to about 30 seconds and increased the rate of complete restoration of hearing. Similarly, a longer period of silence would delay the beginning of and prolong the period of restoration of hearing. Blindfolding seemed to delay markedly the gradual decrease in deafness, in one subject for a period of five minutes consistently, but in no instance did the deprivation of visual cues prevent the process.

For both groups the investigation was continued with a variety of sounds, including electric buzzers, bells, tuning forks, and alarm clocks, as well as the voice of an assistant, with essentially the same results.

An interesting clinical difference between these two groups was their subjective reactions to their auditory difficulties. Those showing primarily progressive increase of deafness tended to ascribe their difficulty to themselves, explaining that the experimenter "seemed to be mumbling," that sounds "seemed to be faint and distant," and that their ears seemed "stopped up" as from a cold or from "getting water in them from swimming," and they would strain to hear, shake their heads, and finger their ears. Those showing primarily a progressive decrease tended, on the other hand, to project their difficulties on the experimenter, explaining their difficulty by complaining that he was speaking inaudibly at first and then gradually raising his voice to an audible level. When questioned about other sounds, the explanation was offered that the experimenter was utilizing an electric control over the intensity of the sounds. No effort was made to correct their views, since only their spontaneous reactions were considered significant.

b. Impairment of spatial localization and time relationships. In all of the subjects showing impairment of hearing there was found to be a marked decrease in the ability to locate sounds spatially and to determine time relationships. Since the findings were essentially the same for all of the subjects, they may be illustrated by the following specific account. One subject, who declared his ability to hear all sounds faintly, was urged to listen carefully and to identify the next noise he heard. The sound employed was that of a concealed alarm clock with an intermittent alarm which rang for one-minute periods at five-minute intervals. Not until some time after the alarm began ringing did he seem to hear it, whereupon he began listening in a strained fashion, first in one direction and then in another, while his eyes searched the floor, the walls, and the ceiling in his endeavor to locate the sound. This behavior continued for a full minute after the alarm ceased to ring. Then, after a sudden start, he listened intently and declared that the sound had ceased. Immediate questioning by paper and pencil concerning the character of the sound elicited the answer, *"I couldn't tell. It was just a faint noise."* There followed the spontaneous observation, *"And what's more, I can't even tell you where it came from."* The suggestion was offered that he "might like to find out what it is," and when the alarm rang again, he suddenly declared, after a delay of some 30 seconds, *"I hear it"* and began to wander about the room in a vague, confused, uncertain fashion, listening intently in an effort to locate the sound. It was noted that he continued his search for about a minute after the alarm had become silent, whereupon he declared, *"It's stopped again,"* nor did he show any apparent realization that his time relationships were wrong. Repeated attempts were made before he succeeded in locating the place of concealment for the clock. Subsequently the clock was secretly removed to a diagonally opposite corner of the room. It was noted that he continued to listen in the direction of the former location and failed to detect the altered direction of the sound even when he approached the supposed place of concealment to listen more closely.

This was followed by the use of two clocks adjusted to ring in immediate succession, the one ringing first located in the original place of concealment, and the second in another corner of the room. The subject was instructed again to find out what the sound was. As previously, after a delay of about 30 seconds, he heard the sound, located it correctly but uncertainly, and failed completely to note any change in location when the second clock sounded. Later the clocks were shifted to various locations, but the first localization achieved in each instance sufficed for the other sound.

Another variation consisted in adjusting the clocks so that the second alarm would follow the first at selected intervals. Since the subject tended to hear subjectively from 30 to 60 seconds after the sound had ceased, it was found that an interval between the alarms greater than this lag was necessary to permit the subject to realize that the sound had ceased and then had begun again. Also, there was found to be no time lag in the detection of the second sound. Various types of sounds were employed, the subject was blindfolded, definite instructions were given to localize sounds, but essentially the same results were obtained. Even the pairing of an electric buzzer with a clock or a tuning fork, although the difference in sound was detected, failed to aid in localization; rather it served only to make the subject more uncertain. A significant additional observation was that those subjects considered by the experimenter to manifest the less satisfactory somnambulistic trances showed less time lag in detecting and the greater ability in localizing sounds, but even these subjects showed a perseveration of first localizations.

c. Impairment of sound discrimination. While investigating the loss of ability to localize sounds in those subjects continuing to hear faintly despite suggestions of a deafness, the experimenter had read aloud slowly from a book while the subject watched and listened intently. At a prearranged passage an assistant concealed behind a screen continued the reading while the experimenter silently mouthed the words. The altered character and location of the sound was not noted even after many repetitions, nor was the use in one instance of a feminine voice. However, cautious inquiry did disclose that during the reading a brief passage had been decidedly more difficult to hear, but that this difficulty had cleared rapidly. Inquiry failed to identify the particular phrases causing the increased difficulty in hearing, but the subject's uncertainties when questioned about the last phrases read by the experimenter and those read first by his substitute were suggestive of auditory threshold changes unperceived by the subjects.

While investigating spatial localization by the use of two alarm clocks, among those used were clocks with different-sounding alarms. This was not detected by the subjects. Tuning forks of different notes were also employed without detection. However, when an electric buzzer was paired with a tuning fork or an alarm clock, the difference was noted but only after a time lag of 10 to 20 seconds. A final investigative measure was to inform the subject that he was to listen to a series of sounds given at intervals of two minutes and that he was to note whether or not they were all the same. During the first two trials he was allowed to watch the experimenter operating a single key on a dummy keyboard while the sounds were actually produced by the secret operation of a concealed keyboard. He reported that the same sound had been made repeatedly. For the additional trials he was blindfolded. In each instance, in a random fashion, different-sounding buzzers, bells, tuning forks, and clocks had been employed, but the only difference reported was that of volume, the subject being quite certain that only one sound had been employed.

3. Selective Deafness

Certain of the subjects were noted to exercise a peculiar selective process in becoming deaf, some doing this spontaneously, and others stipulating, for reasons to be discussed later, that they be allowed to hear certain sounds, a stipulation which in itself is significant.

Three subjects in particular seemed to be unable to accept intellectually the suggestions for deafness. They were amused by the experimenter's inquiries, conversed freely, and demonstrated full hearing ability until a chance incident disclosed that the first of these subjects was hearing only the usual expected sounds appropriate to the situation. The dropping of a pencil, footsteps and voices outside the door, and street sounds were picked up more readily than by the experimenter. However, during the conversation a button was accidentally pushed on a concealed keyboard sounding an electric buzzer. This was not detected by the subject, who laughingly commented on the squeaking of the experimenter's chair as he leaned back. Following this discovery extensive systematic investigations were conducted, and it was found that any number of sounds could be produced without the subject's knowledge. He was given the task of reading aloud slowly and distinctly, while the experimenter ostentatiously timed him with a stopwatch and made extensive notes. During the reading an electric switch was secretly operated, sounding a loud buzzer, almost imperceptibly at first and then more and more noisily, but he failed to notice it or to react to it by raising his voice, although it was noted that an automobile horn, the street car, or other disturbing sounds would evoke this response.

The investigation was continued by blindfolding the subject. Deprived of visual cues, he apparently reacted to his situation as a totally new one in which he could expect anything to happen, with the result that no evidence of any deafness could be discovered. At another session, unblindfolded, he was again found to be deaf to the sounds he had heard when blindfolded.

Similar results were obtained with the other two subjects with the exception that both, after the blindfolding experience, seemed to regard the test noises as expected sounds and hence were no longer deaf to them, but they were still deaf to new test sounds. In addition, it was found with one subject that prolongation of electric buzzer or bell sounds for five or more minutes would break down the deafness, and the subject would slowly begin to hear it and thereafter would continue to be able to hear it. Apparently summation processes developed in this subject.

Another form of selective deafness was that shown by one subject who had an exceedingly strong prejudice against being seen in the trance state by a third party. Previous experience had shown, however, that he was willing to go into a trance in the presence of others providing they were blindfolded. During the experimental work he was found to be deaf to all sounds except the experimenter's voice and to those sounds seemingly constituting a threat to his prejudice, such as a knock at the door, footsteps in the corridor, or someone calling to the experimenter from outside the room, and so strong was his objection that he would tend to awaken immediately despite the fact that he knew the door of the laboratory to be locked. This prejudice suggested the following clinical test. With the subject's eyes cataleptically closed, a visitor, blindfolded to guard against difficulties should the subject awaken, was introduced surreptitiously into the room. A conversation was begun with the subject in which he participated to prove his contention he could hear everything. The visitor joined in the conversation, addressed remarks to the subject, called him by name, but the subject failed completely to perceive the visitor's presence. In a later session the visitor was allowed to touch the subject, who immediately recognized the touch as alien, awakened, at once, but was entirely relieved by discovering that the visitor was blindfolded.

Still another type of selective deafness was shown by a subject from Group *A*. It was discovered that whenever the hypnotic state was induced, he spontaneously developed a total deafness for every sound except the experimenter's voice. There was never any need to instruct him to become deaf, and it seemed impossible for him to hear any sound more than briefly, even when instructed to do so. For example, he was told to converse with a third person while he was in the trance state. The first two or three remarks addressed to him were heard readily, but thereafter he would gradually cease to hear that person's voice even though he could see the speaker's lips moving. Instructed to listen to an electric bell, he would direct his attention as told, but almost immediately a spontaneous deafness would develop. Repeated efforts made to suggest directly a total deafness that would include the experimenter's voice failed completely, but a long period of silence on the part of the experimenter would result in the effective development of such deafness spontaneously. However, after the development of such deafness, continued talking by the experimenter while the subject watched his lips would serve to restore his ability to hear the experimenter, but a similar procedure with other speakers would fail. The results on all other clinical tests indicated total deafness for the subject. Further mention of this subject will be made in Section II of this paper.

4. Hallucinatory Phenomena and Dependence on Visual Cues

Certain of the subjects who reacted to total deafness with panic and shock reactions, to be described later, insisted upon being allowed to retain the ability to hear some chosen sound. When this concession was made, they developed apparently total deafness to all other sounds. Investigation soon disclosed that their wishes could be met by limiting their hearing to the single sound of a special clicking pendulum. Stopping of this pendulum was detected immediately and also invariably interpreted by them as the cue for the restoration of hearing despite instructions to the contrary. Apparently such a procedure was regarded as an absolute violation of the trance conditions. Resort was then had to the following subterfuge: Two pendulums were rigged, one sounding and concealed, the other silent and visible. Both were set in motion simultaneously, and the subject was allowed to associate the sound of the first with the motion of the silent one. Then, after the deaf state had been induced, the subject was given a written statement to the effect that he might watch the pendulum but that as he did so his ears would be stopped so that he could not hear it, and when he had ceased to hear it, he was to inform the experimenter. He was further informed that his ears would then be freed gradually so that he would first hear the sound very faintly and then more and more plainly as he watched the swinging pendulum. This instruction was repeated two or three times until the subject understood fully. Finally, when the subject's ears were fully obstructed, his mouth closed, and even his nose closed for the moment, an assistant secretly interrupted the sounding pendulum, permitting the silent, visible pendulum to continue its motion. The subject's ears were then gradually released while he was instructed to watch the pendulum closely and to inform the experimenter as soon as he heard the first faint sound. As soon as he signified this, his ears were gradually freed entirely. In each instance the subject, convinced by his visual impressions, was content with an hallucinatory hearing of the pendulum sounds, and the substitution was never detected. Nor was the setting in motion again of the sound pendulum detected while the subject was contenting himself with hallucinatory hearing. Stopping of this silent pendulum without the subject's knowledge had no effect upon him, but when he was permitted to see the pendulum stopped, he immediately regained his hearing. Even before the employment of the two-pendulum subterfuge it had been observed that these subjects were dependent upon visual cues, since they consistently refused to be blindfolded for clinical tests without an absolute promise given not to stop the pendulum. Their explanation was that they did not want to be "tricked," an explanation suggestive of their subjective lack of reliance upon auditory experiences.

5. Associated Sensory Changes and Motor Disturbances

Frequently in the induction of hypnotic deafness the subjects would spontaneously develop other physiological changes, apparently as an essential feature of the deafness. Thus one subject, who developed total deafness according to all tests, experienced a distressing decrease in vision. Reading was exceedingly laborious for him, as was writing, and his movements were groping and uncertain. In addition there was much subjective anxiety over his visual loss. Physical examination of his eyes disclosed widely dilated pupils, a failure of focussing, and irregular jerking movements of the eyeballs.

A second subject manifested a generalized anaesthesia, most marked in his arms and legs. Inquiry elicited from him that his limbs were "numb, feelingless, sound asleep," and it was not possible for him to move or to use them spontaneously. Careful tests failed to elicit any evidence of feeling in his hands.

Several of the other subjects manifested sensory losses with the deafness, but to a lesser degree. Efforts were made at first to correct these losses, but it was soon found that suggestions lessening the associated sensory disturbances had the effect of decreasing the degree of deafness. Also it was learned that in these subjects it was not possible to induce deafness unless they were allowed to develop other sensory disturbances. Furthermore, in subjects who previously had failed to develop deafness, a suggestion technique embracing other sensory disturbances—as, for example, combined deafness and anaesthesia—would often be effective. The spontaneous development of these sensory and motor disturbances may reasonably be regarded as confirmatory evidence of auditory changes, since they imply a marked disturbance of general functioning.

6. Apparently Total Hypnotic Deafness

a. Responses to clinical tests. To investigate the apparently total hypnotic deafness manifested by some of the subjects, use was made of a great variety of clinical tests. These may be listed and illustrated by a few examples as follows:

1. Vibration tests:
   a. Detection of and response to loud noises through vibration caused in floor, sounding boxes, etc., instead of response to sound itself.
   b. Lack of confusion of vibratory sensations and sound sensations when sounding tuning fork is held in close proximity to ear while a silent tuning fork is pressed against the mastoid bone and vice versa.
2. "Startle" situations:
   a. Lack of response to joke noisemakers such as inflated rubber bladders placed under chair cushions, trick boxes setting off explosive caps when opened, or making other sudden sounds, etc.
   b. Failure of surprise reactions when, after repeatedly watching a tin pan dropped noisily to floor behind desk, the pan drops noiselessly into a secretly released net.
   c. Failure to start, to turn head or eyes, or to show compensatory withdrawals or tensions to sudden, sharp, unexpected sounds.
3. Voice-raising and -lowering tests:
   a. Failure to raise voice when reading aloud while an irrelevant continuous extraneous noise becomes increasingly disturbing.
   b. Failure to lower voice or to falter at sudden cessation of disturbing continuous extraneous noise when reading loudly.
4. Social situations and involuntary responses:
   a. Failure of response to interruption by a third party to subject's conversational remarks.
   b. Failure to respond with perfunctory courtesies, as for example showing no response or hesitation, while returning his pack to his pocket, to the verbal acceptance of a proffered cigarette following an observed silent refusal.
   c. Failure to show any response to deliberately embarrassing remarks made to subjects known to blush easily.
5. Psychological trickery:
   a. Failure of the subject to include illegitimate data after the following procedure was followed: While the subject was deaf, apparently to inform the assistant, a long list of confusing associated facts, such as a genealogical tree, was read aloud repeatedly with much detailed discussion. A purported carbon copy from which certain data were omitted was given him as a "memory test," which he was to memorize and recall as completely as possible in a given length of time.
   b. Failure to benefit by elaborations, given apparently to assistant, of written instructions.

      c. Failure to benefit by casual assistance given during the oral trans-
lation of a long difficult passage.

      d. Failure to develop sophistication or to show amusement when
subject sees assistant tricked by joke noisemaker.

  6. Conditioned responses:

Simple preliminary experiments on the establishment of conditioned
responses based on auditory cues, and on the evocation of similar
already established conditioned responses, were included as clinical
tests. The significant results obtained gave rise to the experimental
work to be reported in the second part of this paper.

Of the 10 subjects originally considered as showing total deafness, four were
found to be only partially deaf. The remaining six, however, were found to be
consistently deaf to all of these tests. These subjects were all from Group *C*.

    b. Behavior reactions to induced deafness. All of the subjects employed
manifested definite subjective reactions to the hypnotic deafness, and these reactions may be classified for convenience of description under three crude categories—(*a*) curiosity, (*b*) panic, and (*c*) shock—since they appeared in
combination with one or another reaction dominant.

    (a). Curiosity. Those showing predominantly a reaction of curiosity would
manifest a considerable degree of astonishment at the onset of the deafness, and
when reassured by the written statement, *"Everything is all right—just some
experimentation—tell me what you hear,"* would manifest intense and decidedly
childish curiosity and wonderment, dropping objects, listening vainly to watches,
banging things, talking to themselves—particularly this last form of
activity—often so self-absorbed that it was difficult to secure any satisfactory
subjective account from them initially.

    (b). Panic. Those who manifested panic reactions were decidedly difficult
to manage. In producing deafness routine suggestions to allay fear reactions
were always given, but these were worded carefully to avoid possible influence
upon the general state desired, and hence they were often ineffective.

Despite this instruction a number of subjects displayed marked panic reactions, showing marked fright, probing their ears with their fingers, shouting that
they could not hear, and asking importunately what had happened, since they
had complete amnesia for the trance suggestions and often did not realize that
they were at the time in a hypnotic trance. Some, when their hearing was
restored by the proper visual or tactile stimulus, were most emphatic in demanding that no further experimentation in regard to deafness be done with
them. When persuaded to the contrary, much reassurance was required concerning the temporariness of the phenomenon, and the completion of each experimental session was marked by much subjective relief. These same panic
reactions occurred, but to a lesser degree, in some of the subjects showing only
impairment of hearing. Also, certain subjects reacted so strongly that in subsequent experimentation they refused to develop total deafness, insisting that

they be permitted to retain the ability to hear some sounds, which has been described above.

(c). Shock reactions. The third category of behavior was that of shock reactions. These occurred chiefly among those who manifested apparently total deafness, although it was shown to a lesser degree by those who manifested only auditory impairment. Induction of deafness was characterized by the more or less generalized associated sensory changes described above, accompanied by much physical tension, slowing of general reactions, and an appearance and complaints of severe physical discomfort which tended to disappear gradually. When, however, after having been made deaf, they were given a visual or tactile cue restoring their hearing, definite shock reactions appeared. Immediately upon perceiving the cue, there would appear a violent tensing of the entire body, followed often by generalized tremors. Usually the subject would clasp his hands to his ears, and frequently his face would contort as if he were experiencing severe pain. The pulse rate, too, was noticed to increase, sometimes 30 to 40 beats per minute. Respiration was frequently marked by gasping and deep sighing. Almost invariably the subject would speak in a loud tone as if trying to make himself heard above a noisy disturbance. After two to three minutes the subject would begin to relax. Not every subject manifested all of these symptoms—some showed only two or three and others showed all of them. Subjectively, they described it as most decidedly unpleasant and painful. One subject described his experience as *"just like being in the midst of a deep, peaceful silence and then being thrown forcibly into the din of a boiler factory going full blast. It's just painful, and it hurts you all over."* Several subjects who experienced the more painful reactions, after one or two experiences, refused to permit further experimentation because, *"It's too painful."* This refusal was met by developing a technique for slow restoration of hearing which, as sessions were repeated, was gradually abridged to a three- to five-second procedure. One subject, however, would not permit any shortening of the procedure, but insisted on a three- to four-minute period, since otherwise, she explained, she would develop a severe headache. This same subject also insisted, for the same reason, on being awakened slowly from a deep trance, and usually a period of three to five minutes was required to awaken her comfortably. Others did not develop the shock reactions at all, and still others overcame them spontaneously after two or three experiences.

7. Postexperimental Findings

Some weeks after completing the clinical investigations, a systematic inquiry was conducted with the subjects to determine their postexperimental reactions. In each instance the subject was found to have a complete amnesia for the whole experience, the usual report being, *"Well, I reported regularly, you would begin to hypnotize me, and then I would find myself waking up and you would dismiss me. I know sometimes you kept me as long as four hours, but I don't know what happened.''* Extensive questioning by an assistant failed to elicit any other significant information except the fact that frequently they were so fatigued after the session that they had gone to bed immediately.

Inquiry was then made in the form of a hypothetical question concerning their opinion about the possibility of inducing by hypnosis the various phenomena that had been elicited. About 15 of the 30 scoffed at the idea. The majority of these were those who failed to manifest any form of deafness, but most interesting was the inclusion in the group of two of the six showing complete deafness. About half of the remainder were undecided but inclined to be dubious, and these were chiefly those who had shown various degrees of impairment of hearing although one of those showing total deafness was included. The remainder were uncertain but inclined to favor the possibility, advancing arguments best illustrated by the following remarks offered by one of those showing total deafness: "Well, take last Saturday's session. When I sat down for you to hypnotize me, I pulled out my watch and it said 6 o'clock. I started to put it back, and then I took a second look at it and it said 10 o'clock. But before I could figure that out, I noticed that it was dark outside, my coat and tie were off, my sleeves rolled up, and I was just about exhausted, and it really was 10 o'clock. Now, if I could lose consciousness like that, and it's happened lots of times, I think that you could lose hearing or sight or feeling the same way. It's probably the same sort of feeling."

Following this questioning the subjects were asked to behave deliberately as if they were deaf, and thus to impose upon the experimenter the task of proving, against their efforts and without their assistance, that they could hear. To avoid unintentional hypnotic responses an assistant administered the various clinical tests given in the discussion of total hypnotic deafness. All of these tests were failed, usually with full awareness on the part of the subjects of their failures, although in some of the vibration tests and some of the procedures involving psychological trickery the subjects remained unaware of failures. Also, not one of the subjects showed any of the phenomena elicited in relation to impaired hearing. Even a direct suggestion that they simulate impaired hearing failed to secure more than an obvious pretense. Apparently, despite actual past experience, they had no conception of what impairment might mean.

Finally, they were taken into confidence by the experimenter and an assistant and instructed to simulate deafness for the purpose of deceiving a second assistant. Despite the sophistication and coaching effects accruing from the previous attempt the test results were the same, since slight variations in the test procedures served to offset any control of their responses they had established. However, during this part of the investigation three of the subjects who suddenly began passing the tests after initial failures were found to have developed spontaneously a hypnotic trance, and repetition of the tests in an actual waking state resulted in complete failures.

SUMMARY OF CLINICAL FINDINGS

The clinical findings obtained may be summarized briefly in the following two crude categories:

1. *Evidence of Changes in Auditory Functioning.*
   - *a.* Alterations in auditory threshold.
     - (*a*). Fluctuations with progressive increase or decrease in hearing.
     - (*b*). Restriction to certain types of stimuli—"selective" deafness.
   - *b.* Impairment of hearing in:
     - (*a*). Spatial localization of sounds.
     - (*b*). Discrimination of time relationships.
     - (*c*). Discrimination of sound qualities.
     - (*d*). Substitution of inner for outer stimuli—"hallucinatory" hearing.
2. *Evidence of Total Loss of Hearing.*
   - *a.* Appropriate response to vibratory stimulation other than sound.
   - *b.* Absence of "startle" reflexes.
   - *c.* Failure of habitual, ingrained, or voluntary patterns of behavior arising from auditory stimuli.
   - *d.* Complete limitation of responsive behavior to stimuli legitimate to the deaf state.

COMMENT ON CLINICAL FINDINGS

In commenting upon these experimental findings, mention must be made first of the problem central to the whole investigation—namely, the question of the possible identity of *absence of response* and *absence of hearing*. Within the limits of this investigation the one is taken as indicative of the other, and likewise, alteration of response is regarded as evidence of alteration of hearing. Although pragmatically the same, the question of their absolute identity does obtain, but this question does not invalidate the experimental results. Furthermore, definite efforts were made to elicit the responses properly and ordinarily evoked by auditory stimulations, some of which were voluntary, others involuntary. Often no response of either sort could be obtained, and those that were elicited were incomplete, inadequate, or of a character not warranted by or consistent with the stimuli employed in their evocation. Such findings are inexplicable except on the basis of significant neuropsychic changes, induced in the subject by hypnotic suggestions, serving to produce a loss of response to sound identical in character with the loss found in organic deafness.

Because of the varied nature of the experimental findings and the many and diverse questions to which they give rise, comment will be limited to a brief discussion of some of the more significant considerations.

1. *The Hypnotic Technique.* The prolonged, systematic development of the stuporous and somnambulistic trance states, as contrasted to the usual rapid and, in the experimenter's judgment, more superficial induction of such states, probably contributed greatly to the final results. That such a technique served to establish a massive generalized state of "inhibition," rendering the subjects incapable of spontaneous responses and restricting them to limited responsive behavior, is possible, and rather than militating against the experimental findings, it suggests a possible explanation. Also, the obtaining of more extensive results from those subjects responding fully to the complete technique indicates a significant role for the profounder trance states.

2. *Progressive Increase in Deafness.* This finding suggests changes in the auditory threshold rendering previously appreciable stimuli subliminal. Particularly is this indicated by the appearance of the process of summation, which in turn suggests changes in conduction through alterations of synaptic resistances. With such summation processes it is difficult to explain this finding entirely as an inhibition of either responses or perceptual activity.

3. *Progressive Decrease in Deafness.* This finding is in accord with work on changes in sensory thresholds permitting detection, after repeated stimulation, of previously subliminal stimuli. As in the case of progressive increase in deafness, changes permitting processes of summation seem to enter into the condition also, as well as the possibility of various inhibitory processes. Concerning the subjective reactions to both progressive increase and progressive decrease of deafness, whatever the experience was for the subjects they identified it with actual past experience and thus endowed it definitely with a subjective validity.

4. *Impairment of Spatial Localization.* This unexpected finding, for which no suggestions were given, indicates directly a changed character of the auditory stimuli perceived. Whether it derives from failure of perceptual processes or from altered conduction and radiation of auditory nerve impulses is speculative, but its appearance does denote a significant change in hearing.

5. *Impairment of Discrimination of Time-Relationships.* This too, was a spontaneous and unexpected development, and it gives rise to such difficult questions as: What did the subject continue to hear after the sounds ceased? Was the time lag a function of summation processes? Why did the subjective perseveration of hearing of a sound blend into the hearing of a successive and different sound? Speculation is warranted on delayed perceptual processes, threshold changes, and processes of summation.

6. *Failure of Discrimination of Different Sounds.* This finding may be considered as arising at least in part from direct suggestion, but the persistence of some ability to hear and the actual ability to discriminate between immediately successive sounds implies other factors at work. The failure of memory processes indicates definite restriction of perceptual activity and a loss of various sound values for which immediate contrast was necessary. The ability to dis-

criminate between immediately successive sounds of different character suggests
no changes in conduction or radiation of nerve impulses, but the tests employed
were not sufficiently refined to permit the detection of such changes. Hence
conduction or radiation changes could be masked by the crudity of the tests
employed. However, the partial or limited perceptual responses made suggest
that failure of discrimination may be attributable to a number of factors.

7. *"Selective" Deafness.* Somewhat analogous to this finding is the instance
of the person who sleeps soundly through a noisy disturbance yet awakens
readily at the occurrence of a slight preselected sound, or the ability of experienced workmen to converse in natural tones in the overwhelming din of a
noisy factory. These instances from normal life, as well as the experimental
findings, suggest that it is possible to regulate the perception of sounds to those
having certain perceptual values. However, an immediate question is: Is it not
necessary to experience all sounds before a "selection" can be made? Hence
the process would simply be an inhibition of perceptual responses. Or is the
process one of "setting" the auditory thresholds so that it can be sensitive to
only certain stimuli? This is suggested by the experimental findings on the
subject who could hear a voice in the corridor outside the locked door but could
not hear the same voice within the locked room, and hence altered in its secondary auditory qualities. Also, the experimental situation left the subject free
to "select" any sound, but apparently only those sounds having secondary
attributes of "expectedness" or "appropriateness" could be "selected." Apparently hearing depended not only upon sound itself, but upon other qualities.
Briefly the findings suggest that "selective deafness" or, conversely, "selective
hearing" could occur only after the inception of various psychic processes of
a nonhearing character, initiated by stimuli arising independently of sound itself
and not constituting a part of the experience of hearing. Without such preliminary psychic activity sound stimulation remained subliminal in character. This
is indicated also by the summation processes that could be induced. The selective
deafness of the subject who objected to being seen in the trance state indicates
the effectiveness, subjectively, of the deafness, and his ready response to an
alien touch suggests the specificity of the sensory disturbance. The findings on
the subject who developed deafness spontaneously despite efforts to train him
to hear suggest that hypnosis had effected changes in him which precluded the
development of perceptual processes. In brief this disturbance in auditory functioning seems to be one occurring in the states of hearing preceding perceptual
activity and not a process of inhibition of perception.

8. *"Hallucinatory" Hearing.* This finding suggests that the auditory disturbance was of such character that actual sounds could not be differentiated from
sound images, that reality attributes of sound had been lost, permitting an effective substitution of internal for external stimuli. That there was an actual loss
in sound qualities is suggested by the failure of the subject to respond to the
restarting of the sounding pendulum following his hallucination of it. Theoret-
ically there should have been a marked contrast of a disturbing character between

the sound image arising from inner stimuli and the renewed external sound. That there was no such contrast indicates significant changes in auditory functioning.

9. *Sensory and Motor Changes.* The associated sensory and motor disturbances developing spontaneously, either in association with the deafness or the hypnosis itself, may be regarded as significant confirmatory evidence that hypnotic states do alter psychological and physiological functioning.

10. *Apparently Total Deafness.* The totally negative results from a battery of varied clinical tests on six subjects, confirmed by results of similar character but lesser degree on other subjects, indicate that massive alterations may be induced hypnotically in auditory functioning. That auditory nerve stimulation did occur cannot be doubted, but what disposition was made of those stimulations may be speculated upon in the light of the evidence afforded by the lesser degrees of auditory impairment. That the clinical tests employed, despite their variety and directness or indirectness, were entirely adequate to detect complete absence of response is open to question, but the extensiveness of the auditory changes cannot be questioned. The conclusion is warranted that there was produced a condition not distinguishable from neurological deafness by any of the ordinarily competent tests employed. Essentially the problem revolves about the question raised above, namely: *Is being unconscious of a sound* identical with *failure to respond to a sound?*

11. *Subjective Reactions.* While confidence cannot be placed extensively in subjective reactions, even those objectively observed, nevertheless the consistency, the unpleasant character, and the intensity of the reactions manifested by the subjects of this investigation are indicative of subjectively tremendous alterations in neuropsychic functioning. They signify changes beyond the normal control of the subjects which had to derive from actual psychosomatic experiences. Accordingly, these subjective reactions may be regarded as constituting significant evidence of neurophysiological changes.

12. *Postexperimental Findings.* Despite full cooperation and earnest, sincere efforts the subjects failed to duplicate in the waking state the performance made possible by hypnosis, and even to realize the possibility of so doing, despite the fact that, unknowingly, they had undergone very clear experiences. One may venture the hypothesis that their failure in the waking state resulted not from incapacity, since capacity had been demonstrated, but from a mental set, contingent upon wakefulness, precluding the initiation of the remote preliminary mental processes leading to the actual performance.

11. A Study of Clinical and Experimental Findings on Hypnotic Deafness: II. Experimental Findings with a Conditioned Response Technique

Milton H. Erickson

Several weeks after the completion for them of the clinical investigation of hypnotically induced deafness, reported in Section I of this paper, two of the subjects included in Group C, both males, who had manifested total deafness according to clinical tests, were used for further extensive study of the phenomenon by the technique of a conditioned response. These subjects, to avoid the possibility of sophistication, had not been subjected to the preliminary experimentation with conditioned responses reported in Section I, nor had postexperimental attempts been made to secure conscious simulation of deafness. This was done subsequent to the experimental work. Furthermore they were given to understand that the experimenter was now interested in an entirely new problem unrelated to any past work. No new training measures were employed, and the same technique for the induction of the deep sleep, the stupor, and the profound somnambulistic state was employed. Two other subjects were also employed, but for reasons to be given later the findings on them will be reported separately.

EXPERIMENTAL PROTOCOL

The protocol drafted for this part of the study included the following steps:

1. The induction of a profound somnambulistic trance persisting throughout the entire working period.
2. The evocation of a muscular response by an electric shock.
3. The conditioning of this muscular response to an auditory stimulus.

Revised and enlarged from a report given before the American Psychiatric Association at St. Louis, May 6, 1936; reprinted with permission from *The Journal of General Psychology,* 1938, *19*, 151-167.

4. The establishment and removal of a state of hypnotic deafness to determine its effect upon the auditorily conditioned muscular response.
5. Control investigations:
   a. In waking state:
      (a) Evocation of the established conditioned response.
      (b) Establishment of another auditority conditioned response.
      (c) Suject's attempt to inhibit voluntarily this second conditioned response, followed by similar attempt to inhibit the first conditioned response.
   b. In a second hypnotic state:
      (a) Establishment of a third auditorily conditioned response with no suggested deafness.
      (b) Evocation of first, second, and third conditioned responses.
      (c) Subject's attempt to inhibit voluntarily all three conditioned responses.
      (d) Attempt to establish a fourth auditorily conditioned response in a continuously deaf state.

THE APPARATUS

The apparatus employed consisted of an electric resistance coil with a source of current, a two-way electric switch, hand electrodes, an electric buzzer, a recording tambour connected with a special closed rubber tube constructed like a pneumograph, a recording apparatus of highly sensitive electromagnetic markers, a long-paper kymograph, and smoked paper. Screens were used to conceal from the subject all apparatus except the electrodes and the closed rubber tube. By means of the two-way switch two circuits were established. With flow of current in the first circuit, the buzzer would sound and the subject would receive a shock in his hands, while the electromagnetic markers would record both the buzzer and the shock. A flow of current in the second circuit would operate the buzzer and its recording electromagnetic marker only. Hence the subject could receive an auditory stimulus without receiving a shock, but every flow of current to the hand electrodes was in conjunction with the sounding of the buzzer. The special rubber tube was wrapped about the right forearm of the subject and connected with the recording tambour so that the change in the volume of the arm occasioned by muscular contractions was graphically portrayed on the smoked paper of the kymograph. Adhesive tape was used to fasten the electrodes in the palms of the subject's hands, with his fingers fastened in a position of light closure over them.

Using this apparatus a conditioned response was developed as follows: By means of the hand electrodes, an electric shock of sufficient intensity to cause a direct contraction of the flexor muscles of the forearm was administered to the subject. The delivery of each shock was preceded immediately by the sounding of an electric buzzer. Thus the auditory stimulus was established as an integral part of the stimulus-complex evoking muscular contractions, thereby acquiring the same property of evoking muscular responses as did the combined stimuli.

THE EXPERIMENTAL PROCEDURE AND FINDINGS

The subject was hypnotized deeply in a side room and led, with his eyes cataleptically closed, into the experimental room and seated comfortably in a chair. Following the completion of all connections with the experimental and recording apparatus, the subject was instructed firmly that "it was absolutely essential" that he "remain deeply, soundly asleep regardless of anything that may happen" until he received definite instructions to the contrary. He was to sleep deeply and restfully, permitting nothing to disturb his sleep, and moreover, as he did so, he was to "dream in very great detail about some one pleasant childhood experience, *repeating this dream over and over as time passes.*" The purpose of this last suggestion was to establish a pleasant and, if possible, a dominating mental content far removed from the immediate situation.

In subsequent sessions the same general instructions were given, with the added instruction to repeat the previous dream. No other verbal instructions of any sort were given, and the actual experimental work was conducted throughout in silence except for the sound of the buzzer. Immediately after this preparation of the subject the kymograph was started and the first electric circuit, which included both the hand electrodes and the buzzer with their respective markers, was closed and opened at irregularly spaced intervals. Care was taken to have no constant time intervals between stimuli, and these intervals ranged generally from a fraction of a second to 15 or more seconds, although there were occasional intervals of several minutes. Also, any systematic grouping of the stimuli was avoided by grouping rarely and then at irregular intervals. The time required for each session ranged from two to four hours.

Four experimental sessions were held on succeeding days with each subject. The first session was devoted entirely to the giving of the combined stimuli of the buzzer sound and the electric current and to the securing of complete records on the kymograph showing the flow of current, the sounding of the buzzer, and the muscular contractions elicited, a sample record of which is shown in Figure 1.

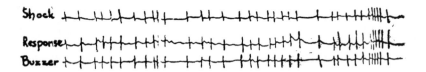

Figure 1. Typical Record to Show Tracings Obtained for the Shocks Given, the Muscular Response Elicited, and the Sounding of the Buzzer. Also, the irregularity of the stimulation may be noted.

During the first session 200 combined stimuli were given, although ordinarily only 15 to 30 are necessary to secure conditioning under similar circumstances. However, it was felt that such long, continued stimulation would serve to establish an exceedingly stable condition response.

On the next day the training of the previous session was repeated to the extent of about 100 combined stimuli for the purpose of reinforcing the learning processes that had been established. The first test was then made for the presence of a conditioned response by operating the second electric circuit whereby the buzzer could be sounded without current being delivered to the electrodes. This auditory stimulus alone was noted to elicit a muscular response. After further reinforcement by combined stimuli, the remainder of the session was spent operating both electrical circuits in an irregularly alternating fashion, and obtaining an adequate record of the presence of the conditioned response. The records obtained disclosed it to be invariably present and sufficiently stable to withstand 20 to 30 seccessive trials before showing much evidence of experimental extinction processes. Complete restoration followed a rest period or further combined stimulation.

Five combined stimuli were given at the beginning of the third session, followed by a single auditory stimulus to determine the persistence of the conditioned response. Although it was found present in each subject, a series of 50 combined stimuli was given for reinforcement, and this was followed by further testing. Finally the subject was given a sharp blow on the shoulder to produce deafness, and a long series of combined stimuli was given, after which his wrist was squeezed to restore his hearing while the combined stimulation continued. This procedure was repeated several times initially and frequently throughout the sessions, with no attempt made to test for the conditioned response, as a measure of preventing the subject from possibly associating the shoulder and wrist stimuli with tests for the conditioned response.

Following this, deafness was produced, and hearing was restored during the midst of series of combined stimuli and series of mixed, combined, and single auditory stimuli, produced by the operation of the two electric circuits alternately in a markedly irregular and confused fashion both as to the number of times and the relationship to the deaf or hearing states established.

The records obtained, illustrated by Figure 2. disclosed the consistent presence of the conditioned response in all hearing states and its equally consistent absence in all hypnotically deaf states.

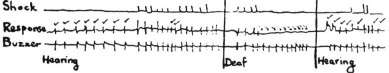

Figure 2. Typical Record Obtained During the Third Session Showing the Presence or the Absence of the Conditioned Response in Accordance with the Subject's Auditory State.

The small check marks indicate the presence of the conditioned response, the arrows, the absence of the conditioned response.

The fourth session began with five combined stimuli, followed by a test for the conditioned response, which was found present in both subjects. Immediately the subject was rendered deaf by the blow on the shoulder, and a long series of combined stimuli was administered, totally 60 for one subject and over 100 for the other. At the close of the series a single auditory stimulus was interjected in the midst of a group of rapidly given combined stimuli to elicit, if possible, a conditioned response. Since this failed in both instances, the procedure was repeated after an even more extensive series of combined stimuli, but with the same negative results. Records obtained are illustrated in Figure 3. There followed then a repetition of the procedure of the previous day to secure more records of the presence or absence of the conditioned response in accordance with the hypnotic auditory state. These were found to be consistent with those of the previous session.

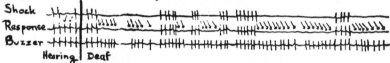

Figure 3. Typical Record Obtained During the Fourth Session Showing the Consistent Absence, After Being Elicited in the Hearing State, of the Conditioned Response During the Deaf State, Despite Long, Continued, and Repeated Combined Stimulation.

Briefly the actual experimental procedure and results may be summarized as follows:

First Session—First Day
1. Series of 200 combined stimuli—shock and buzzer.
2. No test for presence of conditioned response.

Second Session—Second Day
1. Series of 100 combined stimuli—shock and buzzer.
2. Test for conditioned response—(found present).
3. Further reinforcement of conditioned response by combined stimuli.
4. Irregularly alternating operation of Circuits One and Two to secure adequate record of presence of conditioned response—(conditioned response present at every test).

Third Session—Third Day
1. Series of five combined stimuli.
2. Test for conditioned response—(found present).
3. Series of 50 combined stimuli for further reinforcement of conditioned response.
4. Irregularly alternating operation of the two circuits—(conditioned response present at every test).
5. Production of hypnotic deafness and restoration of hearing several times with administration of only the combined stimuli during these initial deaf states.
6. Production of hypnotic deafness in midst of series of combined

or auditory stimuli with continued irregularly alternating operation of the circuits—(conditioned response consistently absent).

7. Restoration of hearing in midst of series of either combined or auditory stimuli with continued irregularly alternating operation of the circuits—(conditioned response consistently present).

Fourth Session—Fourth Day

1. Series of five combined stimuli.
2. Test for conditioned response—(found present).
3. Production of hypnotic deafness.
4. Long series of combined stimuli—60 to 100.
5. Test for conditioned response—(found absent).
6. Further repetition of (4) and (5)—(similar result).
7. Further repetition of (6) and (7) of third session—(similar results).

The completion of this actual experimental work was followed by control studies as planned in the protocol, but in combination with clinical investigations directed to the securing of additional significant data before undue sophistication of the subjects developed from the control procedures.

The succession of steps in these combined clinical investigations and control studies was as follows:

1. Extensive questioning of the subjects in the waking state and in an adjacent room by a third person and the experimenter without discovering any awareness of the entire situation or any specific recollections for the separate experimental sessions.

2. Repetition of this questioning in the experimental room both before and after making the connections with the experimental apparatus and giving the instructions to think freely and talk readily about anything that came to mind, without eliciting any further information.

3. Evocation of conditioned response upon closure of second circuit with a spontaneous subjective belief expressed that an unpleasant electric shock had been delivered.

4. Subject's report of a rapid decrease in the intensity of the shock until it was not perceptible, as the conditioned response was elicited repeatedly by proper stimulation and without reinforcement. Restoration of the feeling of a shock after a rest period occurred followed by a more rapid experimental extinction of that feeling upon continued testing for the conditioned response which remained consistently present.

5. Evidence of experimental extinction processes after 20 to 30 successive conditioned responses.

6. Restoration of conditioned response after rest period but followed

by more rapid experimental extinction.

7. Restoration of conditioned response by combined stimuli, with spontaneous report from subjects that the current had been "turned on again very strong."

8. Rapid learning by subjects to discriminate the presence or absence of electric current but without effect upon the conditioned response.

9. Disclosure by the subjects of only irrelevant associations for the feeling of the shock and no recollection of any similar experience within the recent past.

10. The use of an associate's apparatus to establish a finger-withdrawal conditioned response based on auditory conditioning.

11. Failure of voluntary inhibition of this second conditioned response.

12. Failure of voluntary inhibition of the original conditioned response.

13. Delay of experimental extinction of both conditioned responses occasioned by attempts to inhibit them voluntarily.

14. Induction of a new hypnotic trance with instruction for a complete amnesia for all previous trance experiences and instructions.

15. Evocation of first as well as second conditioned responses.

16. Establishment in this hypnotic state of a third similar conditioned response based on an auditory stimulus.

17. Evocation of this third conditioned response in the waking state without additional training.

18. Induction of another hypnotic trance during which extensive insistent and emphatic instructions were given to the subjects, commanding them to inhibit both in the trance state and posthypnotically all three conditioned responses.

19. Failure both in the trance state and posthypnotically of all attempts to inhibit the conditioned responses.

20. Failure to evoke any of the conditioned responses after the induction of another deep trance and the production of the hypnotic deafness, but reappearance of the conditioned responses upon restoration of hearing.

Since the questioning done in Steps 1 and 2 of the combined clinical investigations had yielded no information, a deep hypnotic trance was induced, and the subject was instructed to recall in complete detail and in chronological sequence every event of each experimental session.

The recollections obtained in this way were essentially the same for both subjects. A statement was made covering the details of bringing the subject into the experimental room, seating him, putting "things" in his hands and around his arm, and telling him to dream. The subject then summarized the rest by stating that a long series of buzzer sounds and shocks had followed, while he absorbed himself in his dream. Further instruction was given that he must verbalize the events fully no matter how monotonous it became until he had actually completed recounting the entire session. There followed a long series of over 100 utterances of "buzzer-shock" irregularly spaced and grouped in a manner suggestive of the actual experience, after which an account was given of the disconnecting of the apparatus. One observation of note was that from the beginning the subject closed his hands each time he said "shock."

The second session was recounted in essentially the same way, with the continued closing of the subject's hands at the word "shock," an item of behavior that remained consistently present during the recollection of each of the experimental sessions.

In recounting the third session, after about 15 minutes of monotonous utterances of "buzzer-shock," the subject was noted suddenly to say "shock" only. Thereafter, in an irregular fashion, found by reference to the kymograph record to parallel crudely the actual experimental procedure, he continued to alternate the utterances of "buzzer-shock" and "shock."

The fourth session was begun with three utterances for one subject, four for the other, of "buzzer-shock," followed by a long series of "shock" alone, finally concluding with an irregularly alternating series of utterances of "buzzer-shock" and "shock."

As an additional measure adequate instruction was given to the subjects to the effect that a recollection of selected parts only of the experimental sessions would now be required, and at the proper verbal command they were to recall the specified part of any particular session. In this manner repetitions of their recollections were obtained in a systematically random order of the first and second halves of each of the four experimental sessions, and these repetitions were found to resemble closely the original recollections.

During the first recalling of the experimental sessions the experimenter had maintained a complete silence. The repetitions of parts of sessions required interruption of the subject by verbal commands, and this led to an unexpected discovery. By chance in the repetition of part of the third session the experimenter attempted to interrupt the subject while he was saying "shock" alone. No heed was given to the experimenter, and the instructions were repeated without attracting the subject's attention. They were again repeated while the subject was saying "buzzer-shock." An immediate response was obtained from him. Thereafter it was found that the subjects' attention, readily obtainable when they were uttering "buzzer-shock," could not be secured by verbal stimuli when uttering "shock." Observation was also made that as the subject shifted his utterance from "buzzer-shock" to "shock" alone, there occurred a marked change in his appearance, his face becoming more rigid and expressionless, his body tense, and his speech slightly slowed.

In brief the recalling of the experimental sessions was literally a reenactment of them with an actual reliving of the experience.

As a separate task each subject was ordered to narrate in complete detail the content of the dream he had been instructed to have during the course of the experiment and to repeat his narration of it as often as he had redreamed it.

The dream of one subject centered around a boyhood play activity, that of the other around an early visit to a theater, both dreams being pleasant, interesting, and rich in detail.

The narration and renarration of the dreams for the first and second sessions showed essentially no significant variations, occasional details being omitted and new ones included. However, in narrating the dream for the third and fourth sessions, certain significant variations in content occurred. Sometimes a small part of a scene, at other times a whole episode, was omitted, causing the previously fluent account to become patchy and even fragmentary in character. When questioned directly concerning these omissions, the subjects could reply only, *"I don't remember dreaming the next part this time. My dream stopped there, and then it began further on,"* and no explanation could be obtained from them. Study of the kymographic record in relation to the occurrence of the omissions of dream content suggested a direct relationship between the omissions and the periods of deafness, and hence the possibility of a different or deeper level of mental functioning. Accordingly the subjects were given additional emphatic hypnotic instructions to recall fully and completely every item of the dream as it had occurred. Following these instructions the narration of the dream proceeded without any omissions, but with certain new inclusions of an unpleasant character, not in keeping with the dream content, and actually constituting apparently inexplicable distortions of the dream. Thus at irregular intervals the subject dreaming of his boyhood play activity interjected the statements of *"He* (one of the dream characters) *hit me,"* or *"He jerked me,"* while the other subject interjected statements about the *"man behind bumping"* him or of his seatmate *"grabbing"* his arm. These interjections were always followed by the change in appearance described above or by the disappearance of those changes. After several manifestations of this behavior an attempt was made to interrupt the subject's narration of the dream by questions. It was found impossible to secure his attention while this change in appearance persisted, but verbal interruption was readily possible at any other time. Careful indirect questioning concerning experimental events disclosed that after such "hitting" or "bumping" the events of the experimental session were consistently recalled as *"shock—shock—shock,"* and that after the "jerking" or "grabbing" they were recalled as *"buzzer-shock, buzzer-shock."* Also, despite elaborate questioning no mention could be obtained of the wrist or shoulder stimuli as such. Rather, they seemed to have been assimilated into the dream content as "jerking" or "bumping" and not recognized for what they were. Also, indirect questioning concerning the sounding of the buzzer alone failed to disclose any realization of such an occurrence.

FINDINGS ON ADDITIONAL SUBJECTS

The findings obtained from the third subject are given separately, since this subject, although not psychotic, was a patient in a mental hospital, had been given slightly different preliminary training, and had not been accessible for postexperimental investigation. The experimental results obtained were definitely confirmatory but were marked by the following peculiarities:

1. The conditioned response obtained invariably underwent experimental extinction after six to 10 trials, and restoration required a considerable amount of retraining.
2. Hypnotic deafness tended to develop spontaneously, seriously handicapping the development of a conditioned response and frequently accounting for an apparent experimental extinction.
3. An extensive hypnotic anaesthesia tended to develop spontaneously, interfering seriously with perception of the electrical stimulus.
4. Hypnotic deafness could be produced or abolished only by slow measures, one to five minutes being required for the development of deafness after the shoulder stimulus had been given, and similarly for the restoration of hearing after the wrist stimulus.

However, extensive experimentation did disclose:

1. That in a deep hypnotic trance a conditioned response based on an auditory stimulus could be produced, and this conditioned response, after undergoing experimental extinction, could be restored promptly upon additional training.
2. That the development of hypnotic deafness, either spontaneously or responsively, abolished this conditioned response and precluded its reestablishment by long-continued training.
3. That restoration of hearing would result in the reappearance of the conditioned response and would permit its reestablishment after experimental extinction.

The fourth subject had been recommended to the experimenter as capable of readily developing exeedingly stable conditioned responses. He was given the same hypnotic training as the original two subjects and underwent the same experimental procedure for the first two sessions, but without developing any conditioned response. At a third session he was given approximately 500 combined stimuli with periodic tests for the presence of a conditioned response. Since even this extensive training failed to establish a conditioned response, a clinical investigation was made. This soon disclosed that the subject, upon being hypnotized, spontaneously developed a deafness for all sounds except the experimenter's voice and that a period of silence on the part of the experimenter would result in deafness even for this voice. Repeated unsuccessful efforts were made to train the subject to retain his hearing, but apparently the spontaneous deafness constituted an essential element of the deep trance for him.

Following these failures, an attempt was made, while the subject was in a deep hypnotic trance, to elicit the other auditorily conditioned responses he had developed in the waking state for the worker who had recommended him. These could not be elicited.

At another session, in the waking state, the subject was tested for the previously established conditioned responses which were readily elicited, although there had been no intervening training. He was then tested for a conditioned response to the training the experimenter had given him, but none was elicited. After several trials, he was given five combined stimuli, and upon testing, he manifested a conditioned response. Reference to his previous learning records disclosed the appearance of a conditioned response after six combined stimuli, and hence no statement can be made concerning any economy in learning.

After the establishment in the waking state of this conditioned response, the subject was given extensive training for several days. Following this, he was hypnotized and attempts were made to elicit the established conditioned response. These attempts failed as did an attempt to reestablish the conditioned response by further extensive training in the trance state. Tests for the previously established conditioned response also failed. Tests made immediately upon awakening disclosed all of the conditioned responses to be present.

SUMMARY OF EXPERIMENTAL RESULTS

The experimental results obtained may be summarized as follows:

1. After repeated stimulation by a stimulus complex consisting of an electric shock and an auditory stimulus, a muscular response in a hypnotic subject was evoked invariably by the auditory element alone, constituting a conditioned response.

2. This conditioned response was consistently present under ordinary hypnotic conditions and was sufficiently stable to permit 20 to 30 successive evocations before showing much evidence of the process of experimental extinction.

3. The induction of hypnotic deafness invariably abolished this conditioned response.

4. The hypnotic restoration of hearing invariably permitted the reappearance of this conditioned response.

5. Various appropriate control procedures disclosed the following results:

   a. Similar and consistent results in relation to other auditorily conditioned responses established either in waking or hypnotic states.

   b. The failure of all attempts to establish an auditorily conditioned response in a susceptible subject rendered hypnotically deaf as a preliminary measure with ready establishment after restoration of hearing.

   c. The failure to inhibit voluntarily in waking or trance states either the experimental conditioned response or those employed in the control studies.

6. Confirmation of experimental results was obtained by further work on two additional subjects, yielding comparable though not identical results.

7. Significant interrelationships were determined between the various auditory states induced during the experimental procedure and the subjects' subsequent hypnotically elicited recollections of the experience.

COMMENT ON EXPERIMENTAL FINDINGS

Comment on the experimental findings, as in the preceding clinical section of this paper, requires the same orientation to the general question of the identity of *being unconscious of a sound* and *failure to respond to a sound*. The experimental findings with the conditioned response technique indicate that, in addition to failure of response, there was an actual failure to receive stimuli sufficiently either to establish the neurological process of conditioning or to activate such a neurological process already established.

However, when it is considered that a conditioned response may be established and evoked without there being a conscious awareness of the conditioning stimulus, the question arises: Is conscious awareness itself an essential element in evoking a conditioned response based on a conditioning stimulus for which there was a conscious awareness? Hence, before any conclusion can be drawn from these experimental findings concerning the identity of being unconscious of a sound and failure to respond to a sound, provision must be made for the possible alteration of the stimulus complex by the loss of the secondary attribute of conscious awareness. Such loss might account for an inability to respond to the stimulus complex. On the other hand the control investigations, as well as the failure of attempts in the experimental situation to build up a conditioned response not including the element of conscious awareness, indicate an actual failure to receive stimuli, not attributable to the loss of an element previously present in the stimulation. Accordingly the experimental findings warrant the conclusion that in addition to being unconscious of a sound there was an actual change in the capacity to utilize sound stimuli, if not an actual incapacity to receive them.

Additional comment is warranted by various of the secondary findings made, and these will be mentioned briefly as follows:

1. *Subjective recollections.* No particular significance may be accorded the waking amnesia for trance events, since such amnesia characteristically succeeds deep hypnosis. Likewise, the detailed recollection of the experience in response to hypnotic suggestion is an expected result. Nor is the persistent nonrecollection of the shoulder and wrist stimuli remarkable, since properly they were only a

small part of a total experience belonging to the training period and hence were not recognized as belonging to the experimental experience. Likewise, the assimilation of those stimuli as part of their dream content illustrates a well-known phenomenon.

However, the peculiar omission of those parts of their recollections directly related to the periods of deafness, coupled with the marked change in appearance and the spontaneous development of deafness, does constitute an item of interest. One may speculate upon the possibility of different levels of cerebration, with suggested deafness causing functioning at a level different from that serving for ordinary deep hypnotic sleep. Contrary to this, the continuance of the dream without actual interruption suggests only a problem of accessibility rather than different levels of functioning. In brief the findings are suggestive of a type of conditioning in which the accessibility of certain experiences apparently depends upon remotely related but closely associated factors. At all events this peculiar amnesia indicates extensive changes in the subject governing and limiting voluntary responsive behavior.

2. *Other conditioned responses.* Although the experiment was centered primarily around a single conditioned response, various others of a more indirect character became evident. The induction of deafness or the restoration of hearing was in essence a conditioning; the closing of the hands at each utterance of the word "shock" illustrates another type of conditioned response; the physical and psychological changes in recounting completely the experiences of the deaf periods represent another type; and the limitation of utterances to the word "shock" while recounting the events of the deaf period and showing the associated physical changes constitutes still another variety of conditioning. Aside from the interest which each of these possesses, their consistency and invariability in this experiment implies a highly organized pattern of behavior in the subject dependent upon many unrecognized factors.

3. *Subjective experience of shock.* The belief of the subjects that a shock had been delivered when only the buzzer had been sounded during the early control procedures raises a difficult question. That the sensory experiences of the shock were conditioned by the buzzer, with this conditioning showing the characteristic processes of experimental extinction and of restoration after a rest period, is a possible explanation. The rapid development of an ability to discriminate between delivery and nondelivery of shocks after combined stimulation suggests the corrective effect of waking awareness, an effect not possible in the hypnotic trance, as was evidenced by the unfailing recollection in this state of all stimuli as including a shock. The appearance of such a corrective influence in the waking state suggests another difference in the neuropsychic organization between the waking and the hypnotic states.

4. *Ideomotor activity.* Throughout the whole postexperimental investigation, extensive ideomotor processes were consistently present. The entire recollection of the trance experience was given in the form of a reenactment and reliving of the experience. Similarly, the recounting of the dream content as a psychic

experience included innumerable complex motor components. The immediate inference to be derived from the spontaneous development of such extensive ideomotor processes is that the entire course of experimental events constituted a valid and vital experience for the subjects. In consequence of this validity there derived extensive ideomotor processes directly attributable to significant changes in the neuropsychic organization.

GENERAL SUMMARY AND CONCLUSION

The findings of this investigation, both clinical and experimental, disclose that the induction of a state of hypnotic deafness results in significant and extensive psychological and neurophysiological changes in auditory functioning comparable in degree and character with those arising from organic deafness. These alterations of hearing are both subjective and objective in character, and range from slight impairment of hearing to total deafness, as evidenced by failure of natural organic responses to auditory stimuli. The findings, although showing differences as well as absolute similarities from subject to subject, are entirely consistent within themselves and with each other, and are illustrative of established psychological and physiological processes.

12. Chemo-Anaesthesia in Relation to Hearing and Memory

Milton H. Erickson

What constitutes psychologically the experience of chemo-anaesthesia has been a question of much interest to this author since the summer of 1932. At that time two events occurred within the same period of time.

A fellow research worker and the author were discussing the problem of memory in general. Dr. A, a Ph.D., had undergone four years of intensive psychoanalysis, three of them under one analyst in the United States and a fourth year, since he spoke German most fluently, under Freud. His assertion that in that period of time he had undoubtedly exhausted all of his past memories was challenged, and this led to a decision to undertake a joint exploration of the possibility that he might recall forgotten past memories under circumstances entirely alien to the analytic situations in which he had explored his memories of the past.

As a pilot experiment two separate tasks were outlined. Dr. A was to make lists of a series of questions concerning possible memories of his childhood and about which he had no personal conscious memories and to list briefly but numerously the memories he had for each year of the first eight years of his life. In turn the author, being a licensed physician, was to take special instruction from a qualified anaesthetist who was fully acquainted with the intended experimental purposes, in the administering of ether anaesthesia to a surgical degree and the maintenance of that degree of surgical anaesthesia. Additionally he was also to make lists of a series of questions which he thought might apply to each of the first eight years of Dr. A's life, since both Dr. A and the author had grown up within a distance of 100 miles without knowing each other until they met in 1932. Both the author and Dr. A had had the same general background. Dr. A's lists of questions and memories were made available to the author but not vice versa.

Arrangements were made for a special recording to be made of the experiment by a secretary who had assisted the author repeatedly on other projects and was trained not only in shorthand but in observing and making notes of concurrent verbal and behavioral activities.

Reprinted with permission from *The American Journal of Clinical Hypnosis*, July, 1963, *6*, 31—36.

The conditions of the experiment included (a) ether anaesthesia of Dr. A to a surgical state as confirmed by a fellow physician whose living quarters were next door (a general precautionary measure), (b) the continuous presence of the recording secretary, (c) Dr. A's numerical lists of questions on possible but not remembered items that appeared as reasonable for a childhood such as his, (d) the author's own numerical lists of questions propounded partly from speculation from his own memories and from what seemed reasonable for a child with a background similar to the author's and coming from an area of the country the author knew.

The plan also included a trial run of ether anaesthesia only with a close study of Dr. A by the author and the next-door physician to determine the probable duration of experimental sessions and Dr. A's period of recovery from the ether with prolonged maintenance of the surgical level and including the effects the next day, since the experiment had to be done outside the author's working hours. These initial findings were that the experiment could best begin at 6:30 P.M., would, with the questioning, last until 3 or 4 A.M. and that weekends were probably the days of choice for the author and the secretary by force of circumstances and best for Dr. A's postexperimental recovery from prolonged ether anaesthesia.

The experimental plan called for 10 such experimental sessions as a method of performing a pilot study which might later serve to interest others in a comparable experiment.

Six actual sessions, not counting the preliminary test session with the ether alone, were completed, each a most laborious task because of Dr. A's apparent surgical state of anaesthesia which was maintained by continued ether administration and tested by the usual measures and the random asking of the questions from either his lists, or from mine, or from both, this being done sometimes separately, sometimes in a mixed, but always a random fashion.

The questions were always asked at least three times, never more than five, sometimes in succession, sometimes in sporadic order, since there was no apparent way to determine whether or not Dr. A was listening or even hearing the questions. The same general casual tone of voice was used, the author sitting at Dr. A's head, and the secretary sitting so that careful watch could be kept on both Dr. A and the author to insure full recording.

After the anaesthesia had reached a surgical state, this was maintained for about 10 minutes to conform to the similar procedure on the preliminary test under the additional observation of the other physician.

Then 20 to 25 questions were asked in various order and with a varying number of repetitions, all of which was recorded by the secretary, including the number of drops of ether administered and the author's yawns, side remarks to the secretary, and the secretary's remarks and yawns.

After the asking of the questions, it became necessary to wait for Dr. A to begin to come out of the anaesthesia so that he could be asked what had occurred. Always the first manifestation was some restless stirring, then thick, slurring, incomprehensive utterances, which later would become understandable utterances, such as "Let me alone," "Want to sleep," and "Don't both me."

Each time he would be reminded patiently that he was undergoing a memory experiment. Sometimes within a few minutes of intelligible speech he would ask, "Did I remember anything?" At other times he would laugh uproariously and declare he had been asked "foolish questions."

In general summary it was learned that he could spontaneously—that is, without any leading question except "Were you asked something else?" or "What did you remember?" or "What comes to your mind now?"—recall questions asked him in deep surgical anaesthesia; that he recalled "forgotten" memories that had not come forth in his analyses; that he could remember 70 to 80 percent of the questions from his list; 50 to 60 percent of the questions from my lists; feelings of resentment when I mixed questions from both lists, and when I changed (deliberately) the wording of questions he had prepared. He also expressed irritation that I had "willfully" alternated questions from the lists, and had asked them in an order different from the actual order of his lists.

Of particular note was the fact that questions from both his and the author's lists had secured repressed or "forgotten" memories that had not come forth in either analysis and of which he disclaimed any memory until the ether experiences. Unfortunately we soon found that such recovery of memories was often transient. More than once, after he had discussed some of these memories, especially if they were traumatic, with the author and even with one or two other colleagues, he would again develop a complete amnesia for them as well as for the fact of even having discussed such topics.

Further use of ether would lead to the recovery of this again-repressed material and even of the fact that he had discussed it only to forget it, and then to deny that he had ever discussed such material.

One such instance concerned an obscene rhyme common to boyhood in that area, and later discovered by the author to be common elsewhere and in previous generations. The recovery of this rhyme came from the author's list of questions. He had speculatively quoted from the rhyme directly but not revealingly in several different questions. These were asked in different sessions but without eliciting more than a memory of the questions, and without evidence of emotional distress.

In the fourth ether session he was asked simply, "What comes after Johnny?" In the recovery phase of the anaesthesia he recalled this question, was obviously distressed by it, but some time elapsed before he repeated the entire rhyme. No additional information was obtained despite cautious questioning about where, when, and how he had learned it. The next day, late in the afternoon, he discussed this rhyme with the author and several others, disclaimed ever having heard it before, recalled having it flash into his mind "sometime last night." He was obviously intrigued by the rhyme and his previous ignorance of it, and those colleagues who did not know of the experimental work being done were allowed to carry the burden of the discussion. The author and the physician next door discreetly kept silent or made only purely casual remarks. The others insisted that surely he must have known the rhyme in his boyhood and Dr. A cooperatively speculated with them at what age he should have learned it. No evidence of emotional distress or hesitation on the part of Dr. A was noted, and he seemed to be merely amused and intrigued by this lacuna in his general knowledge.

Five days later it was learned that Dr. A had completely repressed all knowledge of the rhyme and even of his discussion of it.

At the next (fifth) ether session the same question was put to him while he was in deep surgical anaesthesia. This time upon reaching the stage of articulate speech after the discontinuance of the ether, he suddenly remembered the question, the rhyme, and even told accurately with whom he had discussed that item of memory. Questions of when and where he had learned it yielded nothing again.

Three days later the amnesia was again present for both the rhyme and any discussion of it.

At the sixth proposed ether session Dr. A declared his wish to intrude a new venture into the program. He explained that for several days he felt that he was repressing something vital to him, but what it could be he had not the slightest notion. He apologized for disrupting the ether program but declared some matter of personal interest of unknown origin or character was troubling him intensely, disturbing his sleep, interfering with his work, causing "jumbled, meaningless dreams" if he dozed, and that he was developing a depression. Therefore, he added, instead of ether he wished that the author would do a little mental and emotional exploration by means of hypnosis and that the ether experiment could be continued later.

He was asked why he should not try ether, and his reply was most informative. "I suspect ether is like alcohol. When you get drunk, there's a lot you don't remember the next day or ever until you again get drunk and reach a similar degree of alcoholic saturation." In support of this argument he reported on some intentional laboratory work and some unintentional experiences he and others had undergone.

After this explanation he again insisted urgently upon the use of hypnosis to discover "whatever is troubling me." Apparently he was strongly motivated and reached a deep stage of hypnosis in a few minutes. In this trance he was asked if he knew its purpose, and he replied irritably that he did and that the author should proceed without delay.

With great care many of the questions previously asked, including those that were direct but nonrevealing quotations, were asked. No particular memories were elicited, since only questions previously negative in results were asked. Finally he was asked the original revealing question of "What comes after Johnny?"

Immediately he sat up, still in a deep trance, and urgently asked in what seemed to be a state of alarm, "That's it, let me remember slowly."

His request was acceded to by silence. After about five minutes of obvious emotional experience on his part he said, "Wake me up now, and I will tell you. I remember everything."

Aroused, he recited the rhyme and related how he, at the age of three years, had been carefully coached by some older boys and encouraged to go home where his mother was entertaining female friends, among them the mothers of some of the boys, and proudly to declaim his newly learned recitation. This he had done to the profound horror of his mother and presumably the embarrassment of the guests. With mingled tears, sobs, and profound amusement he told of his mother's irate fury, the corporal punishment by his father, and of being sent to bed without his supper. He recalled crying in bed and wondering why he had been sent to bed in disgrace as was obvious from his mother's and father's behavior toward him. He now realized that he had developed a profound repression apparently almost immediately after the incident.

The recollection of this memory about the rhyme he later verified, including even the names of the boys he had listed as participating. However, some of them had forgotten the incident but some recalled their prank readily. His mother had forgotten it, but his father remembered it after some stimulation. (This information was received by mail much later, and Dr. A some 15 years later still remembered the rhyme but with much amusement at the reactions of his parents. He also stated that two of his sons had, without assistance from him, learned the rhyme from their fellow playmates.)

The results of this so-called "intrusion" into the procedure led to some extensive plans for research as soon as the ether pilot study under way had been completed.

Unfortunately, just before the next ether session, Dr. A received a most advantageous offer to do research elsewhere, and this author kept the records as transcribed by the secretary.

At the time Dr. A received the offer for a new research position this author developed an acute dental distress. Appropriate examination disclosed two adjacent apical abscesses, and the dental recommendation was that one tooth be extracted because the nerve was dead and the abscess at the tip of the tooth root be curetted. Warning was given that the second tooth might need extraction to permit curettage of the adjacent abscess, but the dentist hoped to do this via the cavity of the first abscess.

A medical colleague acted as the anaesthetist, and ether was the anaesthetic of choice, for the reason that the author wished to seize upon the opportunity to compare in some way his own experiences with those of Dr. A. Hence arrangements were made to have the same secretary present to record in full all activity of behavior and speech.

The operation was done in Massachusetts, and after the first can of ether had been slowly dribbled onto the mask, the dentist asked somewhat anxiously, as verified later by special inquiry and the secretary's record, "Good God, man, isn't he under yet?"

Both the anaethestist and I replied respectively "Not yet," and, "I'm just beginning to feel it (meaning the ether).''

A second can was systematically emptied onto the mask, eliciting the question from the dentist, ''Is he a chronic alcoholic to absorb all that ether?'' The anaesthetist assured him that on rare occasions I took a cocktail (he knew nothing about my ether experiment with Dr. A which might have accounted for what was regarded as my unusual tolerance to ether, and naturally the secretary offered no explanation.) When the second can of ether was nearly empty, the anaesthetist requested that a third can be made ready. The dentist declared that two cans of ether was enough for any operation and that he was going to proceed.

The anaesthetist replied ''He's ready, all right. Look at his eyes.'' He looked at the pupils of my eyes, and both agreed that I was deeply anaesthetized. I startled them by saying, so the secretary's notes read, in a slurred voice, ''The hell you say,'' and made a mental note at the time that I could not see light, although apparently my eyes had been opened forcibly, as was indeed the case.

Both the dentist and the anaesthetist laughed at my comment; the anaesthetist proceeded to give some more ether but was interrupted by the dentist, who declared, ''Anaesthetized or not, I'm going ahead. With all that ether, he can't feel a thing.''

The dentist was right. I could not feel anything. Neither could I move or even open my eyes. But I could hear. I heard the forceps clamped to my tooth, but I could not determine any sense of position. I heard the dentist tell the anaesthetist to hold my head firmer, but I could not feel it being done. I could hear what I reasoned to be the sounds of the tooth being loosened from its socket. I heard the scraping sounds of the curettement. The dentist remarked that the second abscess had ruptured into the first and he could do a curettage without a second extraction. I could hear more bone scraping sounds. Also, I could hear someone breathing hard and spasmodically.

Finally the dentist declared that the task was completed, that there would be no packing done, and that I should be returned to the ward. I heard them comment on the heaviness of my inert body, but I did not sense being placed on the surgical cart. I did hear the wheels squeaking, an item I verified the next day but which my secretary had also recorded.

On the way to the ward he encountered someone who inquired about me. I knew that someone spoke but formed no memory of what was said.

The next thing I heard was the anesthetist telling the nurse to keep me under constant observation, to permit my secretary to remain so long as she wished, and that I would ''sleep it off'' during the night, that I was already ''dead to the world.'' It seemed to me to be only a short time before I began trying to talk to my secretary, but she recorded the time as nearly an hour. I tried to give her an account of my memories, but my speech was thick and slurred. She patiently waited until my voice cleared sufficiently, so that by repetitiously asking me to repeat what I had tried to say and by repeatedly asking me if I remembered anything more, she eventually got a full account.

The next morning I awakened feeling rested and refreshed and impatient for the arrival of my secretary. Upon her arrival I gave her as full an account as I could remember. As I did this I realized that we had encountered someone in the corridor on the way to the ward, but I had no memory of whose voice I heard or what had been said.

Transcripts were made of each of the three accounts, the operative, the post-operative, and the account given the next morning. They were read by the anaesthetist, the dentist, and myself. In all three instances they agreed. Neither the anaesthetist nor the dentist had noted the squeaking of the surgical cart wheels, but they verified it by actual investigation. The dentist was embarrassed that I had heard his inquiry about my possibly being a chronic alcoholic. Both the anaesthetist and the dentist confirmed that the dentist's breathing had been labored and spasmodic—that such breathing characterized his operative behavior.

The physician who had encountered us in the corridor and had made inquiries at that time visited me and told me what he had said. It awakened no memories within me. Apparently I had been so set in my interest in the actual experience that I did not include him in the frame of reference. I also learned that the night nurse had asked me about a mouth rinse and had spoken to me several times. She too was not included in my memories. I had overlooked making any provision for her. But for everything for which I had established a mental set on noticing at the levels of hearing, understanding, and remembering, I succeeded. The hearing of the squeaking of the surgical cart's wheels and remembering that, and remembering only that someone spoke whose voice I did not recognize and whose inquiries about me I did not remember both suggest that the squeaking wheels had a highly important personal significance for me, since it meant the undesired operation was concluded. The inquiries of the physician who met us in the corridor at that moment lacked any peculiar personal significance.

My reason for not publishing the above material sooner was simply that neither instance constituted an adequate study. They served merely to indicate that there is an important area for adequately controlled and comprehensive research. However the recent publications that have appeared in this Journal have impelled me to add this account to the literature.

It is also most unfortunate that the original experiment with Dr. A was not completed as a pilot study and a further and a better organized procedure developed. However, it does pose a most fascinating question of why ether could uncover apparently otherwise unreachable memories which the patient could subsequently discuss but fail to integrate into the body of his conscious memories, and how hypnosis could serve to elicit those same memories but in such fashion that they could be integrated.

To summarize very briefly and emphatically, chemo-anaesthesia and mental functioning are as important fields of scientific inquiry as are the fields of chemo-anaesthesia and surgery. Also of equally intriguing interest is the observation that pain as an experience itself and that the knowledge and memory of a painful procedure can be rendered by chemo-anaesthesia into two separate items, only the latter of which is experienced.

13. A Field Investigation by Hypnosis of Sound Loci Importance in Human Behavior

Milton H. Erickson

At the Colorado State Psychopathic Hospital in July, 1929, the author listened to an extensive and very detailed account of six days of seasickness suffered by a resident in psychiatry newly arrived from England. This account was the author's first direct knowledge of the subjective aspects of seasickness reported upon by someone trained in medicine and competent to answer questions informatively.

The information received led the author into prolonged private thinking about various aspects of seasickness, possible seemingly unrelated significances, and possible methods of experimental investigation.

The following September that resident questioned the author about hypnosis.[1] Not only did the resident express interest in learning about hypnosis but volunteered to be a hypnotic subject for the reason that the experience itself might enhance didactic learnings.

This offer to be a hypnotic subject presented the author with a most desirable opportunity for an experiment which he had been in the process of formulating for several weeks but without any expectation of an opportunity to put it to test. Accordingly the offer was accepted, and the resident was informed that an interesting experiment had been under contemplation for some time which might entail some possible, but only transient, discomfort, but which would be decidedly convincing and informative. The resident agreed readily to accede to any plans the author might have in mind.

Reprinted with permission from *The American Journal of Clinical Hypnosis*, October, 1973, *16,147-164*.

[1]Quotations appearing in each account are from write-ups made at the time each case was being seen.

Hypnosis was a topic which the author had been most emphatically forbidden by the authorities of the Colorado General Hospital even to mention under threat of dismissal from his internship and the refusal of his application for examination for a state license to practice medicine. Dr. Franklin G. Ebaugh, now deceased, then the Superintendent of the Colorado State Psychopathic Hospital, however, had given the author freedom of speech and thought, and a special residency in psychiatry after he had completed his internship and secured his state license.

Arrangements were made in the latter part of September to undertake privately the venture the author had in mind in a conference room shortly after the evening meal. That evening the resident was seated in an ordinary chair, while the author took a seat on a low footstool about six feet away, directly in front of the resident, with the author's head level at the subject's chest level. No one else was present in the conference room, and the author spoke in a normal but persuasive tone of voice.

The reasons for the use of a foot-stool at a distance of six feet were the recognitions that when one is seasick aboard ship there is a desire to keep one's distance from others, and that sounds on a ship come predominantly from below.

A trance was quite readily induced by using the hand-levitation technique, which resulted first in a rising of the right hand to the face with instruction that the moment of contact would be marked by a deep breath, a closing of the eyes, a feeling of great comfort, and the development of a deep trance. After a brief period of contact with the face, the hand would slowly descend and come to rest upon the thigh. Thereupon the left hand would duplicate the performance of the right hand, rising slowly to the face, then lowering to the lap. Upon the left hand touching the face, the right hand would simultaneously levitate, reaching the face at just the same moment as the left came to rest upon the thigh. Then the right hand would slowly descend to the right thigh. Five minutes were allowed to pass with the subject enjoying the comfort and restfulness of a deep trance state, knowing that the next task would be the simultaneous levitation of both hands so slowly that almost two minutes would be required for hands-face contact and another two minutes for their descent to the thigh level. All suggestions were limited to, "Soon, very soon, your (right, left, both) hand(s) will begin to move upward from your thigh(s), perhaps sooner than you expect, lifting upward bit by bit, higher and higher, elbow(s) bending more and more, your eyes closing slowly, your hand(s) getting closer and closer to your face, soon touching it, now touching it, now the (right, left, both) hand(s) beginning to lower slowly, coming to rest on your thigh(s), gently, taking a deep breath and going into deep trance with your eyes remaining closed, becoming increasingly comfortable and enjoying the restfulness of a deep hypnotic trance and remaining in the trance until I tell you otherwise."

As the trance induction began, the subject's eyes slowly closed and were completely shut by the time the right hand was halfway to the face at the first levitation; they remained closed with no further suggestions given about the eyes. The room was quiet, there were no interruptions. The suggestions were all given in a leisurely fashion with no special emphasis, there being only a calm, gently persuasive tone of voice. The subject gave every visual evidence of being a readily responsive subject and of achieving a deep trance state rather rapidly, and that responsiveness made unnecessary a rigid abidance to the stated time intervals. The time of the trance induction was approximately one hour after the evening meal, when both the resident and the author were off duty.

All went very well until the simultaneous levitation of both hands was initiated. At this time a new factor was introduced. There was no change in the suggestions or tone of voice, but the author changed his behvaior by silently bending his body back and forth, from side to side, and up and down in a jerking fashion so that the locus of his voice changed constantly from one level to another and from one point to another in an arhythmic fashion. By the time the subject's hands reached a point halfway to the face, a strained and uncomfortable facial expression appeared, and before the hands had actually reached the face, the subject awakened, greatly nauseated, and vomited on the floor. While still retching, the subject explained, "I must have eaten something that disagreed with me. I feel just as sick as I was when I was aboard ship. I'm miserable. I can almost see the waves. I better bathe and go to bed. Maybe we can do this hypnosis bit some other time."

Most reluctantly consent was given for the author "to clean up the mess on the floor," and the resident retired to the hospital living quarters "to bathe and go to bed and get rid of this nausea." The next morning the resident inquired of others if they had experienced gastric distress. Since none, including the author, had, the resident concluded that it was something peculiar to himself.

The following Sunday afternoon, four days later, a "casual conversation" ensued during which there seemed to be no recollection of the previous experience of nausea even though some bananas were consumed. The conversation led gradually to desired comments by the resident. These were, "I had a fine walk this morning, played two sets of tennis, and feel topping. What say we have another go at the hypnosis bit?"

The offer was immediately accepted and a "proper room assuring privacy" was selected. The fact that it also offered a convenient sink did not seem to make any impression upon the resident or to arouse any memories.

Precisely the same procedure as before was employed, with the exception of certain additional suggestions phrased to meet the situation if results comparable to those from the first efforts to induce hypnosis appeared. These were, "At any time this afternoon after your right hand begins to rise toward your face, you will go into a deep, entirely comfortable trance immediately, and any time after that, should I rap on this desk beside which I am sitting, you will go into a deep, sound, comfortable trance. I will now illustrate the rapping (demonstrating) while your hand continues lifting toward your face. If you understand, nod your head in affirmation. If you do not understand, shake your head negatively and I will repeat the instructions." An affirmative nod was made with no alteration in the continued levitation of the hand, which had already risen a full two inches at the beginning of the instructions.

In this manner a posthypnotic suggestion was inserted into the procedure without altering the process itself. Its meaningfulness would be dependent only upon the development of a need for its use. Such a possibility had occurred previously when the resident aroused from the trance upon the development of physical distress. Should there be a repetition of the arousal it could thus be corrected at once.

The author continued, "You will continue in a deep trance a sufficient period of time to meet your didactic and experiential needs, whereupon I shall awaken you with the understanding that any hypnosis thereafter will be in accord only with your own wishes and in accord with matters not necessarily related to today's work. When you awaken, you will have a total amnesia for all that has happened since the very first efforts to induce a trance were made. However you will be given a full account of everything and in a manner that will meet your wishes fully. When you feel certain that you understand these suggestions, your right hand will begin to descend to your thigh after it reaches your face. If you do not understand the instructions fully, your right hand will remain in contact with your face, and the instructions will be repeated."

However, the subject's hand continued to levitate. When the resident had reached the point of levitating both hands, the author began his erratic body movements. By the time the subject's hands were less than halfway to the face, there occurred the same results that had occurred the previous Tuesday evening.

Upon awakening, the resident dashed to the sink and vomited; while still retching, he gasped, "What's happening?"

The author immediately rapped sharply three times on the desk, and a trance state became visibly present, with an immediate disappearance of signs of physical stress.

To explain the situation that then existed, it must be recognized that the posthypnotic cue of rapping on the desk had resulted in the development of a third trance state. Since it was a new trance, there was no physical distress or nausea. The nausea and vomiting belonged only to the first two trances. Use was made of this third trance by giving the resident a mouthwash followed by a drink of cold water to remove any sense of physical discomfort or remaining taste of the mouthwash. The instructions were simply, "Use this mouthwash, please. Now drink this glass of ice water, please." No attention was given to the sink, and in accepting the glass of water, the resident had turned his back toward the sink, and was allowed to continue standing there. The author then took a seat at the desk, ignoring the footstool, which no longer served any purpose. Thus, with the resident standing with his back to the sink, not sitting in a chair with a peripheral view of the sink, and the author seated at the desk with the resident looking at him with only a peripheral view of the footstool, a new immediate reality situation was effected, different from those of either of the first two trances.

At this point it must be noted that the first two trance states were terminated by the development of a state of nausea apparently caused by the arhythmic alteration of the loci of the author's verbalizations. The movements required to alter the loci were not visible to the resident because of eye closure during the trance state. At the arousal of the resident from the second trance state the author discontinued those movements, thus giving the resident no clue for an understanding. The utterance of the bewildered inquiry of "What's happening?" at the termination of the second trance indicated a posthypnotic amnesia for the circumstances of the first two trances and, as it transpired, for nontrance events back to the time just preceding the first trance.

The investigation was continued by the author instructing the resident, "When you arouse from the trance, you may ask any question that might come to your mind. Be curious about anything you wish, and be willing to accept any bewilderment that may occur. I assure you that I will answer all questions and explain everything fully. Is that satisfactory to you? If it is, just nod your head affirmatively." The resident's head nodded slowly. "All right, awaken now!"

The resident slowly aroused, taking about a minute, looked around bewilderedly and asked, "What . . . why . . . how did I get here?"

"Yes, you are here in the laboratory and this is the way it happened. We were reading today's Sunday comic papers and there they are on the desk, and that led to a mention of that new catatonic schizophrenic patient you were assigned last Friday, and that led us to the laboratory here."

"I can see that this is the laboratory and I can see last Sunday's comic papers there, but the last patient I was assigned was that very depressed woman, and she came in today." [That patient had arrived the preceding Tuesday.]

"Now listen carefully and behave in exact accord with what I say, doing no more than I specifically ask. Agreed?"

"If you wish, but I don't understand what. . . ."

"Just do what I ask and you will understand most agreeably, so hop to it quickly. Don't make any comments. Take a look at what's in the sink, keep your mouth shut, don't speak, read the date on that newspaper, keep silent, pick up the telephone there and ask the operator what day it is, quickly now."

With a most puzzled look the resident did as told, then sat down weakly in a chair and said, "She said it's Sunday. Are you and Jack up to your usual?? [Jack was a colleague with whom the author often enjoyed collaborating in practical jokes.]"

The author stated, "I have certain legitimate purposes in which I am interested and which, I assure you, will be fully approved by you. You can judge them as I present them, and if they are nonoffensive and not objectional, you will do them. Okay?"

"I do not understand, but if you say so, I will do as you ask."

"Now write on that sheet of paper three separate sentences giving the day of the week, the kind of patient that was most recently assigned to you, and your knowledge of why you are in this room. Then sign your name to those statements and leave the paper on the desk in a readable position with a paperweight holding it in place."

The resident, very puzzled, obeyed, writing:

1. Today is Wednesday.
2. The last patient assigned to me was a female, manic-depressive, in a depressed state.
3. I do not know why I am here in this laboratory.

The resident was asked to read aloud what had been written and to state if it were correctly stated. The statements were affirmed and the signature was acknowledged verbally.

"Now, Doctor, both you and I know that you wrote those statements and that you have read them aloud with full conscious conviction that they are true. Right?"

"Quite so!"

"We both know about unconscious slips of tongue and pen-slips that reveal what the unconscious mind knows. So now you may rewrite those statements, doing so quickly, writing them with unconscious knowledge."

"I do not understand."

"Your unconscious mind does, so hop to it."

The first sentence was written, "Today is Sunday."

The resident noticed this, looked amazed and puzzled, but rapidly wrote the next two sentences without seeming to be aware of what was occurring. They read: "The last patient was assigned to me on Friday and was a male catatonic schizophrenic. We came to this room for hypnosis." As the signature was appended, the resident exclaimed, "Sunday? Tuesday?" Then, after reading both sets of statements and reading the date on the Sunday newspaper, the resident remarked, "And this is next Sunday's newspaper, but not today's date? I am thoroughly confused. What has hypnosis got to do with being seasick in Colorado?"

The resident was systematically reminded of (a) the seasickness discussed in July, (b) the discussion of hypnosis having begun early in September, (c) the volunteering to be a subject the previous week, (d) the depressed female patient assigned on the previous Tuesday, (e) the events of that Tuesday evening, (f) the male schizophrenic patient assigned on Friday, and (g) "Now it is Sunday afternoon, you had a fine walk and played tennis this morning, then earlier this afternoon we chatted, ate some bananas, and then we came here to the laboratory to try hypnosis a second time."

"A second time? I don't know what you mean! But that wasn't here! It was tonight . . . I mean, I got sick on the floor of the conference room but that sink there . . . please let me compose myself. I'm all mixed up."

The resident was told, "Take all the time you want and recover every memory you need for a complete understanding of this situation."

Shortly the statement was made, "Well, I think I have everything sorted and put together quite rightly except for some seasickness. Just what happened to make me experience being on deck on a ship crossing the Atlantic and being seasick here in Colorado? Twice, too! I really must apologize for that mess you so kindly cleaned up for me. It's embarrassing. I better look to that sink right now. I know you have some kind of explanation for me, so while I do the bit with the sink, please hop to that."

There followed then a detailed discussion of the thinking the author had done following the account of the six-day period of seasickness. The items considered to be of importance and upon which this investigation was based were:

1. One of the basic considerations in the learning of sounds is the identification of the loci of their origin, which includes loci as above, below, in front, in back, to the right, and to the left, as well as every other possible plane which may incorporate combinations of these directional factors.

2. The immediate reality environment on board ship differs in many ways from the immediate reality on land. It requires many and often unrecognized alterations of response to all sensory stimuli.

3. However smooth the ocean may be there is a constant irregular rocking of the ship, necessitating the experiencing of a constant relative shifting of the loci of sound as well as alterations, many unrecognized, of responses to sensory stimuli.

4. Seasickness not only causes physical and emotional distress but in addition alters in some degree established patterns of behavior and causes a sense of loneliness and even an aversion for any contact with others.

The final conclusion reached was that in these two instances in inducing a trance in the resident the slight irregular alteration of the loci of sound appeared to have the effect of a conditioned or conditioning stimulus sufficiently strong to revive the previously experienced seasickness.

Further hypnotic work was done later with the resident, primarily in relation to self-experience and instruction, but only after the author had promised no further investigative work related in any way to the ocean trip. Finally, permission was given for trance induction by simultaneous verbal suggestions and the body movements previously employed from the beginning of the induction, but with the resident's eyes open. This procedure handicapped trance induction, the rationalization being offered by the resident that the body movements resulted in either a sense of amusement or an intellectual challenge to predict the next movements. Thus, whether because of amusement, intellectual interest, or whatever else may have been the actual mental set, the resident's response to the verbal suggestions was diverted or prevented.

This led finally to the resident consenting to trance inductions by the same technique employed in the investigation study. It was also agreed that the tests be made while the resident, eyes closed, facing away from the author, was sitting in a chair and the author was sitting on a footstool, the trance inductions being made in a series. In some of the inductions hand-levitation suggesttions only would be used; in some there would be a combination of levitation suggestions and body movements, with the resident kept unaware of the specific methodology employed until the series ended.

The inductions totaled nine, done over a period of nearly a month, no more than one trance induction in one day and at intervals of at least two days. On the fourth and seventh trance inductions the resident interrupted the procedure because of "liverish feelings." A similar interruption occurred during the ninth induction, when the resident again developed "liverish feelings" which were emphatically asserted as caused by a combination of body movements and verbal

suggestions. The previous "liverish feelings" of the fourth and seventh inductions were also declared to have been unquestionably caused in the same way.
This was a correct statement. The other inductions led only to uncomplicated
trances. The resident refused to permit any further trance inductions in which
body movements were used.

When this same procedure was attempted with other naive subjects whose
only motivation was a desire to cooperate in hypnotic experimentation, the
curiosity aroused by the request that they keep their eyes closed and face away
from the author constituted an obstacle to hypnotic response, despite the fact
that subequently they were found able to develop trance states. Even after this
they objected to turning their backs to the author for trance induction, since
their original curiosity would immediately come to the foreground.

SECOND ACCOUNT

The opportunity for another similar study occurred in 1942. However, it was
a very brief, one-time effort permitting the achievement of similar results but
no opportunity for adequate discussion.

The occasion was a chance meeting at a social gathering. The man was a
university professor with a special interest in any unusual forms of human behavior. The author learned that Dr. X, whose professional interests were related
to psychology and human behavior in general, had traveled on board ship many
times but invariably had suffered from seasickness no matter how smooth the
ocean was. Later in the conversation with him, while discussing various forms
of behavioral manifestations in psychoses, the topic of hypnosis arose, since
Dr. X knew the author by reputation. He inquired about some of the author's
publications which he had read and then asked if it might be possible then and
there to induce in him some hypnotic phenomena that could be explained only
in terms of the effects of hypnosis and not be subject to interpretation in some
other way. After considerable thoughtful study this challenging request was
accepted.

During the early part of the conversation with Dr. X seasickness had been a
minor topic. This had reminded the author of the experience with the psychiatric
resident, but fortunately no mention had been made to that matter. The conversation had first centered on Dr. X's professional field, then turned to the author's
professional experience, and finally to the topic of hypnosis. The author assured
Dr. X that his wishes could be met, and retirement was made to another room
to insure privacy and no intrusion by the other guests present.

In this adjoining room the author positioned Dr. X and himself in the same
manner as had been done with the resident in psychiatry. Then it was explained
that, to achieve specific results explainable only as attributable to hypnosis, two
items of conscious cooperation would be required—namely, closing and keeping
shut his eyes, and listening continuously, intensely, and attentively to everything

the author said even if irrelevant, redundant, or apparently serving no recognizable purpose. Dr. X was informed that this would insure participation by his "unconscious mind" and cautioned that such intent listening might occasion some fatigue and even some transient discomfort, but that he need not be concerned or distressed by any such developments.

Then the author, seated on a low hassock, speaking in a monotonous tone of voice, and bobbing up and down, back and forth, and from side to side, thereby constantly changing the locus of his voice in an irregular fashion, proceeded to give a general discussion of hypnosis. No suggestions were given. All utterances were descriptive of general hypnotic phenomena, with the statement included that the unconscious mind could and would understand meanings not perceptible to the conscious mind and that the unconscious mind could act and would act upon instruction in accord with its own understandings entirely independently of the conscious mind. This statement was reiterated several times, being interwoven with the general remarks about hypnosis.

After about seven minutes of such discussion Dr. X's face showed the typical placid, immobile facies of the hypnotic trance, but within another two minutes the placid hypnotic facies disappeared, and a look of conscious distress appeared, Dr. X opened his eyes, began gagging, hurriedly secured his handkerchief, and placed it to his mouth, rushing to the lavatory as he did so.

Upon his return from the lavatory he remarked, "I just don't know what happened to me. I was listening attentively to what you were saying when a sudden wave of nausea hit me. If I were on board ship, I'd know what was going on, but here I can't understand. The feeling disappeared as rapidly as it appeared. I have no nausea or discomfort now. It was gone by the time I got into the lavatory. It just disappeared as rapidly as it had appeared."

"Perhaps you developed a trance state in which a state of nausea was engendered which, in turn, aroused you from the hypnotic trance. If such is indeed the case, you will unconsciously place your left hand behind your head with the fingertips touching your right ear."

Without noting what he was doing with his left hand, Dr. X explained very earnestly that he had not developed a hypnotic trance, but had only listened to the author's exposition of hypnosis.

"Then why is your left hand behind your head with your fingers touching your right ear?"

Upon noting this, Dr. X dropped his left hand to his lap and replied simply and with a tone of wonderment, "I must have done that unconsciously."

As Dr. X spoke, the author moved from the hassock to a standing position still in front of Dr. X but very definitely to his right.

"Yes, I think you did it unconsciously to signify that you did develop a hypnotic trance," speaking in a manner to keep Dr. X's attention fully upon the author.

"I assure you that I merely listened attentively, but I did not go into a trance."

"Then why is your left hand again behind your head with your fingertips on your right ear again?''

Dr. X turned his face away from the author, glanced first at his left thigh, then at his uplifted elbow, and then slowly lowered his left hand to his left thigh, seeming not to understand the situation.

"Yes, Dr. X, [as he again turned his face toward the author] your left hand by its position indicated and indicates [slowly Dr. X's left hand began to rise toward the back of his head] that a state of hypnosis was induced in you."

"But wouldn't I know it? I certainly don't know it, and you are just assuming that I was hypnotized."

"No, that is not the case. It is simply that you *do not know consciously* something that you *do know unconsciously*. Now listen carefully. Do not make any movement until I tell you what to do. Now move slightly the fingers of your left hand and tell me what you feel with them."

The expression of amazement that appeared on his face as he became consciously aware that his left hand was again behind his head and that his fingers were touching his right ear, indicated that he knew that his unconscious mind did know something that he did not know consciously.

Thereupon the author gave Dr. X an explanation comparable to that which had been given to the English psychiatrist. As this explanation was given, the author had carefully chosen a chair to the right of Dr. X. The explanation was given in a casual, conversational tone of voice. Repeatedly, as the author spoke, Dr. X's left hand would levitate to the back of his head. Each time, as his fingertips touched his right ear, he would self-consciously lower his left hand to his lap, only to position it in the same way again. The author continued his explanatory remarks. His final comment was, "It is evident that in some way you induced a trance by some kind of technique by which you did something or said something to me that I don't know about that makes me keep on doing this [again self-consciously lowering his left hand to his lap] without knowing that I am doing it. Will I keep on doing it? Good heavens! I've done it again!" He was assured that as soon as he was fully convinced of the character of his behavior, it would cease.

At this point of time other matters compelled his departure, and as he put on his hat, his left hand again levitated rapidly to the back of his head, and when his fingertips touched his right ear, he ejaculated, "I'll be damned! I am being stubborn about being convinced."

THIRD ACCOUNT

In mid-March, 1968, the author was visited in Phoenix, Arizona, by Dr. Thomas P. Hackett, now teaching psychiatry and hypnosis at Harvard Medical School. The occasion for this visit was Dr. Hackett's interest in the author's hypnotic teachnique in the treatment of the chronic pain suffered by a patient Dr. Hackett had referred to the author.

However, the author had another chronic pain patient whom he intended to use in initiating a discussion with Dr. Hackett on the use of hypnosis for pain control, especially intractable pain. This patient, Frank, then in his late sixties, had six years previously undergone a right-sided hemipelvectomy. This radical surgery had resulted from a sarcoma of the thigh which had originally been misdiagnosed. When he developed phantom-limb pain, his surgeon, Frank declared, had advised him that he was "old enough and rich enough to live on dope the rest of your life." The phantom-limb pain had been extensively described as an experiencing of a feeling of his toes being severely twisted, his foot being bent double, and his leg being pulled far back behind him and being severely twisted. These feelings occurred irregularly in convulsive episodes and might last from two to three minutes and number from three to 10 times in 24 hours. They often awakened him from sleep. Invariably they were marked by flooding perspiration, particularly of the face, sometimes a fall to the floor even when seated in a chair. Constantly present was a severe aching pain which often became additionally a throbbing pain, sometimes lasting many hours. During the episodic attacks or the periods of severe throbbing pain, there were frequent involuntary outcries which the patient learned finally to subdue usually to a low-pitched moaning. His story was confirmed in all details in separate interviews with his wife.

Treatment of this patient had been limited to pain control and the correction of his drug addiction which had developed within three weeks postsurgically. Various drugs had been prescribed by his surgeon, but it was soon decided that Demerol administered intramuscularly by his wife in amounts ranging from 50 mg. to 100 mg. no oftener than every two hours would probably be the best method of medication.

Frank always carried extra prescriptions with him. His addiction was not a typical addiction. Rather it was a drug dependency. He might take 100 mg. 12 to 16 times in 24 hours for several days in succession, and this period might be followed by several days during which he might take no more than four 50 mg. injections during the night, having been awakened by convulsive episodes. There was no set pattern in his drug dependency. He had an intense fear of "looking or acting like a dope addict—I've seen them all around the world. I am a man, not a freak, I don't want to be torn to pieces by pain and drugs, but I can't last much longer, so do something, anything your conscience allows."

He had tried every possible psychological measure for his pain "from witch doctors, occultism, Zen-Buddhism, stage hypnosis, exotic mysticism, to hypnosis by a competent physician." He was finally instructed by a staff physician at Stanford University Medical Hospital to seek aid "from an experienced internist."

He consulted Dr. T. E. A. von Dedenroth of Tucson, where he was spending the winter. Dr. von Dedenroth, after much effort to induce a trance, referred Frank optimistically to the author.

At the first interview Frank repeatedly apologized for being "a lousy, impossible subject, but I can't help being bossy, stubborn, constantly watchful, and disputatious."

No open or direct hypnosis could be used, since the patient declared himself to be "too disputatious to let anybody take charge of my mind. Any help you give me for my pain and my drug addition you'll have to sneak in when I ain't looking. I've been top-dog so long I can't stop even when it's for my own good. You can knock me out with drugs, anaesthetics, or a baseball bat, but that's no good, I want to enjoy life, but this pain and the drug are interfering. I've read everything I could lay my hands on about phantom-limb pain, and drugs are not the answer. They dull the pain and dull your mind, and that ain't living. After Stanford University Medical Hospital recommended hypnosis, I read up on scientific hypnosis and found that it can permit major operations even though it is a use of psychology. But Dr. von Dedenroth found out that I'm a nut, too hardheaded and too disputatious by nature to be hypnotized. Anyway, he did his best, and I tried my best, too. But he described you as having a hypnotic technique so sneaky that you could keep dry in a heavy rain, and the way he said that, I believed him. So you've got my permission to do anything you can get by with. So you've got a miserable nut on your hands and the light is green, so it's all yours."

While the patient was explaining the situation as he saw it, the conclusion was rapidly reached that the only possible hypnotic approach to him would have to be an interspersal technique (Erickson, 1966) by way of a "casual" conversation.

He was found to be a most charming conversationalist and seemed to know how to make a conversationalist out of anybody he met. He was most sociable and gregarious and, like Will Rogers, had apparently never met anybody he didn't like, including scoundrels. He gave practically no personal information, aside from that of his hemipelvectomy, pain and drug dependency, except that which he disclosed incidentally. Very little of a personal character about him was learned, and this was primarily general in nature. He was a high school drop-out, self-educated by extensive reading covering the fields of art, literature, philosophy, drama, biography, history, science, industry, and business. He owned seven business corporations, two of which were identified as salmon canning and as the importation of many diverse items ranging from rare art objects to the basic needs of industry in general. He had progressed from extreme poverty in his youth to his present status as a multimillionaire. He had endowed orphanages, hospitals, libraries, and museums, had traveled extensively throughout the northern hemisphere, and knew about hunting and fishing in many countries, but he never related any personal experiences. He enjoyed gambling and made repeated trips to Las Vegas, Nevada, but always set the total of his gains or losses at the total of either $3,000 or $5,000 for each trip. Whether winning or losing, when the predetermined figure was reached, he abruptly terminated his visit. He was always intensely interested in the personal lives of others, which made possible the author's hypnotic approach. Another item of absolute importance for this report was his neurotic, fetishistic honesty in relation to anything he said or did, the reason for which the author carefully did not seek to learn, thereby winning the patient's trust, since that patient's frequent references to this attitude seemed to be a testing of the author's willingness to restrict himself to the stated problem of pain and drug use.

Two three-hour sessions were held with the patient before any attempt to use an interspersal technique of hypnotic induction. By the close of the third three-hour session the patient could drift in and out of a trance state without necessarily closing his eyes. It must be added that he developed a full capacity for an amnesia for all matters related to hypnotic procedures and always obeyed any instructions given him readily and unquestioningly, and retained benefits achieved until some uncontrollable condition developed such as illness. He would not accept instruction to foresee such possibilities. While he retained a full conscious memory of the nonhypnotic content of therapeutic sessions, he either chose or was actually unable to be aware of long, unaccountable lapses of time occasioned by prolonged trance states to permit adequate instructions in pain control.

This aspect of his personal behavior was used to devise an investigational approach which might posssibly yield results comparable to those reported in the two preceding accounts, while at the same time serving the purpose of demonstrating a technique of indirect hypnotic induction suitable for resistant patients with chronic pain or other problems. The results were quite serendipitous in that, while serving the primary purpose of an indirect trance-induction technique, an unexpected repressed memory was uncovered. Nevertheless, a confirmation of the two preceding accounts resulted in a completely unexpected fashion.

Several times on later occasions the patient observed with what seemed to the author a most probing tone of voice, "I don't know what you are doing, but my problems are decreasing." An evasive reply was made each time, "Maybe I won't have to do anything." After the first three sessions there was no further discussion of the use of hypnosis for his benefit, but this did not preclude discussion of hypnosis as a phenomenon or in relation to other patients. This, as well as discussion of an almost endless variety of other topics, gave the author ample opportunity to use an interspersal technique for reinforcements or reinstatements of pain control.

Within two months the patient declared he needed no further help. Since he was indeed "a most disputatious character," it was not considered advisable to explain to him the possibility that some adverse event might cause him to lose his new-found ability to control his pain. However, he did agree to return if "anything else" should happen.

Nine months later he returned following a severe attack of Hong Kong influenza and the near death of his adored wife from the same illness, his pain and drug dependency having recurred, as was expected should a stress situation develop. He stated, "I do not know how in hell you talk me out of pain and Demerol, but you sure do, and that damn flu has put me right back to where I was when I first came, maybe worse."

No real effort was made to help him in the first three two-hour sessions. This discouraged him, and he ceased to be wary and overwatchful. He unhappily said that he would "try another couple of sessions, and when they peter out, I'll take your advice about some other drug than this damn Demerol."

At the close of the next session he aroused from a deep trance without awareness of the fact that he had been in a trance, since the author was continuing the casual conversation at the beginning of the session. Suddenly he became startled, looked at his watch, recognized that three hours had passed, then exclaimed, "You son-of-a-bitch, you sneaked past me again when I wasn't looking," and then recited from Kipling's "The Ballad of East and West," beginning with "Oh, East is East, and West is West" finishing with "though they come from the ends of the earth," adding, "Okay, Milton, I'll see you as many times more as you need to tie things down snug and tight." Reply was made, "Right, you do your business your way, and I will do mine my way."

There was a second recurrence over a year later following surgery for an enlarged prostate gland and a resulting secondary infection which required three months hospitalization in his home state. During this period of time he repeatedly received transient help from the author by way of long-distance telephone calls, but this was not fully satisfactory, never lasted more than a week, and could be negatively affected by necessary medical procedures. When he was released from the hospital, he promptly came to Phoenix for a satisfactory reestablishment of his pain relief and freedom from drug dependency.

However, it should be noted that he never did lose his phantom-limb pain completely. Rather, there would be transient minor recurrences, at which time he "would simmer down, get my head straightened around, and get it under control again." These recurrences he stated, "were nothing like the real thing, but bad enough to worry me. I just have to take a little time out, knowing that I can do without them." Any illness or excessive fatigue could bring on such minor recurrences, but they never constituted a real threat to his peace of mind. (This type of experience is typical in the author's experience with other phantom-limb pain patients, and provision is always so made, since perfection is not a human attribute).

There were two other items of interest of great value in the handling of Frank's problems. The first was, "I swore an inviolate oath when I was 16 to be absolutely honest in all my dealings, and thank God I've kept that oath!" No effort was made to ascertain the reason for this oath, but the age of 16 indicated a possibility of some juvenile indiscretion, and his frequent direct or indirect references to truth and honesty, often in poetic quotations, kept the author alert for possible significances. None was learned.

The second item was Frank's hesitation about accepting an invitation to attend the author's class at Phoenix College, where instruction on hypnosis was being offered to physicians, dentists, and psychologists. He had replied, "Oh, I know you won't say anything to embarrass me. So well, why not go? I might as well.

Maybe I might learn something about the way you are handling me!''

No effort had been made to reassure him about the visit to Phoenix College. Additionally the author had observed on many occasions what he considered to be a fetishistic, neurotic striving on Frank's part to be utterly correct in everything he discussed. However, no effort had been made to extract possibly withheld information. In every possible way the author made clear without explicitly saying so that the problems of pain and drug dependence were all that were considered to be in the purview of the author.

In presenting him to the students at Phoenix College no mention was made of his drug dependency—to Frank's obvious relief, since his facial expression of alert wariness disappeared when it became apparent that no such mention would be made. As a result of such restraint and in many other ways Frank had developed an absolute trust in the author. He also developed an open-eyed trance state during the author's lecture at the college, which was most convincing for the students. Some of them made their own tests to be sure of their observations. Frank also, on his own initiative, made a second visit to the class and again developed a trance state which was circumspectly tested by the students.

To meet Dr. Hackett's needs both men were asked separately to meet the author in his office at 9:00 A.M. When they arrived, no explanations were made. They were simply introduced to each other and asked to sit down, which they did promptly but with bewildered expressions on their faces.

Addressing the patient, the author said, ''Frank, I want you to close your eyes and to keep them closed until I tell you otherwise. Is that all right?''

He answered, ''If you say so, all right. You never do anything without having a damn good reason. It ought to be interesting to find out what you're up to. So here goes,'' and with that remark Frank closed his eyes. The author was fully aware that Frank would develop a trance state immediately, since he had been so conditioned in the course of his therapy.

Turning to Dr. Hackett the author said slowly, very slowly, in an even tone of voice, repeating the same jerking movements of back and forth, up and down and from side to side described in the two previous accounts, ''And Dr. Hackett will observe and listen carefully and silently while I instruct you. He will not understand, but your unconscious mind will understand as I speak. You will recall, Frank, a not too terrible thing, but it will be some specific instance long forgotten by you in which you were dishonest or violated the law in some way, an occasion of which you were ashamed at the time and which is now coming back into your mind, and you will recall it fully. It was an occasion for which there was no real reason and for which you were so ashamed that you forgot it. Now slowly open your eyes and tell us the whole story.''

Frank, with a most astonished expression on his face, opened his eyes, saying, ''Well, I'll be damned. How in hell you ever dredged that up I'll never know. And I don't want to know! I forgot it once and I'm going to forget it again. I haven't thought about it for at least 15 years, and I still don't want to remember it. I forgot about it as fast as I could, but now that you have pulled it up, I might as well tell you about that damn peccadillo. Then I am going to forget it again.

"I was sitting in a boat facing the Golden Gate Bridge. The bass were biting like hell. As fast as you dropped your hook into the water, you had a bass snagged. Big ones, too! When I had the limit of 15, I was taking my rod apart to put it in its case, when my friends said, 'Don't do that, Frank. You will never again see a run of bass like this. Keep on hooking them until the run stops. We'll pay the fines if we get caught.' " Well, it wasn't the offer to pay the fines that made me yield like a weak son-of-a-bitch. I just plain wanted to catch bass that were willing and eager to be caught. I just put my rod back together and pulled in another 24 bass before the run ended. Best fishing I ever did, damn it. But I can't say I'm proud of it. I just felt as guilty as hell.

"We weren't caught, but I made damn sure that every fish was properly cleaned and dressed and I personally saw to it that they were delivered to an orphanage. I hope the kids enjoyed those damn fish. I didn't."

Frank was dismissed without any explanation being given to him. His parting comment was, "It beats the hell out of me how you dug that personal history out of me, and I sure don't know why. You've only been interested in my pain and the Demerol before, but I suppose you've got your reasons. You always do. And if you want anything more, you'll dig it out in your own style when I ain't looking, so what the hell? Maybe you've got some idea about publishing it. Well I'm going back to the hotel and get busy forgetting about those damn bass. Makes me sick just to think about them. That's why I never went fishing again."

Nearly a year later, during a social visit, out of context, Frank remarked, "Telling you about those 39 bass took away some of my guilt. When I got back to the hotel, I started looking through that book of your collected papers to get some clue as to how you dug up that peccadillo, but I just got as confused as that Boston doctor looked when I left your office that morning and I don't feel that I have to forget again. I still can't figure out how you dredged it up because I had forgotten it." He did not seem to be really asking for an explanation. No further reference was ever made to that account or to Dr. Hackett, which was most contradictory to the insatiable hunger for information he had always shown in all other situations.

After Frank's departure a brief discussion was offered to Dr. Hackett of the two preceding accounts together with a brief discussion of the processes of learning how to define the focal point of origin of sounds and the usual disregard of such learnings in studies of human behavior. The pertinence of the above account to Dr. Hackett's needs lay only in demonstrating to him convincingly that adequate use of hypnosis is not dependent upon patter, verbiage, what the operator knows, understands, expects, hopes for, wants to do, or the offering of instruction in accord with the operator's understandings, hopes and desires. On the contrary the proper use of hypnosis lies in the development of a situation favorable to responses reflecting the subject's own learnings, understandings, capabilities, and experiences. This can then give the operator the opportunity to determine the proper approach for responsive behavior by the subject. These considerations have been increasingly recognized by the author during the past 20 years as basic requisites in the development of hypnotic techniques and of psychotherapy. Subject behavior should reflect only the subject himself and not the teachings, hopes, beliefs, or expectations of the operator.

DISCUSSION

In any evaluation of these investigations, emphasis must be placed upon the special motivation of each of the three subjects. The first subject was a young English psychiatrist very much interested in learning what psychiatry was like as practiced in the United States. The second subject had a lifelong interest in the many aspects and kinds of human behavior. Both he and the resident had an intense intellectual interest in learning. The author merely offered them a special opportunity to learn something of particular interest to them.

The situation with the third subject was entirely different. He had undergone an emergency hemipelvectomy because of a malignant tumor on his right thigh followed by four years of phantom limb pain and narcotic dependency. His therapy related only to those two problems, and he had twice mistakenly assumed that no unforeseen or totally unexpected occurrences might occasion a return of his symptoms. Hence his motivation was based on emotional as well as physical distress. The freedom from pain after four years of physical anguish and relief of his fear of a continuance of drug dependency resulted in an emotional basis that dominated all relationships with the author.

Also to be recognized is that both times after a trance had been induced and the author had introduced a minor arhythmic alteration of the locus of his voice, the first two subjects had awakened spontaneously with manifested physical distress. Presumably the distress resulted from the randomly altered loci of the author's verbalizations, and it must also be noted that spontaneous amnesias became apparent for the immediately preceding events. However, the amnesia for the first trance of the resident was sufficient to include events of the four days preceding the second trance, even though the memory of the physical distress that had terminated that trance had been retained and proper conscious functioning had remained unimpaired. The amnesia for the resident's second trance became immediately apparent upon arousal from the trance state by the physical distress that had been developed during it, but this amnesia was terminated by the posthypnotic cue which caused the development of a third trance. The amnesia of this third trance state was systematically demonstrated and corrected, at least to a major degree, since no effort was made to discover completely what other items might have been included in that amnesia.

In the first two accounts the random alteration in the loci or origin of the author's voice revivified previous states of physical distress. No thought was given at the time of investigation to the accompanying unpleasant unhappy emotions. In the third account there resulted the recovery of a repressed memory marked by very unhappy emotions, although the associated physical activities were otherwise pleasant. Thus the elements common to all three accounts were the movements transmitted from the ocean, unpleasant emotions, hypnosis, and the irregularly randomly altered loci of the origin of the author's voice.

The first account resulted from the author's association of ideas while reflecting upon the description given him of dizziness during a period of seasickness. The memory of childhood activities with his playmates had come to mind. These activities, so common among schoolchildren, were: (a) squatting down, hugging the knees tightly, and then suddenly springing upright with the fervent hope, if not of actually fainting, of experiencing various changes in subjective feelings, which sometimes included dizziness and (b) of whirling around rapidly in order to enjoy all of the intriguing subjective sensations of dizziness and general physical discomfort, which tended to vary in accord with the position in which the head was held. A refinement of this latter activity was accomplished by the author's affixing a crossbar to one end of a rope, tying the other end to the hayfork track in the barn, twisting the rope to the greatest possible extent and then "riding it down" to insure the greatest number of subjective experiences. One of the most intriguing discoveries was that sometimes the direction from which a voice was heard seemed to be wrong even though the voice was recognized. When the expedient of a whistle was employed by the participants instead of the recognizable voices, there were more frequent difficulties in recognizing the direction from which the whistling came.

To these memories were added recollections of the author's "listening in all directions" when engaged in mischievous pranks or the evasion of responsibilities. It may be that the "dizziness" experiments led to his childhood conception of "listening in all directions."

As the author reviewed these memories and compared them with the similar experiences and learnings of his children and their playmates, he speculated about the possibility of the rolling movements of the ship affecting unnoticeably the psychiatric resident's perception of sound in the same way as had the play activities of his childhood and those of his children and their playmates. Further mulling over these thoughts led to the realization that, unless necessary for an understanding, little attention is given to a precise recognition of minor changes in the locus of origin of sounds. Certainly this would be true in the matter of seasickness. Further speculation led to the question of how a preliminary investigation might be made by using hypnosis to create a situation in which there could be systematic but random minor alterations in the locus of sound origin not likely to be recognized. Three such individual opportunities became possible and were investigated, with positive results that minor random alterations in the loci of sound origin could be an integral but unrecognized part of a larger experience.

Additional studies with the first subject disclosed that similar results could be obtained after an understanding of the original investigation only after elaborate precautions to render the subject unaware of the changes of loci of sounds. Any precaution to prevent awareness precluded similar results. No satisfactory experiments with other subjects could be set up because of intellectual interest or curiosity about experimental procedure.

It must also be noted that both times after a trance had been effectively induced and the author had, in an unnoticeable way, introduced something that presumably led to unpleasant developments for the subject, there had occurred a spontaneous awakening by the subject characterized by an amnesia for trance events. Parenthetically, mention may be made at this point of the pertinence of these findings to the question, if there is one, of the antisocial use of hypnosis. Also, one might think about contentions that there is no such thing as hypnosis and that anything achieved by the use of hypnosis can also be accomplished by the subject in the waking state. All of the significant results obtained by the author's investigation developed out of a trance, without any recognizable suggestion of any sort being given. These were spontaneous nausea and vomiting, spontaneous awakening, and a comprehensive amnesia. All that was suggested was merely hand levitation and eye closure.

Efforts were made to replicate this investigation subsequently with those few trained subjects who customarily developed a trance state with the eyes remaining open and who had a history of seasickness. Such subjects would either fail to develop a trance or would arouse while in the trance. There would be only bewilderment at the author's physical behavior. Having them sit with their back toward the author, in addition to adding a new element to the situation, resulted in no trance and the expressed feeling that "the whole thing seems silly." Insistance upon remaining with back toward the author not only added a new element but required repeated instruction "to be relaxed and comfortable and to remain so continuously," thereby negating possible unpleasant spontaneous developments.

One additional fact needs to be mentioned. This is that further trances could be induced in the resident only after emphatic reassurances that nothing unpleasant would happen. Even then prolonged effort was required, but thereafter trance induction was easily achieved.

Another item of suggestive importance is that three experienced subjects had failed to respond when they were used as subjects, because of amusement engendered by the author's body movements, or because of the intellectual challenge the movements presented in the prediction of the direction of the next body movement, or because of bewilderment or curiosity or some other unknown reason when asked to face away from the author when trance induction was attempted. When they were told the possibility of nausea developing as a consequence of the author's body movements during trance induction, they adopted an attitude of introspection and shortly reported an inner sense of discomfort, which they assessed as similar to the first and second accounts. However, none was willing to continue beyond the first recognition of inner somatic discomfort.

The second account was a hopeful effort to determine if there were a possibility of achieving results that might possibly validate the findings of the first account. However, the author was not too hopeful, since the professor's seasickness was less severe than had been that of the psychiatric resident. Also, he had not been at sea for over a year and he was 23 years older than the resident. Fortunately he was sufficiently interested in hypnosis to be fully cooperative as well as uncritical of the author's specious explanation that he could be more fully attentive if he kept his eyes closed so that he would not be visually distracted while the author was speaking.

The third account differed from the first two. Its primary purpose was to meet Dr. Hackett's needs by demonstrating that hypnotic results could be induced effectively in a chronic pain patient by means of a most indirect technique. The author's previous work with Frank made a trance an easy certainty. The hope was that stimuli not recognizable to the hypnotic subject and not even recognizable to Dr. Hackett until explained could result in some responses that could be used informatively for Dr. Hackett.

The secondary consideration was in relation to the author's belief that the patient was exaggeratedly and neurotically honest and that this obsessive-compulsive honesty quite possibly could be based upon some actual incident, possibly some juvenile delinquency during which "listening in all directions" was quite likely to have occurred. Hence the technique was worded to elicit some such memory "long forgotten" and "not too terrible" in the eyes of a man of wide experience in his late sixties and with an extensive history of philanthropy. The patient was protected by defining the possible incident as "not too terrible." The random, irregular changing of the locus of the author's voice was added to the indirect technique for two reasons. The first was that a specific meaningful incident might be elicited, but this was actually a mere hope not based on any factual knowledge. A second reason was that it might possibly affect the trance state in some informative way. In brief there might be something to gain but nothing to lose, and failure could be corrected by another type of approach. The results were delightfully specific, informative, and confirmatory of the first two accounts, even though they were shown in an unexpected way and served to confirm the author's suspicions of "a neurotic honesty" in the third subject.

SUMMARY

Three unexpected occurrences, one in 1929, one in 1942, and the third in 1968, gave the author an opportunity to further a particular type of field investigation. This was initiated as a result of the train of thought engendered by the first event. As the author had listened to the psychiatric resident's account of seasickness marked by nausea, vomiting, and dizziness, he had recalled some of his childhood experiments and those of his playmates and some of the results of the experiences of his children and their playmates. The question arose about the role of the significance of minor changes in the loci of origin of sounds. This led to a field investigation in three separate instances, each involving only one person.

III. Psychophysiological Processes

The first four papers of this section, which were originally published together in *Psychosomatic Medicine* in 1943, had their source in Erickson's puzzlement about those totally unexpected reactions and seemingly inexplicable complications that all seasoned investigators have observed in hypnotic work. He describes them here as "coincidental phenomena": When one suggests sensory or behavioral alterations in one sphere, the hypnotic subject frequently experiences idiosyncratic patterns of altered functioning in another, apparently unrelated area. Subjects experiencing hypnotic deafness, for example, may spontaneously undergo ocular fixation and loss of peripheral vision, changes in color vision, or alterations in pupillary behavior. Other hypnotically deaf subjects may experience anaesthesias as well as feelings of nausea and vertigo.

In the first paper of this series Erickson attempts a systematic approach by describing typical coincidental phenomena attendant on hypnotically altered visual, auditory, and motor behavior as well as those that tend to accompany certain classical hypnotic phenomena such as age regression, amnesia, analgesia, and anaesthesia. This classification has some value for alerting students about what they may reasonably expect and look for in hypnotic work. The individual differences of hypnotic subjects in their experience of these coincidental phenomena are so great, however, that one initially feels there can be little prospect of ever finding regular, systematic, and lawful relations among them. Yet, since these highly individualized response patterns are so characteristic of psychosomatic medicine, we may assume that the hypnotic investigation of them may yield insights of general validity for this field.

In a detailed case report Erickson illustrates how these highly individual psychosomatic interrelationships evolve naturally out of the typical accidents and learned association patterns in a person's life history. *His conclusions are of fundamental significance for a general theory of psychopathology.* As he summarizes his findings, ". . . they disclose that a disturbance in one single modality may actually be expressed in several other spheres of behavior as apparently unrelated, coincidental disturbances. Hence, seemingly different symptoms may be but various aspects of a single manifestation . . . psychopathological phenomena cannot be understood in terms of the modality of their expression and manifestation alone, but rather that an understanding must be looked for in terms of their fundamental interrelationships and interdependencies."

The other three papers of this series that appeared in *Psychosomatic Medicine* continue with various illustrations of these interrelationships together with hypnotic approaches for exploring them. An outcome of this exploratory work, as is usually the case with Erickson, is the development of hypnotherapeutic approaches to psychosomatic problems. Always the wily badger,[1] Erickson illustrates his indirect approaches in the therapy of an acquired food intolerance. The patient did not know the means by which she was relieved, but Erickson attributes it to the process of providing her with an experience in age regression that permitted an "unconditioning" of an unfortunate learning. We observe in this early case a general paradigm of Erickson's hypnotherapeutic approaches, which will be illustrated in greater detail in Volume IV of this series: Erickson provides the patient with stimuli and situations that will tend to evoke and utilize the patient's own mental mechanisms and learned association patterns to effect the cure. The natural repertoire of psychosomatic interrelations we all have built into us as a result of genetic predispositions and life experiences is the basic stock and storehouse that Erickson utilizes for his hypnotherapeutic effects. Thus the same psychosomatic interrelations and interdependencies that are the basis of psychopathology can be reversed or otherwise used for cure by hypnotherapy. Erickson never or only rarely uses hypnosis to program or suggest something into the patient; hypnosis is best used to provide vivid opportunities to evoke and utilize already existing processes within the patient.

This evocative hypnotherapeutic approach is well illustrated in the other papers of this section on the "control" (sic!)[2] of physiological functions, breast development possibly influenced by hypnosis, and the psychogenic alteration of infertility and menstrual functioning. Erickson tends to use a "shotgun approach," with a variety of suggestions that the patient's unconscious may or may not use. Although he always has a general idea of what class of mental mechanisms he hopes to evoke, he frequently finds it difficult in clinical practice to determine just which suggestion evoked just what therapeutic process within the patient. More recent systematic research in these areas, however, is gradually elucidating these relations.[3]

An interesting illustration of Erickson's penchant for conceptualizing in terms of fundamental psychophysiological processes is in his apparent discovery of the genetic basis of an atypical pattern of the sneezing reflex that could not be altered by hypnosis. His two papers on this subject round out his study of hypnotic interactions with processes on the psychological, physiological, and genetic levels.

---

[1]The badger, a totem some people felt Erickson identified with, was the mascot of his alma mater, Wisconsin University.

[2]"Control" is of course an unfortunate and misleading word in this context, when we are learning that all we actually can hope to do at best is "evoke" and "utilize."

[3]This research is typically reported in *The American Journal of Clinical Hypnosis, The International Journal of Clinical and Experimental Hypnosis,* and other journals throughout the world devoted to research in hypnosis.

14. Hypnotic Investigation of Psychosomatic Phenomena: Psychosomatic Interrelationships Studied by Experimental Hypnosis

Milton E. Erickson

The purpose of this paper is to present an account of various psychosomatic interrelationships and interdependencies frequently encountered as coincidental phenomena during the course of hypnotic experimentation on normal subjects. No effort will be made to review the literature for reports on comparable findings made in neurological studies, in research on sensory and physiological psychology, or in other allied fields of investigation. Nor is there any intention of offering an extensive discussion of the possible significances of the observations reported, since this is primarily an initial report upon extremely complex and varied observations requiring further controlled studies. Briefly, then, the purpose is to report certain phenomena from the field of hypnotic research, of which the literature on hypnosis makes little or no mention.

These coincidental phenomena are not those usual and expected changes in psychological, physiological, and somatic behavior that are essentially common to all hypnotic subjects in profound trances, such as alterations in reaction time, sensory thresholds, muscular tonus, and similar items of behavior. Rather, they are distinct from such psychosomatic manifestations of the hypnotic trance, and they are in all probability expressive, not of the state of hypnosis itself, but of the interrelationships of hypnotically induced behavior and conditions within the trance state. That is, after a profound trance state has first been secured, specific hypnotic instructions can then be given to the subject to elicit responses of a particular sort and in a chosen modality of behavior. However, in addition to the behavior that is suggested, there may also be elicited, seemingly as coincidental manifestations, marked changes in one or another apparently unrelated modality of behavior. Or, equally significantly, hypnotic suggestions bearing upon one sphere of behavior may remain ineffective until, as a preliminary

Enlarged from a report given before the American Psychiatric Association in Boston, May 1942, and released for publication in this journal by the courtesy of the Editor of the *American Journal of Psychiatry;* reprinted with permission from *Psychosomatic Medicine,* January, 1943, *5,* 51-58.

measure, definite alterations are first induced hypnotically in an apparently un-related and independent modality of behavior. Thus, to cite general examples, effective hypnotic suggestions bearing only upon sensory responses would often elicit additional unexpected and apparently unrelated motor responses; or sug-gestions directed toward a sensory sphere of behavior would remain ineffective until hypnotic alterations in a seemingly unrelated motor sphere had been first induced.

These various interrelationships and interdependencies, however, were found to vary greatly from subject to subject and, to a lesser degree, for the individual subject, depending in large part upon the nature and the character of the exper-imental work in progress.

The findings included in this report have been collected over a period of years from a large number of normal subjects. In most cases they were made originally as an incidental part of the development of other research projects, and hence could not always be explored adequately. Whenever possible, however, each of the various findings has been confirmed by further experimental work on the same and other subjects.

These findings to be reported are of two general types. The first type consists of specific instances either observed repeatedly in the same subject and con-firmed on other subjects or encountered from time to time in a number of subjects. The other type consists of a case report of the psychosomatic interre-lationships and interdependencies found to exist between vision, headaches of visual origin, and hypnotically induced psychological states in which the subject was regressed to earlier age levels.

Reporting on the first type of psychosomatic interrelationships and interde-pendencies is difficult, since they constitute essentially individual manifestations which occur under a wide variety of circumstances and in many different as-sociations. Furthermore they are not constant in their appearance for all subjects in the same situation, nor does the appearance of any one phenomenon neces-sarily signify the development of other possibly related phenomena in the same subject. However, the findings do tend to remain constant for the specific mo-dality of behavior under investigation in the individual subject, although repeated hypnotic experiences tend to lessen progressively the extent and duration of phenomena likely to cause the subject discomfort.

With this general introduction we may turn to the experimental situations out of which our findings on psychosomatic interrelationships and interdependencies developed. Many of the findings were made originally in relation to experimental studies on hypnotically induced states or conditions of deafness, blindness, color blindness, amnesia, analgesia, anaesthesia, and age regression. (By the latter is meant the hypnotic reorientation of normal subjects to a previous period of life with a revivification of earlier patterns of behavior and response and with an amnesia for all experiences subsequent to the suggested age level.) Some of these studies have been reported in the literature (Erickson, 1933, 1935, 1937, 1938a, 1938b, 1939a, 1939b, 1939c, 1939d, 1941, 1942; Erickson & Brickner,

1942; Erickson & Erickson, 1938, 1941; Erickson & Kubie, 1939, 1941; Huston et al, 1934), but at best only brief mention has been made of these special findings which have been further investigated by direct studies. Briefly stated, these findings are that the development of any of these special hypnotically induced conditions or states may lead, in addition to those phenomena properly belonging to it, to any one or more of a great variety of responses and manifestations belonging properly to other modalities of behavior—for example, the development of visual and motor disturbances when only hypnotic deafness is suggested.

For purposes of brevity these phenomena will be listed under general headings, and this listing will be followed by a citing of specific examples to illustrate the coincidental developments that may be seen in relation to various induced hypnotic states. The listing is as follows:

A. Altered visual behavior
   1. Decrease in visual acuity with blurring of vision and difficulty in reading
   2. Contraction of the visual field
   3. Difficulty in focusing gaze
   4. Decreased ability in depth and distance perception
   5. Subjective sense of colored vision—that is, addition of chromatic values to visual stimuli
B. Altered auditory behavior
   1. Decrease in acuity
   2. Inaccuracy in localizing sound
   3. Distortions in perception of sound qualities
C. Altered motor behavior
   1. General muscular incoordination
   2. Specific motor disturbances
      (a) Paresis and paralysis
      (b) Apraxias
      (c) Speech disturbances
      (d) Dysmetria
      (e) Ocular fixation, pupillary dilation and nystagmoid movements
D. Other types of altered behavior
   1. Analgesias and anaesthesias
   2. Subjective reactions of nausea and vertigo
   3. Anxiety states and phobic reactions with their various physiological concomitants
   4. Amnesias, usually circumscribed and specific
   5. Revival of forgotten patterns of behavior

To explain the above listing, specific examples will be cited as they were observed in various types of experimental work. However, it must be noted that while some subjects showed many of the phenomena listed above, others showed few or none, depending, apparently, upon the specific type of experimentation. Thus, for example, one subject rendered hypnotically deaf might show many changes in visual, motor, and other forms of behavior, but when rendered color blind might show only one or two disturbances in other fields of behavior, while another subject rendered hypnotically color blind might show many disturbances of motor behavior but no changes in the auditory sphere. Some of these alterations in behavior preceded the development of the hypnotic condition being suggested; some accompanied the process of the development of that intended state; but most frequently they constituted a part of the total picture after the intended hypnotic condition had been established.

In presenting specific examples not all instances will be cited, since this is not intended to be a statistical account. Rather, an effort will be made to select the more typical and informative development. Also, it is to be noted that there was usually a minimum of interference by the experimenter, hence little effort to investigate the unexpected findings. There were two reasons for this—namely, the feeling that more could be learned from simple observation of these spontaneous manifestations which were not readily understood and recognized sufficiently to permit extensive experimental manipulation, and the fact that other experimental work was usually in actual progress.

One of the first instances observed was that of a hypnotically deaf subject polishing and repolishing his glasses and showing peering behavior as if he could not see well. A written inquiry disclosed him unable to read the question, although he examined the paper carefully as if trying to find the writing on it, which actually was somewhat faintly writen. Finally he handed it back to the experimenter in puzzled silence. He was handed a book and a paragraph was pointed at. The subject started to ask if he were to read but showed a startle reaction immediately upon speaking. This was followed by a puzzled repetition of his question as if speaking to himself, whereupon he asked the experimenter what was wrong. Again the pantomimed instructions to read were given, but the subject seemed to experience great difficulty, and he explained that the print was blurred, that the lighting of the room was very dim, and he made anxious inquiry about his voice since he could not hear it. Examination of his eyes disclosed his pupils widely dilated. To prevent disruption of the experimental situation the subject was reassured by the measure of large script on a blackboard.

Subsequently the restoration of the subject's ability to hear restored his visual acuity, and his pupils contracted to normal size.

Another hypnotically deaf subject showed a marked loss of peripheral vision and seemed to have preserved only central vision. Other subjects showed various degrees of peripheral loss, but in no instance was an exact determination made. These subjects also showed ocular fixation and seemed to be unable to move their eyeballs freely.

One hypnotically deaf subject was noted to shift his position, to twist his body and head about, and to make strained efforts whenever he attempted to look directly at an object. Inquiry elicited the subjective statement that whenever he tried to look closely at an object it seemed to blur and to move back and forth as if alternately receding and advancing. Examination of his eyes showed a slow, irregular, alternating contraction and dilation of his pupils.

Another subject, a pyschologist, spantaneously discovered that he seemed to have lost his ability for depth and distance perception, a topic he was studying at the time. He was permitted to investigate this to some extent with available apparatus, and the results obtained indicated a definite decrease in his ability to judge distances. Similar results were obtained with one other subject untrained in psychology. Somewhat comparable was the behavior of another subject who became distressed by her tendency to overreach or to underreach when handed objects, and she was most apologetic about her "clumsiness." The only explanation she could offer was that her body did not "feel right," that her arms and legs seemed numb and stiff, and there were many evidences of general motor incoordination and muscle paresis, but because of her emotional distress extensive investigation could not be carried on without disrupting the general experimental situation.

A subject who had been used repeatedly and successfully in conditioned-reflex experiments failed to develop a conditioned response based upon a pain-light stimulus complex, since he invariably developed a generalized anaesthesia when rendered hypnotically deaf. Another conditioned-reflex subject, reported upon briefly in another study (Erickson, 1938b), invariably developed a progressive anaesthesia when rendered hypnotically deaf.

Two subjects when hypnotically deaf were found to have a subjective sense of colored vision, explaining respectively that everything seemed to have a reddish or bluish hue, and they suspected the experimenter of secretly employing colored light to achieve this effect.

Subjective feelings of nausea and vertigo invariably developed in one subject whenever a state of hypnotic deafness became well established for her. She rationalized this by explaining that her voice did not "feel right" in her throat, but the measure of keeping silent did not lessen her subjective distress. Additionally, she showed nystagmoid movements and pupillary dilation. Restoration of hearing would immediately correct all of these deviations from the normal, and efforts to alleviate her distress tended to remove the hypnotic deafness.

Another subject, who developed hypnotic deafness satisfactorily, seemed to be unable to respond to instructions to recover his hearing. Much effort and investigation finally disclosed that with the onset of hypnotic deafness there occurred an extensive anaesthesia. Until this anaesthesia was corrected he could not recover his hearing except through the experimentally unsatisfactory measure of awakening from the trance state. Several other subjects have shown a comparable inability to recover from induced behavior changes until the coincidental developments were first corrected, unless resort was had to the measure of awakening them from the trance state, usually an undesirable method since it disrupts the general experimental situation.

A peculiar circumscribed amnesia for anything pertaining to the radio was shown by one subject, a medical student, whenever he became hypnotically deaf. He readily detected the sound vibrations of the radio when he happened to touch it, showed a lively curiosity about it, but seemed incapable of understanding any information given him about it. He regarded the radio as some form of a ''vibrator'' such as might be used in physiotherapy and was obviously incredible of the explanations given him by the experimenter. A possibly significant item from his past history related to many reprimands given him by his father for his neglect of his studies in high school because of his excessive interest in the radio. Restoration of hearing always corrected this amnesia. Several other subjects showed somewhat similar circumscribed amnesias in that while in the deaf state they would be unable to call to mind items of memory otherwise readily accessible to them. Thus one subject could never remember when deaf a certain professor's name, and another invariably forgot a certain street address. Comparable findings are reported in a special study on aphasialike reactions from hypnotically induced amnesias (Erickson and Brickner, 1942). Yet in the ordinary trance or waking states none of these subjects showed special amnesic reactions.

More common in hypnotic deafness than the above manifestations were states of anxiety and panic, and phobic reactions with their various physiological concomitants of increased pulse and respiratory rates, tremors, and excessive perspiration (Erickson, 1938a, 1938b). Usually these manifestations would be attributed by the subjects to the experience of finding themselves unable to hear, and they would especially comment upon the unpleasantness of not being able to hear their own voice. Occasionally, however, a subject would show only increased perspiration, tremors, or other evidence of a state of tension, which he would not be able to explain and which were apparently not accompanied by any feelings of subjective distress.

In the development of these types of additional behavior disturbances the time of their appearance varied greatly. Thus several subjects given suggestions to develop hypnotic deafness invariably showed a preliminary state of rigidity and immobility with generalized anaesthesia. As the state of deafness became established, these preliminary manifestations slowly disappeared completely. Any attempt to prevent these preliminary manifestations seemed to preclude the development of deafness, but suggestions leading to such immobility and anaesthesia hastened the appearance of deafness. Another subject was found to be resistant to suggestions of deafness until he had first been given suggestions for a generalized amnesia. Following this, deafness could be induced. In large part, however, the additional behavior disturbances seemed to be an essential part of the established state of deafness, and any disruption of them tended to disrupt the state of hypnotic deafness also. These general findings were found to be true for other special hypnotically induced conditions or states.

In brief, the induction of hypnotic deafness in the normal subject may lead to the development of a variety of other behavior disturbances. These additional manifestations seem to constitute a part of the process of developing the suggested auditory disturbance or of maintaining it, or to be an expression of the imbalance of the psychophysiological functioning caused by the induced auditory disturbance.

In studies of hypnotic blindness, color blindness, amnesia, analgesia, anaesthesia, age regression, and posthypnotic behavior, the coincidental phenomena, depending upon the exact nature of the experimental work in progress, were found to be essentially similar to those developing in relation to hypnotic deafness. Hence they will not be reported in full detail; instead, emphasis will be placed upon those instances found specifically in various of these special hypnotic states.

In hypnotic blindness the coincidental phenomena tended to be limited to fear reactions with corresponding physiological concomitants. However, one subject showed a definite decrease in auditory acuity, another developed a marked increase in muscular tonus with a subjective feeling of stiffness and rigidity, while still another showed an extensive analgesia and anaesthesia of the legs and arms which persisted throughout the state of visual disturbance. In one study (Erickson, 1941) it was found that hypnotic blindness could not be induced except as the culminating feature of an induced acute obsessional hysterical state. In general the feeling of helplessness these subjects experienced and their tendency to become frightened by the situation in which they found themselves made experimental manipulations difficult.

Hypnotic color blindness, like hypnotic deafness, yielded a large variety of unexpected behavior disturbances. Foremost among these were emotional reactions of marked distress accompanied by increased pulse and respiratory rates, tremors, and excessive perspiration. These seemed to derive primarily from the feelings of disorientation and confusion caused by the changed appearance of the experimental setting as a result of the visual disturbance. As was briefly mentioned in another study (Erickson, 1939d), one subject became seriously distressed by her inability to recognize her dress as her own. Reassurances by the experimenter served to allay in large part these manifestations.

In the sphere of auditory behavior two subjects with induced color blindness showed an inability to localize sound correctly, and both commented spontaneously on their subjective feeling that the experimenter's voice did not seem to emanate from him and that his voice had changed markedly in its tonal qualities. Both were observed to turn their heads and listen in the wrong direction to unexpected sounds, ordinarily familiar to them. One subject became greatly interested in investigating the altered character of sounds, periodically interrupting her investigation to ask for reassurances to the effect that the experimenter had full control over the situation. A stopwatch was described as ticking in an unusually muffled way, the tapping of a pencil was regarded as having a "thick, dull" sound, and the squeaking of certain door hinges familiar to her was found to be extremely unpleasant, having a peculiar shrill quality, although in the ordinary trance or waking state she did not react unfavorably to that particular sound.

One special finding in relation to hypnotic color blindness was the unexpected discovery of two instances of synesthesia, the first of which has been reported upon briefly in the study of hypnotic color blindness. This instance was marked by a loss of conceptual values and meanings for the word *three* and its corresponding numeral upon the development of red color blindness. Restoration of color vision restored conceptual values. The second instance was an association of the color red with the numeral 7. Color blindness resulted in a feeling of unfamiliarity for that number despite its recognition, but there was no actual loss of conceptual values. Nor could the subject explain in what way the numeral 7 had changed. Additionally, this subject was found to show synopsia, in that certain sounds always carried a reddish color significance for her. Upon the induction of color blindness these sounds lost their characteristics of warmth and familiarity and in some instances she failed to recognize them, especially in connection with music. A phonograph record played for her was described as having an "incredible number of mistakes," and she wondered why such a recording should ever have been made. When these two subjects were rendered hypnotically deaf, however, the numerical concepts retained their chromatic associations.

In relation to posthypnotic behavior and amnesia a not uncommon finding was the development of a headache when the subject was given an unpleasant posthypnotic task to perform or was asked to develop an amnesia. One example is that of a junior medical student who, because of previous experience as a subject, volunteered for a class demonstration. There were no unexpected manifestations until he was asked to develop an amnesia for all hypnotic experiences including the present one and to awaken with a firm conviction that he never had been hypnotized and that in all probability he could not be. The subject performed this task adequately but soon developed a severe headache, which was readily removed by the simple measure of letting him recover his memories. He later explained that he resented being asked to develop an amnesia for his past hypnotic experience and that he felt that this resentment had caused his headache.

With other subjects who have failed to develop hypnotic amnesias readily, experience has disclosed that the measure of suggesting that they forget some unpleasant thing, to which suggestion the significant qualification is added "even though it causes you to have a headache," often enables the subject to develop additional amnesias previously impossible and without experiencing an associated headache. Other subjects react to amnesias by the spontaneous development of a headache, and still others show peculiar anaesthesias upon the induction of amnesic states even of a limited character. Thus one subject instructed to become amnesic for certain trance experiences developed a persistent anaesthesia of her hands. This was discovered when she attempted to do some writing. Correction of her amnesia enabled her to write. However, this hand anaesthesia developed only when she was given instructions to forget specific items, and it did not accompany spontaneous generalized amnesias.

Two female subjects to whom a phobia for cats had been suggested developed olfactory behavior changes in that one of the subjects became hypersensitive to unpleasant and the other inexplicably interested in pleasant odors until the suggested phobia had been removed. However, suggested olfactory sensitivity did not result in phobic reactions.

Another subject to whom a general disorientation for time and place had been suggested developed a very definite speech defect and stammered, although he had no history of previous stammering. Several months later in another setting the same subject was instructed to become equally confident that a certain specific event which had occurred only once had happened on two distinctly different days and to defend these beliefs emphatically. He again developed his serious stammering, and in addition he became disoriented for time, place, and person with the exception of the experimenter. On still another occasion he was asked to forget that a friend of his had been sitting in a certain chair and to be most confident in his assertion that his friend had occupied an entirely different seat. The subject responded to this task by first developing a stammer, but shortly this disappeared and it was replaced by an amnesia for the identity of his friend. He was shortly given a book to read, and after he had read aloud from it, he was told he would stammer on the next paragraphs. This stammering resulted in the recovery of the friend's identity.

In relation to regression two subjects who are reported in another paper (Erickson, 1943a), when reoriented to a period of life antedating the development of certain food intolerances, were enabled to enjoy the otherwise unacceptable food.

Several adult subjects, when regressed to earlier childhood age levels, have shown marked changes in their motor behavior (Erickson, 1939a). Two other such subjects wrote freely and easily with a backhand slant without error, although special inquiry disclosed that they had changed to a forward slope 15 and 18 years ago, respectively. Another subject who habitually wrote with a backhand slope, in the regressed state wrote with a forward slope. An inquiry proved that this change in her handwriting had occurred at the time of puberty. Efforts in the ordinary trance and waking states to secure duplications of their earlier patterns of writing resulted at best in only fair approximation with many errors.

In brief, the hypnotic induction of disturbances in any chosen modality of behavior is likely to be accompanied by disturbances in other modalities. These vary greatly in their nature and variety and in their relationship to the primary induced behavior disturbance.

CASE REPORT

The report of a case history illustrating various psychosomatic interrelationships and interdependencies may be presented by a listing of the pertinent facts.

The subject was a medical intern who suffered from a high degree of myopia. Whenever forced to do without his glasses, he developed severe headaches. Subsequent to his first hypnotic trance it was learned that he had received his first pair of glasses at the age of 10 years upon the recommendation of his school nurse because of his severe headaches from eyestrain. The original prescription for glasses had been changed for one less strong when he was about 14 years old and these he still wore. His mother, fortunately, had kept his first pair of glasses.

For demonstration purposes before a group this subject had been deeply hypnotized and then reoriented to an age of eight years and awakened in that state of regression.

Promptly upon awakening he removed his glasses, refusing to wear them and seeming to be amazed to be wearing them. When he was persuaded to wear the glasses, he complained that they hurt his eyes, and shortly he became resentful because, he explained, they made his head hurt and he could not see well. Accordingly, he was allowed to take off his glasses and he was then interested in a series of tasks all involving eyestrain, such as reading books held at the wrong distance, threading fine needles, and similar tasks. He cooperated readily for about an hour without subjective complaints. He was then reoriented immediately to his current age and awakened, but he was found to be free of subjective discomfort. As a control measure he was subsequently asked to perform similar tasks in the ordinary waking state without his glasses, but each time he developed a headache after about a half-hour of effort.

A series of trances over a period of weeks then disclosed that the hypnotic regression of this subject to various age levels yielded the following pertinent findings:

I. At 8- and 9-year levels:
   a. Refusal to wear both pairs of glasses and complaints that they hurt his eyes
   b. No subjective symptoms from deliberate eyestrain
   c. Denial of headaches at 8-year age level, but admission of occasional headaches at 9-year age level
   d. No subjective symptoms when awakened from these age levels after eyestrain.
II. At 10- to 13-year levels:
   a. Ready wearing of first but not of second pair of glasses
   b. Prompt development of headaches when induced to dispense with glasses
   c. Complaint of headache when induced to wear the second pair of glasses
   d. Persistence of headaches when awakened from the trance state after eyestrain
   e. Abolishment of headaches when regressed to any previous age level after eyestrain had resulted in headaches

    f. Failure to reestablish headache abolished by reorientation to an earlier age by subsequent reorientation back to the age level at which the headache had been developed unless care was taken to specify the exact date

III. At 14 and subsequent years:

    a. Recognition of first pair of glasses, but subjective complaints when induced to wear them more than an hour, and ready wearing of second pair of glasses with no subjective complaints

    b. Development of headaches upon eyestrain

    c. Persistence of these headaches when awakened from the trance after such eyestrain

    d. Abolishment of headaches immediately upon regression to any earlier age level

    e. Failure to reestablish headache abolished by reorientation to an earlier age by subsequent reorientation back to the age level at which the headache had been developed unless care was taken to specify the exact date

Control tests conducted in the ordinary trance and waking states disclosed the subject to be unable either to dispense with his current pair of glasses or to wear the first pair without soon developing headaches.

When the subject was informed of the experimental results, he was inclined to doubt their validity. He asked that a repetition, while a fellow intern acted as an observer, be made of the various procedures to satisfy him that he could dispense with his glasses without developing a headache when reoriented to an earlier age. The experimental results obtained confirmed the previous results. The subject was much intrigued by the proof offered him that in a certain psychological state he could dispense with his glasses, and he made repeated but unsuccessful efforts on his own initiative in the waking state to achieve comparable results.

These findings are comparable to those reported previously in an account of the apparent development of a state of unconsciousness during the reliving of an amnesic traumatic experience (Erickson, 1937) and in the repeated findings that acquired food intolerances and phobic reactions are not manifested by subjects regressed to a period of life antedating those developments (Erickson, 1943a).

In brief, this case report discloses that, contrary to the actual current physical status of the subject, there were positive and striking correlations between the nonwearing and the wearing of glasses and the development of headaches in accord with past chronological physical states and experiences.

DISCUSSION

Discussion of these findings may be summarized by the statement that they constitute an experimental demonstration of unsuspected and unrealized inter-relationships and interdependencies that exist between various modalities of behavior, an understanding of which is most important in any effort to deal effectively with the complex symptomatology of psychopathological conditions. Particularly do these findings demonstrate that psychopathological manifestations need not necessarily be considered as expressive of combined or multiple disturbances of several different modalities of behavior. Rather, they disclose that a disturbance in one single modality may actually be expressed in several other spheres of behavior as apparently unrelated coincidental disturbances. Hence, seemingly different symptoms may be but various aspects of a single manifestation for which the modalities of expression may properly be disregarded. Just as the hypnotically deaf subject manifested, as a part of his state of deafness, additional sensory or motor changes, so it may be that psychopathological manifestations involving several modalities of behavior are actually expressive of but a single disturbance in only one modality of behavior. Furthermore, just as the experimental approach to one modality of behavior was often dependent upon another apparently unrelated sphere of behavior, so it may be that the primary task in the therapy of various psychopathological conditions may be dependent upon an approach seemingly unrelated to the actual problem, even as hypnotic deafness was sometimes best achieved by first inducing an anaesthesia.

In brief, these experimental findings suggest that psychopathological phenomena cannot be understood in terms of the modality of their expression and manifestation alone, but rather that an understanding must be looked for in terms of their fundamental interrelationships and interdependencies.

15. Hypnotic Investigation of Psychosomatic Phenomena: The Development of Aphasialike Reactions from Hypnotically Induced Amnesias

Experimental Observations and a Detailed Case Report

Milton H. Erickson and Richard M. Brickner

From time to time in hypnotic experimentation, either from direct or indirect suggestions, unexpected and unusual manifestations develop which parallel in many regards the aphasias seen in neurological practice. They are usually of a limited, circumscribed character, cause the subject a certain amount of mental distress, and are recovered from either spontaneously, when the hypnotic experimentation from which they derive is concluded, or upon suggestions from the hypnotist.

Unfortunately the experimental hypnotic situation usually does not permit an adequate investigation of the phenomena, or the nature of the development necessitates an interference with the manifestations. Furthermore there seems to be little possibility of doing this type of experimentation directly and intentionally, since such attempts serve only to alter the total experimental response and the results obtained are in accord with the subjects' understanding of the experimental purposes and the precise instructions given. Efforts made to elicit directly aphasialike reactions secured only amnesias, blocking, or selective restrictions of behavioral responses expressive of the individual's immediate grasp of instructions. To date, despite repeated efforts with subjects who had shown such phenomena spontaneously, direct efforts have failed, except through the measure of having them relive previous spontaneous manifestations.

A number of the spontaneous experimental instances will now be cited, and these will be followed by a case report in which there was opportunity for detailed study of the subject's behavior.

First among these instances is one relating to the induction in a subject of an

Reprinted with permission from *Psychosomatic Medicine*, January, 1943, *5*, 59—66.

amnesia for her name. Subsequently she was called upon, while this amnesia still persisted, to demonstrate automatic writing, the primary object being to disclose the juvenile character of automatic script. By chance the subject was told the sentence she would write would read, "This is Eloise Hospital." She performed as requested but without capitalizing the proper letters. This oversight was regarded merely as expressive of the characteristic economy of effort frequently seen in automatic writing.

Since the subject expressed recurring emotional distress over her amnesia for her name, the suggestion was offered that she might list the names of other persons present as a measure of reestablishing her associations for her own name. She acted upon the suggestion readily, but it was soon noted that no capital letters were used in making her written list. The same observation was made when she was asked to list various cities she had visited. No comment was made to her, but she spontaneously observed that "Something is wrong. Those names don't look right to me. I have a feeling I have misspelled them." She scrutinized the lists and the original sentence uneasily and explained, "Everything seems to be all right. I just have a queer feeling that something is wrong with the spelling." Here she began to spell the various names aloud, shaking her head dubiously each time she did so. In no instance did she seem to be aware of the need for capital letters.

She was interrupted by being asked if she knew the proper, formal, and conventional form for heading a business letter. She replied with amusement that she did. She was then asked to write out in proper fashion and with the proper heading a formal business letter addressed to one of the authors, Dr. Erickson. She did so promptly and correctly with the exception that no capital letters were employed. After writing his middle initial, however, she inquired specifically if it was correct as she had written it. She was given the casual reply that his middle name was "Hyland," and she was asked, "Does that answer your question?" She replied, "Yes, but somehow there seems to be something wrong here the way I have written it. Just like that there (pointing to the other written material). The spelling is all right, the punctuation is correct, and the margin is O.K., but I have a most uncomfortable feeling that it is all wrong and I don't know why." Nor could she verbalize her feelings further.

Unfortunately no further investigation was made. Upon restoration of her memory for her own name she wrote it correctly at the request of a member of the group.

A second example concerns a stenographer to whom an amnesia was suggested for material just dictated and recorded by her in shorthand. Later that day, and before she had transcribed her notes, she was called upon by a colleague to take more dictation. A serious state of emotional distress developed when she discovered that not only could she not write shorthand but that she could not read even the shorthand in her notebook which she was fully aware she had already transcribed. Because of her emotional distress it became necessary to induce a new trance and to readminister the amnesia instructions, limiting them carefully to the content of the material. Indeed, the subject promptly sought out the hypnotist to report her problem and to ask for aid.

Another stenographer was told to forget the names of all her teachers, and she was further told that this amnesia would persist for several days, the purpose being to make a study of amnesia. Upon being awakened from the trance, she was given the task of filing data, and when this job had been completed, she was asked to take dictation. The discovery was made at once that she had a complete amnesia for shorthand. She was so frightened by this loss that it became necessary to rehypnotize her and to give her specific instruction to remember her shorthand ability. (It is to be noted in this case and the preceding instance, as well as in other similar instances, that the immediate availability of the hypnotist, of which there was full awareness on the part of the subjects, served to preclude them from reacting too unfavorably to their emotional distress and from spontaneously correcting the difficult situation in which they found themselves. Knowledge that the hypnotist was available for prompt intervention helped them to endure their distress until aid was given. Otherwise, as is shown in the detailed case report, when aid was refused, the subject simply made a spontaneous recovery).

The discovery was made that a patient was planning to escape from the mental hospital. Since he was a trained hypnotic subject, he was hypnotized deeply and the entire matter discussed at length with him. This discussion resulted in the patient's abandonment of this plan. The next day, by chance, it was discovered that the patient had lost his ability to recognize keys, did not know how to use them, and showed an extremely lively childish curiosity about them. Unfortunately no systematic investigation was made, and on the following day the patient was found to have recovered fully his understanding of keys.

Another instance, somewhat similar to the detailed case report, relates to a 19-year-old boy with less than normal intelligence who was instructed to forget his age. While this amnesia persisted, it was found that he could neither read nor write the number or the word signifying his age. Nor did he recognize the number when it was spoken to him. Correction of the amnesia caused the immediate disappearance of this manifestation.

DETAILED CASE REPORT

This subject was a 19-year-old boy, C. L., whose I.Q., as determined independently by several psychometrists, was in the lower 80's. Nevertheless he was a remarkably good hypnotic subject and had often been used for demonstration work.

On one such occasion he was told in a series of graduated suggestions, the content of which may be summarized as: "Forget how old you are. Just forget your age and don't remember how old you are until you hear me snap my fingers five times. Understand? You don't know how old you are—you've just forgotten completely." The experimental purpose in mind was merely to demonstrate the possible development of a limited amnesic state.

Later, after he had been awakened from the trance state, but before anything relating to his age had been said, the subject was asked to write automatically a number of dictated sentences, and thus to demonstrate the juvenile character of such handwriting. At the completion of this task he was asked by chance to number the sentences. He manifested immediate willingness but seemed to be inexplicably confused, uncertain, and hesitant. Cautiously, since his behavior was not readily understandable, he was urged "go ahead, go ahead." After a few uncertain, confused movements he seemed to omit from further consideration the first sentence and proceeded to number correctly the next four sentences as 2, 3, 4, and 5. Pausing, and seeming to study the task, he returned to the first sentence and numbered it with a zero. This apparently did not seem to satisfy him entirely, but he resumed the task at the 6th sentence and continued numbering correctly until he reached the 9th sentence. Thereupon another state of confusion developed, which he finally resolved by numbering it with a 0. At once he seemed to realize he had done the same for the first sentence. Laboriously he erased the first 0 and replaced it with another, as if correcting an error. Noting then that the 9th sentence was marked by a 0, he promptly erased it and replaced it, again as if he were correcting an error.

In looking over his work, he suddenly observed with bewilderment that there were still 0's for the 1st and 9th sentences. Promptly he declared, "There's a mistake here, something's wrong" and he seemed rather dismayed. He was told, "Never mind, just go ahead with your job."

Still glancing hesitantly at the 1st and 9th sentences, he proceeded to number the 10th and last sentence with two 0's. As he handed the sheet to the hypnotist, he became aware that the 10th sentence was wrongly marked and corrected it by an erasure and a replacement of the two 0's. Then, again glancing over the sheet, he became increasingly puzzled and uncertain, and he repeated his statement that "something's all wrong."

Disregarding his protest, two more sentences were dictated to him and he was asked, "just keep on with the job and number those sentences also." The 11th was given two 0's but the 12th was correctly numbered. Without giving him any opportunity to pause he was told, "Just keep on writing numbers in the right order until I tell you to stop. Just make neat columns up and down the page, going on from where you left off with the sentences."

In this way it was found that all other numbers could be written correctly with the exception that 19 was omitted entirely, while 29, 39, etc. were written as 20, 30 etc. The number 89, actually written 80, was followed by a figure comprised of three 0's. At this point he was told to stop and was asked, "How far have you gotten?" He replied "one hundred" and then repeated his answer several times, with a very peculiar emphasis on the "one."

Before anything could be said to him, he began looking over his handiwork. In a puzzled fashion he placed his forefinger successively on 81, 71, 61, etc., finally announcing in a dismayed tone of voice the he had discovered "some mistakes." Seizing the eraser, he proceeded to remove all 0's and to replace them energetically with the numeral 1. As he completed this task by changing the three 0's for 100 into 111, he became even more bewildered and explained "That don't seem to work out right. It's still wrong." He was urged, "Just keep on trying and see if you can work it out right. Just take your time. Start at the beginning and don't hurry."

Laboriously he set about the task, muttering "one hundred-one-that's right." Starting with the first sentence, he declared it correctly numbered. The 9th, however, he declared was wrong "Because one, that's where you start, it's the first number and this ain't the first sentence." Passing hesitantly on to the 10th and 11th, he declared them wrong "because they're two numbers like those," pointing to 12 and 13. Continuing he explained "They're both elevens that way, and one should be a ten so you write '10' this way," suiting his action to his words.

He proceeded with his task by running his pencil down the column of numbers, but he failed to observe that 19 had been omitted. Instead he became interested in the two sucessive 21's, resulting from the alteration of the numeral 20 by the replacement of the 0 with a 1. After making the proper correction, he continued with his inspection of the column. Pausing at 29, actually written now as 21, he compared it visually with the correct 21.

Apparently puzzled by their identity, he began counting rapidly to himself, omitting as he did so 9 and 19, and he followed the numeral 28 with 30. This led to the discovery that, in addition to the 21 written between 28 and 30, the number 30 was actually written as 31. Distracted by this error he embarassedly corrected it, explaining, "It's just like that 20. I got too busy with the eraser and didn't watch what I was doing."

Returning to the problem constituted by the two 21's, he repeated his count as before and then explained, "I must've been in a hurry and stuck in an extra 21." Thereupon he erased it neatly.

Continuing his checking of the column, he soon discovered 31 in place of 39. Apparently, however, he observed at the same time the two 41's, since immediately he glanced back at the corrected 30 and then the corrected 20, pointing them out to himself with his index finger as he did so.

This apparently suggested a new idea to him, for at once he glanced ahead to note the 51 and the 61 in place of 50 and 60 respectively. Simultaneously he discovered that there was a third 41 representing a 49, adjacent to the 51 and a comparable error in the 50's, 60's, etc.

He commented with marked embarrassment, "That's a funny lot of mistakes to keep making. I sure must be dumb today. I must be going nuts if I can't write numbers right." Slowly, systematically, and with laborious care he proceeded to make erasures and corrections, concluding the task by changing 111 to 100.

Handing the sheet to the hypnotist he declared, "It's O.K. now."

He was asked if he could count. He flushed as he replied earnestly, "It sure don't look it after all those mistakes, but I can."

Accordingly he was asked, "Well, just count for me slowly and carefully and point to each number as you have it written there while you do the counting."

Confidently he began this task, but as he reached the numeral 8, he apparently glanced ahead and saw the 1 still in the place of 9.

Interrupting himself, he declared with marked embarrassment, "There's an extra 1 I forgot to erase when I was erasing those other extra numbers. I sure must be nuts." Promptly he erased it and hastily checked through the rest of the numbers, as if to assure himself that no other errors had been overlooked. Finding none he declared, "It's really O.K. now."

He was asked to continue his counting. He proceeded, omitting 9, 19, and all numerals ending in nine. So far as could be judged, there was no hesitation or faltering in his voice in relation to the omitted numbers. When, however, he followed 88 with 100, he became aware that something was amiss, declaring, "Say, there's something wrong here. You don't say 88, 100, but. . . ." Here he interrupted himself to repeat a second and a third time his count, beginning with the numeral 1, ending each time with "88, 100." With many puzzled shakes of his head he repeatedly declared that something was "awful wrong." What this might be he could not define other than to say "88, 100, that don't sound right, it don't sound natural."

The measure of having him count from 100 to 200 yielded comparable results. However, the sequence of "188, 200" made him declare that perhaps he merely thought he was not counting correctly.

The suggestion was offered that he could prove to his own satisfaction that he could count correctly by enumerating aloud his fingers. To this he replied, "Sure, I got ten fingers—everybody's got ten fingers if he ain't lost them in an accident. I'll count mine if you want me to."

Asked to do so, he began readily, but when he enumerated the ninth finger as number 10, in consequence of the omission of the number 9, he embarrassedly remarked, "I must've got mixed up when I changed hands there, so I'll start over again." After two further efforts leading to the same results, the subject became more distressed than embarrassed, reiterated his explanation of getting confused when he shifted from the right to the left hand in ticking off his fingers, and glanced repeatedly in a worried fashion at the sheet of paper bearing the marks of many erasures.

To prevent a disruption of the situation through the development of a strong emotional reaction he was reassured by the simple measure of having him count separately the fingers on each hand and then add the totals. This apparently restored his general self-confidence and relieved his emotional distress.

His attention was then called to a wall calendar showing the current month on the upper half and all the months on the lower half.

To avoid ddetailed description, the various tasks the subject was called upon to perform will be listed below in chronological order. In addition the nature of his performance of each will be indicated. Also it may be added that the subject was deliberately hurried from one task to the next in a most urgent fashion to prevent emotional disturbances or any spontaneous disruption of his existing mental state.

1. State the number of months in a year. (12)

2. Read aloud rapidly, apparently at random, as indicated by the hypnotist, all of the dates in various months on which each of the days of the week fell. (Correctly performed. Care was taken by the hypnotist to avoid any column containing 9's.)

3. State the number of days in a month. (30, 31)

4. Confirm the fact that the lower half of the calendar showed the months arranged in 4 rows of 3 each or 3 rows of 4 each. (He agreed and also declared that 4 times 3 is 12 and that 3 times 4 is 12.)

5. Reaffirm the number of his fingers. (10.)

6. Read aloud rapidly the days of the month. (Correctly done, except 9 was regarded as an "upside down 6 and a mistake," 19 as "another 16 with the 6 upside down like that other 6," and 29 as "26 again, upside down too, that is, the six is upside down like those other sixes. There's an awful lot of mistakes. I didn't know they made mistakes on calendars.")

7. Count the months of the year. (13, "what the hell—" repeated count of 13.)

8. Count hypnotist's finger. (11, 11, 11—"That ain't right.")

9. Count days of the current month by counting all the Sundays, then the Mondays, etc., instead of following the numerical sequence. (33 days—"I sure get mixed up in my counting." Care was taken by the hypnotist to obscure each numeral by covering it in large part with his fingers so that it could be seen in part but not really read.)

10. Count days of the next month. (34—"I'm getting worse. I must be awful dumb today.")

11. Count in numerical order the days of the month ("1, 2, 3, 4, 5, 6, 7, 8, there's that upside down 6 that should be a 10—then this 10 would be 11—that makes all these other days wrong—and this upside-down 16—and this other 26—say, you can't count on this calendar with all these mistakes. No wonder I got 33 days. I thought that was kinda funny, but it wasn't my fault at all. Where did you get a phony calendar like that?")

12. Discover through silent assistance on the part of the hypnotist that all other calendars, even books and newspapers were similarly numbered. (Cumulative, obvious, and troubled distrust of hypnotist and general fearful uneasiness and bewilderment.)

13. Discover that without the "mistakes," each month would have too few days. (Unable apparently to meet the intellectual task involved.)

14. Repeat count of months of year and of hypnotist's fingers. (13-11, and increasing distrust and fear).

15. Arrange paper clips into 3 rows of 6 each, and then alongside of the first

row place 4 additional clips, with 3 additional for the second row and 2 additional for the 3rd row, and then to determine the total number of clips in the first and third rows by addition, not by counting. (10-8)

16. Determine number of paper clips in second row. (Bewilderment, hesitation, confusion, with muttering of "it ain't 10 and it ain't 8. 6 and 5 are 11, so it ain't 11, but its got to be something. There's something awful phony here," and he announced his desire to depart without delay.)

17. Place the paper clips from the second row, one at a time on the days of the month as shown on the calendar, beginning with the first of the month, announcing the total number of clips placed as he laid each down. ("1, 2, 3, 4, 5, 6, that's all of that row, do I use them three too—7, 8, say this last one goes on that upside down 6. What the hell is going on here? And another one makes it a even 10. And what are you (the hypnotist) doing all that writing for (taking of notes on his behavior)? I don't like this a bit, and I'm going to get the hell out of here right now." However, he yielded to persuasion to remain when finally assured he had nothing to fear.)

18. Discover "just what you think this whole business that's puzzling you is all about?" ("About counting and all these mistakes in the calendar and the books and what I wrote.")

19. Count the slips in the first row. ("Don't need to, there's 10.")

20. Count the clips in the first row. ("1, 2, 3, 4, 5, 6, 7, 8, 10,—11—there it goes again, just like your fingers and my fingers. I got too many days in the month too. I even counted the months wrong. I don't like it. Are you giving me a brain test like you do the patients here? There's something phony going on here." Reassured again, he consented to stay a while longer.)

21. Discover "just what you think this whole business that's puzzling you is all about?" ("I guess it's this counting business, specially this upside-down 6. It looks like a mistake to me but the calendar's got it, all the books got it, and I sure as hell can't count straight today, so it looks like there's something wrong with me.")

22. Attempt reading. (Failed to recognize the word nine in any form, complained that he did not read well, since many words were too big and he had only gone to the 6th grade. Nor did he recognize "nine" or "nineteen" when these words among others were spelled to him.)

23. Look further into the matter. ("Well, all these upside-down numbers—let's see the numbers I wrote for you—there ain't none there—just the places where I made a lot of mistakes." Then, after rapidly checking aloud his written figures, he declared, "Nope, this is all O. K.")

Apparently his intellectual endowment was not sufficient to permit his spontaneous appreciation of the situation. Then, by the measure of letting him count out in groups of five each a total of 100 paper clips and similar such concrete expedients, it became possible to demonstrate systematically to him the falsity of his method of counting. As this procedure continued, the subject became greatly worried and frightened and seemed to have much difficulty in thinking.

Accordingly, much to his relief a casual conversation was begun, and after a while he was asked if he knew the date of his birthday.

His reply was, "I sure do. It's December 4th," and he offered various reminiscences.

After still further conversation he was asked, "By the way, what year were you born?"

After a startled pause, he stammered bewilderedly, and in his confusion and uncertainty it became necessary to question him simply and carefully before coherent replies could be obtained. It was learned that he did not know:

1. The year of his birth, although he was certain of the day of his birth.

2. The current year, although he knew the current day and the month. (The calendar had been carefully put aside, but even so, he tried to find it.)

3. He did remember that he had been 17 years old, he was confident that he had also been 18, and he was equally confident that he had not yet been 20. Rather he was "between 18 and 20 years old, and it's June now, and my birthday ain't until December so you might say I'm 18½. But that don't sound right. It's just like that counting business you made me do. It's just all mixed up. All I want to do is go home and sleep and get over all this. It ain't doing me any good, and I'm getting a headache from trying to figure things out, and it don't do a man any good to find out he don't even know when he was born."

Recognizing the underlying request and significances of this remark, the subject was dismissed. When seen the next day, he had apparently spontaneously recovered his memory for his age and all related facts. When an attempt was made to ascertain his recollections of the previous day's work, the subject related that the hypnotic demonstration had left him a bit "dizzy" and suffering from a headache which got him "all muddled up." "All I remember is that I did an awful lot of counting and figuring for you, and it didn't seem to make much sense. It just made my headache worse, and that's about all I remember."

Subsequently in a trance state he was asked to explain. This he did by declaring that he had really forgotten how old he was, but he could offer no explanation regarding the forgetting of the nines and nineteens. This, he stated, he did not understand himself.

He recognized that there was a certain relationship between his age and those numbers. He explained that when his age was forgotten, so were those numbers, and that the sight of them had impressed him as nonsense figures, until he had recognized the 9 as a 6 upside down. Thereafter he had continued to think of 9 as an inverted 6.

DISCUSSION

Occasional opportunities present themselves with which to explore further the nature and functions of what has been termed the "neurointellectual system." The observations just described appear to furnish such an opportunity.

> The 'neurointellectual' system is thought of as acting in a manner comparable with that of the neuromuscular and neurosensory systems. The implication is that the nerve impulse may affect similarly the neurone beds underlying intellectual, muscular, and other functions. This in turn implies that these functions, although they differ greatly in their outward manifestations largely because of their manifold end organs, are identical from a neural standpoint. All of these systems are thought to operate by the same laws and to be subject to the same physiological and pathological influences. It is thought possible that our greater knowledge of muscular than of intellectual function may be largely due to the fact that muscles and their actions are more concrete than ideas. Hence our comprehension of the physiology and pathology of the neurointellectual system may gain if we study it in the image of the neuromuscular and neurosensory systems (Brickner, Rosner, et al, 1940).

This concept of a neurointellectual system helps to elucidate phenomena like those shown by the patient C. L., and conversely, his behavior illustrates in a hitherto unexplored way the behavior of that system. Previously neurointellectual functions were studied in two main ways—by observation of patients after lobectomy and lobotomy (Ackerly, 1935; Brickner, 1936, 1939a, 1939b; Freeman & Watts, 1942) and by certain intellectual processes resulting from cortical stimulation and release (Brickner, 1938, 1940; Foerster, 1928). In the cases of stimulation and release the stimulus was usually the epileptic process. It was found that streams of ideas could be elicited by that process which appeared comparable in every basic way to the muscular movements resulting from the action of the epileptic process upon other neurone beds. In other instances phenomena in which intellect played a large but not exclusive part were evoked by electrical and mechanical stimulation (Brickner, 1938, 1940); and in still others by that postencephalitic process which produces oculo-gyric crises (Brickner, Rosner, et al., 1940). All of these observations led to the deduction that the neurointellectual system followed the same laws of reaction to stimulation and release as the rest of the nervous system. These reactions could be traced out in considerable detail.

The present instance gives an example of the throwing out of function of a specific, exquisitely isolated chain of neurones underlying the formation of ideas. It appears comparable to the more readily visualized exclusion from function of neuromuscular or neurosensory chains which can also be produced hypnotically or hysterically. Under those conditions we speak of paralysis or anesthesia. The same terms would be applicable to the present conditions except that the neurointellectual system cannot consistently be called either motor or sensory. Its motor or sensory rank depends upon what it is doing in any given instance. However, the terminology we apply to the superficial appearances is less important than knowledge of the fact that one can manipulate a discrete neurone chain, whose function is the pure production of ideas.

But alignment with muscular and sensory phenomena of the intellectual operations shown by this patient is not all that is revealed. We can also discern the actual, neural reality of some of the ideational components of a total idea. When the neural bed which the patient had to use to think of his age, 19, was thrown out of action, the beds needed to think of the two numbers, 1 and 9, were similarly thrown out. This fact shows, in this particular case, the close anatomical association between the neurone beds for the numbers 1 and 9 and the total concepts "nineteen" and "age nineteen." 1 and 9 rested upon two distinct anatomical settings, because 1 returned to function long before 9 did. Under other circumstances a different thing could have happened to the neurone organizations for 1 and 9; they could each have been still able to function, but not to unite into either of the two total ideas "nineteen," or "age nineteen." This would be comparable to conscious inability to synthesize thought, which has been described in a case of right frontal lobe tumor (Brickner, 1959).

In addition the actuality of processes of thought which never reach consciousness is shown. This has been illustrated in another case (Brickner, Rosner, et al., 1940, Case L). To the patient it was never known that the concepts of the two numbers were indispensable components of the concept of his age, all to be manipulated, preserved, or lost together. Thus it is clear that the individual thoughts which served as components for a total thought were never so perceived by the individual harboring them, but were unconscious thoughts, as far as he was concerned. Nonetheless, these same thoughts were available to his consciousness at other times, when they served as total thoughts in themselves (thoughts of 1 or 9 as such) instead of as components of something else. This point supports the hypothesis that, as thinking develops, individual items which are consciously known at first later lose their conscious identity when they combine with other items to form a more complicated unit. Then, the new, more complicated unit is the thing of which one is conscious. Nonetheless the discrete components can still reach consciousness when activated in their old form as complete units in themselves. In this sense they resemble complex muscular movements such as those required to drive an automobile. Although they are consciously and laboriously learned as individual components at first, all that is conscious later is the total combination of them. Yet any one of them can be selected and perfectly executed at any time as a total unit in itself—for example, in demonstrating a single movement to a novice. But that isolated movement must be serving in a total capacity at the time in order to be successful. If each component of, for example, gear shifting is brought to consciousness as an isolated movement while the total act of setting the car in motion is going on, that total act cannot be carried out successfully. Another comparable example is the difficulty encountered in buttoning or unbuttoning when one isolates any one of the various automatic movements and makes it fully conscious.

If we keep in mind these neural interpretations of the phenomena shown by C.L., some suggestions can be derived from the cases mentioned at the beginning of the text. The patient who lost the concept of capital letters when experiencing amnesia for her name and the one who forgot the number representing his age show a situation very similar indeed to that of C. L. With the two who forgot shorthand, the same identical neurophysiological principles would appear to have been involved; however, the material forgotten was of much larger mass, and apparently very large chains of neurones were thrown out of action. The loss of the concept of keys appears to be of the same category, possibly leading to the domain of the concept of symbols. Such cases as these two are illustrative and instructive, but the very complexity of the material for which there was amnesia would blur the point they illustrate, were it not for the clue supplied by a case like that of C.L.

From a clinical standpoint some additional aspects emerge from these observations. Reference is made to the patient's own response to his symptoms. As with all or most other cortical deficits, this patient was unaware of what was missing; he knew only that something was wrong or missing. This is so well seen in cortical deficits resulting in aphasia, hemianopsia, and other disturbances that it requires little comment.

It is also of interest to observe the genesis of projection (the calendar had mistakes in it, etc.), confusion, and anxiety bordering on panic, all as the result of the recognition by the patient that something was wrong with his mind which he could not identify. Although for the purposes of the experiment an explanation was not given to him, it is obvious that these secondary symptoms would have disappeared immediately, if it had been. Equally clear is the diagnostic puzzle such a patient would have presented, had he appeared in the clinic with his secondary symptoms, the origin of them unknown to the physician as well as the patient.

SUMMARY

1. Cases are described, one in detail, in which amnesia for a specific thought or class of thoughts was induced by hypnosis.

2. In all of the cases amnesia was also developed for certain collateral thoughts. This had not been suggested by the hypnotist.

3. A neural interpretation of these observations is given. The nature and functions of what is thought of as the neurointellectual system are further described in the light of these observations.

16. Hypnotic Investigation of Psychosomatic Phenomena: A Controlled Experimental Use of Hypnotic Regression in the Therapy of an Acquired Food Intolerance

Milton H. Erickson

Repeated experiences have often demonstrated that hypnotic regression can be used as an effective procedure in the exploration and also therapy of various psychopathological conditions, such as minor disturbances and maladjustments, phobias, amnesias, and even an hysterical depression of psychotic degree (Erickson, 1937, 1939a, 1943c; Erickson & Brickner, 1942; Erickson & Kubie, 1941). By such regression is meant the hypnotic reorientation of the subject to an earlier period of life with a revivification of those patterns of behavior belonging to that period and with an amnesia for all experiences subsequent to the suggested age level.

Usually the utilization of regression constitutes only a single, though perhaps major aspect of the total explorative and therapeutic effort, so that no clear determination can be made of the specific role it had in securing the final results. Nor does the psychotherapeutic situation lend itself readily to a rigid control of variables. In the following case report, however, there was an opportunity to deal with an acute, distressing personality problem by means of a controlled experimental procedure intended to test hypnotic regression as possibly the most significant factor in the handling of that problem. Additionally, the subject was not allowed to become aware of any experimental intentions, nor did she realize that the author was even interested in her problem except at the unsatisfactory superficial level of polite but unwilling attention to her request for therapy. Several instances comparable to the following account, one actually centering about the same food intolerance, have also been observed with similar findings, but none in such full detail as the following example.

Reprinted with permission from *Psychosomatic Medicine,* January, 1943, *5* 67-70.

CASE REPORT

A subject in her early twenties was inordinately fond of orange juice and drank it at every opportunity. One day, because of gastrointestinal distress, she decided to try self-medication and proceeded to take castor oil, first mixing it with orange juice to disguise its taste. Unfortunately this concoction caused acute gastric distress: She became violently nauseated and she vomited repeatedly. Following this she went to bed. The next morning she felt much better and very hungry. She went to the kitchen to get her customary glass of orange juice. Quite unexpectedly she found that the sight, smell, and taste of orange juice caused immediate nausea and vomiting, and she could not drink it.

Instead of making a spontaneous recovery from this acute violent distaste for oranges, she continued to manifest it until it became almost phobic in character. She could not endure the thought of oranges in the refrigerator, and her family had to cease using them. Even the sight of oranges in fruit markets caused her to develop feelings of nausea.

After about a month of such experiences she related the foregoing facts to me and asked how she might "uncondition" herself, and she suggested that hypnosis be used to free her from this problem.

(Additional material making clear the background for the development of such a violent reaction was also revealed to the author. This additional information concerned a highly charged emotional problem which had resolved itself within a few days but without lessening her distaste for orange juice. Since this data bears primarily upon the causative aspects of her difficulty and is not actually relevant to the experimental procedure employed, it will not be reported. Mention of these facts is made so that there can be a ready understanding that an adequate psychological background to account for such violent reactions had existed at the time of the first developments, and still served to maintain her present problem despite the resolution of the original emotional situation.)

In reply to her requests the unhelpful suggestion was offered that it might be better if she were to try to solve her problem entirely through her own efforts. Reluctantly she agreed.

About two weeks later she reported that she had made many efforts to develop control over her reactions by walking past fruit stores, asking her mother to keep oranges and orange juice in the refrigerator, inducing friends to drink orangeade in her presence while she drank lemonade, and even by forcing herself to sip orange juice. All of these efforts, she found, seemed to intensify her tendency to develop nausea and vomiting.

On one occasion I rubbed my fingers well with orange peel and, at a suitable opportunity, held them under her nose. This caused her to develop acute nausea, which, she declared, should force me to believe her story, and she demanded therapeutic hypnotic intervention. Again she was evasively urged to rely upon her own efforts. She consented, but expressed a feeling of resentment over my refusal, pointing out that, on at least three occasions since she had first asked for help from me, I had not hesitated to call upon her to demonstrate hypnosis for my own purposes. Incidentally, in none of these demonstrations was hypnotic regression induced, nor did the subject have access to the records made of those demonstrations, in which only the more common simple hypnotic phenomena were elicited.

Sometime later she reported that she had attended a dinner party at which a salad containing oranges was served. She had immediately pushed the salad aside, but the sight of other guests eating the salad had slowly caused her to develop a nausea that had forced her to leave the table.

About a week later I learned that she had been invited to a social gathering to which I was also invited. Accordingly, I made arrangements with the host, whom I knew intimately, to serve no drinks or refreshments or to allow these to be in evidence until I so indicated. I also suggested that during the course of the social conversation he was to watch his opportunity to introduce the topic of hypnosis and, if the guests seemed interested, to ask that I demonstrate hypnosis. I also told him that, should I hypnotize somebody, he was to wait until the demonstration was well under way and then, at a given signal from me, he was to declare, in his customary jovial way, that I deserved to be rewarded for my efforts with a special drink that he had invented. In preparing this drink he was to bring out on a tray a glass half full of any drink he wished. Also on the tray was to be a half-dozen or more oranges, a sharp knife, two other glasses, and an orange squeezer. This tray was to be placed on a stand which I would arrange to have in front of my chair. He was then to expound to the group that the final touch in preparing this special cocktail was the adding of freshly squeezed juice from chilled oranges directly to the already mixed ingredients and that the proper technique in drinking was to sip it slowly and to keep adding a little orange juice from time to time. Since it was well known that he delighted in mixing drinks, this task was entirely in accord with his rèputation and would not seem to unusual. Additionally he was told that, as he squeezed the oranges, he was to stack the peels neatly on the tray and to fill both of the empty glasses with orange juice.

Because of our close acquaintanceship no explanation of this eccentric request was necessary, and the host readily consented.

After the party was well begun, the topic of hypnosis was raised spontaneously by one of those present and with seeming reluctance I consented to demonstrate hypnosis if somebody would volunteer to be hypnotized. My subject, however, was obviously unwilling to volunteer, possibly because of her previously expressed resentment, even though since that outburst she had consented to another group demonstration. However, some of those present knew that she had been my subject previously, and they soon persuaded her, as was fully expected.

A trance was readily induced and the more common hypnotic phenomena demonstrated. Shortly in accord with a previous arrangement, the request was made by one of the group that I demonstrate "age regression."

This I proceeded to do by carefully and systematically reorienting my subject to a period of two years before. (For a discussion of the techniques and problems involved in securing such reorientation, see Erickson & Kubie, 1941.)

After the subject had been in this "regressed state" about 20 minutes, during which time she had been extensively questioned by the group, I signalled my host. He responded by declaring that my efforts warranted a special reward—namely, a drink he had recently invented. He went to the kitchen and returned with the tray previously described, which he placed upon the stand directly in front of us. He then proceeded with elaborate explanations to get everything in readiness, squeezing out two full glasses of orange juice. Everybody including my subject watched him with much interest. Finally the drink was handed to me with proper instruction for drinking, and I was invited to pass judgment upon it. I approved it, complimented my host upon his ability and continued to sip it slowly, replenishing it from time to time with one of the glasses of orange juice.

While this was going on my subject kept glancing furtively at me and at the second glass of orange juice. Very soon a member of the group protested that she had contributed as much as I had and therefore was fully entitled to a drink too. The host embarrassedly expressed his apologies and immediately offered to get her any drink she wished, naming a variety of choices. She replied that if I did not need the second glass of orange juice, she would greatly prefer that. Immediately our host assured her that he could readily secure more orange juice for me before I could possibly need an additional supply and urged her to take the second glass. She promptly accepted the offer and drank the orange juice with such obvious relish that a second glassful was prepared, which she also drank readily.

For some 15 minutes after the drinking of the orange juice the subject was kept busy by the group, who were still trying to fathom the puzzling psychological problem her "regression" behavior constituted.

Following this she was taken into another room out of range of hearing, and an explanation was given to the group that an experiment had been conducted; that it was most important that the subject not be given any inkling of what had occurred during the trance session; and that it would be most desirable if the members of the group would not discuss the events of the evening among themselves for at least a week. To all of this they agreed.

The subject was then recalled, reoriented while still in the trance state to her current chronological status, and thanked courteously for the work she had done. Then indirect suggestions were given to the effect that after awakening she would have little or no interest in what had occurred while she was in the trance, and that she would have a comprehensive amnesia covering the period of time that she had been in a trance.

She was then awakened, and the host very ably provided adequate distraction at once by serving refreshments, from which oranges in any form were excluded.

During the rest of the evening the subject's behavior was somewhat remarkable. Her facial expression was frequently puzzled and reflective, and she kept rolling her tongue about her mouth and passing it gently over her lips as if she were trying to sense some elusive taste. Nothing further developed.

Several days later she was seen, and she related at once that she had attended a dinner the previous day at which a mixed fruit salad had been served. Her immediate reaction had been one of disgust and nausea, but she determined to overcome this by carefully sorting out the orange and eating the rest of the fruit. When she had done so, she realized that she had unquestionably eaten fruit flavored with orange juice, and this realization had led her to conclude that, in some unknown way, she had "spontaneously unconditioned" herself. This conclusion she had put to test immediately after her return home, and she then discovered that she had regained her original liking for orange juice.

Indirect inquiries disclosed her to have no understanding of the possible genesis of her "unconditioning," and no attempt was made to give her any information. The whole incident was allowed to close with her believing that she had made a spontaneous recovery and that the author had probably been wise in letting her assume the responsibility for her problem.

SUMMARY

The pertinent facts of this case report may be summarized briefly as follows:

1. The patient, a hypnotic subject, was exceedingly fond of orange juice.
2. She had an acute, highly charged emotional problem, which resolved itself in a few days.
3. She developed, while this emotional problem still existed, an acute gastrointestinal disturbance for which she treated herself by taking a dose of castor oil mixed with orange juice.
4. This concoction nauseated her, and she vomited repeatedly.
5. The next day and thereafter the sight, smell, or even thought of oranges caused nausea and vomiting and phobic reactions.
6. After a month of such experiences she sought hypnotic therapy, which was refused, and she was told to try to correct her problem herself.
7. She continued to act as a hypnotic subject, but developed resentment over the continued refusal of hypnotic therapy.
8. At a social gathering she was induced by others to act as a hypnotic subject.
9. During the demonstration hypnotic regression was induced.
10. While in the "regressed state" a prearranged plan culminated in her drinking orange juice.
11. She was reoriented to her current age, comprehensive instructions were given to cause her to develop an amnesia for all trance events, and she was awakened.
12. The subject showed no knowledge of what had happened, but was

observed to roll her tongue about her mouth and to pass it over her lips as if trying to detect some elusive puzzling taste.
13. The next day, in a situation which had previously accentuated her symptomatology, she regained her liking for orange juice. This she reported to the author as a "spontaneous cure," nor did she seem to realize that there might be another explanation.

DISCUSSION

Exactly what occurred to effect a therapeutic result is difficult to define despite the experimental controls employed. The patient's own efforts, the resolution of her other problem, the use of hypnosis itself, the patient's resentment over refusal of therapy, and the effects of a social situation are all ruled out by the procedure as ineffective. The one significant item left of the whole experimental procedure is the hypnotic regression, which permitted the patient to drink the orange juice with that pattern of response belonging to a previous time. Once the orange juice had been swallowed, time was allowed to elapse, and, perhaps unnecessarily, an amnesia for having drunk it was induced. The only significant bit of behavior shown was the patient's attempt to discover subsequently some elusive taste in her mouth. The speculation may be offered that once the orange juice was swallowed, its absorption resulted in various physiological responses not accompanied by her recently acquired emotional reactions. Thus the original pattern of behavior was reinforced sufficiently to permit her to discover successfully that she had "unconditioned" herself. The conclusion seems warranted that the somatic or physiological components of a total psychopathological manifestation can be of great importance.

17. Experimentally Elicited Salivary and Related Responses to Hypnotic Visual Hallucinations Confirmed by Personality Reactions

Milton H. Erickson

Full reliance cannot be placed readily upon the results of experimental studies obtained under conditions in which the subject is aware of what behavior is desired, if such knowledge can possibly aid in manifesting the desired behavior. Especially is this true in experimental hypnotic work, where the transcendence of ordinary waking capacities and the subject's suggestibility and cooperativeness may contribute greatly to a possible vitiation of the experimental findings. In brief, too much care cannot be exercised to insure that the investigative results derive from the experimental situation itself and not from simple cooperation in manifesting behavior in accord with the knowledge of what is expected.

In the following account a report is given of an experimental study in which the subject's initial responses could easily be attributed to an able demonstration of the behavior obviously called for by the situation, and hence their validity is open to question. Fortunately the events immediately subsequent to the discontinuance of the experiment led to the development of an entirely nonexperimental personal situation for the subject, which permitted, on this new basis, a duplication of the apparently significant results of the experimental procedure. Thus there were secured further findings, confirmatory of the experimental data, which derived from personal and social reactions to a general situation and which were expressive of the subject's efforts to satisfy her personality needs rather than to cooperate with experimental objectives. Additionally, these further findings serve to demonstrate effectively the reality for the subject of the original experimental situation, which in itself is a most important consideration in this type of experimentation. Thus, the unplanned and unanticipated developments arising from the experimental procedure served to confirm both the results obtained and the validity of the procedure itself.

Reprinted with permission from *Psychosomatic Medicine*, April, 1943, *5*, 185-187.

CASE REPORT

One evening, during a hypnotic demonstration in the author's home before a group of professionals who had not witnessed hypnosis before, several members of the audience were used as demonstration subjects. One of these was called upon to demonstrate the somnambulistic state, and at the conclusion of her task but while she was still in the trance state she was thanked for her work. A member of the audience remarked humorously that the simple thanks were not enough, that she was entitled to a substantial reward. The author agreed at once and, knowing her great fondness for candy, stated that as a reward she could have first choice from a platter of homemade candy that had been provided for the evening. The subject was then asked what her favorite homemade candy was, and the polite hope was expressed that it was actually included in the varieties that had been prepared. The subject, still in the somnambulistic state, expressed a marked preference for divinity fudge, and even as she spoke she was noted to salivate freely in anticipation. The salivation was observed independently by several of the medically trained persons present. Stepping into the next room as if to check, the author called back with an expression of satisfaction that there was divinity fudge, and she was told that as her reward she could help herself freely. Then she was asked if she wished the candy served at once or later. She replied smilingly, "So far as divinity fudge is concerned, immediately is scarcely soon enough."

She was taken at her word, and without any attempt to awaken her the author stepped into the room bringing napkins and acting as if he were carrying a platter of candy, explaining with social cheerfulness that he hoped for a variety in appetites since there was a variety of homemade candies. Stepping over to the subject, the author told her that in return for her services she was to be served first, and that properly, as her just due, she was to select the largest pieces of divinity fudge.

With the juvenile directness, earnestness, and simplicity so characteristic of behavior in the somnabulistic state, she replied that she would. After scrutinizing the imaginary platter carefully, she made her choice of a piece and, upon urging, a second and a third, but she explained that she was taking only a small piece for the third.

The imaginary platter was then carefully passed to all of the group, each of whom went through the pretense of taking and eating candy. The medically trained members unobtrusively watched the subject, and all agreed upon her increased salivation and were much amused to see her use the napkin on her fingers after eating, an act that the group duplicated.

When all had been served with the imaginary candy, the act of placing the platter on the table, fortunately on the far side of the room, was carried out, and the subject was allowed to continue in the somnambulistic state.

One of the other subjects mentioned that she would like to be hypnotized and induced to do automatic writing, a task in which she was interested but had previously failed.

Accordingly she was rehypnotized, but when an attempt was made to have her write, she explained that she was having difficulty in writing satisfactorily while holding the paper in her lap. Meanwhile the first subject became disinterested in the proceedings and restless and finally reacted to the situation by offering the use of her chair since it had arms which could be used as a support for the paper. Her offer was accepted and she relinquished the chair, but instead of taking another, she began to wander about the room aimlessly, looking at the books in the bookcases, to some extent repeating the somnabulistic behavior previously asked of her. This soon brought her beside the table where the imaginary platter had been placed. Soon she seated herself in the chair which happened to be there. In the meantime two of the medically trained members of the group had been instructed to watch her closely but unobtrusively, since the author was busy with the other subject and wished to be kept informed of her behavior.

Shortly she was observed to look at the table and then to turn hesitantly toward the author, whom she found to be absorbed in his work with the other subject.

After some hesitation and in the manner of a small child who wishes another helping of candy, she kept looking furtively and uncertainly first at the author and then at the imaginary platter. Finally, with a slight gesture of resolution she leaned forward, scrutinized the platter carefully, and proceeded to go through a performance of selecting carefully and eating several pieces of candy, now and then glancing in a hesitant, semiembarrassed fashion toward the author, who continued to be busy. The two medically trained observers agreed independently in their observations when questioned about the validity of her performance, and both emphasized the increased salivation and swallowing the subject manifested. Carefully veiled glances by the author made him aware of what was occurring.

At the conclusion of the automatic writing the author expressed his intention of passing the candy again, suiting action to the word. As it was passed to the first subject, she remarked unnecessarily, "I believe I will, but this time I'll take another kind since I like chocolate fudge too." Again she gave what appeared to be a valid performance of eating candy with proper salivation and deglutition.

Shortly the demonstration was concluded. All subjects were awakened and refreshments were served.

DISCUSSION

Since the subject's physiological responses in the experimental situation presented nothing unusual, discussion will be limited to the significances of the subject's postexperimental spontaneous behavior.

In the initial situation the subject could conceivably have behaved in simple accord with the experimental demands. When, however, the experiment was concluded and the subject had been displaced from her position of central interest for the group, her reactions of disinterest, boredom, restlessness, and possibly jealousy were quite understandable. Thus there could and obviously did arise within her a need for some form of satisfaction, a need which could be satisfied by something possessing reality values for her. Hence the original choice of candy as an hallucinatory reward had been fortunate, since it was in keeping not only with the preceding experimental situation but actually with her well-established habitual practice of keeping a supply of candy available. Consequently, when she found herself beside the table where the hallucinatory candy had been placed, there was then an opportunity for her to satisfy personality needs in a well-accustomed way if that hallucinatory candy possessed any reality values for her. That it did possess such values and was not an experimental pretense was evident from her furtive behavior, her guilt reactions, and her overcompensatory remark about chocolate fudge as well as from her salivation and related behavior. Thus in a significant nonexperimental situation the subject confirmed her experimental behavior.

Additionally, these findings suggest the informativeness of clinical developments from an experimental procedure as a possible technique for indirect experimentation in situations where a subject's knowledge of experimental objectives constitutes an important variable, and, likewise they suggest the desirability of *so devising experimental procedures that they fit the personality structure of the subject.*

18. Control of Physiological Functions by Hypnosis

Milton H. Erickson

My topic for this afternoon is "Control of Physiological Functions by Hypnosis." I am also listed later for "Hypnotic Approaches to Therapy." Actually, I have the feeling that it is rather a difficult separation to make, because in any approach to physiological control one also makes use of therapeutic approaches. I am not therefore going to attempt to make a differentiation or to give you a set lecture on the subject. Both topics involve a question of techniques, and they are both concerned with the adequate functioning of the individual as a personality and his functioning in a desired manner. Therefore the two presentations will be separate but will overlap, although I shall try to place emphasis accordingly.

It must be borne in mind that one's appreciation and understanding of the normal or the usual is requisite for any understanding of the abnormal or the unusual. Just as a knowledge of normal physiology constitutes a background for a knowledge and an understanding of pathological conditions, similarly a knowledge of the approach to an understanding of normal physiology constitutes a means of approaching an understanding of abnormal physiology. Any approach to either must be based upon a knowledge of techniques, perhaps fundamental in character but varying according to the conditions. I want to amplify that. When I say "varying according to the conditions," I mean according to the personality of the individual, the psychological situation *at that particular time,* and the psychological situation of the hypnotist as well as of the patient or the subject. One simply cannot handle those things without having an understanding of all of them at the time.

Since I am a psychiatrist as well as a psychologist—I am primarily engaged in psychiatric practice—I shall rely chiefly upon my experience as a psychiatrist. I am going to try to avoid, as much as possible, any reference to my previous publications. Those are available to you, and it would only be using up your time to keep referring to them, but I shall occasionally make reference.

First I shall consider the matter of physiological functions and the control of

Originally presented at a hypnosis symposium at UCLA Medical School, June 25-27, 1952. Reprinted with permission from *The American Journal of Clinical Hypnosis,* July 1977, *20,* 8–19.

them. I don't think that is a problem that should be taken too lightly. I've seen a person in the laboratory with his hands in the plethysmograph and told in the hypnotic trance, "Make your right hand smaller and your left hand larger," and have seen excellent results in the hypnotic trance because the blood vessels shrank in one hand and dilated in the other. That seems to be an excellent demonstration of the proof of the possibility that hypnotic measures are bringing about physiological changes. When I questioned the subject, however, his statement was, "I can do that without being in a trance." He very neatly and carefully demonstrated it. What was his way of doing it? The man had a very vivid imagination. He thought about holding ice in one hand and getting his arm very, very cold. He thought of the other hand being in warm water. Naturally vasomotor changes took place, and the hypnosis had nothing to do with it.

I've seen subjects who would dilate the pupil of one eye and contract the pupil of the other in hypnotic trance, when looking at the same light. My question, however, is, "Can this be done at will without the presence of the trance state?" I have seen people who were not in a hypnotic trance who could look at a light and dilate one pupil and contract the other. It was a matter of personal, voluntary control of physiological functions.

The anesthesias that you can develop in hypnosis, I have seen occur in the ordinary state. When I was working my way through college, a workman offered to stick pins into his skin with no pain reactions. I had enough knowledge of psychology at the time to know something about pupillary contractions with pain reaction. He would stick the pins through the skin of his legs, through his cheek, and so on for a package of cigarettes; and the chap didn't need hypnosis to do it. I am always therefore exceedingly suspicious.

I remember one carefully controlled experiment in inducing blisters on the arm by a friend of mine in the army. He wrote me that he kept the subject under absolute observation for 24 hours, and the man produced the blister in the area drawn on his arm with a pencil. My first question was "Was he kept under observation for 24 hours?"

"He was."

I was extremely specific about it. How many times a day did the man go to the lavatory? Who went with him, and who watched him? The man had some cigarettes concealed, he lit a cigarette, and he produced his blister, but it wasn't hypnotic in origin; 24-hour observation means 24 hours and four minutes per day to be scientifically accurate.

Another item is the question, How do you define normal physiological reactions? How much do you know about them? How can you decide what is normal and what is induced? I think one of the best tests you can set up is the production of perspiration. Place a subject in a nice cool room and talk with your subject about various topics so that you are sure there is no sign of perspiration. For example, last week one of my patients was commenting on how cool my office was and how comfortable he was. We talked about various subjects, and my purpose in talking to him was to see if I could produce a sudden flow of perspiration. He was comfortable, at ease—decidedly at ease—and we were talking about his home town, whom he knew, and so on. I threw in a casual question about a relative of his wife. Immediately he drew out his handkerchief and started wiping the perspiration. I had obtained the name of the relative of the wife from a letter the wife had written me. The patient wiped his brow and said, "What happened? Has the cooler been turned off? It seems awfully warm."

I said "It's probably some reaction that you've had. Never mind."

We continued discussing and talking about a trip that the relative made. I then commented that I had heard his name mentioned at luncheon that day by Dr. Stafford Ackerley. I mentioned Louisville, Kentucky, and that Dr. Stafford Ackerley lives there. Immediately he started perspiring, and he wondered why. I knew why. His wife's letter had given me the information that informed me why he should perspire at the mere mention of Louisville, Kentucky, and the mention of his wife's relative.

I think that kind of physiological control is much more reliable than when you try to have subjects increase their heartbeat or their blood pressure or something of a similare nature. One of my subjects could increase his pulse rate by ten points if requested to do it. I also found out that he could do it in the ordinary waking state at the request of a friend of mine whom he didn't know was a friend of mine. He could increase it 20 points, within a range of error of one to three points. He could increase his blood pressure, and hypnosis had nothing to do with it. He fantasied walking up a certain hill, and that would raise his pulse rate a certain amount. He could fantasy running up that hill—really fantasy it very vividly—and increase it 20 points. He could raise his blood pressure by a very simple mechanism, that of contracting his abdominal muscles, which you didn't notice ordinarily under his clothes. It was beautifully done, but he himself was not aware that he was doing it.

I placed him in a hospital bed, checked on the increase in blood pressure, and had a nurse check on his abdominal musculature at the time. He thought she was giving him a message, but she was actually checking his muscles. He had a skin condition that made the procedure seem appropriate. He could really raise his blood pressure by the very simple means of contracting his abdominal musculature.

You may know that during insurance examinations patients will become terribly tense, their muscles will tighten up, and as a result their blood pressure goes up. Often after the conclusion of a physical examination blood pressure when taken again will be lower by 20 points or even 40 points because the tension has gone. Any physiological manifestation that you can produce in the ordinary waking state should not be credited to hypnotic suggestion.

I have had subjects who would raise their blood pressure and increase their rate of perspiration by thinking about situations that produce anger. Watching Lester Beck's film this afternoon, I thought about subjects who had made use of a similar situation by recalling deliberately a past traumatic experience that put them in a cold sweat and altered their blood pressure. That isn't hypnotic suggestion; that's normal physiological behavior.

I think the most valid physiological changes—that is, changes in physiological function—are those that are brought about by unconscious processes. I think mentioning Louisville, Kentucky, and this chap named Gene from Alabama was a much more valid measure of producing a physiological change than any direct effort. In fact it is my feeling that in hypnotic research one should resort to indirect method as much as possible to keep the subject from ever cooperating with you intentionally and complacently to give you the desired results.

The following will illustrate the point. A brilliant GI student was failing badly in all courses. One night he leaped downstairs to join a beer party. Two weeks later he came to the Veterans Administration with which I was associated for an examination. He tired much too easily; he was worried about his heart; and examination soon disclosed that he had a "stocking anesthesia," or complete numbness of both feet. I examined his feet and made my own diagnosis: he had fractured bones in both feet. I had another physician check him over, and he also reached the same conclusion. So we looked up the X-ray man and explained to him what we wanted done. I gave this GI student a very nice talk about this skin condition, the swelling of the skin of his feet, and told him that I was going to have the X-ray man give him a skin treatment. The X-ray man was most cooperative, so we obtained an X-ray that verified the fracture of the bones of the feet. But that stocking anesthesia was a very, very important thing. In investigating his past history we found out that he had a personality collapse if he cut his finger or if he nicked himself in shaving. He was practically laid up for a day or so from a razor nick. He was the type of person who just simply collapsed at the slightest physical injury. His discharge from the army was a medical one, based on that, and yet here was a man who had been walking around on badly fractured bones in his feet for two weeks.

Eventually he produced a certain change in himself that enabled him really to attend classes. What I did was to put him in a trance and give him a long, deceptive story about the skin disease and my worry about it, and that the treatment was medicated gauze protected by a cast with iron supports in it so that he could walk around. He attended classes and progressed well. The result was that I accepted that particular physiological condition, didn't try to correct it, but merely gave him a certain type of invalidism from which he didn't have to collapse. He made A's in all of his courses, as he should have done, for he was a brilliant chap.

In discussing the numbness of his feet and the skin condition in the trance state, I gave him an overwhelming urge to want to enjoy it and to preserve it until the medicated gauze had healed it completely, so that as his feet healed and a new sensation in his feet developed, he would not have to drop out of school and become an irascible invalid. Had he been told that he had broken bones, he would have been in bed and thoroughly incapacitated.

Another patient in her thirties with an irregular menstrual cycle presented a similar problem. Each period resulted in daily severe headaches, vomiting, gastrointestinal disturbances, and actual invalidism for five days; no invalidism the first day and no invalidism the last day. She wanted medical help, but she did not want psychotherapy. However, she consented to go into a trance to please me. I was perfectly willing to be pleased. A deep trance was induced in her, and she was instructed that on any Saturday night she chose she would have a dream in which she would telescope time. In the dream she would experience a whole week's menstrual invalidism; that is, the dream would seem to last five whole days. She would be invalided, she would dream that she was vomiting, having diarrhea, cramps, and everything else that went with her past history; but that she would sleep soundly and wake up the next morning rested, refreshed, and energetic. Moreover, she would awake with an amnesia for the dream experience, and the dream experience itself would result in a satisfactory menstrual period later.

Two weeks later she was surprised to find herself menstruating without any difficulty, without an invalidism, with no pain, no discomfort. She came to me and asked me what I had done, what had happened. She had had a lifelong experience of having painful menstruation, and here she was feeling like a queen—perfectly comfortable, perfectly at ease. Why didn't she have cramps? What was wrong? In the trance state she knew exactly what I had done, but consciously she had no awareness whatsoever of it. Since then, and that was several years ago, she has had no painful menstrual periods whatsoever. Everything has gone along perfectly all right. She is regular in her menstruation and has no pain, no discomfort, no distress. I think that she can readily come under the heading of controlled physiological functioning. The measure was indirect, but the history certainly warrants the belief that if I hadn't done that sort of thing, she would have continued to have painful menstrual periods.

Our third example is that of a normal 18-year-old girl who had not shown any evidence of breast development. She was very much distressed. Her father was a physician, and when she was 12 years old he had loaded her up with every kind of hormone imaginable. No breast development of any sort occurred. This was continued for three more years but was then terminated. At 18 she was making an extremely schizoid adjustment, withdrawing completely. She has an extremely disagreeable, unpleasant mother whom she hated thoroughly. Her doctor-father brought her to me and asked "What can you do to keep my daughter from becoming schizophrenic?"

It took about an hour to get the girl to tell me that she didn't have any breast development whatsoever. She did agree, however, to go into a trance. So I spent another couple of hours putting her into a trance, very cautiously and very indirectly, until she was in a deep trance. While she was in that deep trance, I explained to her how ignorant a man is about what a breast feels like; that he can't have any idea how it feels to grow a breast; that he can't know what a breast feels like during the menstrual period; that he cannot know what a woman's nipple feels like during menstruation. I spent a great deal of time stating very repetitiously that since she was a girl somehow or other she must have the right nerves, the right blood vessels. I showed her pictures of anatomy showing the difference between the vascular distribution of the chest of the male and the female, and explained that she did have the background for breast development. I told her what I wanted from her was a complete amnesia for everything I had said to her in the trance state; but when she was alone in the privacy of her room, especially at night, where her mother would not annoy her—because her mother was very rigid about sleeping in a certain part of the house—she would some way, somehow, get a tremendous surging feeling in the breast area; that some way, somehow, the rudimentary nipples would feel warm, and that she would have the feeling that something was happening. I told her very honestly I didn't know what that feeling was, but that she could find out, and that she would do that and that she would get that tremendous surging feeling, growing feeling—whatever it was—and drift off to sleep very comfortably.

Another thing I added to that was to show her how I put my hand on my shoulder, and then point out that when a woman does it she does not touch her shoulder with her arm in direct contact with her chest but raises it with her elbow slightly about the breast area as she puts her hand to her shoulder. I told her that she would have a tremendous unconscious need to put her hand on her shoulder in that fashion, but she wouldn't be aware of it. Sometime during the course of the day or perhaps the evening, if she happened to get a mosquito bite on her shoulder or an itch, she would unconsciously raise her elbow, and within the course of the next few weeks she would have the thorough conviction that she was growing breasts—really growing breasts.

I saw her once a week. Usually we talked it over and usually I put her in a trance and said "We've discussed this matter before. I'm just reminding you that we have discussed it. Why should we talk about it any more? I just want you to know that we've really discussed it, and that you're really going to try out all my instructions—even though I don't know what I've instructed you to do."

I saw her once a week for two months, at the end of which time she had very well-developed breasts. In the trance state she told me she had them and wanted to know if I wished to examine them to see if they were real. I told her no, it wasn't necessary, that she would do all of that examining and that she could be much more critical of them than I would be; that they belonged to her and that she should reserve to herself the right to criticize her breasts.

I ceased seeing her at the end of two months, but three months later she came back and said "Dr. Erickson, I came to see you quite a while ago. I was awfully withdrawn. I liked to sit in corners and hide behind the piano, and I avoided company. I just wanted to report to you that I don't do that any more. I'm dating regularly."

Her father, the medical man, came to me and asked "What hormones did you use?"

I told him I was a variation of a Christian Scientist, that I healed from a distance.

What did I do to that girl? I think that I brought about a change in physiological functioning. I certainly produced tremendous changes in her. She has well-developed breasts, she is very proud of herself, her schizoid state has been corrected, and I have her father's statement that he himself has examined those breasts and that they are perfectly good breasts. Moreover I have the word of a number of young men who said they would *really* like to examine the breasts.

How great a part did raising the elbow play in it? How much did the idea of a surging feeling in the chest wall have to do with it? There's nothing more vague, really. Yet she had had hormone therapy, discontinued several years before; she had menstruated regularly since the age of 13. She just hadn't developed breasts. Yet in two months' time, I think it is reasonable to assume, my suggestion brought about in her a control of physiological functioning.

Another case that I want to cite concerns a young man who had married an exceedingly attractive girl. His weight was 170 pounds. Nine months later he came in to see me weighing 120 pounds. He said he couldn't stand it any longer and wanted to have a psychiatric interview. His story was very simple. It was to this effect: "Every time I try to consummate my marriage my bride goes into a hysterical panic. It's just driving me crazy, and I can't take it much longer. I lie awake nights wondering how to please her. Every night she promises me, and every night she throws a hysterical panic."

I told him to bring his wife in to see me and to have her bring every bit of information that she could about her menstrual cycle. The astonishing thing was that she had started to menstruate at the age of 11 and that she had kept a diary all those years. She was 19 at the time. She menstruated regularly every 33rd day, according to that diary. Usually she began to menstruate between 10:00 and 11:00 A.M. When I looked through her diary, I began to wonder about her personality and to understand more about her panic reactions. I understood how she must have felt when her husband wanted to consummate the marriage. She had a seven-day period.

I had an interview with her husband, and then I had an interview with her in which I made a rather serious mistake. I discussed sex relations with her and I laid down the law to her thoroughly. Both of them were seen together, and they were instructed to consummate the marriage that night as soon as they got home. It was seventeen days before the next period. They lived two miles from my office. Halfway home she started to menstruate.

That kind of reaction medically is not too uncommon. An unexpected early menstruation to avoid consummation of marriage, or the failure of menstruation because of desired pregnancy, takes place fairly often. However, this girl with a long history, verified by her diary that she had kept, had her menstrual period that night about 8:00 P.M., seventeen days ahead of time.

She had a normal period, and when she came back at the end of the period, I apologized very greatly for my error, my mistake, my failure really to understand. I was right in that, because I had failed to understand. I told her that she and her husband should consummate their marriage, that they should do it on

Saturday night, or Sunday night, or Monday, or Tuesday, or Wednesday, or Thursday—I would prefer *Friday,* or Saturday, or Sunday, or Monday; but I would prefer *Friday.* I repeated that several times, just to drive home a point that she couldn't possibly recognize.

Of course, nothing happened Saturday night, or Sunday night, or Monday night, or Tuesday night, or Wednesday night. Thursday is very close to Friday night, and she had already demonstrated that I couldn't dictate anything to her. When I said I preferred Friday, and it was Wednesday night and nothing happened, she had no choice because I already mentioned Saturday and Sunday too.

They consummated the marriage; they have two nice children, and they are happily married now. Her husband reported that since nothing happened Saturday, Monday, Tuesday, Wednesday—that he was beginning to get sick of me and thought that he should see some other psychiatrist who might be some good. However, on Thursday night he was taken by surprise.

One could make various ribald comments here, but it led to a happy marriage, regular sex relations, and the enjoyment of sex relations. She had taken the initiative, and she had placed so much emphasis upon sex since the age of 11 that she had kept a monthly diary of her menstrual period. So again I think I interfered with, or altered, or changed physiological functioning.

I want to stress the emphasis that I placed upon *my* preference for Friday. I had no right to express any preference whatsoever. I think that in hypnotherapy and in experimental work with subjects you have no right to express a preference; it is a cooperative venture of some sort, and the personality of the subject or the patient is the thing of primary importance. What hypnotists or therapists think, or do, or feel is not the important thing; but what can they do to enable the subject or the patient to accomplish certain things is important. It's the personality involved and the willingness of the therapist or the hypnotist to let the subject's personality play a significant role.

Another area of control of physiological functioning concerns the knee-jerk. A lot of people can inhibit the knee-jerk—that we know physiologically—and can do a perfectly beautiful job of it. A naive person who has never studied physiology can control the knee-jerk so that it is not exhibited. However, there's one thing the naive person doesn't know, and that is the item of summation of nerve impulses. I remember a patient of mine to whom I had given anesthesia of the legs! I brought in a professor of physiology to see him because he couldn't walk. The physiologist said that the knee-jerk is a spinal reflex, and you cannot interfere with it. A very careful examination was made and checked by another professor of physiology. The knee-jerk was tested. There was no contraction of the muscles, no apparent inhibition. Then the physiologist said, "Well, apparently there is an inhibition of nerve impulses. There's one other test that should be tried." He tried the phenomenon of summation.

If he timed the blows correctly, 13 or 14 rapid, properly timed blows resulted in a kick; otherwise there was no knee-jerk. In other words the synapses had been separated in some way so that anesthesia was present. I know that Sears has done his work on anesthesia and the psychogalvanometer. What do you do to test anesthesia or a functional loss at a psychological level? You want to produce psychological deafness that's real, so you render a subject hypnotically deaf. But the test isn't the fact that subjects show you that they're deaf and don't hear anything. Do they make any responses to sound that are unexpected? For example, you can ride on a bus, and as you look at the people sitting in the seats ahead of you, you notice that so-and-so doesn't turn his head at the honk of a horn. Why? You notice further that he still doesn't turn his head at the sound of another car horn. You begin to question his ability to hear.

In psychological deafness hypnotically induced I think one of the neatest and meanest trick of all is to render somebody hypnotically deaf and then tell him a whole series of riddles, stories, hokes; and when the hand is palm up, he hears, and when the palm is down, he can't hear.

I've done that with cases of psychological deafness. I've given them a series of 500 articles, palm up and palm down, and if you try to sort them out in your memory, you find it almost impossible. When you test the subjects indirectly for the items you said when your palm was up and for those you said when your palm was down, they remember the items when your palm was up, but they can't remember those said when your palm was down. Think how very, very difficult it would be for any one of you, listening to several people sitting here conversing, later to be asked what was said in that conversation and who said it. It would be very confusing. Your hypnotically deaf person can actually do that. Selective deafness? Yes. Is it because they select out the things that they are not going to hear, or is it that their hearing depends upon certain other things?

I think one of the best examples I can give of that is my son Robert a couple of years ago. We served a new dish at the table. He took a mouthful, tasted it, was uncertain. He closed his eyes and took another mouthful. He was still uncertain. He held his nose and took another mouthful. He tasted it; then he sat down on the floor and tasted it. It was good, just as he'd suspected in the first place, but he wasn't sure of it. In psychological deafness hypnotically induced how many other things enter into hearing? When a speaker speaks in a low tone of voice, what is the tendency but to close the eyes and listen so as not to be distracted. What does hypnotic deafness do but interfere with certain other functions that interfere with the hearing process?

Another item in the array of physiological controls is the matter of delayed menstruation. One week I had two cases come in to me of delayed menstruation. The patients were frightfully worried about it, terribly distressed, and they wanted to be certain that everything was all right. Hypnotically, what did I do? I avoided the question entirely, and I think I should have because I wanted to relieve the minds of those two women. I suggested to them that it would be very, very nice if they went on a swimming party next Saturday, and I built up that swimming party into a gala event, a wonderful experience. I did everything

I could to drag together all of their childhood happy memories about going swimming, all the happy times they ever had swimming. Then I suggested that they would definitely go to a certain swimming pool in Phoenix, go swimming, and recapture all the joys of their childhood, girlhood, and young womanhood that they ever knew when they went swimming. After I had built that up very, very carefully, I put into their minds the fear that they might menstruate that night.

That may have been a mean trick, but what was my problem? It was to correct a rather serious fear. The result was that both girls menstruated before Saturday night. They missed the swimming experience.

Another technique I have used in that same measure: A girl or a woman comes to me and says she's missed her period. She's never done it before in her life, and she's very worried. You get her menstrual history and find she was always regular as clockwork, and you raise the question, "Have you got a Kotex with you? Would you mind going and putting it on—just in case?" Then you have her sit down in the office, and you have her explain to you in detail all the sensations she ever has had about menstruating. She'll tell you how her breasts feel, how the nipples feel, about the ache in her shoulders, the congestion in her back—innumerable things peculiar to the individual. I have had more than one woman start menstruating in the office! Why? Because I had built up that picture of what menstrual feelings really were so strongly that her body had to respond in that particular way.

Now I want to cite another case, that of a young man 30 years old. He came to me as a patient, and he didn't want to be my patient because he didn't want it known or even suspected that he was going to a psychiatrist. In his work he had to enter a certain tall building and had to take the elevator up to the seventh floor. It was a rapidly moving elevator; friends of his got on that elevator. He usually fainted when he entered the building, or he fainted in front of the elevator, or when he got into the elevator he fainted. It was a very distressing thing, and he didn't like it. Could I do something about it? What I did was very simple. He was an excellent hypnotic subject, and I agreed that I wouldn't be a psychiatrist but just an ordinary hypnotist. I put him in a trance, and in the trance state I asked him to describe to me not the feeling of the elevator going up but the feelings he had when the elevator came down. He never fainted, his history disclosed, when the elevator came down—he was so relieved and so thankful that he was going to get out of that building. So he described it to me over and over again, the somatic sensations that he experienced going down. I told him that the next time he entered that building it would be impossible for him to think of anything except the peculiar, pleasant, comfortable feeling of going down in an elevator. He hasn't fainted since. Why should he?

The cause of his fainting, I have since learned—because he finally decided it would be perfectly all right to be the patient of a psychiatrist—was a conflict in his home.

I do not know whether you would put fainting under the heading of controlled physiological functions, but I think it belongs there because it is a failure of function in a certain sense of the word.

Not long ago a dentist called me up and said that he was really distressed. He had hired the perfect assistant—and I think when a dentist finds a perfect assistant he has found something. She had one fault. Every time she saw a bloody tooth she fell flat on her face in a faint, and he became tired of picking her up off the floor and reviving her. His question was "Can you do something about the girl?" I told him I was perfectly willing to try.

The girl came to my office and said, "You're a psychiatrist and you're a hypnotist. I want it distinctly understood that I don't want psychiatric treatment. I want hypnotic treatment, and I want to get control of myself so that I don't fall down flat on my face every time I see a bloody dish or a bloody tooth or something of that kind. Several times I've had a nosebleed as a result, and fainted again."

What did I do for the girl? The treatment I used should be described in my next lecture because it concerns a technique, a therapeutic approach. I merely had the girl describe her problem and then told her to go into a deep trance. She went into a very nice deep somnambulistic trance. I told her that I was tired, and would she mind if I smoked a cigarette. She agreeably told me to go ahead and smoke. I told her while I was smoking the cigarette that I wanted her to review everything that was traumatic or connected with blood or fear of fainting, and to review it in her mind, and to review it without having any awareness of what she was reviewing. It was just to flash through her mind like a thought flashes through your mind. You see a person on the street and the thought flashes, "I know that person," or "Wait a minute. What was that I was going to say?" She was to have that same sort of reaction. She agreed that she would do that. So for the next 20 seconds I smoked a cigarette and let her do that. I awakened her and we chatted about the dentist, Phoenix in general, this and that, and then I told her my bill.

"Well," she said, "you haven't done anything for me. Don't you think that's pretty steep?"

I agreed with her that it was. Well, then, I *should* have done something for her. There was no question about it: if I charged a fee like that, I *should have done something for her*. We went round and round on that point. I really *should* have done something for her. Of course, the girl didn't realize that was in itself a posthypnotic suggestion. She left the office rather discontentedly. She hasn't fainted since.

The next morning the dentist handed her a tray full of teeth—she took it, dumped out the teeth, washed out the tray, brought it back to him, and she said "Why I didn't faint! What's the matter with me?"

He said "I don't know, but that's right."

Now what did I accomplish there? Physiologically speaking, in a very short period of time, which I shall take up in my next lecture, I induced a rapid process of thinking concerning blood, trauma, injuries—all those things had passed through her mind while apparently I was smoking. I interrupted that and just emphasized that my fee indicated that I *should* have done something for her. And that was the thing that really convinced her. *I should have!* She walked out in about 10 minutes' time. Nine minutes, about, were spent in inducing the deep trance, then about 10 to 20 seconds in letting her review distressing times, then awakening her and emphasizing by my fee that I should have done something for her. What could the girl do except alter her vasomotor behavior? How I did it, I don't know. Neither does she. We're all very ignorant on that subject.

One of the things in physiological control in which I am tremendously interested is unilateral visual changes and unilateral auditory changes. I haven't done any of that yet; I haven't had the apparatus. I think that would be one of the most interesting and the most startling things that could be done. Using a stethoscope, one side of which has been plugged up but the patient doesn't know it, you could really "go to town on him" in hypnotic deafness in one ear. At the University of Michigan they have an apparatus that I was going to use in which, by the use of mirrors, you can look through and see what you thought you saw with your right eye you were really seeing with your left eye. That would be a wonderful thing to do, and I hope that some day somebody is going to do that. In that sort of experimentation, just to try to induce blindness by telling a subject, "You're getting blinder by the moment"—I don't think that that is the right way of proceeding because it isn't quite fair.

To produce physiological changes one ought to go about it with the realization that those physiological changes occur in the total body and in relationship to the total psychological picture that exists at the time. I don't like to tell a person that he is becoming blind, that he's not going to be able to see, because he too easily and too readily cooperates with me. I'm not going to get a valid picture until a person becomes deaf and can cooperate with me and simply ignore sounds. What I try to do is to build up the picture first. How does a deaf man sit in a chair? Just how? We go into that in great detail, because a deaf man sits differently than one who is in full control of his hearing. You very carefully build up that certain muscular rigidity, that certain lack of response to extraneous sounds. You build that up and built it up, and then you call attention to the fact that certain sounds that are close by, you hear with a certain quality, and sounds more distant you hear with another quality, and sounds remote you hear with still another quality. You get that idea across to them very carefully until they begin to appreciate that deafness isn't just a closing down, but is a matter of circumscribing, circumscribing, bit by bit, until finally the subject begins to look at your face and study your lips.

"You spoke, didn't you? I didn't quite hear you. Do you mind speaking louder?"

You take a deep breath and speak a little bit softer. He looks at you again. "You'll have to speak louder." You merely shift your position, your attitude, and you lean forward. The first thing the subject knows, he is convinced, and he starts leaning forward, and he starts cupping his ear. Why shouldn't he? You want psychological deafness and you want it to be very genuine.

Similarly with blindness, you use the same technique. The direct technique I don't think is very satisfactory, because the subject can fake it so well. What you want to do is give the idea with every action that the light is poor or failing . . . "Will you look please? Because it's come back on again." Just give that suggestion by your total behavior. You test out the switch on the wall to see if the light is really on. You go through all manner of suggestive behavior. You then raise the question "how would you act if you were blind?" What sort of groping movement, for example, should I make if I were blind and reaching for this notebook? I can't do it very well because I'm not blind. I'd have to learn. Serious-minded subjects will take that as a very definite project, and the first thing they know they have built up a generalized pattern of behavior. How much do your arm movements, your foot movements, your shoulder movements, your head posture, the way you bend your neck enter into your vision, your hearing, your speech?

For example, suppose you are walking behind somebody who has on a brand-new suit. You don't know who it is until he starts talking to somebody in front of him. You recognize the characteristic head movements. You know who it is, not because you heard the voice, but because you unwittingly recognized the characteristic head movements which in the past you learned to relate to that person but never differentiated from his voice.

We use soundproof rooms for that sort of thing. I know at Menninger's Clinic they use soundproof rooms, and that question came up while I was instructing there. They brought in a number of people that I knew, differently dressed, and had cautioned these people to keep their hands beside them. Their heads were very carefully draped, very tightly draped, so that I couldn't even see the color of their hair, or get a look at a profile, or anything of that sort. I had them start talking. All I did was watch for characteristic head movements while they talked, and I identified the people in my soundproof room.

In the control of physiological functioning I think it is tremendously important to pay attention to all of the little things that enter into physiological functioning. Consider the idea that speech comes from the mouth. It doesn't come just from the mouth: the neck is involved, respiration is involved, the shoulder movements are involved, and the tension of the hands is involved. Everything is involved. Once you start that pattern, you can learn a great deal about it. But to isolate it, as so many psychologists do, as a single unitary thing, I think is wrong experimentally; because you're dealing with a human being who is a physical creature and a psychological creature who is a personality responding to you and to the room in which you are. Lecturing in a totally dark room is one thing. Lecturing in a room with windows is an entirely different thing. Your behavior is going to be entirely different, no matter how interested you are in giving the lecture to the group. Hence when I try to induce physiological changes, I try to start at the beginning; that is, as far as I personally can understand the beginning of those things. I try to build it up, to build it up in such a general fashion that my subjects or my patients can translate it into their own experiential life.

19. The Hypnotic Alteration of Blood Flow: An Experiment Comparing Waking and Hypnotic Responsiveness

Milton H. Erickson

In medicine, dentistry, or psychology, the primary purpose served in the experimental and clinical use of hypnosis is the communication of ideas and understandings for the purpose of eliciting responsive behavior at both psychological and physiological levels. This responsive behavior differs significantly from seemingly comparable behavior elicited in the ordinary waking state. This difference between hypnotic and waking responsive behavior derives from the actual but easily overlooked dissimilarity between their reality backgrounds and the purposes to be served by them.

In waking responsiveness, the experiential background of learning and conditioning has been one of receiving ideas and understandings out of a *total reality situation* and reacting by placing on the responsive behavior a meaningful significance which, in turn, is to be integrated into the reality situation.

Hypnotic responsiveness is, however, of quite another character. The reality situation in which the hypnosis occurs is, in itself, essentially an *"extrapolated reality"* sometimes deriving only from experiential processes within the subject and having little or no relationship to objective reality. Additionally, this hypnotic reality situation is limited by and restricted to the subject's understandings of what is required in the hypnotic situation with an exclusion of, or unresponsiveness to, objective realities that may be regarded as irrelevant, coincidental, or merely concomitant.

Of even greater significance in differentiating between waking and hypnotic responsiveness is the nature of the purposes and goals achieved. Waking responsiveness tends to be goal-directed towards an integration with objective reality in some form, while hypnotic responsiveness tends to be its own goal, complete in itself and without need for integration into objective reality. For example, the instruction in the ordinary waking state to blush and then to feel cold and develop "goose-flesh" would be most likely to elicit responses only indirectly related to the behavior sought. The same instructions to the same

Unpublished paper presented at the American Society of Clinical Hypnosis Annual Meeting, 1958.

person in a profound trance, however, could easily elicit the requested behavior.

AN EXPERIMENTAL APPROACH

To illustrate from actual laboratory experimentation, the following is cited:

Seven college students—two women and five men—were employed as experimental subjects. One of the women and three of the men were somnambulistic hypnotic subjects. The other three were unacquainted with hypnosis, but after the first experimental procedure they were also trained to develop profound hypnotic trances.

The entire experiment was conducted separately with each student. The first step involved introducing the subjects to a colleague inexperienced in hypnosis who in turn induced each of them to act as a subject for a physiology experiment involving the simultaneous use of a plethysmograph upon each hand. They were unfamiliar with the apparatus, were given no understanding of the experiment, and the volumetric recordings made were outside their visual range. Once the apparatus was functioning, the subjects were instructed simply: "For five minutes, in silence, you are to watch that clock and, while doing so, you are to make your right hand cold and your left hand hot. Then for another five minutes, you will reverse the procedure by making the right hand hot and the left hand cold."

RESULTS

1. Waking State with No Trance Training

The volumetric recordings obtained disclosed no instance of significant changes. The subjects had shown only puzzled interest.

2. Hypnotic State

The next procedure that followed the hypnotic training of the three originally hypnotically untrained subjects was merely a repetition of the first procedure. This time, however, each subject was in a profound somnambulistic trance with instructions to be able to hear and understand the colleague. The volumetric recordings obtained this time, for all seven subjects, were in accord with vascular dilation and contraction in direct correlation to the instructions given them. The subjects were awakened from the trance state and dismissed with an amnesia for the events of the experiment.

3. Waking State After Trance Training

The third procedure was conducted in the waking state and was a repetition of the first procedure. Significant volumetric recordings were obtained from four of the subjects, but it was also noted that they had developed spontaneous trances. When questioned about this, they explained that the task was "impossible when awake" and hence they had resorted to a trance state in order to obey instructions.

4. Awake State with Dissociated Arms

The fourth procedure was similar to the first except that the colleague urged them to avoid falling asleep. Two subjects positively produced significant volumetric records and, when questioned, explained that they had followed instructions by "carefully keeping awake while just my arms went asleep". In this way they felt that they had obeyed both the instructions to stay awake and the instructions about their hands.

5. Autohypnosis After Trance Training

The final procedure was to explain the experiment to the subjects and to suggest that they investigate their own abilities. They soon demonstrated their ready abilities to bring about volumetric changes in their hands if they first developed trances. When questioned about how they accomplished these results, they explained with varying degrees of clarity how they withdrew from objective reality and created out of their memories and ideas an "experiential reality" that "resulted" in their hands becoming either hot or cold.

DISCUSSION

Similar experimental findings have been reported over the years, so that these results constitute no new or special development. Judging from these and other experimental findings, as well as from a much greater wealth of clinical observations, the hypnotic state is conducive to a responsive functioning by the person in direct accord with, and relationship to, the stimulus itself. In the ordinary waking state, however, it appears that the responsive functioning occurs in relationship to the stimulus as emerging from, and constituting only a part of, a much greater and seemingly more significant reality background.

For example, the experimental subjects as described in the third and fourth procedures "withdrew" from the reality of the physiology laboratory and its setting. Then, out of their own past experiential learnings and conditionings, they "created a reality" that permitted a responsive functioning in accord with the demands of the experiment. Even against a background of actual physiological achievement they still resorted to the establishment of an "experiential reality" as opposed to objective reality in order to accomplish their tasks.

In other words, the hypnotic state derives from, or results in, an attentiveness and a receptiveness to ideas and understandings as well as a readiness to function responsively to the ideas themselves without a need to establish them as stimuli emerging from and constituting a part of the existing objective reality external to the self. As a result, the reality or validity of ideas and suggestions in hypnosis which act as stimuli to elicit responses based upon experiential learnings transcends in importance and significance the irrelevant, coincidental, or concomitant aspects of objective reality.

20. A Clinical Experimental Approach to Psychogenic Infertility [1]

Milton H. Erickson

I will present today a clinical experimental approach to psychogenic infertility that evolved out of many years of clinical and experimental observations. I will first outline these clinical and experimental observations and then describe my therapeutic program dealing with psychogenic infertility and my results with 20 cases.

CLINICAL OBSERVATIONS

A clinical observation that has been repeatedly discussed in the literature is the not unusual occurrence of a pregnancy following the adoption of a child after a long period of infertility. In those instances with which this writer is acquainted, the mothers' general attitudes and behavior before the adoption of a child were characterized by marked tension and anxiety related to the fear of infertility. Their descriptions of their sexual behavior also emphasized marked physical tension and anxiety. Following the adoption of a child, especially an infant in arms, there usually occurred in the mothers a marked decrease in tension and anxiety with the emergence of a definitely increased state of physical relaxation. This general improvement was also found to extend into the sexual sphere.

EXPERIMENTAL OBSERVATIONS

All of you are aware of the fact that you can suggest to a patient in the trance state that he is cold, and you can get evidence that he is cold. You can suggest that he is warm, and get evidence that he is warm. You can suggest that he have a muscle spasm, that he have a muscle paralysis; you are aware that you can induce gastrointestinal activity; that you can alter the flow of urine; that you can alter the flow of blood; that you can do any number of

[1]Edited from a presentation made at the American Society of Clinical Hypnosis Annual Meeting, October 4, 1958.

things in altering the physiological behavior of the individual. You can make him hungry; you can make him satiated without the benefit of food. You know that the dentist can decrease the capillary flow. The preceeding speaker spoke of the decreased flow of blood in the Caeserian operation. In experimental work you can demonstrate with the use of plethysmograph the volumetric changes in blood flow that take place when you ask a subject to make his right hand hot and his left hand cold, and vice versa.[2]

From the background of the above clinical and experimental observations, and the general knowledge available on the interrelationships between tension and anxiety states and spastic reactions, a clinical experimental procedure was devised as a possible therapeutic approach to selected cases of infertility. Briefly, my basic hypothesis was that the anxiety and tension these infertile women experienced could be manifested as tubal spasms that interfered with the normal transport of the ovum to the uterus; this was the psychosomatic basis of their infertility. My therapeutic approach to their problem was to place these women on a program of hypnotic training designed to increase muscular relaxation and blood flow so that their hypothesized tubal spasms would be reduced.

Clinical Subjects

Twenty patients were referred to me over a number of years because of infertility. All these patients had been infertile for at least four years, one for fifteen years, another for twelve years (see Table 1). All of these patients had anxiety and tension, fear, distress, and unhappiness. Some of them had been operated on to see if there was anything wrong with their ovaries. They had undergone various medical regimens. They'd been recommended to psychiatrists for psychotherapy, but they didn't want pschotherapy—they wanted a baby.

On the whole these patients, both the successes and the failures, were a homogeneous group. They all complained of being "nervous," "anxious," "worried," "tense," "frustrated," "hopeless," "easily upset," "tired," unable to relax or to sleep well, easily reduced to tears, and always feeling that "things are just too much, too overwhelming." All were either definitely overweight or underweight. Their general health, however, despite complaints, was fairly good.

Of the total group, the two oldest patients, both successful, and three of the other women, were married to men who had fathered children in previous marriages. Three of the successes and four of the others had borne a single child, conceived during the first year of marriage, and followed by periods of infertility

---

[2]See previous paper, "The hypnotic alteration of blood flow: An experiment comparing waking and hypnotic responsiveness."

ranging from four to eight years. A few had practiced contraception during the first year of marriage only.

METHOD

The actual methodology employed with these patients is difficult to describe since it was based upon the presentation of ideas, the establishment of good interpersonal relationships and the use of hypnosis to facilitate and ensure adequate responses. Also, each patient was handled separately, and the duration and rapidity of therapy varied from one patient to the next, as did the exact order of procedure. The preliminary step in each case, however, was the same: A slow, carefully worded explanation was offered to each of them; much of their previous medical treatment served to give weight to the ideas presented. To each patient it was emphasized that the failure of conception might derive from tension, particularly muscular, from spasms, particularly tubal, and from faulty blood circulation that in turn would result from the spasms and muscular tension. Because of these significant possibilities, it was proposed that we employ hypnosis as a special aid in dealing with these psychosomatic manifestations. The purpose of this explanation was not a presentation of established scientific facts, but merely a communication of ideas in general to elicit patient cooperation.

The procedure with each patient was as follows:
1. Hypnotic training resulting in trances which varied from light to medium and deep. Sometimes, only a utilization of hypnotic fixation of attention was required to induce trance.
2. A reorientation of the patient concerning the purposes of therapy. They had all been referred for psychotherapy because of tension, anxiety, nervousness, and general maladjustment. The explanation was given carefully and slowly that their need for psychotherapy was a secondary need, that their primary need was maternal satisfaction, and only in the event of absolute failure in this regard would they need psychotherapy.
3. The reaching of an agreement with each of them to the effect that an earnest experimental procedure would be employed with them in an effort to meet their primary needs.
4. A systematic hypnotic training in which each woman was taught what was described as "basic, easy, tensionless physiological functioning ordinarily learned spontaneously but, in your case, requiring special effort and instruction."
5. A systematic progression from commonly known physiological manifestations related to altered blood flow such as blushing to a postulation and suggestion of less familiar but comparable manifestations of altered blood flow and blushing in different parts of the body, particularly the pelvic area.

HYPNOTIC TRAINING

The actual initiation of hypnotic training was essentially the same for each patient. Since they all complained of tension and fatigue, the "beginning step" was to teach them simple relaxation by employing an hypnotic technique of body relaxation. Once this had been learned and their interest well enlisted, the experimental procedure was developed in the following steps, each one being repeated again and again if necessary to meet the patient's learning needs:

1. Relaxation of entire body with feeling of restfulness and comfort.
2. Transformation of that feeling of comfortable relaxation into one of physical heaviness, sluggishness, inertia, and "utter tiredness."
3. Restoration of feeling of comfort and relaxation.
4. Teaching the "partitioning of the body," i.e., simultaneously, "right leg comfortably relaxed," "left leg painfully tired, heavy, sluggish and inert;" "right arm feeling normal," "left arm rested and full of energy."
5. Teaching of rigidities, i.e., simultaneously "right arm stiff and rigid as an iron bar," "left arm relaxed and comfortable;" "left leg fixed and rigid and immoveable," and "right leg at ease and comfortable and mobile."

The above training was relatively easily accomplished. Depending upon the patients' capacities to learn, the procedures were repeated until they seemed to comprehend adequately. However, the next step in the hypnotic training was more difficult. Their capacities for visual, auditory, and tactile imagery were tested and appropriate suggestions were offered to each patient, according to individual abilities, to experience vividly a sense of coldness and "goose bumps," of warmth, hotness, and perspiration, of blushing, shame, and embarrassment, of sunburn, hotness, and pain, of the roughness of sandpaper, and of rasping.

When all of this seemed to have been learned adequately as a general phenomenon, the patients were asked to learn it in the same "partitioned" manner as the relaxation had been learned. Thus, each patient was systematically taught: "Right hand cold, left foot hot, face warm, hands cold, face blushing, body cold, right breast cold, left breast warm, all embarrassed and all cold, all happy and all warm, all embarrassed and all warm," until the patient was ready to accept and act upon any experiential suggestion given.

The patients were then finally allowed to extend whatever manifestations of heightened blood flow they could experience to the pelvic area. Thus some learned to experience warmth, hotness and perspiration in their pelvises while others experienced blushing, embarrassment and sensual warmth. In the next section I will describe in more detail the experiences of Anne as a typical case illustrating the above process.

RESULTS AND CASE STUDY

Table 1 summarizes the pertinent data on the successful patients.

In summary, of the twenty infertile women with whom I worked, the ten who stayed with me all became pregnant within a range of two to thirteen months. Ten of those twenty women had children. Of the ten that did not become pregnant the longest I treated any one of them was five months. These unsuccessful cases terminated their work with me because they became discouraged that hypnotic therapy didn't seem to be working fast enough. They wanted their pregnancies too soon—often expecting success within the first month. The following case study of Anne was typical of the clinical course in the successful cases.

ANNE: A CASE STUDY

Anne had been married twice, the first time to a man who had been divorced from his first wife by whom he had fathered several children. Anne married him and they lived happily for a while, but she desparately wanted a baby. All of their endeavors produced no pregnancy, despite Anne's wandering from one physician to another. She stayed with one good physician for a whole year, and then she sought out another good physician for a whole year. Finally she divorced that first husband because she wanted a baby, and she married another divorced man who had fathered several children by his first wife. Seven years

TABLE 1
CHARACTERISTICS OF THE INFERTILE WOMEN SUCCESSFULLY TREATED

Patient Identity	1	2	3	4	5	6	7	8	9	1
Age (in years)	25	28	28	31	31	33	33	34	36	3
Infertile Period (in years)	4	5	6	3	11	7	8	8	12	1
Previous Children	0	1	1	0	0	0	1	0	0	
Treatment Period (in months)	7	2	13	3	10	5	6	2	2	

went by with this husband, and there was no baby. So she had spent twelve years in all trying desparately to conceive. Finally, because of the severity of her tension, anxiety, and fear, her physician sent her to me for psychotherapy. Anne stated clearly that she didn't want psychotherapy, she wanted a baby—she had tried plenty of psychotherapy in the past.

Hypnotic Training

So, utilizing all the things that I knew about what you can do to physiological behavior with hypnosis, I trained Anne to go into a nice profound hypnotic trance, telling her that she could think about the various parts of her body separately. I pointed out to her that her right arm could get very very cold, and her left arm very very hot. I taught her that her right arm could get very very tense and her left arm could get very relaxed. Then I taught her to separate the various parts of her body in different fashions . . . left leg being relaxed, right arm being very tense, the left arm being very hot, the right leg being very cold. And I bounced these various physiological reactions around in her body until she really understood. Then I taught her that she could sit quietly in her chair and she could get a feeling of intense blushing in her face. I suggested that she get a feeling of intense warmth in her thighs, which would mean a blushing of her thighs; then a coldness in her chest, and then a warmth in her breast, so that I bounced these various physiological processes around within her. Then I explained to her something about the physiological processes of menstruation. And I suggested that she really learn how to relax her pelvis, and to relax it completely, thoroughly, to get a tremendously warm feeling in her pelvis, then let go of that relaxation, and then re-develop the relaxation and the warm feeling, until Anne had the feeling that she could relax her pelvis completely, and have it feel warm and comfortable.

My motivation for using this technique came from my suspicion that there might possibly be a tubal spasm. So I told Anne that, and I spent quite a number of hours with her during the first month of therapy. For the first time, she had a normal menstrual period without cramps. She was very pleased with this, but she informed me that she wanted that sort of thing to stop (menstruating). And I told her it would, but that she should practice this matter of pelvic relaxation and this feeling of comfort, and that during sexual relations there should be a tremendous feeling of comfort and relaxation throughout her body, and especially in her pelvis.

Anne had first come to me in October at which time she was just completing a period. She had normal periods in November and December. Then she came to see me just after Christmas and said, "I got my Christmas present—you made me pregnant!" Then she flushed and said she didn't mean it the way the words sounded, but that she had had such enjoyable sexual relations, and that it felt so relaxed and so comfortable, that she was absolutely certain that the physiological relaxation that I had taught her had enabled her to become pregnant.

Now I think all of you ought to consider this matter of re-educating the physiological responses of the body. If we can do it in one area, we can do it in another. If we can correct constipation, if we can correct retention of urine, why can't we correct tubal spasm. The point is, we ought to *expect* to find solutions rather than passively accepting a decree of "uncurable." Such an attitude of expectancy is far more conducive to our task of exploration, discovery and healing.

21. Breast Development Possibly Influenced by Hypnosis: Two Instances and the Psychotherapeutic Results

Milton H. Erickson

Common experience has demonstrated repeatedly that unconscious attitudes toward the body can constitute potent factors in many relationships. Learning processes, physical and physiological functioning, and recovery from illness are, among others, examples of areas in which unrecognized body attitudes may be of vital significance to the individual. Hence the question is pertinent: To what extent can specific forms of somatic behavior be influenced purposefully by unconscious forces, and what instances are there of such effects? The two following cases, aside from their hypnotic psychotherapeutic significances, are presented as indicative of a possibly significant problem for future research concerning unconscious purposeful influence upon breast development.

CASE 1

A 20-year-old girl was brought by her older sister for a single hypnotherapeutic interview because of failure of breast development, despite good nipple development. The girl was found to be seriously maladjusted emotionally, had failed some of her college courses, and was afraid to seek employment. She was, and since childhood had been, deeply religious, but her religious understandings and convictions included an undue element of austerity and rejection of the physical body. Additionally, it was learned that she was engaged to be married to a 47-year-old alcoholic welfare recipient, because, as she resentfully declared, with no breasts she was not entitled to more.

She readily developed a medium-to-deep trance and manifested a markedly passive attitude. The suggestion was offered to her that she read carefully and assiduously the Song of Solomon, and that she recognize thoroughly that it glorified the Church, and before the time of the Church, it glorified the human body, particularly the female body in all its parts. She was admonished that

Reprinted with permission from *The American Journal of Clinical Hypnosis,* January, 1960, *11,* 157–159.

such should be her attitude toward her body, and that perhaps an attitude of patient expectancy toward her breasts might aid in some further development. It was further explained to her that as she obeyed instructions she was to feel with very great intensity the goodness of her body, particularly the goodness of her breasts, and to sense them as living structures of promise, and in which she would have an increasing sense of comfort and pride. These suggestions variously phrased were repetitiously presented to her until it was felt that she had accepted them completely.

The outcome almost two years later of this one hypnotherapeutic session may be summarized as follows: (1) The breaking of the engagement to the alcoholic; (2) weekly reading of the Song of Solomon; (3) return to college and successful completion of the courses previously failed; (4) enlargement of social and recreational life; (5) successful employment; (6) recent engagement to a young man of her own age group whom she had known for several years; (7) independent reports from her and her sister that breast development had occurred to the extent of "one inch thick on one side, about one and one-half inches on the other side."

Comment

That significant therapy was accomplished for this patient cannot be doubted. That her breasts actually enlarged is not a similar certainty, since an objective confirmatory report was not obtainable. But there is a definite possibility that physical processes, comparable in nature and extent to those which occur in "psychosomatic illness," may have resulted in what might, as a parallelism, be termed "psychosomatic health."

CASE 2

A 17-year-old girl was first seen in her home because of her seriously pathological withdrawal responses to the failure of her breasts to develop, despite the adequacy and maturity of her physical development otherwise. She had a history of extensive medical treatment, extending over five years, with much experimental endocrinological therapy. The only results had been an increasing failure of emotional adjustment, and the possibility of a mental hospital was under consideration.

She was found hiding behind the davenport, and upon her being discovered there, she rushed behind the piano. When she learned that "no more medicines or needles" would be employed, superficially good rapport was established, possibly because she regarded the situation as offering a better means of escape or withdrawal. She was found to be a good hypnotic subject, readily developing a light-to-medium trance.

The first interview, after several hours' effort in winning her cooperation, was spent primarily in appraising her personality assets, both in and out of the trance state. During the interview she was found to have a Puckish sense of humor, with dramatic overtones, and this was utilized as the opening gambit for the therapeutic approach. This was initiated by reminding her of the old song about how the toe-bone is connected to the foot-bone, etc. When her interest had been fully aroused, a paraphrase was offered in relationship to the endocrine system, and it was pointed out that, even as the foot-bone is connected to the ankle-bone, so is the "adrenal bone" connected with the "thyroid bone," with each "supporting and helping" the other.

Next she was given suggestions to feel hot, to feel cold, to have her face feel uncomfortably hot, to feel tired, and to feel rested and comfortable. She responded readily and well to these suggestions, whereupon it was suggested effectively that she develop an intolerable itch upon her feet. This itch she was then to consign with dramatic intensity, not to the nethermost depths, but to the "barren nothingness" of her breasts, a fitting destination for so intolerable an itch. However, in further punishment of it, the itch would become a constantly present, neither pleasant nor unpleasant, noticeable but undefined feeling, rendering her continuously aware of the breast area of her body. This involved series of suggestions was formulated for the multiple purposes of meeting her ambivalences, puzzling and intriguing her, stimulating her sense of humor, meeting her need for self-aggression and self-derogation, and yet doing all this without adding to her distress and in such fashion and so indirectly that there was little for her to do but to accept and to respond to the suggestions.

Then the suggestion was offered that, at each therapeutic interview, she was to visualize herself mentally in the most embarrassing situation that she could possibly imagine. This situation, not necessarily to remain constant in character, would always involve her breasts, and she would feel and sense the embarrassment with great intensity, at first in her face, and then, with a feeling of relief, she would feel that weight of embarrassment move slowly downward and come to rest in her breasts. She was given the additional posthypnotic suggestion that, whenever she was alone, she would regularly take the opportunity to think of her therapeutic sessions, and she would then develop immediately intense feelings of embarrassment, all of which would promptly "settle" in her breasts in a most bewildering but entirely pleasing way.

The rationale of these suggestions is rather simple and direct. It is merely an effort to parallel in relationship to her breasts, but in a pleasant, constructive manner, such unfortunate destructive psychosomatic reactions as "terrible, painful knots in my stomach over just the slightest worries."

The final set of hypnotic instructions was that she was to have a thoroughly good time in college. (By these suggestions all discussion of her withdrawn behavior and college attendance was effectively bypassed.) It was explained that she could, in addition to handling her academic work adequately, entertain herself and mystify her collegemates delightfully by the judicious wearing of tight sweaters and the use of different sets of "falsies" of varying sizes, sometimes not in matched pairs. She was also instructed to carry assorted sizes in her handbag in case she decided to make an unexpected change in her appearance, or, should any of her escorts become too venturesome, so that she could offer them a choice with which to play. Thus her Puckish activities would not lead to difficulties.

She was first seen in mid-August and given weekly appointments thereafter. The first few of these were used to reiterate and reinforce the instructions previously given her and to insure her adequate understanding and cooperation.

Henceforth she kept, by permission, three out of four appointments "in absentia." That is, she would seclude herself for at least an hour, develop, in response to posthypnotic suggestions, a medium-to-deep trance state, and in this state, as far as could be learned, she would review systematically and extensively all previous instructions and discussions and whatever "other things" that might come to her mind. No effort was made to determine the nature of those "other things," nor did she seem to be willing to volunteer information, except to the effect that she had thought of a number of other topics. The other appointments she kept in person, sometimes asking for information, sometimes for trance induction, almost always for instructions to "keep going." Occasionally she would describe with much merriment the consternation she had caused some of her friends.

She entered college in September, adjusted well, received freshman honors, and became prominent in extracurricular activities. During the last two months of her therapy she kept her visits at the level of social office calls. In May, however, she came in wearing a sweater and stated with extreme embarrassment, "I'm not wearing falsies. I've grown my own. They are large medium size. Now, tell them to stop growing. I'm completely satisfied."

Her college career was successful, and subsequent events are entirely satisfactory. At the writer's request she underwent a complete physical examination, with special reference to her breasts, a report of which was sent this writer. She was physically normal in every regard.

Comment

Whether or not the hypnotherapy had anything to do with her breast development is not known. Quite possibly the development may have been merely the result of a delayed growth process. It may have been the result of all the medication she had received. Or it may have been a combined result of these, favorably influenced by her altered emotional state. But at all events the psychotherapeutic results that derived from getting her to enter college and to enjoy life, instead of a continuing of her previous pattern of psychopathological withdrawal, cannot be denied.

However, in all fairness it must be recognized that there is a significant possibility that the therapy she received, through the mobilization of unconscious forces by hypnosis, may have contributed greatly to her breast development.

22. Psychogenic Alteration of Menstrual Functioning: Three Instances

Milton H. Erickson

That menstruation may be precipitated, delayed, interrupted, or prolonged by strong emotional stress is a common observation. Usually such effects are unexpected and seemingly beyond the volitional control of the individual. Unquestionably, speaking biologically, lack of volitional control is as it should be. Nevertheless, the readiness with which an abnormal alteration of some physiological functioning is effected is often in sharp contrast to the difficulty encountered in attempting medically a purposeful directing of those same processes. Hence any instances indicating an intentional purposeful control, whether conscious or unconscious, of physiological functioning ordinarily beyond volitional influences suggest the possibility of significant research.

Following are three separate clinical accounts of an intentional, purposeful interference with the menstrual cycle. Two of the women deliberately employed hypnotic experience to effect special personal purposes, while the third utilized in a new fashion a psychosomatic pattern of reaction established in other relationships, doing this just after she had been carefully trained hypnotically for a possible correction of this pattern.

CASE 1

A young woman, an experienced hypnotic subject, had many times been much annoyed by the insistent sexual importunities of a certain man. His behavior on one occasion had disclosed to her that he had an extreme olfactory aversion for menstruation and that he invariably detected the odor and would resort to laborious methods to avoid even the slightest physical contact with a menstruating woman. She had also learned that he kept a timetable on his female acquaintances.

She was invited to a physically confining 10-day social function, which hap-

Reprinted with permission from *The American Journal of Clinical Hypnosis,* April 1960, *2,* 227–231.

pened to be scheduled for the same time as the midperiod of her menstrual cycle. After she had accepted, a letter from the man apprised her of the fact that he, too, was an invited guest, and in this letter he suggested that they see much of each other during the entire social gathering.

She consulted this writer about the possibility of "having an early period." The frequent effects of psychological attitudes and reactions upon menstruation were explained to her, and it was then suggested posthypnotically that, throughout the week preceding the social function, she think and feel and sense and function as if it were the week immediately preceding her menses. She agreed to this, and the posthypnotic suggestions were reinforced by a detailed explanation to her, in a state of ordinary awareness, of what she could expect her body to do.

She accepted the man's invitation after amending it in her reply to include daily afternoon and evening "cheek-to-cheek" dancing, an item which he fervently promised her in the return mail.

At the social affair some hours after she had induced the man to declare boastfully to the guests that he was "really out of circulation" because of a "promise to dance cheek-to-cheek" with Miss X, her menstrual period began and lingered for 10 days instead of the usual five or six, during which time she thereby thoroughly punished the man for all of his previous affronts.

Comment

That the alteration of her menstrual cycle was simply a coincidence appears improbable. She was well aware of what she wanted to accomplish before she sought professional advice. This was given on an experimental basis. The subsequent events were in actual accord with her wishes and were also a reasonably logical outcome of the suggestions given her. Subsequent inquiry in both the trance and waking states yielded no significant information except that she had accepted the suggestions and her body had "felt the way it always does a week before my period. But I don't know how I did it."

CASE 2

An artist's model with a regular menstrual cycle and a history of profuse flow with the first few days was offered an unexpected assignment in nude posing on the second day of her period. She had had previous unsatisfactory experience with intravaginal tampons and was about to refuse the assignment when she recalled her previous experimental work with a physician interested in hypnosis and psychosomatic medicine. This led her to accept the assignment with the intention of employing autohypnosis, with which she was experienced, to inhibit her menstrual flow. A telephone call to this writer confirmed her in her intention, but no helpful advice could be given to her except that she should rely upon the capacity of her unconscious mind to function competently.

Shortly before reporting for work, she developed an autohypnotic trance and in some manner unknown to her conscious mind she inhibited the flow from 7:00 P.M. until her return home at 11:00 P.M., after 2½ hours of posing in the nude. She employed no precautions; and, as she explained, she "forgot" her period "both psychologically and physiologically." "I didn't remember after I came out of the autohypnotic trance that it was my menstrual period, and I didn't recall that fact until the flow steadily resumed as I was preparing for bed. I just forgot it as completely physiologically as I did psychologically. I still don't know how I did it."

On another occasion, where the values of the situation were significant, this same young woman discovered that her regular menstrual period would intervene and bar her attendance. Again she consulted this writer, who explained that the appearance of the menses was often temporally altered by various physiological forces, and hence, in view of her past experience in inhibiting menses, she might try the experiment of delaying her period. Instead, because she thought it the safer procedure, she induced her period 10 days early.

Subsequently she postponed her period experimentally for 10 days, beginning the period of delay the day before her period was to begin, and after the usual molimina had indicated that the menses were about to begin.

Comment

This second account is essentially an experimental study on the part of the woman. She was interested in her body and what it could do. Her knowledge of psychosomatic medicine and her extensive knowledge of hypnosis provided an ample background for her own personal investigation. How she accomplished her various purposes is not explained by her simple assertion of "forgetting physiologically." Yet one can draw somewhat of a parallel with the "forgetting" of intense hunger that can be effected by a pleasing interest. At all events her findings suggest that experimental investigations of psychosomatic alterations of physiological functioning are feasible.

CASE 3

An out-of-state woman, much in love with her husband, invariably reacted with severe physical symptomatology, prolonged from one to three weeks, whenever she became sufficiently distressed emotionally. Her symptomatology variously included marked hematuria, protracted diarrhea, severe nausea and vomiting with excessive weight loss, and disabling headaches and backaches. These conditions invariably developed suddenly, almost always after a quarrel with her husband because of her unwarranted and unreasonable jealousy. As she explained, "My sickness, no matter what kind, disappears like magic just as soon as I feel punished enough. In an hour's time I'm well, but I'm usually pretty washed out." She sought therapy to free herself from this psychosomatic pattern, and she had arranged to be away from home an indefinite length of time.

In taking her general history, she was found to have a pain-free 30-day menstrual cycle with almost exact regularity, and she carried a small calendar appointment book in which she had marked for the entire year the date of her expected periods with a notation of their actual date of occurrence. Her book was examined from January to September, and in two instances the expected date and the actual date differed by one day only.

She was found to be an excellent somnambulistic hypnotic subject, and the second and third interviews were spent in training her hypnotically for therapeutic work. On the evening of the third interview, in accord with a previous arrangement, she attempted to reach her husband by long-distance telephone and failed. (She had not made allowance for the difference in time zones.) She developed a furious rage, went out walking, encountered a strange man, and for the first time in her life engaged in illicit sex relations. She reported this to this writer the next morning with much contrition, and added that her period was due in three days and she hoped she would not become pregnant. She postponed further interviews, stating that she would call after the second day of the expected period.

Six days later she came in to declare that she was pregnant and that she was going to seek employment and pay her own expenses throughout the period of her pregnancy. She demanded that she be placed in a deep trance and instructed emphatically that this pregnancy be impressed upon her as the final somatization of her emotional outbursts. She explained that the pregnancy would give her an adequate period of time in which to mend her "habit of always and always taking my mad out on my body." When doubt was expressed about the certainty of the pregnancy, she was emphatic in asserting that her intense awareness of her own physical experience with three previous pregnancies (the last one eight years previously, contraception since then) left no doubt in her mind. The only instruction given her in the trance, in response to her request, was that she meet her situation adequately.

She secured employment that day and was not seen until six weeks later. She brought in letters addressed to the writer from two independent obstetricians, each of whom stated that she gave good physical evidence of pregnancy and both of whom commented, at her request, upon her unusually extensive and unusually early breast engorgement in relation to her pregnancy. After the letters were read, she requested that the writer call each of the obstetricians and verify the letters, but without betraying to either that she had been examined by another physician. The telephone calls merely confirmed the letters, but one obstetrician recommended a laboratory test as "confirmatory alone." The other, when asked about this, stated that he was confident about his examination findings, but would order a laboratory test if desired. Both expressed surprise at the extent of her breast development and stated an interest in following the breast development, which seemed to indicate a pregnancy much further advanced. This was related to the patient, and she listened quietly, then asked that she be hypnotized. In the deep trance she asked that she be instructed to discuss everything on her mind.

This was done, and she launched into a discussion of her wishes and fears concerning an abortion and her aversion to such a procedure. She debated the matter back and forth, then took up the plans she was formulating for giving birth to her child secretly and in some way securing an adoptive home for it. She wanted no advice or instruction from the writer, except in the form of encouraging her to pursue her ideas as freely as she could. She finally asked to be aroused from the trance with an amnesia for what had been discussed. Out of the trance she explained that she would telephone for an appointment "some time."

Eight weeks and four days from the expected date of the missed period, she came in for an interview, bringing letters, again from two different independent physicians. These letters contained the statement and a laboratory report to the effect that physical examination showed normal menstruation and that this was confirmed by a laboratory report of vaginal smears. She asked that a telephone call be made to each of them, again with the request that no betrayal be made that she had consulted another physician. Each physician confirmed his report and expressed curiosity as to why any woman would want a medical and laboratory examination and a special examination of her breasts to confirm a normal menstrual period. Both mentioned that, since she was an out-of-state patient, the suspicion had arisen that something illegal was involved, and hence the examinations had been most thorough. However, when she requested the letters which were to be addressed to the writer, it was apparent to them that her problem was emotional rather than legal.

The patient explained, "I just wanted you to be certain I hadn't secured an abortion, so that you would listen to me. Four days ago I woke up that morning and I knew I wasn't pregnant. I realized that I had just punished my body the way I always do when I get mad. I felt my breasts. They were smaller, the swelling had gone out of them, and they were just tender around the nipples, the way they always are just before I menstruate. So I called my boss and said I was sick and I couldn't come in, and I just stayed in my room to enjoy menstruating. It started about 11:00 A.M. and in just the usual way. And that afternoon I called doctors for appointments and explained I wanted a laboratory examination made of my vagina. I got the appointments for the next day because I always flow very lightly until after the first night. Then I had to wait until I had the lab reports, and that's why I only got here this afternoon. But now something makes me think you should hypnotize me so I can tell you what's in my unconscious mind."

In the trance state the patient explained that the sexual episode had been seized upon "to teach me a lesson. I just remembered every feeling I ever had in my pregnancies and I just made my body have those feelings, and that made me believe I was pregnant and that helped me to feel all the pregnancy feelings better. I even noticed how I started to walk like I was pregnant. I just got every one of the feelings that I learned when I was really pregnant. And I was so worried about being pregnant and what I would do and how I could stick to my job. Finally, I went to bed one night feeling just completely whipped, knowing I'd have to take my responsibilities absolutely completely. I fell asleep exhausted, and the next morning I woke up feeling wonderful, knowing I wasn't pregnant. Tell me I'm all through punishing my body. I know I am, but I want you to tell me, too." There was some additional discussion, but the above contains the essential communications.

A friendly correspondence has been maintained with this patient at fairly regular intervals for more than four years. She has had no further physical symptomatology in relation to the emotional distress. Her pathological jealousy has disappeared. Her husband's acquaintance has been made, and he also assures the writer that his wife's previous emotional outbursts and physical reactions are past history and that she is remarkably happy and well-adjusted.

Comment

This case report is a definite instance in which a patient adapted an established pattern of severe, prolonged, somatic disturbances of sudden onset and disappearance, in reaction to states of emotional stress, to a new and different personality problem involving a special order of physiological processes. It presents the intriguing problem of how extensively and how elaborately unconscious forces and motivations can be utilized to mobilize physiological functions in a systematically directed fashion. Considerable information exists in the literature about laboratory procedures in the conditioning of body behavior, but there is little available information on how the learnings derived from body experiences can be utilized to influence or direct selected physiological processes.

SUMMARY

These three case reports indicate, each in a different way but each in relationship to hypnosis, that somatic learnings derived from body functioning can be utilized meaningfully but in an unknown fashion. Additional such case reports could conceivably serve in the further confirmation of these findings and in the development of more understandings in this important, complex field.

23. The Appearance in Three Generations of an Atypical Pattern of the Sneezing Reflex

Milton H. Erickson

The purpose of this short note is to report the observation in a young woman of an atypical pattern of the sneezing reflex which was originally considered to be strictly a personal mannerism or habit of marked individuality. The error of this assumption, however, was disclosed by the reappearance of this same peculiar pattern of sneezing behavior in her new-born daughter and the subsequent discovery that an essentially identical pattern was exhibited by the young woman's mother. The situation which led to the making of this report was as follows:

Close observation of the young woman over a period of years disclosed her sneezing behavior to be that of always expecting and usually experiencing, generally within one to two seconds, a second sneeze in rapid succession to the first. Inquiry disclosed that this pattern of paired sneezes was of lifelong duration, that she had taken pride in it as a child, and that she could not remember ever having observed similar behavior in others, including her family. In this last recollection, however, she was mistaken, since, after this study had been completed originally, the author discovered by direct observation and inquiry the same peculiarity in her mother's sneezing behavior.

As a consequence of this peculiar pattern of sneezing, the young woman has developed a definite modification of her general behavior, in that on the occasion of a sneeze she arrests her activity to await a second sneeze, and should it fail to occur, she experiences a somewhat distressing sense of incompleteness. This same feeling of expectancy is also described by her mother.

Those fully aware of this young woman's oddity in sneezing tended to regard it purely as an individualism, an acquired habit based upon some chance oc-

Reprinted with permission from *The Journal of Genetic Psychology*, 1940, *56*, 455–459.
Previous to the submitting of this report inquiry made of the young woman had found her mistakenly confident that no one else in her family showed this peculiar pattern of sneezing behavior. Recently an opportunity for direct inquiry and observation disclosed that the sneezing behavior of the young woman's mother was essentially identical with that of the daughter and the granddaughter. Unfortunately, however, no day-by-day record could be secured. Further direct inquiry disclosed no other instance of such unusual behavior in the family.

currence in her early childhood, and fostered until it had become an ingrained habit. She herself regarded it as an innate, rather than as an acquired, pattern of behavior over which she had no control, constituting nothing more than an amusing physiological peculiarity and she offered the explanation that it might be similar in character to the sneezing reflex encountered in relation to bright light or to temperature changes.

Exposure without her knowledge to nasal irritants, particularly substances to which she is allergic, does not alter this sneeze pattern, but serves rather to bring it markedly into relief, as does upper respiratory infection.

In 1938 this young woman became a mother. About three weeks later, upon her return home from the hospital with the baby, the infant was observed to sneeze twice in rapid succession. No particular attention was paid to this except to note it casually. During the next few weeks, probably because of various allergic reactions shown by the baby, many observations were made of paired sneezes in the infant and of the persistence, after the first sneeze, of the general muscular tension and facial grimaces suggestive of an anticipatory response to another sneeze, all very much in duplication of the sneezing behavior of the mother.

When approximately two months old, the baby developed an upper respiratory infection and sneezed frequently and consistently in sets of two, with the time interval between sneezes never longer than a single, usually sharp, inhalation of breath. On relatively rare occasions this inhalation would be spasmodic in character and then, instead of a single sneeze, there would be a series of two to six in rapid succession, a finding also true for the mother.

When interest was first taken in the baby's paired sneezes, both parents began watching for singles. By the time the infant was three months old a total of three single sneezes had been noted, while there had been scores of pairs. During the next few weeks, however, a constantly increasing frequency of single sneezes was noted and led to the making of a belated record of every sneeze heard. This account was begun when the baby was slightly more than four months old. A similar record was kept on the mother, the two records differing only in completeness, since all of the mother's sneezes were listed, while only those heard by either of the parents when with the baby could be recorded. Unfortunately, however, no day-by-day record on the grandmother could be secured, and it was necessary to rely upon careful inquiries. As a control measure, close attention was paid to the sneezing of five other people, two of whom suffer from numerous allergies, to note the occurrence of paired sneezes. In addition the author watched carefully for double or multiple sneezing among his numerous associates, but in no instance was a pattern of double sneezing discovered.

After the record had been kept for a considerable length of time, another peculiarity, not shown by the mother, was noted in the baby's sneezing—specifically, a light reflex sneeze. This type of sneeze tended to occur upon sudden exposure to bright light, such as being taken out-of-doors into the bright sunlight, the turning on of the electric lights at night, or the sudden flashing of a bright light into the child's eyes, and, as far as could be determined, the distribution of single and paired sneezes followed the general pattern. After making this discovery, the parents tended to avoid sudden light stimulation, reducing somewhat the previous frequency of sneezes. In Table 1 the sneezes listed as light reflexes are known instances only. In all probability the actual total is greater.

Other observations made while keeping the record, which extended over a period of nearly four months, were that for both cases the ratio of paired to single sneezes remained essentially constant from day to day, and that upper respiratory infection and exposure to allergens served only to increase proportionately the frequency of both types of sneezes. It is also of interest to note that previous to the keeping of the record the mother believed that only rarely did she herself sneeze singly. In addition, despite the close watch kept on the sneezing behavior of a large number of people, no similar pattern was found, although a few instances of occasional multiple sneezing were observed.

COMMENT

Frequently in a specific type of behavior involving organic and psychic patterns of response, the differentiation is difficult between the behavior constituting a functioning of innate physiological and neurological processes and the behavior constituting a response of the personality itself to organice processes over which it may have little or no control. Nevertheless the attitude taken by the personality may serve markedly to alter or to distort the strictly somatic aspects of the total behavior process, and particularly is this considered to be the case when some relatively simple form of physiological behavior involving definite psychic responses manifests a striking individuality peculiar to the person.

Hence when some process of physiological or neurological behavior shows apparently purposeless and illogical variations in accord with what could reasonably be expected to result from personality factors, the assumption is made

TABLE 1
DISTRIBUTION OF SNEEZES

	Mother	Daughter
Single sneezes	32	125
Paired sneezes	105	212
Triple sneezes	17	20
Multiple sneezes (more than three)	4	5
Light reflex sneezes	0	20

that the personality has seized upon that innate behavior and added to it learned behavior serving other and remoter purposes of the personality, as is often to be noted in psychoneurotic symptomatology.

At first thought this might seem to be the case with the young woman, especially so since her mother's sneezing behavior could furnish an opportunity for an imitative performance. However, the appearance of the same pattern in the granddaughter long before the possibility of imitation clearly indicates either an inheritance or a remarkable coincidence. In this connection references may be made to the recent extensive experimental studies on the startle pattern by Landis and Hunt (1939), who found that, "Complicated bodily responses exist and are exhibited in a pattern-like fashion—startle, Moro reflex, sneezing, coughing, and so on," and that the general pattern of these responses tends to remain constant regardless of age, sex, and race. To this may be added that variations in the pattern may be inherited.

24. An Addendum to a Report of the Appearance in Three Generations of an Atypical Pattern of the Sneezing Reflex

Milton H. Erickson

In the *Journal of Genetic Psychology* in 1940 this author reported the appearance in three successive generations of an atypical pattern of the sneezing reflex. A young mother, her infant daughter, and the grandmother all show a pattern of occasional single sneezes, a large number of paired sneezes, a few triple sneezes, and rare multiple (more than three) sneezes. Respiratory infections, allergens, and the light-reflex sneeze did not alter the character of the sneeze pattern of the infant.

There was available no information on the grandmother's siblings, male or female. The grandfather, the father, and the young mother's two brothers showed only the usual sneeze pattern.

Since the publication of that paper four more children were born to the young mother, two boys, two girls. None of these showed any unusual sneeze pattern.

In addition there were three slightly older step-children, two boys and one girl. The publication of the original paper aroused their interest and they spent much time and effort in attempting to learn to sneeze in pairs or triples. None succeeded.

The author employed hypnosis on a variety of Ss to teach them a double or triple sneeze pattern or any other variation from their established pattern. He also attempted by hypnosis to abolish the pattern of light-reflex sneezing shown by some people—that is, sneezing when stepping out of comparatively dim light into bright sunlight, or of responding by sneezing when an electric light is suddenly turned on. All such hypnotic studies resulted in only transient successes eventuating in failure, or else in no alterations at all.

In the years that have passed since the infant's noticeable sneezing pattern led to the publication of the observations, the infant has grown up and become the mother of a baby boy who also manifests his mother's, his grandmother's, and his now deceased great-grandmother's sneezing pattern, which remained in all of them a continued phenomenon. This child's father has a normal sneeze

Reprinted with permission from *Perceptual and Motor Skills*, 1964, *18*, 309-310.

pattern. Obviously then, the pattern is not sex-linked as was originally tentatively suggested.

Since preparing this report a mother and her only daughter have been encountered, both of whom consider their double sneeze pattern as completely normal. The mother's parents and siblings, however, did not sneeze double and neither did the daughter's only child, a son, nor her husband. The report was validated by the author's own observations and inquiries.

This paper may be concluded with the same final statements as the first study, namely, ". . . references may be made to the recent extensive experimental studies on the startle pattern of Landis and Hunt (1939) who found that, 'Complicated bodily responses exist and are exhibited in a pattern-like fashion . . . startle, Moro reflex, sneezing, coughing, and so on,' and that the general pattern of these responses tends to remain constant regardless of age, sex, and race. To this may be added that variations in pattern may be inherited.'' One more statement can now be added, namely, that such variations are not necessarily a sex-linked inheritance.

IV. Time Distortion

Time distortion has been described as the first new hypnotic phenomenon to be discovered in over 100 years. The first paper in this section, published in 1948 by Linn Cooper, is his initial report of this remarkable discovery. The second paper, published two years later in 1950, has Erickson as a junior author for his collaborative work with Cooper. Erickson had recognized immediately the value and validity of Cooper's work because, as Erickson reports in this second paper, years earlier he had accidentally stumbled upon the therapeutic value of time distortion but without understanding just what it was.

Erickson was tremendously stimulated by the prospect of using time distortion as a method of gaining access to the experiential life of his subjects and patients. Since time is a central facet in all subjective experiences, he hoped the phenomenon of time distortion could be used to explore questions such as the following:

> What constitutes subjective reality? Of what seemingly pertinent and irrelevant elements is it composed? In what way is it integrated into the total life of the person? What self-expressive purposes does it serve for the personality? What determines its validity? How does it differ from a memory, a dream, a fantasy, and from retrospective falsification?

It is evident from these questions that Erickson hoped to stimulate a broad program of basic research into mental life. He felt time distortion could be quantified so that carefully controlled studies in the areas of learning, memory, and conditioning might be possible along with an exploration of subjective realities. In his clinical utilization of time distortion in the cases reported in this second paper he provides hints about some of the parameters of this research program, but to this day his early hopes have not been realized. During the initial period of excited discovery he published a major paper, "Pseudo-orientation in time as an hypnotherapeutic procedure" (which appears in volume 4 of this series), which was undoubtedly stimulated by his thinking about time distortion even though it is a phenomenon of a different category. Or is it? And what of the classical hypnotic phenomenon of age regression? Is this a different category of response or is it related in some way to time distortion? Linn Cooper was apparently concerned about carefully defining and distinguishing his discovery of time distortion from all other hypnotic phenomena. While this attitude was important in the initial work, more systematic investigations in future work may uncover relationships between all hypnotic phenomena dealing with alterations in the subjective sense of time and place.

The last paper of this section deals with Elizabeth Erickson's recognition of an oversight in Cooper's original concept of time distortion. Cooper's original conception was essentially *time expansion:* A short period of "real" clock time was subjectively experienced as a long period of mental time during which many events could take place and many things could be done mentally. Elizabeth Erickson's contribution was to recognize and establish with her husband, Milton, that the reverse, *time condensation,* was also possible. A long period of "real" clock time could be subjectively experienced as taking place very quickly so that a lengthy period of childbirth, for example, could appear to pass quickly. Milton Erickson then used this approach to greatly reduce the suffering of painful terminal illness, and since that time it has become one of the standard means by which he deals with pain. It is evident from the four papers of this section as well as Cooper's original work (Cooper, 1948–1959) that only the most preliminary studies have been made of the twin phenomena of time expansion and time condensation. Much needs to be done to further explore Cooper's and Erickson's early hopes for their utilization in the general study of our world of subjective experience.

25. Time Distortion in Hypnosis: I

Linn F. Cooper

Despite the fact that time perception is one of the most basic of human experiences, it is subject to wide variations. The commonest of these is observed in the dream, where the subject may experience many hours, or even days, of dream-life in the course of but a few minutes of solar time. Another instance of the distortion of time perception is found in cases where persons in danger have related how the scenes of their life passed slowly before their eyes in a matter of seconds or minutes. Such experiences are encountered by near-drowning persons or those having falls. Time passes more rapidly for the aging than for the young, and certain drugs, notably marijuana, are said to alter time perception. Disorders of time modality as a personal experience are found in organic brain lesions, the psychoses and psychoneuroses, and in delirium and toxic states. Pleasure may shorten the sensation of time, and pain increase it. "Time flies on Love's wings," and yet, "The watched pot never boils."

The following studies were begun in an attempt to determine whether or not time sense could be deliberately distorted in the hypnotized subject, and, if so, whether the subject could utilize "slowed" time by engaging in mental activity. As will be seen, an affirmative answer was obtained in both instances.

ABBREVIATIONS AND DEFINITIONS

W. T.—world time—solar time as measured by watch or metronome.

P. T.—personal time—subjective, experiential, or psychological time.

E. P. T.—estimated personal time—estimate, by the subjects, of the length of an interval of their experiential time.

S. P. T.—suggested personal time—a time interval suggested to the subject under hypnosis, as in, "There will be 10 minutes between the two signals," or, "You will have 10 minutes for this."

A. T.—allotted time—the time, in world time, that is allotted to a test by the operator. It is not told to the subject. Thus it may be sug-

Reprinted from *The Bulletin, Georgetown University Medical Center,* 1948, 1, No. 6, April and May, pp. 214-221.

gested to the subject that she will have 10 minutes for a problem, while the actual interval between signals is only 10 seconds.

D. R.—demonstrated rate—in the counting experiments the subject was frequently asked to demonstrate, by counting aloud, the rate at which she counted hallucinated objects. This was done both during trance and posthypnotically. In the former instances the subject had finished the test and was presumably not in a phase of response to suggestion.

(D.R.)(E.P.T.)—demonstrated rate multiplied by estimated personal time—a product used in the counting tests. It indicates the count that would be reached if the subject counted at the demonstrated rate for a period equal to the estimated personal time.

A description of a test will illustrate the use of these terms. Example:

The following suggestions are given:

"You're back on the farm and are going to churn some butter."

"Tell me what you see." (Subject describes the scene in some detail. She is sitting on the back porch, with a crockery churn half full of milk. She mentions the paddle with the "cross-piece on it," and the hole in the top of the churn through which the paddle passes.)

She is interrupted at this point by the observer, who continues:

"Now just stay there for a while and listen carefully. You're going to churn that milk, and it's going to take you 10 minutes, which will be plenty of time. While churning, you're going to count the strokes. I shall give you a signal to start and another signal, at the end of 10 minutes, to stop. Here comes the signal—Start."

Three seconds later, by world time, the "stop" signal is given as follows:

"Now stop. The 10 minutes are up."

"Now make your mind a blank. Your mind is a blank."

"Now tell me about it. Tell me what you did, how high you counted, and how long you were churning."

She reports that she counted 114 strokes and churned for 10 minutes. Everything was very real to her. The churning became more difficult toward the end as the butter formed, and this slowed things down. She heard the churning and had plenty of time. At the "stop" signal the entire scene faded from view.

When asked to demonstrate, by counting aloud, the rate at which she operated the churn, she counted to 60 in one minute, adding that toward the end the strokes became slower because of the increased resistance from the butter.

Continuing:

"I'm going to wake you up by counting to 10. You will remember all about this experience and tell me about it."

On waking she is again asked to give a report. Her story is similar to the above, including the number of strokes counted, the time estimate, and the demonstrated rate.

In this example, then, the world time (W. T.) and the allotted time (A. T.) was 3 seconds, the suggested personal time (S. P. T.) 10 minutes, the estimated personal time (E. P. T.) 10 minutes, and the demonstrated rate (D. R.) 60 strokes per minute.

The product of the demonstrated rate times the estimated personal time (D.R.)(E.P.T.) is 600. Yet the subject insists that she took only 114 strokes, that she counted each stroke individually, and that she was occupied for the full 10 minutes. When asked, posthypnotically, about the discrepancy, she has no explanation to offer.

METHOD

In brief an inquiry was made into the relations between the "world time" and the "subjective" or "experiential" time involved in various experiences suggested to the hypnotized subject. The "experiences" were listening to a metronome, counting hallucinated objects, and a diverse group of familiar activities. In some cases a time interval (S. P. T.) was suggested; in others, none. An "allotment of world time" (A. T.) was employed in many of the tests.

The subject was a young woman of 36 years of unimpeachable integrity, known to the writer for 10 years. She had had a high school education and worked as a secretary-stenographer. During the earlier tests she had no idea as to the purpose of the experiment, and accepted the suggested time intervals as real. Later she was told the truth and expressed great surprise. It was her first experience with hypnosis. The experiments were done daily for eight days and were consecutive except for an interval of one day between the first and second session. Hypnosis was induced 33 times, the trances lasting from five minutes to 45 minutes. Induction was very easy, and suggested experiences were clear and "very real." She not only "saw" clearly, but could "hear" conversations and other sounds, and could "feel" things she handled. She was unaware of odors or tastes. Emotions were "felt," sometimes spontaneously, and she was always aware of the passage of time. In comparing her suggested experiences to dreams, she described them as "making more sense," and added that "I lived them, whereas in a dream I'm more of an onlooker." It was noted that the simplest suggestions caused a rich and detailed hallucinatory production on all occasions. For this reason simple suggestions such as "You're standing in the street in Memphis" were generally employed, the subject spontaneously supplying details.

Invariably there was amnesia concerning the trance unless the suggestion was given under hypnosis that recollection would be retained posthypnotically. Such a suggestion was frequently given and is to be inferred wherever the subject is reported to have described her trance experiences while awake.

World time was measured by a stopwatch or a metronome.

"Personal time" was determined by asking the subject to estimate it.

Hypnosis was deep enough to produce amnesia, and catalepsy if suggested, but light enough to permit free discussion by the subject.

Because of the very nature of the experiments mathematical analysis cannot be applied to the results. The tabulation of measurements and calculations is done merely to show general trends.

METRONOME EXPERIMENT

A metronome was started at one stroke per second, and the hypnotized subject was told the rate. The suggestion was then made that the metronome was being "slowed down" to one stroke per minute. The subject confirmed this apparent slowing. She was then told that she would be given a signal (tap on the forearm), at which time she would start to review in her "mind's eye" some of her schooldays during the fifth grade, seeing in her imagination the school, the teacher, and her companions. She would do this for 10 *minutes*—that is, 10 strokes of the metronome—at the end of which time she would be notified to stop.

The metronome was stopped after 10 beats—10 *seconds,* world time—and the subject was waked up. On questioning, the following significant experiences were recounted:

a. The metronome was most certainly "slowed down."

b. A good 10 minutes had elapsed between signals.

c. She had "lots of time," and saw clearly the school and her classmates.

d. She expressed great surprise when told that the metronome had not changed rate and that actually her experience had taken only 10 seconds.

Observations similar to the above were repeated on numerous occasions, and subsequent studies showed the following:

a. With the "suggested rate" of the metronome at one stroke per minute the subject, asked to count the strokes aloud, did so at a rate of about one every five seconds rather than one every 60 seconds.

b. When the "slowed" metronome was stopped without the subject's knowledge, she continued to "hear" it and count the beats.

From this it was concluded that the "slowing" of the metronome experienced by the subject was an hallucination of hearing, and that during this hallucination the actual striking of the instrument was inaudible.

EXPERIMENTS IN COUNTING

There were two groups—an earlier one, Group A, made up of some 15 tests, and a later one, Group B, consisting of four tests, and which will be considered first. In all, a group of objects was suggested to the subject, and she was directed to count them.

Group B

The technique employed is similar to that illustrated in the example given in the section on abbreviations. Table 2 shows the results of four tests run at one session. The following comments are in order:

a. It is probably quite impossible for the average waking person to count 137 objects, "one by one," in three seconds of world time, much less 862 objects. Not only did the subject allege just this, but she insists that she did not hurry. For instance, in counting the cows she "walked around the edge of the field. They were very close together." With the cotton—"I used both hands and moved the bag accordingly. I picked only the ripe bolls, leaving the green ones alone. Sometimes I stopped and looked under the leaves to make sure that I had not missed any." We have already mentioned how the churning slowed down as the butter formed. It is quite obvious that the subject truly "lived" these experiences.

b. The product (D.R.)(E.P.T.) is invariably larger than the count. In other words, if the subject had counted at the demonstrated rate for the estimated time, she would have counted far higher. Yet she insisted that she kept busy throughout. She had no explanation to offer for the discrepancy, nor do we.

Group A

Prior to the above, many tests on counting had been run, but a different form of suggestion was used, and different signals. Table 1 shows the results of four of these. An example follows:

"You now see a bushel basket of potatoes."

"Now tell me what you see." (Subject here describes the scene.)

"When I give you the signal, those potatoes are going to be turned out onto the floor and you're going to count them. Take your time about it."

"I now raise your left arm. It will stay raised until you have finished counting, when it will drop to your side."

"Here's the signal—Start counting."

And, as the arm dropped,

"All right, make your mind a blank. Now your mind's a blank."

The time between the signals was noted and recorded.

The essential difference in the technique is that here, in Group A, no time interval is either allotted or suggested to the subject. She merely counts until the task is finished. Furthermore, whereas the signal to start is given by the operator in both groups, in Group A there is no true stopping signal, although the subject does indicate when she has finished by dropping her arm.

But why is there such a vast difference in rate of counting? It will be noted that in Group B the allotted time (A. T.) was rather short—three seconds. This figure was chosen because in other tests—i.e., taking walks—with a suggested personal time in one hour the task was completed in an allotted time of five and three seconds. When the allotted time was cut much below three seconds, however, the subject reported that she had been interrupted before her hour was up. Now, it is of great interest to note that in the Group B tests three seconds of allotted time (A. T.) sufficed, whether the suggested time (S. P. T.) was 10 minutes or an hour and 20 minutes. This makes one wonder whether, for a given individual, a suggested experience may not be "lived" within a more or less fixed interval of world time—i.e., three seconds.

We were unable to induce our subject simply to count at a specified rate. In response to the suggestion, "In the 10 minutes following the signal, you will count to 800. I'll let you know when time is up," the subject counted merely to 29 in 10 seconds, world time.

Group A included a number of counting tests. Objects counted other than those mentioned were books in bookcases, persons passing in a crowded street, sheep, houses passed while walking or driving, freight cars, sewing machine stitches, etc. There was almost always a marked discrepancy between the estimated personal time and the number of objects counted in that time. When asked about this, the subject not infrequently explained her slow counting by reporting that "I had to move the potatoes in the top layer before I could count the ones below," or, "The cattle got in each other's way at the gate," or, "I had to get down on my knees to count the books on the lower shelves," or "I had to lift the chicks out of the incubator and set them down on the floor as I counted, and that took time." These reports were all obtained while the subject was awake. Special precautions were taken, incidentally, in all the reporting to make certain that the subject was not unconsciously adding new "experiences" to those she was supposed to be recalling from her trance. On repeated occasions reports taken during the trance were compared with those taken posthypnotically, and there were never any appreciable differences.

Notes concerning the counting tests:

a. Where there was no allotted time or suggested personal time, that is, in Group A (Table 1) the counting rate in world time was slower than in Group B (Table 2), where there was an allotted time of only three seconds.

b. As shown by the demonstrated rates, 36 to 76 for Group A and 60 to 80 for Group B, the subject thought that she was counting fairly slowly. Yet actually she was often "counting" very rapidly, the average rates being 204 and 6120 per minute for Group A and B, respectively.

c. She "lived" these experiences, and they were, to her, very real. At no time was she aware of hurrying.

d. On posthypnotic interview she stated that the "counting" and the "thinking" she did during trance differed in no way from normal counting and thinking.

PROBLEMS

In these tests the subject was presented with a problem to consider, and given both an allotted time (10 seconds, world time) and a suggested personal time

TABLE 1

Group A.	W.T.	S.P.T.	Count	E.P.T.	D.R.	(D.R.)× (E.P.T.)
Counting cows	65 sec.	—	664	30 min.	36 min.	1080
Counting soldiers	82 sec.	—	90	10 min.	72/min.	720
Counting churn strokes	100 sec.	—	115	10 min.	76/min.	760
Counting cotton bolls	217 sec.	—	719	80 min.	56/min.	4480
	464		1588	130	240	7040

Average rate of counting (world time)—count/W.T., 3.4/sec., 204/min.
Average rate of counting (subject's time)—count/E.P.T., 12/min.
Average demonstrated rate (world time)—60/min.

See Table 2 for explanation of abbreviations.

TABLE 2

Group B.	A.T.	S.P.T.	Count	E.P.T.	D.R.	(D.R.)× (E.P.T.)
Counting cows	3 sec.	30 min.	137	30 min.	60/min.	1800
Counting soldiers	3 sec.	10 min.	112	10 min.	80/min.	800
Counting churn strokes	3 sec.	10 min.	114	10 min.	60/min.	600
Counting cotton bolls	3 sec.	80 min.	862	80 min.	68/min.	5440
	12	130	1225	130	268	8640

Average rate of counting (world time)—count/W.T., 102/sec., 6120/min.
Average rate of counting (subject's time)—count/E.P.T., 9.4/min.
Average demonstrated rate (world time)—67/min.

W.T.—world time.
A.T.—allotted time.
S.P.T.—suggested personal time.

E.P.T.—estimated personal time.
D.R.—demonstrated rate.

(10 minutes) for its completion. The following example will illustrate the technique:

"I'm going to give you a problem to solve in 10 minutes. After I tell you the problem, you will receive a signal, at which you will start working on it. At the end of 10 minutes I shall give you the signal to stop. You will have plenty of time."

"Now here is the problem. A young girl is in love with a young man who wants to marry her. However, the girl has an invalid mother who is dependent upon her and to whom she feels obligated. She hesitates to marry because she does not wish to burden her fiance with her mother, and yet she is very anxious to get married and does not wish to sacrifice her entire life to her mother. These young people want your advice."

"When I give you the signal, you're going to think this situation over from all points of view and afterward tell me what conclusion you came to."

"Here comes the signal—Start."

Ten seconds, world time, later she was told,

"Time is up. Now tell me about the problem."

The subject reported that she saw and talked to a young man and a girl about this, their problem. She discussed the matter at length with them, asking the girl various questions and receiving answers. She suggested that the girl work after marriage in order to support her mother, who, she felt, should not live with the young people but rather with some friend her own age. She did not think that the girl should give up her life to her mother, but on the other hand she shouldn't shirk her responsibility. She should marry by all means. She talked mostly to the girl. "The boy didn't have much to say."

Her account of this experience was amazing in the fullness of detail and the amount of reflection that it apparently indicated. This was especially surprising in view of the fact that in waking life the subject is not prone to speculate on matters. When told that she had thought the problem through, not in 10 minutes but rather in 10 seconds, she was astounded.

Numerous other problems were presented from time to time, among them the following:

Should a young girl, daughter of well-to-do parents, seek a job?

What are the relative merits of government and private industry employment?

Are you in favor of compulsory military training?

What do you think about segregation of the Negro in the South?

In every case the reports gave evidence of careful and thorough consideration,

TABLE 3

Activity	W.T.	S.P.T.	E.P.T.
Walking	65 sec.	30 min.	30 min.
Picnic	130 sec.	"all day"	9 hrs.
Day's activities	115 sec.	day	9½ hrs.
Walking	10 sec.	none	30 min.

See Table 2 for explanation of abbreviations.

TABLE 4

Activity	S.P.T.	A.T.	E.P.T.
Walk a.	1 hr.	5 sec.	1 hr.
Walk b.	1 hr.	3 sec.	1 hr.
Walk c.	1 hr.	1 sec.	"30 or 40 min."

See Table 2 for explanation of abbreviations.

and the estimated personal time interval was always the same as the suggested one. She didn't have to hurry. She always "saw" something—that is, she saw and talked to the young couple; she saw the girl who was discussing the job; she saw a government office building and a factory; in considering the segregation problem she was watching a group of poor and shabby blacks in a small southern town. A fishbowl with names in it appeared while she was considering compulsory military training.

The last test done was given a suggested personal time of 10 minutes but an allotted time of only three seconds. The subject reported that she seemed to be working on it for 10 minutes, and gave a very complete account of her "thoughts."

OTHER EXPERIENCES

All sorts of activities were suggested to the subject, among them the following:

Reviewing previous periods of her life in her "mind's eye."

Listening to a band.

Taking walks.

Going on picnics.

"Reliving" periods of her life.

Dreaming.

Sometimes she would be told to engage in a given activity for a suggested length of time, and to signal by dropping her raised arm when the time was up. Table 3 shows the relation between suggested personal time and world time in some of these cases.

Usually there was both an allotted time (A. T.) and a suggested personal time (S. P. T.), the interval being designated by signals. Almost without exception the subject's estimate of the interval was the one that had been suggested to her. However, where the A. T. was too short, the estimated personal time would be less than the suggested one "because you interrupted me before the hour was up." This led to a series of "one-hour walks" with gradually decreasing allotted times. "The walks," incidentally, were over the same "route" each time. Table 4 shows the results.

Ine one test the subject was simply told that a band was playing and that she was to listen to it. She was interrupted after 30 seconds and reported that she had been listening for nine minutes. No time had been suggested to her.

On several occasions dreams were experienced as the result of suggestion. Time in these dreams showed the same sort of distortion that is seen in normal ones. Their duration was indicated by the subject dropping her arm when the dream was over.

DISCUSSION

We do not feel qualified to say what the nature of hypnotically induced experience is. What, if any, relation does the "counting," and the "thinking" of this subject, under hypnosis, bear to such activities carried out by her while awake? What is this amazing state of affairs that permitted this subject—"in her mind," of course, but with complete sense of participating—to pick and count 862 cotton bolls in three seconds, carefully selecting each one and occasionally looking beneath the leaves "to make sure that I had not missed any"? We do not know.

We are certain, however, that our subject's sense of time was altered, more or less at the will of the operator, and that in this altered time which he bestowed upon her she had experiences that were very real to her. These, while occurring at a normal rate as far as she was concerned, actually moved incredibly fast according to world time. Furthermore they were experiences that, to a considerable degree at least, "made sense." This in itself is indeed intriguing and causes one to wonder if, under hypnosis, judgments may not be made, and decisions arrived at, in a mere fraction of the world time ordinarily required. Also, it makes one wish that ideas could somehow be introduced into the human mind with a speed proportional to that of the mental activity of this hypnotized subject.

26. Time Distortion in Hypnosis: II

Linn F. Cooper and
Milton H. Erickson

GENERAL INTRODUCTION

In a previous communication (Cooper, 1948) findings were presented which indicated that time sense can be deliberately altered by hypnotic suggestion. Thus a 10-second interval by the clock might seem to be one of 10 minutes to the hypnotized subject. Furthermore the individual concerned might report that he had had an amount of subjective experience in the form of hallucinated activities, thought, feeling, and the like—all proceeding at a normal rate—that was more nearly appropriate to the subjective 10 minutes than to the brief 10 seconds recorded by the clock. One of the inferences from these results is that mental activity, under the conditions described, can take place at extremely rapid rates while appearing, to the subject, to progress at customary speeds. In the present paper a further inquiry is made into this phenomenon. After a brief consideration of time it proceeds to the presentation of experimental results, followed by an analysis of the findings and a discussion of their significance.

Notes on Time and the Concept of Time Distortion

Einstein has made the following statement: The experiences of an individual appear to us arranged in a series of events; in this series the single events which we remember appear to be ordered according to the criterion of "earlier" and "later." There exists, therefore, for the individual, an I-time, or subjective time. This in itself is not measurable. I can, indeed, associate numbers with the events, in such a way that a greater number is associated with the later event than with an earlier one. This association I can define by means of a clock by comparing the order of events furnished by the clock with the order of the given series of events. We understand by a clock something which provides a series of events which can be counted. (Barnett, 1950).

Reprinted with permission from *The Bulletin Georgetown University Medical Center,* 1950, *4,* 50-68.

While the hands of a clock move frm one position to another, an infinite number of other changes take place in the cosmos. And wherever that phenomenon which we call awareness exists, there is probably a sense of the passage of time, and a sense of sequence. In other words subjective experience seems to be inseparably interwoven with time sense, which, as is true of other primary experiences, is indefinable. Yet we all know what it is, and we apparently conceive of it as a magnitude, for we speak of a long or a short time, and readily compare intervals one with another. And our perception of it as a magnitude differs from that of another magnitude—space—in a strange way. Time seems to be of us, and inseparable from our very existence. Furthermore one is tempted to think of subjective time as extending from future to past in a direction at right angles, so to speak, to all other experience.

Although we cannot at present measure subjective time, we can gain some idea of the seeming duration of an event or interval by asking a person, "How long did it seem?" He may then reply, "It seemed like 10 minutes," meaning, of course, that his sense of the passage of time was approximately that which he generally experiences when the clock hands advance a certain distance—i.e., 10 minutes. Were we to inform him that actually the clock had advanced by only five minutes, he might reply, "It seemed longer than it was [by the clock]." Thus we all come to associate a certain quantity of subjective time with a given amount of movement of the clock hands. Exactly how we do this is not known, but certainly we are aided by observed changes in the physical world. At any rate it is common experience that a given world time interval may seem longer or shorter, depending upon the circumstances. When the difference between the seeming duration of an interval and its actual duration is great, we say that time distortion is present.

Time distortion is most commonly seen in the dream, where many hours of dream-life may be experienced in but a few minutes by physical time. Furthermore, the phenomenon is not infrequently encountered in times of danger or narrow escape, where intervals of but a few seconds may seem to be greatly prolonged. In such cases the long subjective interval may be filled with thoughts and images proceeding at an apparently normal rate, and movement in the physical world, actually often very rapid, may appear to be in "slow motion." It is by no means rare for the individual involved to report that in the emergency his performance was improved because he seemed to have more time for decisions.

There are numerous other conditions under which time distortion occurs. Thus a given interval may seem to be prolonged in the presence of pain, discomfort, anxiety, anticipation, or boredom. On the other hand it may seem shortened during pleasure, amusement, or interest.

The perception of time may be altered also by organic brain lesions, certain drugs, the psychoses and psychoneuroses, delirium, and toxic states. In general time seems to pass more rapidly for the aging than for the young.

Welch (1935–1936) has made a study of time distortion in hypnotically induced dreams, and Erickson (1937) has reported the phenomenon in a hypnotized subject who was reliving past events. Inglis had a subject who claimed to be able to bring about an apparent slowing of observed physical phenomena at will, and to have employed this ability to advantage while boxing, when it aided him in placing blows.

Finally, time sense can be deliberately altered by hypnotic suggestion and a predetermined degree of distortion thus effected, as reported in an earlier communication.

Depending upon the circumstances, certain changes in subjective experience may accompany time distortion. The following outline presents some of the more important of these:

The Narrow Escape.
  A given world time interval seems prolonged.
  Sensory experience.
    All sensory experience may seem to be slowed down, action appearing to occur in "slow motion." Actually, high speeds in the physical world are often involved.
  Non-sensory experience.
    Thought, imagery, etc. are often much increased in amount per unit of world time. As far as the person involved is concerned, the activity seems to proceed at a normal rate.
The Dream.
  A given world time interval may seem much prolonged.
  Sensory experience.
    Physical stimuli are usually not experienced as such.
  Nonsensory experience.
    Much dream activity may take place in a short world time interval.
    This activity appears, to the dreamer, to proceed at the normal rate.
Hypnosis (with "slowed" time).
  A given world time interval may seem much prolonged.
  Sensory experience.
    In the few cases where sounds have been "injected" into hallucinatory experiences, their apparent duration was increased.
  Nonsensory experience.
    Much activity may take place in a very short world time interval.
    This activity appears, to the subject, to proceed at a normal rate.
Boredom.
  A given interval seems prolonged.
  Sensory experience.
    No change.
  Nonsensory experience.
    No change.

DEFINITIONS AND ABBREVIATIONS

W.R.—world time—solar time as measured by watch or metronome.

P.T.—personal time—I-time—subjective, experiential, or psychological time.

E.P.T.—estimated personal time—estimate, by subjects, of the length of an interval of their experiential time.

S.P.T.—suggested personal time—a time interval suggested to the subject under hypnosis. In these experiments the subjects came to think of this as "special time." Hence such expressions as "You're going to spend 20 minutes of your special time . . ." were frequently used.

A.T.—allotted time—the time, in world time, that is allotted to a test by the operator. It is not told to the subject. Thus it may be suggested to the subjects that they will have 10 minutes for a problem, while the actual interval between signals is only 10 seconds.

D.R.—demonstrated rate—in the counting experiments the subjects were frequently asked to demonstrate, by counting aloud, the rate at which they counted hallucinated objects. This was done both during trance and posthypnotically. In the former instances the subject had finished the test and was presumably not in a phase of response to suggestion.

(D.R.) (E.P.T.)—demonstrated rate multiplied by estimated personal time—a product used in the counting tests. It indicates the count that would be reached if the subject counted at the demonstrated rate for a period equal to the estimated personal time.

(D.R.) (W.T.)—demonstrated rate multiplied by world time—the count that would be reached if the subject counted at the demonstrated rate for a period equal to the world time.

Time Distortion—a marked difference between the seeming duration of a time interval and its actual duration as measured by the clock.

A description of a test will illustrate the use of these terms:

"You now see a large bag full of jelly-beans on a table. . . . Now tell me what you see." The subject describes the scene.

"Stay there, please, and listen to me. When I give you the starting signal by saying 'Now,' you're going to spend at least 10 minutes (of your special time) taking them out of the bag one at a time, counting them as you do so, and placing them on the table in piles according to color. Please don't hurry. At the end of 10 minutes I'll give you the signal to stop." "Here comes the starting signal. 'Now.' "

Ten seconds later—"Now make your mind a blank please. Your mind is now a blank. Tell me about it, please."

The subject reports that he counted 401 candies and gives the approximate number in the black, white, and red piles. Others were blue, yellow, green, and pink. He tells how the piles were located, and notes that some of the black ones fell on the floor. He tells of wondering whether the spotted white ones, which he used to know as "bird's eggs," are still flavored with banana. He counted "one by one," without hurrying, counting for what seemed to be about eight minutes. There were no omissions. When asked to demonstrate, by counting aloud, the rate at which he worked, he counts to 59 in one minute.

In this example, then, the world time (W.T.) and the allotted time (A.T.) was 10 seconds, the suggested personal time (S.P.T.) 10 minutes, the estimated personal time (E.P.T.) 8 minutes, and the demonstrated rate (D.R.) 59 per minute.

SUBJECTS

The subjects were divided into two groups, an earlier one of four, which worked for a period of seven weeks, and a later one of two, which worked a little over a week. All except one had had a college education. All were much interested in the experiments, cooperative, and eager to improve their performance. They were paid by the hour.

Subjects A, B, C, D were not informed concerning the nature of the problem until the end. With subjects E and F, on the other hand, this was discussed at the start.

Table 1 gives further information about them.

METHODS

In essence the experiments consisted in suggesting to the hypnotized subjects that they perform certain hallucinated activities and in studying the relationship between the experiential and the physical time involved. In the majority of tests an allotted time (A.T.) was used. In a few instances the hallucinated activity was explored by means of injected sound signals.

TABLE 1

ct	*Age*	*Sex*	*Marital*	*Education*	*Occupation*	*Interest*	*Number of tests*	*Experimental hrs.*	*Prev. hypnosis*
	25	M	M	College	Student	Psychology	213	39½	Some
	23	F	M	College	Student	Psychology	202	31	None
	23	F	S	College	Student	Psychology	184	32	5 hrs.
	32	F	M	College	Teacher	Music	139	35	None
	18	F	M	High School	Housewife		41	12	None
	28	M	M	College	Student	Psychology	29	7	Some

There follows a partial list of the activities used:
Buying various things
Counseling
Counting various objects
Dancing
Dreaming
Free association
Group discussion
Housework
Listening to a metronome
Listening to music
Making decisions
Mathematics
Painting
Sewing
Seeing movies and plays
Thinking
Walking and riding
Watching games
Writing letters

Induction of a simple trance state was effected by suggestions of sleep. Post-hypnotic amnesia was routinely suggested with the earlier group of subjects, but was only partially successful. The later group was told that they could remember the trance experiences if they so desired.

As a rule the suggestions were read from cards to insure uniformity. Timing was done with a stopwatch. There were two kinds of sound signals used, one the striking of a (damped) tumbler with a metal knife; the other a note on a pitch instrument.

The work was done in the afternoon, the usual session lasting an hour. During trance the subjects lay supine on a bed with their eyes closed.

Notes on Suggestions

In the following discussion a completed activity is one which progresses to the fulfillment of certain stipulated or implied conditions (none of them concerning the duration), at which point it reaches completion. Examples are drawing a picture, making some toast, counting a given number of objects, walking a certain distance, etc.

Incomplete, or continuous, activities are those which do not progress to such a limit.

It will be noted that we have defined the completed activity as being limited by considerations other than duration. This is done in order to permit a special treatment of the time factor.

The degree of time distortion and the amount of subjective experience occurring within the experiential time interval depend upon various factors. Important among these are the absence of presence of an allotted time (A.T.) and its duration, the assigning of an incomplete or a completed activity, and the absence or presence of a suggested personal time (S.P.T.) and its magnitude. A classification of suggestions according to these considerations will be given below.

Suggestions were introduced by the expression, "Now give me your attention please. When I give you the starting signal by saying 'Now,' you are going to. . ." The activity itself was then suggested. If it was felt advisable to "clear" the subjects' minds of residual scenes before the above introductory statement, they were told, "Now any scenes that you've been witnessing are disappearing from view. They have now disappeared, and your minds are now a blank."

The method of termination of an activity depended upon the absence or presence of an allotted time.

(a) In the absence of an allotted time (A.T.), and when the suggested activity was a completed one, the subjects were instructed to notify the operator when they had finished the assignment. They were told, "When you've finished, you'll let me know by saying 'Now.' " This was also done with incomplete activities without an allotted time (A.T.), which were always given a suggested personal time (S.P.T.) in these experiments.

(b) In the presence of an allotted time (A.T.) the termination of the activity was, of course, brought about by the operator. It was our practice to say nothing to the subjects concerning the fact that they would be told when to stop. One may, if one wishes, say, "After a while I'll tell you to stop." Or, in those cases where a suggested personal time (S.P.T.) is used, "At the end of so many minutes [constituting the S.P.T.], I shall tell you to stop." The actual terminating suggestion, given when the allotted time (A.T.) had expired, was "Now make your mind a blank. Your mind is now a blank." No mention of the allotted time (A.T.) as such was ever made to the subjects while in trance.

In assigning a suggested personal time (S.P.T.) to an activity the following form was used: "—you're going to spend (at least) 10 minutes (of your special time) watching a baseball game." The phrases in parentheses were used frequently in the later experiments. The "at least" gives a certain leeway to the subject, and the "special time" gives expression to the uniqueness of distorted personal time, a concept which the subjects came to appreciate of themselves.

In the classification of activity suggestions, code designations are built upon the following symbols:

A.T.0—no allotted time was used.

A.T.+—an allotted time was used.

A—an incomplete activity.

B—a completed activity.

1—no mention is made concerning the duration of the activity.

2—subject is told, "You'll have plenty of time," or, "There'll be plenty of time."

3—a definite suggested personal time (S.P.T.) is assigned.

Thus A.T.0, A1 means that no allotted time was used, that the activity was incomplete, and that no stipulation was made concerning its duration.

Classification of Suggestion Types

I. Without Allotted Time.
    Incomplete Activity.
    Without suggested personal time. (Code A.T.0,A1.)
    "—you're going to go walking."
    With suggested personal time (Code A.T.0,A3.)
    "—you're going to walk for 10 minutes."
    Completed Activity.
    Without suggested personal time. (Code A.T.0,B1.)
    "—you're going to draw a picture."
    With suggested personal time. (Code A.T.0,B3.)
    "—you're going to spend ten minutes drawing a picture."
II. With Allotted Time.
    Incomplete Activity.
    Without suggested personal time. (Code A.T.+,A1.)
    "—you're going to go walking."
    With suggested personal time. (Code A.T.+,Ae).
    "—you're going to spend 10 minutes walking."
    Completed Activity.
    Without suggested personal time. (Code A.T.+,B1.)
    "—you're going to draw a picture."
    With suggested personal time. (Code A.T.+,B3.)
    "—you're going to spend ten minutes drawing a picture."
    Termination suggestions.
    I—as in paragraph (a) above.
    II—as in paragraph (b) above.

After a test activity was finished, the subjects were asked to report on their experience. The following form of request was used: "Now tell me about it please," or, "Now tell me what you did."

Other questions were then asked, such as the following:

"Was it real?"

"Were there any omissions or gaps?"

"Did you hurry?"

"How long was it?"—"How long did it take?"—"How long did it seem?"

"Were you aware of the sound signal?"

"How high did you count?"

"Did you enjoy it?"

RESULTS

Introduction

In these experiments the results consist of the reports of our subjects plus the actual time observations by the experimenter. The reports in turn are descriptions of subjective experiences while responding to suggestions in hypnosis. So amazing are they, when their time relations are considered, that the opinion has been expressed in connection with previous, similar work that the subjects, in reporting, probably resort to restrospective falsification, elaborating on a very meager original experience in order to please the operator.

Thus we are faced at the start with the question—"Did these subjects really have the experiences they say they had?" The question is one of the utmost importance and is, by its very nature, most difficult to answer. The difficulty arises from the fact that purely subjective phenomena cannot be shown to another person and thus proven to exist by demonstration. It is true that, because we all claim to have such experiences as dreams, emotion, thought, sensation, and the like, we readily grant that our neighbors also have them. Consequently these phenomena have come to be accepted as realities that are experienced by mankind as a whole. However, the sort of experience reported in this and in a previous paper has been had by too small a group to attain acceptance in this manner. Moreover we cannot at present know these alleged phenomena "by their fruits," for they have not yet been correlated sufficiently with behavior, nor has "operational" mental activity yet been demonstrated to occur more rapidly in "prolonged" time than normally.

The best we can do under the circumstances is to give an account of our subjects' reports, which are fairly numerous and uniform, and to hope that the reader will find them interesting and will speculate upon their significance. Indeed, our ignorance of the nature of subjective phenomena per se is abysmal. Yet in a sense these are the most "real" part of existence. Our relatively great knowledge of the physical world has been won largely as the result of our ability to apply to it the process of measurement. This process, unfortunately, can be used only indirectly in the study of the subjective time to be in the nature of a magnitude—which won't stand still long enough to be measured. It is obvious that we need some other tool for our work, possibly a tool of new and strange design.

Table 2 gives some of the significant data on certain tests. These were selected because they show the performance of the subjects at their maximum proficiency after adequate training.

Generalizations from Results

The following generalizations can be made on the basis of our results.

TABLE 2

Sub-ject	Code	Activity	W.T.	A.T.	S.P.T.	E.P.T.	Count
A	A.T.0 B1	Walking one mile	59″			13′	
A	A.T.0 B1	Watching movie short	1′35″†			12′	
A	A.T.0 B1	Walking to school	1′ 6″			20′	
B	A.T.0 B1	Walking to school	1′ 53″			20′	
B	A.T.0 B2	Painting a picture	43″			15′	
B	A.T.0 B1	Counting 200 flowers	3′ 26″			15′	200
C	A.T.0 B1	Listening to music (piece)	2′ 45″			10′	
C	A.T.0 B1	Walking to school	2′ 17″			30′	
A	A.T.+ A1	Group discussion		1′		13′	
A	A.T.+ A1	Reliving		1′		1 hr.35′	
A	A.T.+ A1	Reliving		20″		15′	
B	A.T.+ A1	Group discussion		1″		10′	
B	A.T.+ A1	Free association		1′		15′	
B	A.T.+ A1	Picnic		2′		20′	
C	A.T.+ A1	Group discussion		20″		14′	
C	A.T.+ A1	Shopping		20″		10′	
D	A.T.+ A1	Watching races		10″		5′	
A	A.T.+ B1	Considering problem		1′		20′	
A	A.T.+ B1	Counseling		10″		12′	
B	A.T.+ B1	Morning routine		10″		10′	
B	A.T.+ B1	Making a pie		1′		15′	
B	A.T.+ B2	Swim		1′		25′	

†—*indicates correction of error in previous printing.*

There is a marked difference between subjects as regards their ability to produce the various phenomena under study. This is to be expected, and it is mentioned here in order to call attention to the fact that the amount of training required is variable within wide limits. Thus one subject may require only three hours training while another may require 20.

In all cases the reports were simple narrative accounts of a recent experience, given in much the same way as any waking person might go about answering the request, "Tell me what you did this morning?" The amount of detail varied with the individual. Because of the time required for complete reporting, the subjects were usually asked to be brief.

All subjects showed the phenomenon of time distortion, and all were able to engage in mental activity during the prolonged subjective time intervals. This activity proceeded at a rate considered normal or usual so far as the subject was concerned, yet its amount was greatly in excess of what the world time interval would ordinarily permit.

TABLE 2—(Continued)

Code	Activity	W.T.	A.T.	S.P.T.	E.P.T.	Count	D.R.
A.T.+ B1	Counseling		20″		10′		
A.T.+ B1	Counseling		10″		10′		
A.T.+ B1	Listening to music (piece)		20″		5′		
A.T.+ B1	Watching ballet (scene)		20″		10′		
A.T.+ B1	Problem		1′		15′		
A.T.+ A3	Watching football game		10″	10′	10′		
A.T.+ A3	Counting candies		10″	10′	8′	402	60
A.T.+ A3	Visiting friends		10″	10′	5—10′		
A.T.+ A3	Counting candies		10″	10′	10′	127	
A.T.+ A3	Watching races		10″	10′	10′		
A.T.+ A3	Swimming		10″	10′	8′†		
A.T.+ A3	Dancing		10″	10′	10′		
A.T.+ B3	Counting pennies (50)§		10″	10′	3′	28	19
A.T.+ B3	Considering a decision		30″	1 hr.	1 hr.		
A.T.+ B3	Counting flowers (150)§		10″	10′	10′	145	
A.T.+ B3	Counting pearls (200)§		10″	10′	10′	100	

world time.   E.P.T.—estimated personal time.
allotted time.   D.R.—demonstrated rate, in terms of items counted per minute.
-suggested personal time.   §—*subject to count at least this number.*

In all cases performance improved with practice.

All four subjects who worked with the metronome were able to effect marked slowing of the instrument. With two of these, practice was required.

Four out of the five subjects who practiced counting activities during time distortion achieved satisfactory results. The fifth had difficulty but showed progressive improvement, and there is reason to believe that she would succeed with further training.

All subjects were astonished by the things they did, some of them strikingly so, when informed of the facts.

Sound signals could be introduced into hallucinated experiences in all cases in which this was tried with sufficient care. Their position in the experiential time interval corresponded fairly well to that in the world time interval.

Individual Reports

The following two case reports are presented:
(1) "What would you like to do now?"
"My husband molds bullets for his gun. I could be counting them as he makes them."

"For how long do you want to do this?"

"For 10 minutes."

The following suggestions were then given:

"When I give you the starting signal by saying 'Now,' you're going to spend at least 10 minutes of your special time counting bullets as your husband makes them."

"If the sound signal is given, you will be aware of it."

"Here comes the starting signal—'Now.' "

The pitch instrument was sounded from the fourth to the seventh second.

At the end of 10 seconds—"Now make your mind a blank. Your mind is now a blank."

"Now tell me about it."

"It was at a molding party of the club. There was quite a crowd there. I counted for maybe six minutes and ran out of bullets, so I waited for more. I didn't count the full 10 minutes. While I was counting them, this other boy walked up—he was talking and waving his arms. The pot of lead tipped over. It burned his foot rather badly. I got up but then sat down again and continued counting. The others were running all over the place. The remainder of the lead we put back on the stove. I counted 493. That's when I stopped and waited. Then later I got up to 546."

"Did you hurry?"

"I didn't hurry too much as I was counting, but I kept busy."

"Was it real?"

"Yes."

"When I give you the signal to start, please show me, by counting aloud, how you counted the bullets. Now."

Subject counted at a rate of 54 per minute.

"Were you aware of the sound signal?"

"When they spilt the lead, it sizzled a lot."

"How long was the sizzling?"

"It seemed like three or four minutes."

(This interpolation of the sound signal into the hallucinated activity will be discussed later.)

(2) "What would you like to do now?"

"To package some cookies. I used to do this."

"For how long?"

"Twenty minutes."

The following suggestions were then given.

"When I give you the starting signal by saying 'Now,' you're going to spend at least 20 minutes of your special time packaging cookies. As you do this, you'll count them. If the sound signal is given, you will be aware of it. Here comes the starting signal—'Now'."

The pitch instrument was sounded from the fifth to the eighth second.

At the end of 10 seconds—"Now make your mind a blank. Your mind is now a blank."

"Now tell me about it please."

"I was down in the basement. There were worktables. I was counting. I counted them as I put them in the smaller sacks. I counted 1,003. That was all I got. In the middle the telephone outside rang on and on. Just after that there was so much cookie dust all over that I started to sneeze. I sneezed 10 or 12 times. I just couldn't stop. I dropped one package. I didn't answer the phone."

"When I give you the signal to start, please show me, by counting aloud, how you counted the cookies. 'Now'."

Subject counted at a rate of 60 per minute.

"How long did the telephone ring?"

"It must have been five or six minutes. No one answered it outside."

"When I say 'now,' please recall parts of the scene and see if you can tell me what the count was when the phone started ringing and when it stopped."

"It was about 498 when it started, and 889 when it stopped."

"Was it real?"

"Yes."

"Were there any omissions?"

"None."

"How long was it?"

"Probably 23 minutes."

The code designation for the two above tests, and for the one below, is A.T.+,A3.

The following account gives one an idea of the richness of these subjective experiences:

Having said that she would like to spend a half hour riding in an automobile, the subject told how she and her sister, both children at the time, sat on the back seat of the car and counted cows seen along the way. Her sister won the game, counting 45 to her 42. Then they decided to count license numbers bearing the letter C. This was slow, for there was but little traffic. They both saw the same ones, 14 in all. Then they stopped at a roadside stand to buy lemonade from a little girl with pigtails and several missing teeth because they "felt sorry for her." The experience was continuous, without omissions of any kind, and seemed to last "a half hour easy." Asked if she enjoyed it, she replied, "Oh yes!"

Actually this elaborate response to the simple suggestion "You're going to spend at least a half-hour of your special time riding in an automobile, and it's going to be a nice ride," took place in an allotted time of 10 seconds.

Counting

By far the most dramatic results were those obtained in the counting experiments. These were usually run as incomplete activities, with a short allotted time (A.T.) and a moderately long suggested personal time (S.P.T.) In a few instances, however, the suggestion was put in the completed form by saying,

"Since you can easily count 30 in a minute, you will have no difficulty counting at least 300 in 10 minutes. Please take your time and don't hurry." This was generally done during training in an attempt to utilize the performance-increasing value of the completed activity.

Generally the subjects were given a "preview" of their surroundings in the following manner:

"You now see several large bags of gum drops on a table. Please tell me what you see."

Then, after a brief description by the subject, "Stay there now, and listen to me."

The activity suggestion was then given.

Table 3 shows the more important data on the counting tests done after proficiency had been attained.

It will be noted that the count, although much greater than the product (D.R.) (W.T.), is almost invariably less than (D.R.) (E.P.T.). Sometimes the subjects had no explanation for this. At other times they ascribed the discrepancy to the fact that part of the time was occupied otherwise than by counting.

TABLE 3

Sub- ject	Code	Counting	A.T.	S.P.T.	E.P.T.	Count	D.R.	D E
A	A.T.+ A3	Flowers	10″	10′	8′	140		
A	A.T.+ A3	Flowers	10″	10′	7′	41	48	
A	A.T.+ A3	Flowers	10″	10′	10′	35	42	
A	A.T.+ B3	Pennies (50)§	10″	10′	3′	28	19	
A	A.T.+ A3	Potatoes	10″	10′	5′	165	60	
A	A.T.+ A3	Candies	10″	10′	5′	140	60	
A	A.T.+ A3	Candies	10″	10′	8′	402	60	
A	A.T.+ A3	Candies	10″	10′	3′	75	60	
C	A.T.+ B3	Flowers (150)§	10″	10′*	10′	145		
C	A.T.+ B3	Pearls (200)§	10″	10′	10′	100		
C	A.T.+ As	Candies	10″	10′	10′	127		
C	A.T.+ A3	Candies	10″	10′	8′	49		
C	A.T.+ A3	Candies	10″	10′	10′	127		
E	A.T.+ A3	Flowers	20″	20′*	20′	115	54	I
E	A.T.+ A3	Flowers	20″	20′*	20′	40	35†	
E	A.T.+ A3	Strawberries	20″	60′*	50′	600		
E	A.T.+ A3	Tomatoes	20″	60′*	40′	225		
E	A.T.+ A3	Bullets	10″	10′*	10′	546	54	
E	A.T.+ A3	Flowers	10″	15′*	15′	973	60	
E	A.T.+ A3	Cookies	10″	20′*	23′	1003	60	I
F	A.T.+ A3	Nuts	20″	20′*	20′	400	66	I
F	A.T.+ B3	Candies (200)§	10″	10′*	60′	2500	72	4
F	A.T.+ A3	Flowers	10″	10′*	10′	60		

W.T.—world time.
A.T.—allotted time.
S.P.T.—suggested personal time.

E.P.T.—estimated personal time.
D.R.—demonstated rate, in terms of items counted per
*—time suggestion was preceded by the phrase "at lea
§—subject to count at least this number.

Sound Signals

The idea of exploring hallucinatory activities by means of injected sound signals was suggested to us by Dr. J. B. Rhine.

In one group of tests the subjects were told to take a familiar walk—from house to school. No allotted time (A.T.) or suggested personal time (S.P.T.) was used. Thus the code designation is A.T.0, B1. A single short sound signal, produced by striking a damped glass with a metal knife, was employed at various intervals from the start. The subjects were then asked to estimate, at the end of the test, the personal time of the entire experience and the approximate location of the sound signal. The latter they usually did by considering where, in their walk, they were when they heard the signal. The accompanying figure shows the relation of the signal to world and experiential times.

In other cases a pitch instrument was sounded for a known length of time during an activity with an allotted time. The subject was later asked to estimate its duration. Some of the results are shown in Table 4.

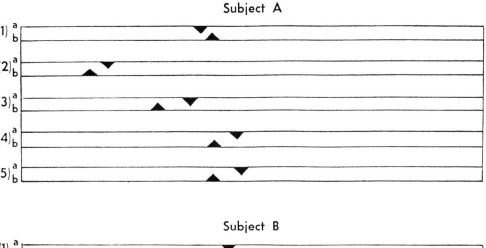

Subject A

Subject B

Subject C

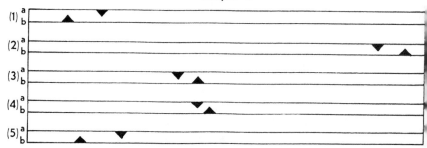

The pairs of lines represent the world time interval (a) and the personal time interval (b) for a given test. The markers show where the sound signal actually occurred in relation to the world time interval (on lines a), and its location in the personal time interval (on lines b), as determined by asking the subject how long it seemed from the beginning of the activity to the signal. Note that the subject locates the signals with fair accuracy. The chart above is based on the following data:

	World Time (secs.)		Estimated Personal Time (min.)	
	Signal	Total	Signal	Total
Subject A				
(1)	60	155	5	12
(2)	20	105	1.5	10
(3)	60	164	3.5	12
(4)	90	192	5	12
(5)	120	252	5	12
Subject B				
(1)	60	133	10	20
(2)	90	135	14	20
(3)	110	133	17	20
(4)	30	107	4	20
Subject C				
(1)	30	163	3	30†
(2)	120	137	28.5	30
(3)	60	159	13	30
(4)	90	210	17	37
(5)	46	196	4	30

TABLE 4

Subject	Activity	Code	A.T.	S.P.T.	E.P.T.	Sound Signal		
						Time	Appearance Form	Est. Duration
E	Baking cake	A.T. + B3	15″	15′	10′	5th to 10th sec.	Auto horn stuck	3 or 4′
E	Mowing lawn	A.T. + A3	10″	10′	10′	3rd to 5th sec.	Squeaking	2′
E	Counting bullets	A.T. + A3	10″	10′	10′	4th to 7th sec.	Sizzling lead	3 or 4′
E	Picking flowers	A.T. + A3	10″	15′	15′	5th to 8th sec.	Bird singing	5′
E	Embroidering	A.T. + A3	10″	15′	15′	4th to 7th sec.	Radio static	3 or 4′
E	Counting cookies	A.T. + A3	10″	20′	23′	5th to 8th sec.	Telephone ring	5 or 6′
F	Watching basketball	A.T. + A3	10″	10′	5′	5th to 6th sec.	"Funny noise"	1′
F	Picnic	A.T. + A1	20″†		20′	10th to 15th sec.	"Like a train"	"Quite a while"

The subjects, even though forewarned, were not always aware of the sound signal, and when they were, it was experienced in various forms.

Striking the glass, to some subjects, sounded exactly as it does normally and did not take on any significance in the hypnotic scene. More often, however, it was heard, as a somewhat similar sound, such as a tumbler dropping on the floor, one striking the side of the pitcher, an object falling on a hard surface, etc. Sometimes, however, the actual sound signal acquired an entirely different significance, e.g. the sizzling of the lead and the ringing of the telephone noted above.

Since the subjects had been led to expect a sound signal, they quite possibly anticipated it and included appropriate "properties" in their hallucination. Thus in three successive counseling scenes glass was present either as a tumbler or a pitcher.

Even so there is much food for thought here, for an object must fall before it can strike the floor and make a noise, and there must be some cause for the fall. Somehow or other all this is arranged in a most skillful way. Interestingly enough, to one subject the sound signal came just as he struck a pole with a stick. After telling about it he added, "I had anticipated hitting the pole, for I saw it in the distance." It may be that there is a definite lag between the communication of the signal to the brain and its entry into the hallucinated world as an appropriate part of the picture.

Similarly with the pitch instrument, at times it was unchanged, but more often it was altered.

The presence in our group of two musicians, one with "absolute pitch," gave us the opportunity of determining whether a sound, coming into the hallucinated world of altered time sense, would itself be altered in tone, i.e., lowered, by virtue of the new time relations. (Suggested by P. F. Cooper, Jr.). The answer apparently depends upon the degree to which the sound is disguised. In hallucinations where it was heard as a horn and an air-raid "all clear," the pitch was recognized as C. Usually, however, there was little resemblance to the original, the pitch instrument being heard variously as a bird, a fan, a squeaky lawn-mower, the buzzing of a crowd of people, etc.

Of considerable significance is the fact that almost always the duration of the sound seemed much longer than it actually was. This is what we would expect in the presence of time distortion and in a way confirms the reports of the subjects. Here too we have the awareness of a physical phenomenon during time distortion, and the event seems to be slowed. Compare this with reports from persons following a narrow escape, who may say that world events appeared to be in "slow motion."

Not always was the intruder welcome, for on several occasions the hallucination was completely destroyed. On others the subject would become "nervous," irritated, or apprehensive.

In fact one subject reported that in subsequent walks, whenever he passed the spot at which he had previously been "jolted" by the sound signal, he had a sense of impending trouble. Here apparently we have an instance of conditioning to a hallucinated environment. This is evidence of the subjective reality of the experience.

Metronome

Initially a metronome was started at 60 strokes per minute, and the following suggestion then given: "You now hear a special variable speed electric metronome striking at 60 strokes per minute. Please listen to it. - - - - I'm soon going to slow it down gradually. When it's going very slowly, please let me know by saying 'Now.' "

At varying intervals thereafter this suggestion might be given—"It's going slower and slower, slower and slower—."

The metronome, of course, continued at its initial rate of 60. Three of the four subjects who were thus tested reported marked slowing. However, for one of these, the slowing did not always occur.

Next four subjects were trained to "imagine" that they were listening to a metronome. This was accomplished with little difficulty. The following suggestions were then used:

"When I give you the starting signal by saying 'Now,' you're going to imagine that you hear that metronome beating at 60 strokes a minute. As you listen, it will go slower and slower. It will slow down fairly rapidly. When it's going very slowly, you'll let me know by saying 'Now.' As you listen, you will count the strokes to yourself."

All four subjects reported marked slowing, usually after an interval of less than two minutes. Along with this they almost always had visual hallucinations, generally involving a metronome. In the case of some subjects these were bizarre and elaborate and included pendulums with sliding weights, large and small hammers striking in counterpoint, flexible and adjustable shafts, men swinging hammers or beams, airplanes looping, etc. The subjects were asked to state the count and to demonstrate the initial rate and the rate during the last five or ten beats. The count generally averaged much less than 60 per minute.

Finally all four subjects were again allowed to listen to the real metronome and were given the suggestion noted in the first paragraph of this section, plus instructions to count the strokes to themselves. No further "slowing" suggestions were given. All reported slowing, and there was usually an appropriately low count. Actually the rate was unchanged.

There were, however, occasional reports in the last two exercises described above where the subject reported marked slowing although the count was not proportionately reduced. In view of the fact that these subjects could very closely approximate a rate of 60 per minute, the conclusion is inescapable that there was a purely subjective lengthening of the interval between sounds, whether real or hallucinated. Two of the subjects studied in previous experiments, incidentally, showed the same phenomenon.

Review and Practice

A few pilot experiments were run in an effort to learn whether our subjects could review for a history examination in distorted time. The results were inconclusive, but it led one of them, a professional violinist, to attempt to reivew certain pieces and to practice these while in a self-induced trance, using her "special time" for this purpose. Her own account of the procedure follows.

> I put myself into a trance and then practiced in several different ways. I might see the music before me and mark the spots that needed extra practice. I would then play the different spots over and over until I got them—which helped my finger memory because I was actually playing in the trance. [This was hallucinated activity only. In other words she was "actually playing" only in the hallucinated world and did not in the physical world.]
>
> I did "passage practice"—picking hard passages and playing them in several ways to facilitate speed and accuracy.
>
> Then I went through the whole composition for continuity. In doing this in "special time" I seemed to get an immediate grasp of the composition as a whole.

Thus she was able to practice and review long pieces over and over in very brief world time periods, and she found that not only did her memory improve strikingly, but also her technical performance. This remarkable result is attested to by her husband, himself a musician. In other words she felt that hallucinated practice of these pieces, learned years ago, improved her subsequent performance.

It is impossible at present to evaluate these reports which, if confirmed, carry important implications for facilitation of the learning process. They suggest at least two possibilities for making use of distorted time in the hypnotized subject.

The first is that the memorizing of new material might be speeded up by hallucinating the frequent repetition, either in visual or auditory form, of whatever is to be learned. The second, of course, is that hallucinated practice and review be used to aid in the acquiring of new motor skills. So important are these considerations that we feel obliged to mention them, however far-fetched they may be, for their experimental investigation is fairly simple.

Coincidental Happenings

Not infrequently certain fortuitous and sometimes unwelcome things occurred and were reported. They are listed here because they so convincingly bespeak the reality of these experiences, all of which occurred during time distortion.

While rowing a boat, the subject lost an oarlock.

While picking up shells, he stepped on a jellyfish.

While getting out of the way of an automobile, he tripped over the curb.

"Mother helped me on with my coat. It wouldn't button. Dad buttoned the vest."

In changing a tire he found only three lugs in place. Later he found the fourth one in the hubcap.

"I hurried to get past a hayfield which was irritating my nose."

In changing electric light bulbs, the one he threw into the scrap-basket broke.

While drilling, the man next to him "passed out" from heat prostration.

Asked to sing a hymn in church, "I stood on the platform and announced to the Baptists that I was going to sing a Jewish chant. I sang it all the way through." (In an allotted time of 10 seconds!)

While burning trash, he watched the match burn down, after striking it on his pants.

"I shaved but I didn't wash my face afterward. I didn't have authority to do that." (Suggestion: "You're going to shave." A.T., 10 seconds.)

"The barn door stuck because it had been raining."

"While getting shaved, the barber spent so much time talking to the other barber that the lather began to set."

While pulling up and counting iris, "the reason it took so long was because I had to get the dirt off them."

While watching a football game, his attention was drawn away from the play by a fight in the stands.

In counting potatoes, as he removed them from a basket and placed them in a sack, some fell back into the basket and hit the rim. "I had to count them over again."

While counting candies as he removed them from a box, "there was a strawberry cream that had mashed and cracked and had run a little bit. What to do with it passed through my mind."

In counting gum-drops, he noticed that some were stuck together. "I pulled out the whole bunch and broke them off and put them in separate piles."

While picking berries, the carton got so full that they kept falling out.

While riding the waves during a swim, she hit the bottom.

While washing the baby, she spilled all the water.

In making sandwiches, she cut her finger with the knife, and it bled.

In counting chickens, she noticed that one had started sprouting wing feathers, and one was sick.

In playing truth or consequences, "they blindfolded me and a fellow kissed me and embarrassed me."

"The Victrola started slowly. I had to wind it again."

While roller-skating, she fell down.

While crocheting, the thread broke.

In buying shoes, she tried on four pairs first.

A student who came for counseling said, "I want you to know that I'm not here because I'm crazy."

While counting chickens, the first one defecated in his hand. Asked what he then did, he replied, "I wiped it off on the second chicken."

SPECIAL INQUIRY

After a subject had completed his or her report, various questions were asked of them, designed to clarify certain aspects of their experiences. The following section is devoted to a presentation of the knowledge thus acquired.

Falsification

One who hears a number of these accounts soon becomes intuitively convinced of their truth and of the actual existence, for the subject, of the alleged experiences. The subjects were honest individuals, interested in the research, and their waking reports agreed with those given under hypnosis. They all insisted that the reporting was an entirely different event from the original experience, and that they did not elaborate. They repeatedly resented the implications of questions directed to the discovery of possible retrospective falsification. Incidentally, during the reporting they saw scenes from the activity, but they were generally "stills." Questions directed to the "subconscious" concerning the presence of falsification were invariably answered in the negative. Finally, the locating of the sound signals, the coincidental happenings, the apparent conditioning, the spontaneous expression of emotion during reporting, and the subsequent amazement on learning the true time relations, all render retrospective falsification unlikely.

Realness

In the accomplished subject the hallucinations possess a high degree of "realness," which is fairly consistent. At times, however, reports will mention a lack of clearness in the imagery. Such instances are on the whole infrequent. Often, however, the definition and clarity will be confined to those things which occupy the immediate attention, the background remaining vague.

As training develops the ability to hallucinate, so also it aids in the production of scenes that are real and true to life. Thus, with practice, there comes an increase in detail and in color. To encourage this, we daily gave our subjects the following suggestion—"In this trance any scenes you see will be very clear and any experiences you have will be very real, so that you will actually live them."

One very striking evidence of the realness of the activities is the frequent reporting of accidental or coincidental happenings. For instance, the subject who is crocheting breaks her thread, and later cuts her finger while making sandwiches or spills the water in which she is bathing her child. Another one, asked to burn some rubbish, strikes the match on his pants and watches it as it burns, or while walking past a hayfield begins to sneeze. The chalk that the angry teacher throws strikes the blackboard and breaks, and the little boy whose ears stand out so far scratches his head as he strives to find the answer to his problem. Such telltale details were frequently mentioned, and a partial list of them is given elsewhere.

It was not uncommon for the subjects to say how much they enjoyed an activity and how much they regretted its termination. At other times they would get tired or become bored. In one case a subject who had been waked was telling about an activity in which he seemed to be quite young. After telling how rough the ground was over which he had been dragging a bushel basket of apples, he asked, "Did I breathe hard?" When answered in the negative, he replied, "Then I guess I must have just imagined it." Thus the subjective reality of the experience was so great that even in the waking state he expected physical manifestations of it.

Continuity

Action was continuous in all but a very few hypnotically suggested experiences. This was ascertained by frequent questioning. In fact the subjects themselves would usually volunteer information concerning an omission or a skip. When these occurred, there was generally a shifting of scene without apparent transit from one location to the other. Another form would be a "floating" from one place to another instead of walking. One subject did this when she became bored.

In several instances a shift of scene apparently represented an amnesia, for on being asked to relive the action, the subject reported the missing experience.

The hearing of rather long pieces of music without omission by musicians is most suggestive of true continuity. One of our subjects was a skilled professional violinist, and another an accomplished amateur. They frequently reported that there were no omissions in the familiar pieces they heard or played in trance. Other subjects gave similar testimony concerning familiar popular music.

Another point that bespeaks continuity is that injected sound signals invariably arrived during hallucinatory action. In other words this type of exploration revealed no action-free intervals.

The counting experiments also support the view that continuity is present.

Time Sense

For successful "utilization" of experiential time by increased mental activity it is probably mandatory that the subjects be totally unaware of their surroundings and of world time. With some subjects this is difficult at first; with others it is easy. Three of our subjects were apparently helped by a brief talk on the relation between subjective and physical time, the dream being cited as the most familiar example of the variability of the former. The transition period which preceded the full acceptance of "special time" in these subjects was most interesting, as the following accounts will show.

The efforts of these subjects to get away from world time are worthy of note. One of them, who said she seemed always to be aware of world time, would hallucinate a weird cellophane covering for herself, into which to "escape." With this pulled down over her, she was able to hear several minutes of music, in normal tempo, during but a few seconds of world time. Her difficulties disappeared one day, and with them the necessity for these odd creations, while she was counting silently the strokes of an hallucinated metronome. She counted 27 metronome strokes in 55 seconds, and as she did so, found herself watching a "sky-writing" pilot in the air. She was much impressed with what she saw. "Here I am counting by myself in one kind of time and watching an airplane do fancy loops, and it seemed to me that he had so much time to kill between strokes. He had time to do all kinds of fancy loops and things, and it didn't seem strange at all. If he had been writing a word, which he wasn't, there were enough loops to take care of a six- or seven-letter word." Later she said, "I think the thing that convinced me most [of the reality of another sort of time] was seeing the airplane and noting how easily, effortlessly, or unhurriedly it was looping in between strokes. He seemed to have so much time to kill. Now I really realize that the thing to do is to relax and accept the fact that there is more than one kind of time."

Another remark that is worthy of record was made by a subject who, while in trance, refused to demonstrate the rate at which she picked flowers. When asked why she couldn't do so, she said, "I'll try, but I tell you I picked 145 in 10 minutes and I can't repeat it now because I don't have a time limit right now—neither a time limit nor a limit on the flowers I might pick. It doesn't coincide. But there I'm in a certain frame of mind—and it can't be repeated here. I can't do it incomplete—in a fragment. It's impossible. I can do it again too!"

Then, after waking, she said, "Well, I consider this a unique experience with a certain time limit and a certain amount of work to be accomplished. If the time limit or the amount of work or both are eliminated, it is not the same experience anymore, so I can't show you in a fragment how it went, or how it was."

Some weeks later she was crystal-gazing in a trance and was asked to see herself picking the same flowers, and to count them aloud as she did so. Under these circumstances she readily complied. The demonstrated rate was 42 per minute.

Another subject, in the transition period, once tried to escape world time by "going off from the main shaft of a mine." His difficulties were further revealed in the following remarks: "Here's a funny thing now. I was conscious that the physical time was perhaps 11 seconds, but the hallucinated time seemed to be about two minutes."

"And I was able to move these marbles, one at a time, without taking a handful or anything like that and without hurrying."

"Were you aware then of two time factors?"

"Yes—I was aware of the consciousness of physical time and also of hallucinated time."

"Would it be fair to say that you weren't completely lost in the hallucinated experience?"

"No—I was engrossed in the hallucinated experience, but yet some other factor seemed to indicate that it was merely 10 or 11 seconds."

"Were you aware of that while you were counting marbles?"

"No—but when I said [while reporting] 'two minutes,' the other factor came into play and gave a quiver—a physical shock—to my body, and then the idea of 11 or 10 seconds came."

In some of the tests the subjects spontaneously hallucinated a watch or a clock. In others, these instruments were suggested to them. Usually, but not always, the time indicated by the hallucinated timepieces was appropriate to the subjects' experiences.

Thought

All our subjects felt that the thought processes they employed in their hallucinations were comparable to those of the waking state. In fact some of them felt that they were possibly of a superior type, there being an increased ability to consider situations as a whole. One said, "Considerations are weighed out mentally instead of verbally." We were, unfortunately, unable to give this matter the attention it deserved.

We feel that this is true thought. If such indeed be the case, then it is obvious that this all-important mental activity, at least a form of it, can take place at very rapid rates, while appearing to proceed normally. It is obvious also that such thought can deal only with concepts available through memory. Yet it is possible that the increased accessibility of material from the unconscious might be advantageous under certain circumstances. Creative thinking likewise might be aided.

To date the ability to perform mathematical thought more rapidly while time sense is distorted under hypnosis has not been demonstrated.

Hallucinations and Dreams

We do not consider these hypnotically induced experiences to be identical with dreams, and we have never used the word "dream" in a suggestion unless we wish to produce such an entity. That our subjects were in most cases aware of a difference is evidenced by the fact that they occasionally, while resting, would say, "I went to sleep and had a dream." However, these dreams had no connection with the experimental work. Between assignments it was customary to give the suggestion, "Now let your mind wander whither it will—to pleasant scenes," in response to which they usually engaged in desultory hallucinated activity, which they did not consider the same as dreaming.

Five of our subjects were asked to compare these two types of activity, and all felt that there were differences. Their remarks follow.

Concerning hallucinated activities in hypnosis:

Hallucinations are,

—"better organized."

—"more real than dreams."

—"directed dreams."

—"very true to life, and the experiences carry on as if they were really happening."

"You are conscious of what you are doing and can control the situation better."

"They make sense, whereas dreams are often silly and impossible."

Concerning dreams:

Dreams are,

—"less meaningful."

—"often far-fetched."

"They contain nonsense and extraneous things."

"They show less continuity."

"They contain something impossible or unreal."

"In dreams the mind jumps from one subject to another, and it is as if the dreamer were looking on instead of participating in it."

"Most dreams are next to impossible."

Awareness of Surroundings

The subjects with the best performance all reported that while engaged in an assignment they were completely unaware of their surroundings. The ones who were unable to lose touch completely with the physical world had difficulties with time distortion.

Miscellaneous

The subjects all said that the hallucinated activity never started before the starting signal and that it invariably ended abruptly at the termination signal.

As an example of the sudden cessation of action, one subject told how the signal came as he was reaching for something, and his hand was in midair as the hallucination disappeared.

Aside from their intrinsic significance, these findings speak against retrospective falsification.

ANALYSIS OF RESULTS

Experiential Time

If we simply assign a completed type of activity to subjects and ask them to let us know when they have finished it, we shall find the following to be true:

a) They will complete the activity
b) It will appear to proceed at the usual rate.
c) It will probably take less than three minutes by world time.
d) It will seem to the subjects to take much longer.

In other words there will be definite time distortion even though the suggestion made no stipulation whatever concerning time.

These relations are shown in an analysis of 55 tests in which the activity was a completed one, and in which there was no allotted time (A.T.) or suggested personal time (S.P.T.).

	World Time.	
	Average	127 secs.
	Maximum	270 secs.
	Minimum	35 secs.
	E.P.T.	
	Average	17 min.
	Maximum	45 min.
	Minimum	3 min.

E.P.T. was invariably longer than W.T.

It is thus seen that in hallucinatory activity in hypnosis there is apparently an inherent tendency for time distortion to occur.

Another basic consideration is the fact that the subjects will try their best to carry out whatever is suggested—to "obey orders," in other words. Thus if, with a given activity, we use an allotted time and gradually decrease this in repeated tests, assuring the subjects that they will not have to hurry and will have plenty of time, they will learn somehow to adjust their hallucinated action to the short world time interval. They will "fit it in," so to speak. Yet they will continue to complete the assignment without hurrying, it will appear to be real in every way, and the experiential time will be appropriate. Use is made of this in training subjects, and it is of considerable importance for this reason.

A little reflection will reveal that in assigning a completed activity we assign not only a definite amount of action, but also in effect an appropriate amount of experiential time. This is especially true if we tell the subject not to hurry. The reason for this, of course, is that the awareness of action or change is invariably accompanied by a sense of the passage of time.

On the other hand, time sense itself may be prolonged without the awareness of an equivalent amount of action. This is seen in the dream, where there is often a relative poverty of action. It is also true in those hypnotically induced hallucinations where, on occasions generally involving a suggested personal time (S.P.T.), the amount of activity, though large, is still much less than would be expected when one considers the estimated personal time (E.P.T.).

We can see from the above that, in hypnotically induced hallucinations, the experiential time is influenced by some inherent factor and by the assigned activity itself.

A third consideration, and a most effective one, is the direct suggestion of a subjective time interval—the use of a suggested personal time (S.P.T.).

Amount of Action

Where an incomplete activity is used, and there is no suggested personal time (S.P.T.), the accomplishment depends upon the rate at which the subjects choose to carry out their hallucinated action and the allotted time (A.T.) or world time (W.T.).

On the other hand, where an incomplete activity is used and a suggested personal time (S.P.T.) given, the subjects will strive to fill up their suggested interval with action. Most of our counting experiments are of this type and are indeed remarkable.

With a completed activity the most important factor determining the amount of action is of course the assignment itself. Within undetermined limits, a proficient subject will complete activities as requested.

Summary

The essential points in the above discussion of the relation between type of activity, S.P.T., amount of activity, and E.P.T. are recapitulated below.

I. Incomplete activity.
   1. Without S.P.T.
      Amount of action depends upon subject's chosen speed of hallucina-
      tory action, and upon A.T. or W.T.
      E.P.T. will be appropriate to the action.
   2. With S.P.T.
      Amount of action will be consistent with S.P.T. where the subject is
      proficient.
      E.P.T. will equal S.P.T.
II. Completed Activity.
   1. Without S.P.T.
      Amount of action is determined by the suggested activity.
      E.P.T. is appropriate to the suggested activity.
   2. With S.P.T.
      Amount of action is determined by the suggested activity.
      E.P.T. equals S.P.T.

It is understood of course that the subjects have had enough training to have become proficient. Thus in a sense the above statements apply to the "ideal" subject. The commonest shortcoming is an inability to accept fully a suggested personal time (S.P.T.). It is important to note, furthermore, that in these experiments the allotted time (A.T.) was never less than 10 seconds, and only rarely was the suggested personal time (S.P.T.) over 30 minutes. No attempt was made to explore the limits of performance.

It is clear from the above that hallucinated action and subjective time are to a certain degree interrelated.

Time distortion as effected in these experiments is accompanied by a marked increase in the ratio E.P.T./W.T. It is usually accompanied by an appropriate increase in hallucinated activity. In order to produce these results, then, the following conditions should be fulfilled:

For an incomplete activity:
   A familiar activity
   S.P.T.—long
   A.T.—short

For a completed activity:
   A familiar activity the completion of which requires a relatively long period
   of time
   S.P.T.—not of primary importance. If used, it should be appropriate.
   A.T.—short

In general:
   Subjects often find that the suggestion "Please don't hurry, you'll have
   plenty of time," reassures them and helps them to relax.

TRAINING

The following suggestions may be helpful in the training of new subjects.

Keep concurrent reporting—that is, reporting while an hallucination is actually in progress—to a minimum. This will give the subjects an opportunity to become accustomed to dissociating themselves from their physical surroundings and becoming wholly engrossed in the hallucinated world. Without the ability to do this, satisfactory time distortion cannot be obtained. We used concurrent reporting only in the "previews" to the counting experiments.

In teaching a subject to hallucinate, a good expression to use is, "I now want you to imagine that you're in such and such a place." After a brief interval—"Now make your mind a blank. Your mind is now a blank. Now tell me what you saw."

After the ability to hallucinate has been acquired, it is best to start with either simple incomplete or continuous activities, such as looking in shop windows, with a long allotted time (A.T.) or with a simple completed activity without A.T. By a long allotted time (A.T.) we mean one or two minutes. An estimated personal time (E.P.T.) should be asked for after each activity. It will almost invariably show distortion fairly early during training. It might help to point out this distortion to the subject, who will then realize that there is nothing amiss in experiencing a subjective time interval that is out of proportion to world time.

We have usually postponed the suggestion of a personal time until subjects have acquired some proficiency with simpler procedures, on the theory that failure might discourage them.

Throughout the training, advantage is taken of the following:

a. The inherent tendency toward spontaneous time distortion in hallucinated activities.

b. The effort and the need on the part of the hypnotized subject to carry out suggestions, especially to finish a completed activity.

c. The fact that, at the beginning at least, familiar activities are more readily hallucinated than unfamiliar ones.

d. The fact that the interest and curiosity of the subjects, and their feeling of being productive, tend to improve cooperation and performance. Advantage can be taken of this by giving them sufficient understanding of what they are doing so that they accept and do not reject it.

e. The tendency to improve with practice.

As training progresses, a series of tests is run with completed activities, and a gradually decreasing allotted time (A.T.), but without a suggested personal time (S.P.T.). As mentioned elsewhere, it is not necessary, and is possibly not desirable, to give the subjects any notice to the effect that the operator is going to tell when to stop. We generally began with an allotted time of one or two minutes and cut it down by 10 to 30 seconds at each step. The subjects, "caught short" at first, will soon learn to adjust to the shorter allotted time (A.T.), and will fit their hallucinatory experiences into the interval allowed them, without hurrying or compromising in any way. In this way they learn to work with short allotted times. How far this process can be carried is not known at present.

The next step is the giving of a suggested personal time (S.P.T.). This is of special importance with incomplete activities. Some subjects readily accept this early in their training; others have difficulty doing so. The difficulty seems to arise from at least two factors—a residual awareness of surroundings and consequently of world time, and a deep conviction that it "just ain't so." Practice, and use of a deeper trance, will help overcome the first difficulty. With the second it may help to point out to the subjects that they have on many occasions during their training experienced the variability of subjective time in relation to world time. The results of some of their earlier tests will convince them of this, when shown to them. In addition, it may help to give them some such explanation as the following, which proved to be of definite assistance with some of our subjects.

> There are two kinds of time, one, the time the clock tells us, the other, our own sense of the passage of time. The first of these is known as physical, or solar, or world time. It is the time used by the physicists and the astronomers in their measurements, and by all of us in our workaday life. The second is called personal, or subjective time. Einstein refers to this as "I-time."
>
> It is this subjective time that we are most interested in here. One of the most important things about it is that it is very variable. Thus, if several persons are asked to judge the length of a five-minute interval as measured by a clock, they may have very different ideas as to the duration of the interval, depending upon the circumstances in which they find themselves. To those who were enjoying themselves, or who were absorbed in some interesting activity, the interval might well seem shorter. On the other hand, to those in pain or discomfort or anxiety, the five minutes would seem much longer. We call this time distortion, and the most familiar example of it is found in the dream. You yourself have probably often noticed that you can experience many hours of dream life in a very short time by the clock.
>
> Now, it has been repeatedly demonstrated that subjective time appreciation can be hallucinated just as you can hallucinate visual or auditory sensations, in response to suggestion during hypnosis. The subjects thus actually experience the amount of subjective time that is suggested to them. So in a sense you have a "special time" of your own, which you can call on as you wish. Moreover you have an unlimited supply of it. It is the time of the dream world and of the hallucinated world, and since it is readily available, you will never have to hurry in these tests. Furthermore it bears no relation whatever to the time of my watch, which, consequently, you will ignore.
>
> Knowing these things, you can now relax and take your time.

CONTROLS

As a control our subjects were asked to estimate both short and long world-time intervals while engaged in various activities. With the short intervals, which varied from 10 to 30 seconds, the activities were counting small objects, sorting cards, talking, and reading. The instructions, incidentally, were patterned after those used under hypnosis in assigning activities. With the longer intervals, ranging from 15 minutes to several hours, ordinary daily occupations were engaged in.

It is quite obvious from the results in Table 5 that the estimated times are in far closer agreement with the actual world-time intervals than under the type of time distortion studied in this report.

TABLE 5
Controls
Estimation of Short Intervals (10-30 seconds).

Subject	Maximum Error (%)
A	120
B	85
C	100
D	150
E	100
F	66

Estimation of Long Intervals (15 minutes to several hours).

Subject	Maximum Error (%)
A	80
B	30
C	—
D	25
E	25
F	25

SPECIAL DISCUSSION OF PSYCHOLOGICAL AND PSYCHIATRIC IMPLICATIONS

Milton H. Erickson

The discovery or development of every new concept in science poses the difficult question of what will be its eventual significance and application. The publication of the senior author's first experimental study of time distortion impressed this writer with the possibility of new and better understanding of certain psychological functionings and consequently, of different and more searching procedures and methodologies in dealing with psychological problems. Long experience in the fields of experimental and clinical psychology and in psychotherapy has repeatedly demonstrated the tremendous importance of experiential realities in human living and, at the same time, the laboriousness and often futility of any attempt at reaching a measurable understanding of them. Certainly the findings made in the original study and confirmed by this second report suggest the definite possibility of new, readily available avenues for the examination of those inner experiences that constitute so large a part of life, and which are so difficult to study in a rigorously scientific manner. However, no attempt will be made to offer an elaborate discussion of psychological and psychiatric implications of these two studies. Rather, a number of them will be mentioned briefly with the hope that readers will accept the task of considering for themselves those implications bearing upon fields of special interest to them.

Foremost to this writer are the implications of time distortion in the field of psychotherapy. Certainly no one questions the importance of the subjective experiential life of the individual, nor the present unsatisfactory, laborious, time-consuming, and unscientific methods of studying it.

What constitutes a subjective reality? Of what seemingly pertinent and irrelevant elements is it comprised? In what way is it integrated into the total life of the person? What self-expressive purposes does it serve for the personality? What determines its validity? How does it differ from a memory, a dream, a fantasy, and from retrospective falsification? In what way is it distorted by present methods of concurrent or retrospective reporting, and how much time does it require? All of these considerations are touched upon either directly or indirectly in this study, and each of them constitutes a significant problem in psychotherapy, to say nothing of psychology in general.

The girl who, in an allotted 10 seconds, subjectively experienced in voluminous detail a 30-minute automobile ride upon which a report could be made with "stills" of the scenes, demonstrated a challenging possibility of a new approach to the exploration of the experiential past of the individual.

The subject who found it impossible to demonstrate in the waking state her experiential behavior in picking flowers because it was under a "different" time limit and work limit, and yet, weeks later in a trance state was able to demonstrate in actual accord with the previous findings, discloses the possibility of controlled studies of subjective realities.

Delusions and hallucinations have long constituted intriguing problems. They are subjective realities accepted by the person as objective realities. Yet one of our experimental subjects experienced dragging a basket of apples with such vividness that he expected the experimenter to note his forced respirations, which, similar to the basket, were only subjectively real. Nevertheless he recognized the total experience as entirely subjective but did so without it losing the experiential feeling of its objective reality. Experimental studies patterned from this and the other similar findings above might lead to a better understanding of pathological delusions and hallucinations.

Theories of learning and memory are constantly in need of revision with each new development in experimental studies in those fields. In this regard the findings on the subject who in an allotted 10 seconds took a long walk and developed a conditioned-response reaction by being "jolted" by an interjected sound signal, pose definite problems for research on learning, memory, and conditioning.

Similar is the instance of the violinist who, in allotted 10-second periods, subjectively experienced playing various compositions with practice effects as attested by a competent critic. Subsequent to this study she made use of her "special personal time" to experience subjectively practicing a difficult, long-forgotten composition, and then to play it successfully in reality from memory without having seen the written music for years.

In this same connection one may speculate upon the role of motor functioning in mental learning, since this violinist subjectively experienced the total process of playing the violin, studying the written music, and memorizing it, while lying supine and inactive, and yet demonstrated the actual effects of reality practice.

A tempting experimental study based on these findings would be the exhibition of a form board to naive subjects and having them in special personal time, at a hallucinatory level, practice assembling it. The findings of this study warrant the assumption that, even as motor activity facilitates learning in everyday reality, subjective motor activity, as contrasted to objective, is an effective aid to memory and learning.

Another interesting, actually significant finding bears upon the validity of the experiential realities to the subjects, negates assumptions of retrospective falsification, and serves to confirm the findings of various competent experimenters that hypnosis cannot be used to induce antisocial behavior. This was the discovery in several instances that suggested hallucinatory activities were unexpectedly regarded as objectionable by the subjects. The reactions were essentially the same in all cases and can be illustrated by the following example.

The subject was instructed to experience herself in the role of a psychologist counseling a client relative to a problem involving epilepsy. Although willing to serve as a counselor, the experiential reality of the situation was so great that she could not tolerate the task of dealing with the problem because she felt that epilepsy was beyong the rightful scope of a psychologist and that any counseling she might offer would be unethical. Accordingly she referred her hallucinatory client to a medical man and developed intense resentment and hostility toward the experimenter for calling upon her to violate, even at a subjective level, her personal code of ethics.

While much could be said about the implications of time distortion and the experimental findings reported here in relation to concepts of gestalt psychology, the molar psychology of Tolman, Hull's modern behaviorism, and Freudian psychology, this will be left to the special interests of the reader. Time and its relationships constitutes a significant element in all psychological functioning no matter from what school of thought it is viewed. Hence any study dealing with the element of time itself in psychological functioning must necessarily have important bearing upon every school of thought, and this concept of time distortion offers a new approach to many psychological problems.

A final item of special interest to this writer centers around the problem so pertinent in research in clinical psychology and psychotherapy—namely, the problem of how to create for a subject or a patient a situation in which to respond with valid subjective reality. Certainly this study indicates the possibility of much more rigorous controlled research with time as aid rather than as barrier.

To conclude, this writer in all modesty—since the conception, plan, and organization of this study was entirely original with the senior author—can express the opinion that the experimental findings reported in this paper offer a wealth of highly significant ideas and concepts for extensive psychological research and clinical psychiatric application.

SUMMARY

The relation between experimental time and world time during hallucinated activity in hypnotized subjects was studied.

Various hallucinated activities were suggested and were carried out by the subjects, a record being made of their duration. In activities which did not involve a completed act a personal time interval was often suggested to the subject. The hallucination was terminated either by the subjects themselves or by the experimenter. In some instances the period of action was explored by injecting sound signals into the hallucination. In another group of tests the suggestion was given that a metronome, either real or hallucinated, would slow down. A brief study was made to determine the value of hallucinated review of previously learned material. An interesting attempt to improve motor function by hallucinated practice is reported.

The most important findings were that the investigator can control within limits the subject's sense of the passage of time, and that in a prolonged experimental time interval an appropriate amount of subjective experience, hallucinatory or otherwise, may take place. The suggested slowing of the metronome was accepted. Thus the findings of our initial report were confirmed. The sound signals often were apparent in the hallucination, their position in the subjective interval roughly corresponding to that in the world-time interval. Continuous sounds were definitely prolonged, as was to be expected. In one case the sound signals set up a conditioned stimulus in the hallucinated environment.

Inquiry was made into various aspects of the hallucinatory experiences. They were found to possess both realness and continuity. Time sense was strikingly altered. Thought seemed quite natural in distorted time. Subjects felt that their hallucinated activities in these experiments differed from nocturnal dreams. Subjects were unaware of their surroundings during their hallucinations.

The findings as a whole are analyzed.

Suggestions are given concerning the training of new subjects.

The experiments are discussed from a psychological and psychiatric point of view.

CONCLUSION

In view of these findings, the following statements are probably true:

1) Results reported in an earlier communication on time distortion in hypnosis (Cooper, 1948) can be duplicated in the majority of subjects. Time sense can be deliberately altered to a predetermined degree by hypnotic suggestion, and subjects can have an amount of subjective experience under these conditions that is more nearly commensurate with the subjective time involved than with the world time. This activity, while seeming to proceed at a natural rate as far as the subject is concerned, actually takes place with great rapidity.

2) Retrospective falsification does not enter into the subject's reports.

3) The continuity of these subjective experiences during distorted time is good.

4) Thought, under time distortion, while apparently proceeding at a normal rate from the subject's point of view, can take place with extreme rapidity relative to world time. Such thought may be superior, in certain respects to waking thought.

27. The Clinical and Therapeutic Applications of Time Distortion

Milton H. Erickson

INTRODUCTION

The discovery or development of a new concept in science poses difficult questions concerning its definition and its eventual significances and applications. In the experimental work constituting the major part of this book the term "time distortion" has been used as offering a reasonably concise way of expressing a methodology for a study of time itself as one of the essential elements in the experience of human living. To so emphasize time as an integral part of human experience may be considered trite, but it is not trite to recognize time as an element fully as worthy of investigation as any other factor in human living. Yet such investigative studies have been seriously neglected. From recognition of this oversight and long interest in the experiential significance of time came the senior author's impetus for the foregoing experimental studies.

In sharing with him a small part of the experimental studies, this writer became interested in the question of the clinical and therapeutic applications of the experimental findings. The publication of the first experimental study (Cooper, 1948) suggested definite possibilities of new and better understandings of psychological functionings and consequently of different and more searching procedures and methodologies in dealing with psychological problems. Subsequent experimental studies and tentative applications of the findings to clinical work confirmed that first impression. In the second experimental study (Cooper and Erickson, 1950) these impressions have been discussed in the form of a general summary as follows:

> Foremost to this writer are the implications of time distortion in the field of psychotherapy. Certainly no one questions the importance of

Written with L. Cooper. In *Time Distortion in Hypnosis*. Baltimore: Williams & Wilkins, 1954. Reprinted with permission of the publisher.

the subjective experiential life of the individual, nor the present unsatisfactory, laborious, time-consuming, and unscientific methods of studying it.

What constitutes a subjective reality? Of what seemingly pertinent and irrelevant elements is it comprised? In what way is it integrated into the total life of the person? What self-expressive purposes does it serve for the personality? What determines its validity? How does it differ from a memory, a dream, a fantasy, and from retrospective falsification? In what way is it distorted by present methods of concurrent or retrospective reporting, and how much time does it require? All of these considerations are touched upon either directly or indirectly in this study, and each of them constitutes a significant problem in psychotherapy, to say nothing of psychology in general.

The girl who in an allotted 10 seconds subjectively experienced in voluminous detail a 30-minute automobile ride upon which a report could be made with "stills" of the scenes, demonstrated a challenging possibility of a new approach to the exploration of the experiential past of the individual.

The subject who found it impossible to demonstrate in the waking state her experiential behavior in picking flowers because it was under a "different" time limit and work limit, and yet weeks later in a trance state was able to demonstrate in actual accord with the previous findings, discloses the possibility of controlled studies of subjective realities.

Delusions and hallucinations have long constituted intriguing problems. They are subjective realities accepted by the person as objective realities. Yet one of our experimental subjects experienced dragging a basket of apples with such vividness that he expected the experimenter to note his forced respirations, which, similar to the basket, were only subjectively real. Nevertheless he recognized the total experience as entirely subjective but did so without it losing the experiential feeling of its objective reality. Experimental studies patterned from this and the other similar findings above might lead to a better understanding of pathological delusions and hallucinations.

Theories of learning and memory are constantly in need of revision with each new development in experimental studies in those fields. In this regard the findings on the subject who, in an allotted 10 seconds, took a long walk and developed a conditioned response reaction by being "jolted" by an interjected sound signal, pose definite problems for research on learning, memory, and conditioning.

Similar is the instance of the violinist who, in allotted 10-second periods, subjectively experienced playing various compositions with practice effects as attested by a competent critic. Subsequent to this study she made use of her "special personal time" to experience subjectively practicing a difficult, long-forgotten composition, and then played it successfully in reality from memory without having seen the written music for years.

In this same connection one may speculate upon the role of motor functioning in mental learning, since this violinist subjectively experienced the total process of playing the violin, studying the written music, and memorizing it while lying supine and inactive, and yet demonstrated the actual effects of reality practice.

A tempting experimental study based on these findings would be the exhibition of a form board to naive subjects and having them in special personal time, at an hallucinatory level, practice assembling it. The findings of this study warrant the assumption that, even as motor activity facilitates learning in everyday reality, subjective motor activity, as contrasted to objective, is an effective aid to memory and learning.

Another interesting, actually significant finding bears upon the validity of the experiential realities to the subjects, negates assumptions of retrospective falsification, and serves to confirm the findings of various competent experimenters that hypnosis cannot be used to induce antisocial behavior. This was the discovery, in several instances, that suggested hallucinatory activities were unexpectedly regarded as objectionable by the subjects. The reactions were essentially the same in all cases and can be illustrated by the following example.

The subject was instructed to experience herself in the role of a psychologist counseling a client relative to a problem involving epilepsy. Although willing to serve as a counselor, the experiential reality of the situation was so great that she could not tolerate the task of dealing with the problem because she felt that epilepsy was beyond the rightful scope of a psychologist and that any counseling she might offer would be unethical. Accordingly, she referred her hallucinatory client to a medical man and developed intense resentment and hostiltity toward the experimenter for calling upon her to violate, even at a subjective level, her personal code of ethics.

While much could be said about the implications of time distortion and the experimental findings reported here in relation to concepts of gestalt psychology, the molar psychology of Tolman, Hull's modern behaviorism, and Freudian psychology, this will be left to the special interests of the reader. Time and its relationships constitutes a significant element in all psychological functioning no matter from what school of thought it is viewed. Hence any study dealing with the element of time itself in psychological functioning must necessarily have important bearing upon every school of thought, and this concept of time distortion offers a new approach to many psychological problems.

A final item of special interest to this writer centers around the problem so pertinent in research in clinical psychology and psychotherapy—namely, the problem of how to create for a subject or a patient a situation in which to respond with valid subjective reality. Certainly this study indicates the possibility of much more rigorous controlled research with time as aid rather than as barrier.

Since the publication of the above, opportunities have arisen from time to time to utilize or to adapt various experimental findings in clinical and therapeutic work. However, it must be noted that experimental studies and clinical work belong to different categories of endeavor. In the former rigorous controls must be exercised, and the object is the determination of possibilities and probabilities. In clinical work the welfare of the patient transcends all other matters, and controls and scientific exactitudes of procedure must give way to the experiential needs of the patient in the therapeutic situation. Another type of measure of validity, different from the controlled scientific methodology of experimental procedure, holds in clinical work. Such a measure is constituted by the therapeutic results that can be definitely related to the procedure employed and which are understandably derived from it.

GENERAL CONSIDERATIONS OF CLINICAL APPLICATIONS

Since the clinical situation of psychotherapy is not a Procrustean bed, utilization of experimental findings and concepts must necessarily depend upon the patient's needs and desires and the attendant circumstances. It cannot be a matter of furthering special interests of the therapist. Hence any utilization must await the opportunities and occasions presented by the patient and not represent a planned procedure established out of context with the developing needs of the patient in therapy.

Furthermore the concept of time distortion does not constitute in itself a form of psychotherapy. Rather it offers a method by which access can be gained to the experiential life of the patient. Any therapy resulting derives from a separate process of reordering the significances and values of the patient's experiential subjective and objective realities.

The following case reports are those of patients who presented an opportunity to investigate the applicability of time distortion to psychotherapeutic problems. These reports are presented relatively briefly, and emphasis is placed upon the dynamics of the individual case, since the purpose of the reports is to demonstrate as clearly as possible the problem, the situation, and the circumstances which led to the utilization of time distortion, and the results obtained.

PATIENT A

The first case history illustrates an unwitting and unintentional spontaneous utilization of time distortion by a patient previous to Cooper's initial publication.

It is presented because it demonstrates not only the use of time distortion but how, in the ordinary course of psychotherapy, an opportunity can arise for the utilization of time distortion. Needless to say, at the time of this occurrence this writer was at a loss to understand what had happened, but it laid the foundation for a profound interest in Cooper's first publication four years later.

The patient, an arist in his early thirties, sought therapy primarily for marital problems and secondarily for personality difficulties. During therapy, despite his success in the field of portraits, landscapes, and still life painting, he felt extremely frustrated because he had not painted a circus picture. For more than ten years, even previous to his marriage, he had hopelessly desired to paint such a picture but had not even succeeded in making a preliminary sketch. He had not even been able to think sufficiently clearly on the subject to speculate on what figures or scenes he might wish to portray. The entire project remained a vague, undefined "circus picture."

Although his other problems were clarified during months of therapy, nothing was accomplished in this regard. Even profound somnambulistic hypnotic trances, with various techniques, elicited only the explanation, "I'm completely blocked mentally. I can't think any further than 'circus picture.' " He could not even sketch a possible composition plan of vertical and horizontal lines, his usual method of working out preliminary sketches.

Since the patient wished further therapy in this connection, a deep trance was induced and he was given the following posthypnotic suggestions:

> 1. Stretch a large canvas in the neighborhood of 24 x 40 inches. It may be larger or smaller—possibly a golden rectangle.
> 2. Secure a more than adequate new supply of paint tubes and pigments and set them up as if in preparation for painting.
> 3. Make out a daily hourly schedule for the next three months, blocking out hours that might be used for painting the circus picture (his usual procedure in planning a new painting).

He was then awakened and dismissed with an amnesia for trance events.

A few days later, with no realization of the posthypnotic nature of his performance, he reported that he had made a time schedule for the next two months. This schedule would permit him, if he worked hard, to finish his present commitments within two weeks. Then over the remaining period there would be blocks of time totalling 70 hours which he would reserve absolutely for an effort to paint a circus picture. No mention was made in relation to the other posthypnotic suggestions.

He was hypnotized deeply and instructed to fulfill his current commitments adequately. Then he was to set about this proposed project, working slowly, carefully, and painstakingly as he always did, without rushing or hurrying. In so doing the 70 allotted hours would pass with utter and incredible speed. Yet he would work satisfyingly and at a normal tempo. (The intended purpose of this instruction was to prevent him from feeling the burden of a long-continued task.)

All of this instruction was emphatically and repetitiously given to insure adequate understanding.

Two days later a highly excited telephone call was received from him, asking for an immediate interview.

His story was as follows: While completing a current picture, he ceased work to eat his lunch of sandwiches in the studio. While so doing he decided to stretch a new canvas, thinking vaguely that he might use it for the projected picture.

This done, he picked up the remainder of his sandwich and found it inexplicably dry. Puzzled by this, he chanced to look at the stretched canvas and was utterly amazed to find a freshly completed oil painting of a circus scene. With intense curiosity he examined it carefully, feeling exceedingly pleased and satisfied with it. Suddenly he saw his signature in the corner (which he ordinarily appended ritualistically only when he had given his final approval to his work) and noted at the same time that the style of painting was his own. Immediately he had rushed to the telephone, observing on the way that the clock gave the hour as 6:00 P.M. All the more bewildered, he had telephoned, saying, "Something's happened. Can I see you right away?" To this account he added, "What happened? What happened?"

Since he had brought the picture with him, he was questioned about it. The performing dog in it was really a neighbor's; the equestrienne was his recently acquired second wife; the clown was himself; and the ferriswheel was one his present wife had recently described in a reminiscence. Yet the painting as a circus picture was more than satisfying to him as a person and as a critical artist. (At art exhibitions in various states critics have all been most favorable in their comments.)

He was much puzzled by his replies to the questioning and kept reiterating, "It's the circus picture I've always wanted, but it's got nothing to do with any ideas I ever had about a circus picture. It's mine; it's a circus picture; it's what I want. But what happened?"

He was hypnotized and asked to explain.

> When I had the canvas stretched like you told me to, I knew I had plenty of time. So I worked on it as slowly and as carefully as I could. I painted just the way I always do—slowly. And I had trouble, too. I knew the clown's coat had to be blue and the ribbon and the ferriswheel also. They had to be the same shade of blue but a different blue. I used different pigments for each one, and it was an awful slow job mixing those different pigment combinations to get the same shade of color. And I had trouble with the horse's mane. I wanted to work out an entirely new technique for that, and I finally succeeded. [The critics also commented favorably on that item of technique.] But I didn't have to hurry because I had plenty of time. And then when I had it finished,

I studied it a long time, making sure that it was all right, and when I was finally sure, I signed it. Then I picked up my sandwich and woke up. I didn't remember a thing, and when I saw the picture I got puzzled and scared. I even examined the studio doors—they were still locked on the inside. So I knew that I had better see you in a hurry. But it is a good picture. Be sure you help me to know that I really painted it.

While he now knows he painted it, his general understanding of the entire matter is sketchy and vague, but his satisfaction is unchanged. A year later he commented on the "curious fact" that in daylight the three shades of blue are identical but that under different lighting effects they are dissimilar. From this he had "deduced" that he "must have used different pigments."

Therapy was terminated a few sessions after the completion of the picture.

Comment

Regardless of the dynamics involved, the hypnotic suggestions given, and the purposes served for the patient, one fundamental fact remains. This is that a task conceived of as requiring, on the basis of long experience, a total of about 70 hours, was accomplished in six with no known preliminary preparation, at a totally unexpected time and in a fashion alien to established patterns of behavior and work. The parallelism between this report and many of the experimental findings reported in the first part of this book is at once obvious and pertinent.

PATIENT B

This next case report is decidedly different. It is an example of the intentional therapeutic use of time distortion as a consequence of a failure to secure results by other methods. And since therapy was the desired goal, there was no opportunity to utilize the clinical situation to demonstrate time distortion *per se*. Rather its existence as a reality in the situation was assumed, and all efforts were directed to the securing of therapeutic results as a direct outcome of its utilization.

The patient was a 30-year-old twice-married woman who was known to have suffered from recurrent episodes of hysterical amnesia characterized by essentially complete personal disorientation. These attacks dated from two years prior to her second marriage six years ago. Since it had been a hasty wartime marriage, her second husband knew practically nothing about her past except that she was a widow with two children and that she had recurrent "sick spells when she didn't know nothing."

She was first seen in consultation while hospitalized with amnesia. She gave the date as 1934 and described herself as a woman but could give no other information. She did not recognize her name, her husband, or her children. She complained of a severe headache, and her appearance and behavior corroborated this complaint.

She made, as was usual for her, a sudden spontaneous recovery after three weeks in the hospital and left hurriedly in a state of terror upon discovering where she was.

She was seen at home the next day. She was fully oriented but still frightened. She explained that many times in the past she had suddenly awakened in a hospital after being unconscious for days at a time or even weeks. However, she was uncooperative about further questioning or therapy.

She was seen again five months later. During that time there had been a number of brief amnesic periods during which she had been cared for at home by constant supervision. Now she was again amnesic, and the only information that could be elicited was that she was a woman and the year was 1934. She was hospitalized and heavily sedated for a week. She then made her usual sudden spontaneous recovery, but this time she was cooperative about therapy.

She was interviewed daily for the next three months from two to four hours each day. Only a scanty outline history of her present marriage could be obtained. As for her previous life experiences, she knew only that she had been widowed, but not the year, although she knew the birthdates of her children. Nothing more of apparent significance was elicited. Mention of the date 1934 was without any apparent meaning to her. She expressed doubts about the correctness of her first name. This lack of knowledge of her past was most frightening to her, and every inquiry caused her intense anxiety.

Concerning her amnesic states, she regarded them as periods of unconsciousness. She described them most unsatisfactorily. Typical of her accounts is the following: "When I woke up in the hospital, the last thing I remembered was walking down the street when a truck came along." Or, it could have been going to the store or reading a newspaper.

During those first three months every possible effort was made to secure some understanding of her problem. Since she proved to be an excellent subject, every hypnotic technique known to the writer was employed, to no avail. While she could be regressed in age, such regression was limited to the relatively normal happy periods of the past eight years. Indeed, every effort to reconstruct her past by whatever technique was restricted to some limited period of the recent past. Automatic writing and drawing, crystal gazing, dream activity, mirror writing, free association, random utterances (i.e., every fifth, eighth, or tenth word that comes to mind), depersonalization, disorientation, identification with others, dissociation techniques, and other methods were futile. It was obvious that she was trying to cooperate, but only relatively meaningless material of the recent past was secured.

Additionally during this time she developed frequent amnesic states of one to three days' duration. During them she always gave the date as 1934. While she could be hypnotized deeply in these states, and hypnotic phenomena elicited, these were restricted and limited in character to various aspects of the actual office situation. Thus she did not recognize the writer but did regard him as a possibly friendly stranger. She viewed the wall calendar as "some kind of a joke," since it did not read 1934. She could hallucinate readily and would count the books in an hallucinatory bookcase. She would write simple sentences upon request, but did not seem to understand what was meant when efforts were made to have her write her name, geographical location, or age. Nothing that impinged upon her personal life seemed to be comprehended. However, to a colleague experienced in hynosis but unacuquainted with her, she was obviously in a strance. She would awaken from these trances in the amnesic state.

These amnesic periods usually terminted after a night's sleep, or if more than a day in duration, responded to heavy sedation.

On one occasion, in the writer's presence, she chanced to see through the window a Borden's milk truck, and immediately she developed a three-day amnesia. Several days after her recovery, during an interview, she happened to see on the writer's desk, purposely placed there, a small calendar advertising Borden's milk. Another three-day amnesia occurred. Later she was asked to copy a weekend sales advertisement. Upon reaching the item of Borden's milk, a third three-day amnesia ensued. Still later, while discussing recipes, Borden's milk was mentioned by the writer with a similar result. Finally she was asked what a male hog was called and what a bear slept in. She gave the correct answers. She was then asked, with careful emphasis upon the key words, "What would happen if you put a boar in a den?" Her reply was simply, "I guess the bear would eat him."

However, the amnesic states were frequent and were apparently caused by a variety of other stimuli not recognized by the writer.

Every effort was made to secure some measure by which the amnesias could be interrupted or aborted. Finally a very simple measure was found. Since she could be regressed to a previous age within the eight-year limit, and since she always gave the date as "sometime in 1934" when amnesic, the regression technique in reverse was employed. Thus she would be hypnotized and in a systematic, repetitious fashion be told, "Yes, it is 1934, and the seconds and the minutes are passing one by one, and as the seconds and the minutes pass, so do the hours, and with the passage of the hours, so do the days pass. As the days pass, so do the weeks. The weeks come and go and the months pass and 1935 is coming closer and 1934 is passing, passing. And after 1935 will come 1936, which will pass, and then it will be 1937," etc., until the current time was reached. Frequent need to utilize this technique rapidly reduced the initial period of 30 minutes to less than five in bringing her out of her amnesic state. On two occasions, when she wandered away from home and was picked up amnesic by the police, her memory was promptly restored by this technique.

A laborious, futile effort was made, following this success, to regress her from 1934 to 1933 or earlier. Then an effort was made, after getting her to accept the argument that there were years antedating 1934, to induce her to forget 1934 and to experience the date as 1930, with the hope of building up from that date. This and numerous variations of the general idea failed.

After three months' failure to make recognizable progress with her it was decided to employ time distortion.

In the guise of sharing personal satisfactions in past professional experimental work, several prolonged sessions with her were devoted to presenting the general concepts and experimental procedures of time distortion, all as something of only intellectual interest to her. In so doing it was hoped to avoid any measures of defense against this therapeutic approach.

This was done in both the waking and the hypnotic states. When she seemed to have a good comprehension of world, solar, clock, special, experiential, and allotted time, time distortion, and time distortion experiments, the suggestion was offered that she might like to engage in an experiment comparable to those that had been read and explained to her. She agreed readily and seemed to be under the impression that the project was essentially a mere continuation of the already published study.

The next day she was hypnotized deeply and instructed as follows:[1]

You have many times taken a trip in a car and enjoyed it immensely. The car was moving very rapidly. You saw this sight, you saw that scene, you said this, you said that, all in an ordinary way. The car moved fast, but you were sitting quietly, just going along. You could not stop the car, nor did you want to. The telephone poles were so many feet apart and they came along one by one and you saw them pass. You saw the fields and they passed by, large fields, small fields, and you could only wait quietly to see what would be in the next field, and to see whether the next house would be brick or frame. And all the time the car went along and you sat quietly, you saw, you thought, all in your own way, at your own speed, just as it happened, and the car just kept going. You did not need to pay attention to the car, *just to what next would happen,* a field, a house, a horse or *whatever was next.*

"However, this experiment will not be a car ride. I have just used it to explain more fully to you. I could have described going through the cooking of a dinner—peeling potatoes, washing carrots, putting on pork chops—*anything that you could have done.*

"Now I'm going to give you much more time than you need to do this experiment. I will give you 20 seconds world time. But in your special time that 20 seconds will be just as long as you need to complete

---

[1]These instructions are probably much too elaborate, but a first experimental therapeutic effort with a new methodology is not an occasion for economy. They are presented rather fully in order to demonstrate the effort at comprehensiveness.

your work. It can be a minute, a day, a week, a month, or even years. And you will take all the time you need.

"I will not tell you yet what your experiment or task is. As soon as you nod your head to show that you are ready, I will start the stopwatch and give you the signal *now,* and very rapidly I will name the task and you will start at the beginning of it, the very beginning, and go right through to the end, no matter how far away it is in time. Ready? All right, listen carefully for the click of the watch, my signal, and the name of the task. *Now—from Childhood to Now—Remember!"* [The *Now* was repeated as literally a double signal.]

Her response was a tremendous startle reaction, a gasp, a marked physical slumping in her chair and a frozen facial expression.

Twenty seconds later she was told, "Stop," and was asked, "Through?"

"Yes."

"Will you tell me if I awaken you?"

"Yes."

For several hours there was a tremendous outpouring of her past traumatic memories. These were related in a most remarkable fashion. She detailed them as if they were actually in the course of happening, or as if they were items of the very recent past, and at the same time, in a dissociated fashion, she offered comments and interpolated remarks bearing upon much later events. For example, she began her account with:

My dress is pink. It's my birthday. I'm sitting in a high chair. I'm going to eat my cake. My daddy is going to kiss me. He falled down. That's what happened. My father died of heart failure. I was three years old. Pink dress. When Deborah [her daughter] wanted a pink birthday dress, I forgot everything and I went to the hospital. I couldn't think. My head ached. . . .I'm going on a train ride. Mummie is taking me. It's fun. See the pretty trees. There's cows, too. Mummie is coughing. She's sick. Her handkerchief is all red. [Pulmonary hemorrhage.] I'm scared. My mother is so sick. And every time Elaine [her second daughter] had a nose bleed, I got sick. . . . I'm so tired and thirsty—he keeps doing it—he's going to kill me—I wish somebody would come." [This was a long story of being tied hand and foot to a bed for three days and repeatedly raped by a man named Borden.]

Another account was that of her delivery in 1934 of her stillborn child resulting from the rape, and her vivid report of the delivery scene and her grief over it. "That's when everything in me died. I couldn't stand to remember."

Three more instances that may be cited are her first husband's infidelity and the finding of a love letter from his paramour in his effects, and her present husband's receipt of a letter from a former fiancée, with a consequent amnesia resulting for her; the suicide of one of the girls in the maternity home during her own stay there by hanging from a chandelier, and her own daughter of similar age tying crepe paper to a chandelier as a Christmas decoration; and the inexplicable death of her third child while lying in bed one night, and reading a newspaper account of a similar instance. All of these were vividly described in the present tense and then related to actual amnesic episodes.

There were many more comparable traumatic experiences recalled and discussed, all in chronological order. This required many hours before she could complete her review of her past. Various of the events could be verified, some appeared to be hysterical fantasies of a morbid character, and yet later some of these were found to be true.

Her therapeutic response to this catharsis was decidedly good. However, there were several more brief amnesic episodes, but each time she recovered promptly and was able to define the precipitating stimulus and to relate it to either an incompletely discussed trauma or to one that had been overlooked. In each instance the precipitating stimulus lost its effect upon her. For example, upon moving to a new location, she readily purchased her milk from the Borden truck that traveled that street.

Shortly after all this her husband deserted her. She responded by divorcing him, securing employment, and supporting her children adequately. Her employers thought highly of her.

Therapy was discontinued upon her gaining employment, except for brief casual visits at long intervals.

In final appraisal, two years after termination of therapy, she was still an hysterical personality type, but well controlled and functioning at an adequate personal, social, and economic level.

Comment

What happened during that eventful 20 seconds after months of futile effort, and how it happened, can be speculated upon best in terms of the experimental findings reported in the first part of this book. That the previous work with the patient quite probably laid the foundation for the final outcome does not militate against the significance of what occurred in 20 seconds time.

Her narrative of what happened, extended over many hours, was given largely in the present tense. Yet at the same time it was given with interpolated comments and explanations relating long-past events of her life with those of the recent past. This indicates that the narrative was not a simple initial revivification of the past. Rather it strongly suggests that in those 20 seconds she had achieved a sufficiently comprehensive recollection of her life history to be able to see it in meaningful perspective. Then, in her narrative, couched in the terms in which she had reacquired her memories, she communicated it to the writer for his understanding and at the same time achieved for herself an effective catharsis of her experiential past.

Before utilization of time distortion, therapy was a clinical failure. Twenty seconds of time distortion, whatever that may mean clinically, resulted in a therapeutic success of a known two years' duration.

PATIENT C

This case report concerns a relatively circumscribed emotional problem for which the concept of time distortion was employed as an expeditious and experimental measure.

The patient, a 25-year-old student working his way through college, was primarily interested in the field of entertainment. His voice was fair and he accompanied himself on a guitar. Because of his promise as a singer, a night club gave him regular weekend employment. Unfortunately, as the weeks went by, his performance showed no improvement, and he was notified that he would be replaced at the first opportunity.

This had caused him much discouragement, anxiety, and depression, and he sought therapy because of his hopeless attitude.

His history disclosed nothing of immediate significance except that his studies and his regular week-day employment on a late shift, in addition to the weekend engagement, gave him practically no time for practice.

Further inquiry disclosed that his late shift was characterized by spurts of activity followed by intervals of idleness.

This fact suggested a possibility for utilizing time distortion. Accordingly the question of hypnosis was raised with him, and he dispiritedly expressed his willingness to try anything. He proved to be a good hypnotic subject and was easily trained in hypnotic phenomena.

This accomplished, he was systematically instructed, under hypnosis, in Cooper's experiments on time distortion until his understanding of the general concepts was good. The suggestion was offered that he might participate in a time distortion experiment. He was disinterested in the idea but did consent reluctantly. He preferred that attention be given to his problem.

Accordingly, on a Monday, while in a profound trance, he was given a series of posthypnotic suggestions. These were that he was to utilize, from time to time, each night the idle periods at work to develop brief 10- to 30-second trances. During these trances, at an hallucinatory level, he would have adequate special personal time to practice extensively both his singing and his playing. Since the trances would be brief in clock time, and since his practicing would be hallucinatory in character, his fellow-workers would not note more than that he appeared momentarily self-absorbed.

He was awakened with a total amnesia for the trance instructions and given an appointment for the next Monday.

He reported excitedly at that interview, "I've got a new lease on life. Saturday was the best night I have ever had. Sunday night I did so well that the boss said that if I kept on that way, I could be sure of my job. I don't understand it because I didn't get a chance all week to practice. But Sunday I got out my tape recorder and made a new recording. Then I played it and some of my old recordings for comparison. Sunday's sounded as if I had had a lot of practice. I was amazed to find out how much I had improved. I must have unconsciously ironed out some emotional kink that was interfering."

Hypnotized, he explained that he had averaged at least three long, as well as several brief, practice sessions per night. During the long sessions he went through his repertoire, and the brief sessions were used for the practice of individual selections. Each time everything seemed to proceed at a normal tempo. Additionally, he frequently made an hallucinatory tape recording which he "played back" so that he could listen to his practicing and thus note errors for correction. At no time had any of his associates seemed to notice his periodically preoccupied state. He expressed his intention of continuing with this method of practice and supplementing it with ordinary practice.

At the present time, many months later, he still has all of his jobs and his weekend stipend has been greatly increased. He has enlarged his repertoire, and he practices at every opportunity in the ordinary state and in posthypnotic trances in time distortion.

He is still unaware of his trance activities but is greatly amazed at the rapidity with which he learns new selections.

To date he has made no effort to apply this special learning in any other way. Nor has such a suggestion been offered to him, since the excellent therapeutic result might possibly be jeopardized by other experimental efforts.

Comment

This case report is essentially a parallel of some of the experimental findings reported by Cooper. While the validity of this report rests upon the bare facts of the patient's statements and his continued employment at an increased stipend, there can be no question that the concept of time distortion served a significant personality purpose for the patient. Additionally, of particular note is the fact that the patient elaborated the suggestions given him by including an hallucinatory tape recorder to further still more the hallucinatory practice sessions, and that he has continued to utilize time distortion in learning new selections.

PATIENT D

The manner in which this patient sought therapy was both challenging and baffling. Her seemingly impossible demand was met by the utilization of time distortion, which resulted in amazing and surprisingly rapid therapeutic results.

She was a 19-year-old girl employed in a dental office, and she suffered from a severe reaction to the sight of blood. Usually she fainted, although occasionally she became only nauseated and greatly distressed. Otherwise she was a competent and willing employee and genuinely interested in dental work. She was directly referred for therapy by her employer, who expressed a hope to retain her services and at the same time a fear that her behavior of the past few months precluded any such hope.

She arrived at the office accompnaied by a chaperone. She seated herself and smoothed her dress down with exaggerated modesty and was utterly brief and final in her statements. She declared that she had come for therapy, that this was to be accomplished in a single interview, and that hypnosis was to be employed.

The protest that she was demanding a miracle was disregarded by her. She merely reiterated her demand.

When asked for her history, she replied, "The doctor [her employer] has already told you over the phone. All the time I've worked for him, I've fainted every time I saw blood, and I hate being picked up off the floor over and over again. I'm going to lose my job and I want to work in a dental office. That's my ambition. That's all you need to know. Now, I want to be cured. I want you to hypnotize me right away and cure me." It was as if she had indicated an aching tooth and was demanding an extraction.

A deep somnambulistic trance was induced with remarkable ease. Asked if she were ready for therapy, she shook her head negatively and asked that "things" be "changed." This cryptic request led to an inquiry about the chaperone's presence. She asked that the chaperone be dismissed "tactfully."

When this was done, she hastily and with great urgency declared, "I'm scared—I don't know why—I'm afraid to think *and I won't think*. You have got to hypnotize me some more or I'll wake up—I just can't stay asleep. Just keep me asleep and *don't let me wake up*. You have got to help me, *but don't let me know about it until it's all over,* and do it fast or I'll wake up and faint. *I don't want to know anything and I don't want you or anybody else to find out what's wrong.* So don't try to find out and don't let me wake up." Much of this was repeated with emphasis.

She was assured that her wishes would be met to the fullest extent. The suggestion was offered that first of all it might be well to have her experience, as a means of keeping her hypnotized and as a measure of giving her satisfaction, the various common phenomena of the hypnotic trance. She agreed readily as if being given a reprieve, but admonished the writer not to forget the problem of therapy afterward.

For 50 minutes she enjoyed thoroughly experiencing a great variety of the common hypnotic phenomena. Care was exercised constantly neither to impinge upon her personal life in inducing the hypnotic manifestations nor to seek any understanding of her as a person.

She was then told, while still in the trance, that there remained a couple more phenomena which she could enjoy. One of these was related to time and would really center around a stopwatch, which was exhibited to her.

With every effort to be instructive, she was reminded of the rapidity with which time passed when she was pleased, how slowly when bored, the endlessness of a few seconds' wait for an intensely regarded outcome of a matter in doubt, the rapidity with which a mere word could cause to flash through the mind the contents of a well-liked book or the events of a long, happy trip and the tremendous rapidity and momentum of thought and feelings.

Against this background a detailed elaboration was presented of the concept of distorted, personal, special, or experiential time as contrasted to clock time. Extensive discussion was also offered of the "normal tempo" of distorted or experiential time.

When she seemed to understand, the explanation was offered that this hypnotic phenomenon could be initiated for her by giving simple instructions which she could easily accept fully. These instructions would be followed by the starting signal of "Now," at which time the stopwatch would be started. Then, when the phenomenon had been completed, she would be told to stop. This explanation was repeated until she understood fully.

Then with compelling, progressive, rapid, emphatic, insistent intensity she was told, "Begin at the beginning, go all the way through in normal experiential tempo with a tremendous rush of force, skipping nothing, including everything, and reach a full complete understanding of everything about *Blood—Now.*"

She reacted to the word "blood" by a violent start, trembled briefly, became physically rigid, and clenched her fists and jaw. She appeared to be in acute physical distress but too rigidly involved physically and mentally to break into disruptive actions.

Twenty seconds later, at the command "Stop," she relaxed, slumped in the chair, and breathed hard.

Immediately she was told emphatically, "You now know, you understand, you no longer need to fear. You don't even need to remember when you are awake, but your unconscious now knows, and will continue to know and to understand correctly, and thus give to you that ease you want."

She was asked if she wished to awaken or to think things through.

Her reply was, "I've done my thinking. Wake me up."

Her waking remarks were, "I'm all tired out. I feel simply washed up. Where is Miss X [the chaperone]? What's been going on—did you put me in a trance—did she see me?"

The reply was made that she had been hypnotized and given an opportunity to learn hypnotic phenomena, but that Miss X had not been a witness. She asked that Miss X be summoned and some unimportant demonstration be given to show Miss X what hypnosis was.

When this had been done, she remarked, "I suppose I owe you a fee, but I don't even know why. But I am going to make you wait for it. I don't know why."

She was told to return in one month's time. She replied, "I suppose I will, but there is no reason to do so," and thereupon took her departure.

Late the next day her employer telephoned, stating, "Whatever you did, worked. She has assisted all day in comfort, handling extracted teeth, washing out bloody trays, and even picking up bloody teeth and examining them. I haven't said a word about you nor has she and I don't think it wise."

Three weeks later part of the fee was received. A week later she came in to say, "I don't know why you want to see me. There is no reason. I've had to get another job. My boss is going into the Army. So I've got another job. It's with Dr. Y [a dentist who does extractions]. I like being a dental assistant."

A few days later a telephone call was received from her. She inquired about the balance of the bill and expressed regret for having overlooked it. Asked about her work, she declared that it was wonderful and that she would place a check in the mail immediately, as, indeed, she did. Her good adjustment is known to have continued for more than a year.

Comment

To discuss this report without emphasizing the obvious is difficult. One can readily state that it demonstrates that sometimes brief psychotherapy can be remarkably effective; that the dictum that the unconscious, if therapy is to be achieved, must be always made conscious warrants serious doubt; and that the concept of time distortion lends itself in a remarkable way to clinical therapeutic work.

What the patient's problem was and the nature of its causes remain unknown, even to her conscious mind. Equally probable is that therapy by other methods, given more cooperation, could have led to a similar therapeutic result. However, the fact remains that, whatever her problem was and how the therapy was achieved, the concept of time distortion proved applicable and effective under adverse conditions in meeting adequately the patient's needs.

PATIENT E

The following case is reported for two reasons. It illustrates a problem comparable to the preceding case history in that, despite much previous therapy, the entire therapeutic result was determined by the handling of a single session. Secondly, the crucial situation was one in which time distortion could have been used most advantageously but was not, since it antedated Cooper's experimental work. Viewed in retrospect, however in terms of what happened and the final result, the utilization of time distortion could easily have resolved the ominous difficulties that developed.

Two young women in their mid-twenties had been intimate friends since early childhood. Now they were roommates and engaged in the same occupation. Each had influenced the other in the choice of work. Both were members of a minority group and had grown up in a community rife with prejudice. Both encountered prejudice in their daily work. Each confided in the other, and they regularly exchanged sympathy and encouragement. Their identification with each other was remarkably strong, and their relationship was definitely sisterly in type. Their adjustment within their own group was good, but they were both regarded as decidedly neurotic and they themselves recognized their neurotic patterns of behavior. Each encouraged the other to seek psychotherapy but neither had the courage to do so for herself.

Their neuroses deepened, and one night Kay complained that all day she had felt strange and different. Peg tried to comfort her but found her peculiarly unapproachable. The next morning Kay was even more disturbed, and on the way to work her erratic behavior attracted the attention of the police. When hospitalized she manifested an acutely catatonic state.

For about a month Peg brooded over Kay's condition, wondering obsessionally if she should "let myself go like Kay did." Her work performance failed greatly, and she spent much time staring into space.

Finally, and reluctantly, she decided to seek therapy. Four psychiatrists were consulted, two of whom stated that their schedule was too full. The other two declared that they did not have the training requisite for her problem. She was then referred to the writer. Inquiry of the other psychiatrists disclosed that they felt that she was an "incipient, if not an actual catatonic," and not amenable to therapy at the time.

Hypnotherapy was employed from the beginning, but progress was slow, uncertain, and difficult. Frequently she appeared on the verge of an acute psychosis. Repeatedly during interviews, both in the waking and the trance states, she would ponder the idea of "giving up" and "letting myself go just the way Kay did."

One evening she entered the office for her usual appointment wearing a completely new outfit, including even hat, shoes, and handbag. Most seriously and in a frightened manner she declared, "I don't know what I'm doing. I can't afford these clothes. Either I'm going to improve or I'm having a last fling before they lock me up. Maybe my unconscious knows."

With this remark she closed her eyes and developed a deep hypnotic trance.

She was asked why she had purchased the new clothes. She answered, "I don't know. Either I'm going to get well or I'm going to get worse. Wake me up."

She aroused with an apparent amnesia for her trance state. Immediately she asked, "Instead of working, can't we have a little casual conversation?"

However, after a few commonplace remarks she declared suddenly that she had just remembered that she had dreamed the previous night. This dream, she knew, was tremendously important, but she could not recall its content. Perhaps a little reflection would enable her to remember it.

After a couple of minutes of thoughtful silence she leaped to her feet and screamed, "No, no, I won't remember any more. I won't. I won't. It's too horrible. I'm going to forget it so that I can never remember the rest of it. It's too horrible. I'd go crazy if I remembered it."

Then, speaking to herself, she proceeded to utter a whole series of auto-suggestions, patterned after the writer's technique of suggestions, to induce an amnesia. She concluded then with a self-satisfied remark, "I've just forgotten something, I don't know what it was even about, but I do know that I can't even think of what it might be. It's completely forgotten."

In a subdued, frightened way she continued. "I know I've done something I shouldn't have done, but I don't know what it was. It was something about forgetting, but what I don't know. It was wrong, but I'm glad I did it, awfully glad. But now I will have to give up therapy because there is no hope for me, and I'm glad. Good night!"

With difficulty she was persuaded to remain at least long enough for a social visit, but she kept declaring, "It's no use."

However, she was finally induced to review superficially and disinterestedly some of the work of previous sessions, but was adamant in her refusal to permit further hypnosis.

Finally she was persuaded to allow the writer to try to find out what she had done that was wrong and which had made everything "all over" for her. She agreed reluctantly, but again stipulated that hypnosis was not to be employed.

A whole series of speculations was offered to her, among which, in random order, were included, dreaming, remembering a dream, and forgetting a dream. She listened attentively and thoughtfully but discarded every possibility named.

She then announced her intention of leaving at once and going to visit Kay, "because I'm going to do something horrible when I get to her ward."

The plea was offered that she stay a little longer to please the writer. She yielded reluctantly but began pacing the office. She smiled to herself, pirouetted, waved her arms, giggled, and now and then stared abstractedly into space. Her attention could be secured fairly readily, although only briefly.

At last, after much persuasive effort, she consented to be hypnotized but declared that she would terminate the trance and walk out of the office, never to return, if there were any hint at therapy or even investigation of her ideas.

A number of trances were induced and utilized to elicit demonstrations of the common hypnotic phenomena in an impersonal manner.

When an effort was made to induce crystal gazing, she protested that that measure had been used therapeutically with her. She was reassured by having her hallucinate a rosebush and count the roses on it.

However, any attempt at depersonalization, disorientation, or regression elicited prompt protest and threats of waking and leaving.

More than four futile hours were spent in laborious efforts to gain control of the situation. In retrospect the concept of time distortion could have been readily and easily utilized. With the first development of her adverse reaction there could have been made a shift from the therapeutic situation to a simple experimental situation involving distorted time. Then in all probability her behavior would have paralleled that of Patient B or E.

However, after this extensive effort with her, a solution of the situation was finally reached by means of a simple, fortunate stratagem.

She was told, "Since you are terminating therapy and I shall not see you again, I would like to ask a parting favor. I hope you will grant it. It is this. You entered the office wearing a new outfit and I was glad to see you. Now I would like to hypnotize you and send you out of the office to enter it again as you did earlier, so that once more I can have the pleasant feeling I had when I first saw you tonight. Will you do this?"

She agreed and a deep trance was induced. She was instructed, "Leave the office, walk up the hall a short distance, turn, and then *come down the hall and enter my office in exactly the way you did upon arriving, feeling and believing as you enter that you have just arrived, and give me the same initial greeting.*"

In her willingness to grant this parting favor she was so attentive to the actual wording of the instructions that she failed to perceive their significant implications.

She obeyed the instructions exactly and thus reentered the office regressed in time to the moment of her original arrival. Thereby an amnesia had been effected for everything that had already occurred in the office.

In this new psychological setting it became relatively easy to guide a second course of developments.

By techniques of dissociation, depersonalization, disorientation, and crystal gazing, the patient was enabled to achieve adequate insight into and understanding of both the dream and the uncooperative, disturbed behavior related to it.

Thereafter the course of therapy was favorable and rapid, and it was soon terminated as successful. More than eight years have verified this judgment.

Comment

Perhaps technically this case report, like that of Patient A, may be regarded as not belonging properly to this series. However, it illustrates, and all the more clearly since it is in retrospect, how the concept of time distortion, had it been available, could have been applicable and effective in an extremely difficult therapeutic situation. In its absence hours of futile anxiety, which certainly did not benefit the patient, had to elapse until a fortunate stratagem of psychological maneuvering met the patient's needs. Otherwise the probable outcome would have been regrettable.

Furthermore this case presentation illustrates the constant need, in every field of endeavor, to review the past in terms of newer understandings and thus to achieve a better comprehension of both the old and the new.

PATIENT F

This final case report concerns a difficult psychiatric problem in which therapeutic progress was exceedingly slow and difficult until resort was had to the utilization of time distortion.

The patient, in his mid-twenties, complained of a variety of symptoms. He suffered from overwhelming obsessional fears of homosexuality; he had frequent disabling headaches; he was extremely fearful and shy; he lived from day to day without any interests; he was both agoraphobic and claustrophobic; and he was afraid to look at women because they became hideous creatures in some inexplicable way that caused him to be afraid to look at them.

These symptoms, of more than six months' duration, had developed rapidly some 18 months after he had completed his military service, but he could not attribute them to any particular set of circumstances nor to any particular time. They had merely developed with such distressing rapidity that he was not able to remember their onset nor the order in which they appeared.

The personal history he gave disclosed little of recognizable significance, nor was he at all interested in discussing it. His concern was a repetitious recounting of his present condition.

However, it was learned that his military history was creditable and that he had had active combat experience. Upon discharge from the Army he had systematically visited numerous relatives in the East and then had come to Arizona for employment.

Shortly thereafter his father and stepmother had moved to Arizona because of his father's health. While he did not live with them, he visited them weekly until shortly before entering therapy, and he supported them willingly. His relationship with them both had always been and still was good.

His mother had died "when I was just a little boy. It was on my tenth birthday. She was awful good to us kids. There were eleven of us. She died suddenly, I guess it was her heart. We were awful poor and it was a really tough struggle. We were glad when Dad married Mom. Things got easier then."

Further extensive questioning elicited one other item of possible significance. This was that shortly prior to the onset of his symptoms, contrary to his usual habit, he had slept poorly and had had most disturbing dreams, none of which he had remembered subsequently.

Then one morning on his way to work he saw a pretty girl, but a closer look disclosed her to have the hideous appearance of a "rotting corpse." This terrified him. Further down the street he saw another girl approaching, and as they met she too assumed the appearance of a "rotting corpse." Doubts of his sanity came to his mind, and these were reinforced by the discovery that every female he met became transformed into a similar revolting sight. When he finally reached the large factory room where he worked with a score of other men, he felt protected and most grateful to them, but drawn to them emotionally in a "horrible, sentimental way."

Thereafter journeying back and forth and working became nightmare experiences for him.

On payday he had to stand in line in a small office to receive his check from a young female clerk. He became oppressed by the small size of the room and felt hopelessly trapped. Following this he was unable to sleep in his room unless the windows were open and the door slightly ajar, and repeatedly during the night he would awaken to see if all were well.

He sought therapy because he felt himself on the verge of insanity, with suicide the only other possible alternative.

Therapeutic interviews for many weeks yielded little more than a compulsive, repetitious recounting of material already related. He was averse to hypnotherapy and insisted that if he talked long enough, he would succeed in "talking it out."

Finally, since his funds were being exhausted, he was persuaded to permit hypnosis as a possible stimulant to more rapid progress. However, he emphasized that actual therapy must be limited to the waking state. Accordingly it was agreed that the hypnosis would be employed simply to give him access to unconscious material which could then be discussed in the waking state.

He proved to be a good subject and, after intensive training to insure a good hypnotic performance, his permission was asked for a therapeutic investigation. This was refused, and he insisted anew on only waking therapy.

Accordingly he was told that an experiment requiring 10 to 20 seconds' time could be done that would undoubtedly enable him to get at the core of his difficulties. Reassured by the brevity of the time required, he consented readily.

He was systematically taught a working knowledge of time distortion in much the same fashion as has been described above.

When this had been completed, he was given the following instructions:

> With this stopwatch I will give you an allotted world time of 20 seconds. In your own special experiential time, those 20 seconds will cover hours, days, weeks, months, even years of your experiential life. When I say "Now," you will begin the experiment. When I say "Stop," you will be finished. During that 20 seconds of world time you will sit quietly, neither speaking nor moving, but mentally, in your unconscious, you will do the experiment, taking all the experiential time you need. This you will do thoroughly, carefully. As soon as I give you the starting signal, I will name the experiment and you will do it completely. Are you ready?
> "Now—Go through all the causes of your problem. *Now.*
> "Stop."

Immediately he awakened, sighed deeply, wiped the perspiration from his face and stated, "It was my mother. She always told me to trust her. I was so mad when she died and I hated her."

He paused, and then went on to explain, very much as Patient B did but with much less tendency to vivify so intensely. He employed tenses in a comparable fashion and interpolated explanations similarly.

A summary of his utterances is as follows:

> I was a little boy sitting in her lap. I came home from school and I fell and bit my tongue and she told me to trust her. That was her way of comforting, I suppose, but I didn't understand. The cat scratched me [rubbing his hand]. Always she said "Trust me." She promised me a birthday party when I grew up. I waited and waited—hundreds of days. I can feel that waiting right now. It was so long. I waited for her to tuck me in bed—she is good. I waited for her to get me a penny for candy—I waited and waited. Always she said "Trust me." It all happened right here in this room, but I thought I was back in Pennsylvania. I had to run home from school because I played too long and I was late. And always, always, always I heard her say, "Always trust Mother, just trust Mother, you can always trust Mother." She is just saying it to me over and over and over all the years.
>
> I have just been growing up from a little boy. Everything that happened to me that made mother say "Trust me" has just been happening right here.
>
> There were so many of them. I can tell you them if I should, I don't need to because they all led to the same thing. [He was assured that other details could be given later.]
>
> I was 10 years old that day. Mother promised me a special birthday dinner and cake. We were too poor to have those things. I wanted it so bad. She kept telling me all day, "Trust Mother to make your cake, the best cake you will ever have in all your life." She is going in the kitchen, she stopped, I saw her get pale. She said her arm and shoulder hurt and she went to bed and I sat and watched her die. The last thing she said was "Trust me." I was mad at her—she promised me and she always told me to trust her and I did and I didn't have my birthday. I hated her—I was sad, too. I didn't know how to feel and I was scared. But I forgot all that. I just remembered it here.
>
> And then Dad and Mom came to Arizona. I visited them regular. Then one day he told me confidentially that he had cancer and that the doctors said he had only a month left to live. [Actually the father lived nearly a year.] I was feeling bad about this. I heard him tell it to me just the way he did then. Then later Mom said, "This is the tenth birthday of our marriage," and I froze up stiff and I just now heard her say it again just like she did then. Then I was going to bed and trying to sleep, but I kept waking up because I kept seeing dead bodies. I hated them. They were my mother. And every one of them kept saying "Trust me." And I tried to run to my Dad and climb into his lap and I wanted him to love me and comfort me and put his arms

around me. And I could not find him anywhere and everywhere I looked, I saw Mother dead and saying "Trust me."

And the next day everything began. The girls on the street, my crazy ideas.

That's how my problem started. Now it's over with.

The patient was right. Therapy was complete except for a few more interview. During these he reviewed various incidents of the past and discussed his confused thinking and emotions as a child and his consequent development of intense guilt reactions.

A year has passed. he is engaged to be married and is happy and well adjusted.

Comment

One can only speculate on how long a time therapy by other methods would have required. Equally well one can wonder how time distortion, in 20 seconds, could effect a removal of such massive repressions and activate into seemingly current reality so great a wealth of experimental life.

Undoubtedly the preceding efforts at therapy and the established rapport constituted a significant and essential foundation for the therapeutic results obtained. It does not seem reasonable to this writer that in this kind of a problem time distortion could be used as an initial procedure. But the results do indicate that time distortion has definite clinical and therapeutic applications.

GENERAL SUMMARY

Perhaps the best way to summarize these clinical studies is to refer the reader to the conclusions at the end of the experimental section of this book.[2] In so doing the parallelism between the experimental findings and the clinical findings is easily recognized.

Study of the concept of time distortion by controlled experimental research led to findings of definite psychological interest and significance. The same concept was utilized independently in the totally different field of clinical and therapeutic problems. It yielded results confirmatory and supplementary of the experimental findings. The therapeutic results obtained indicate the validity of the concept of time distortion and its applicability to psycho-pathological problems.

---

[2] From *Time Distortion in Hypnosis*. Baltimore: Williams & Wilkins, 1954. Reprinted with permission of the publisher.

There remains now the need for further and more extensive and varied study of time distortion both as an experimental psychological problem and as a useful concept applicable to clinical and therapeutic work.

28. Further Considerations of Time Distortion: Subjective Time Condensation as Distinct from Time Expansion

Milton H. Erickson and Elizabeth M. Erickson

Shortly after the publication of the first edition of this book one of the authors of this new section (E.M.E.) noted a definite oversight in the development and explication of the concept of time distortion and its clinical applications. This new section is intended to correct that omission and to clarify, from a slightly different angle, the concept of time distortion and other aspects of its clinical application.

In both the experimental and the clinical sections of this book the concept of time distortion has been developed unilaterally in relationship to the "lengthening" or "expansion" of subjective time. The converse manifestation—that is, the "shortening," "contraction," or "condensation" of subjective time—has received no direct recognition or elaboration, except for brief mention in discussions to establish contrast values. However, the implications to be derived from, and the deductions warranted by, the experimental and the clinical sections of this book make apparent that time distortion as an experiential phenomenon may be either in the nature of subjective "time expansion" or its converse, "time condensation."

Though not then recognized as such, the first experimentally and clinically significant instance of hypnotic time condensation known to these writers occurred some years previous to the initial work basic to the first edition of this book. The situation was that of a young woman trained as a hypnotic subject for the delivery of her first child. No suggestions of any sort had been given her concerning her perception of time except that she would "have a good time" and would "enjoy having her baby."

Nevertheless, spontaneously she experienced the following subjective phenomena:

Reprinted with permission from *The American Journal of Clinical Hypnosis*, October 1958, *1*, 83–89. Published simultaneously as an additional section in the second edition of *Time Distortion in Hypnosis* by Linn F. Cooper and M. H. Erickson, published by The Williams and Wilkins Company, Baltimore (first edition, 1954).

1. The 20-mile automobile ride to the hospital seemed to be remarkably rapid, despite her repeated checkings of the speedometer, which always disclosed a speed within established limits.

2. The elevator ascent to the maternity floor seemed to be unduly rapid and in marked contrast to the definite slowness of subsequent rides in that elevator.

3. The delivery room preparation of the patient seemed barely to begin before it was completed.

4. Nurses seemingly dashed in and out of the hospital room, orderlies appeared to run rapidly up and down the corridor, and everybody apparently spoke with the utmost rapidity. She expressed mild wonderment at their "hurried" behavior.

5. The obstetrician "darted in and out" of the room, "hastily" checking the progress of her labor, and he seemed scarcely to complete one examination before beginning the next.

6. The minute hand of the bedside clock appeared to move with the speed of a second hand, an item of bewilderment on which she commented at the time.

7. Finally, she was transferred to the delivery room cart and was "raced" down the corridor to the delivery room, where the minute hand on the wall clock was also "moving with the speed of a second hand."

8. Once in the delivery room the transfer to the delivery table, the draping of her body, and the actual birth of the baby seemed to occur with almost bewildering rapidity.

Actually the labor lasted a total of three hours and 10 minutes and had been remarkably easy and unhurried. Detailed inquiries to the mother subsequent to delivery, supplemented by various pertinent comments she had made during labor, served to furnish an adequate account of the greatly increased subjective tempo of all the activities comprising her total experience. All of this, she explained, had "interested" her "mildly," but she had been much more interested in the arrival of her baby. The interpretation offered at that time of her subjective experience was the simple jocular statement that she "obviously just couldn't wait for the baby."

Cooper's development of the concept of time distortion, however, makes apparent the fact that the patient, in her eagerness to achieve motherhood, spontaneously employed the process of subjective time condensation, thereby experientially hastening a desired goal.

The above case report is a strikingly illustrative example of spontaneous experiential condensation of subjective time. However, this phenomenon is one of common experience in everyday living. We all readily recognize how pleasures vanish on fleeting wings, but to date it has been primarily the poet who has best described time values, as witness: "Time travels in divers paces with divers persons. I'll tell you who Time ambles withal, who Time trots withal, who Time gallops withal, and who he stands still withal." [Shakespeare, *As You Like It*, Act III, Sc. 2, lines 328 ff.]

A common general recognition is easily given to time condensation in daily living. The vacation is so much shorter than the calendar time, the happy visit of hours' duration seems to be of only a few minutes' length—indeed, too many pleasures seem to be much too brief. Unfortunately, in the very intensity of our desire to continue to enjoy we subjectively shorten time; and conversely, in our unwillingness to suffer we subjectively lengthen time, and thus pain and distress travel on leaden feet.

These spontaneous, untutored learnings from everyday experiences suggest the importance of a continued and even more extensive study of time distortion in both of its aspects of subjective expansion and condensation.

In our experience, as well as the experience of various colleagues, the ready reversal of the usual or ordinary learnings of subjective time distortions seems to be limited primarily to learnings achieved in relation to hypnosis. In this regard a wealth of observations has been made on hypnotic subjects in both experimental and clinical situations.

To cite an example, a dental patient who had an extensive knowledge of hypnosis and who was definitely interested in subjective time expansion sought hypnotic training for dental purposes. The results achieved did not derive from the actual hypnotic instructions given but were expressive of the patient's own wishes for subjective experiences. Dental anaesthesia and comfort were achieved by a process of dissociation and regression, by which she subjectively became a "little girl again and played all afternoon on the lawn." As for the dental experience itself, as she remembered experiencing it subjectively, she adjusted herself in the dental chair, relaxed, opened her mouth, and was astonished to hear the dentist say, "And that will be all today." She surreptitiously checked her watch with his clock and then another clock before she could believe that an hour had elapsed. Yet at the same time she was aware of the prolonged, dissociative, regressive, subjective experience she had had as a child for an entire afternoon.

Thus within the framework of a single total experience both subjective time expansion and time condensation were achieved to further entirely separate but simultaneous experiences, that is, simultaneous as nearly as the writers can judge.

Another subject, untrained in time distortion, was employed repeatedly to demonstrate hypnotic phenomena at the close of an hour long lecture. After the first few occasions the subject developed a trance state at the beginning of the lecture which persisted until the demonstration was concluded. By chance it was discovered that thereafter the subject inevitably misjudged the lapse of time by approximately the duration of the lecture. After repeated observation of this manifestation inquiry elicited the significant explanation from the subject, "Oh, I just stopped the clock. I didn't want to wait all that time while you lectured." By this she meant that she did not wish to experience the long wait for the close of the lecture. Instead she had arrested subjectively the passage of time and thereby reduced it to a momentary duration. Or, as she expressed it in her own words, "You see, that way you start the lecture, I go into a trance and stop the clock, and right away the lecture is over and it is time for the demonstration. That way I don't have to wait." In other words she had subjectively arrested the passage of time and thereby had reduced the duration of the lecture to a seeming moment.

That report is but one of many similar accounts that could be cited. One of us (M.H.E.) has repeatedly encountered over a period of years, while assisting in conducting postgraduate seminars on hypnosis, volunteer subjects, themselves physicians, dentists, or psychologists, who have spontaneously developed time condensation. Furthermore they have done this without previous training in hypnosis or in time distortion.

Usually the situation in which this manifestation developed was one wherein the teaching needs of the lecture period required the repeated withdrawal of the instructor's attention from the volunteer subject.

One such subject, in a post-trance review of his hypnotic activities in an effort to develop a more adequate understanding of hypnotic phenomena, inquired at length about the nature and genesis of his apparently altered visual perception of the lecture room clock. He explained that during his trance state he had been distracted and fascinated by his discovery of a repeated sporadic movement of the minute hand of that clock. This hand, he explained, did not consistently move slowly and regularly. Some of the time it did—specifically, during those periods when the instructor kept him busy at various tasks. When left to his own devices because the instructor's attention was directed to the classroom, he noted that the minute hand "would stand still for a while, then jerk ahead for maybe five minutes, pause, and then perhaps jerk ahead for another 15 minutes. Once it just slid around a full 30 minutes in about three seconds' time. That was when you were busy using the other subject [a second volunteer]. It annoyed me when you kept demanding my attention when I wanted to watch that clock." Inquiry disclosed that his awareness of the passage of time had greatly decreased. In other words he, too, had "stopped the clock."

Another example of the experiential values of time condensation relates to the experience of a dentist who employed hypnosis extensively in his practice. Unfortunately, in the individuality of his personal technique in maintaining a trance state he conditioned his patients to a continuing succession of verbalizations. Even more unfortunately, as he became absorbed in the intricacies of his work on the patient, he would find himself unable to verbalize. The result was that his patients would arouse from the trance state, to the mutual distress of both dentist and patient. One of the writers (E.M.E.), on the basis of her own personal experience, suggested that he employ time condensation by teaching it to his patients so that they might abbreviate the time between his verbalizations and thus become unaware of his silences. The results for that dentist were excellent.

Two further instances of the clinical use of time condensation in the therapy of individual patients can be cited. The first of these is the report by one of us

(M.H.E.) given before the Arkansas Medical Society in May 1958 on "Hypnosis in Painful Terminal Illness" and accepted for publication in 1959 by *The American Journal of Clinical Hypnosis*. In this report an account is given of the teaching of time condensation, in association with other psychological measures, to a professional man in the last stages of painful terminal carcinomatous disease. The clinical results obtained in this patient definitely indicated a highly significant relief of the patient's distress, a part of which was directly attributable to time condensation. Particularly for this patient did time condensation appear to preclude variously a subjective awareness, memory, and anticipation of pain. The usefulness in this one case suggests the possibility of its utilization as a clinical measure of reducing subjective awareness of physical distress and pain.

As a final illustration of time distortion involving both subjective time condensation and time expansion in a complementary relationship, a clinical history from the practice of one of us (M.H.E.) is cited. In this report an account is given of the experimental-clinical therapeutic procedure employed in the alleviation of a symptomatic manifestation.

The patient, a 50-year-old socialite, was referred by her family physician for hypnotherapy. For many years she had suffered a yearly average of 45 severe incapacitating migrainous headaches, for which there had been found no organic basis. She had often been hospitalized for these attacks because of severe dehydration and uncontrollable vomiting, and the attacks lasted from not less than three hours to as long as three weeks.

Although the patient was desirous of therapy, she was incomprehensibly demanding, dictatorial, and actually uncooperative as far as psychotherapeutic exploration was concerned. She wanted all therapy to be accomplished, very definitely so, within four visits at intervals of two weeks. Hypnosis and any hypnotic procedures considered valuable by the therapist were to be employed, with the exception of any psychological investigative procedures. The entire situation was to be so handled that she was not to have any seriously incapacitating attacks—that is, attacks of over three hours duration—in the six-weeks period of her therapy.

However, it was also her demand that, since she had these headaches for many years with great regularity, she wanted them to continue, but in such fashion that they would serve to meet her "hidden personality needs" but without interfering with her as a functioning personality. (The patient was intelligent, college-bred, well-informed, happily married, and a devoted grandmother.) She suggested that the character of the headaches might be changed but not the frequency. However, this was but a suggestion, she declared, and she was content to rest this responsibility upon the therapist.

In reply to her the demand was made that the therapist required as a special consideration that she report yearly to him as a form of insurance of her therapy. After careful thought, she agreed to do so for two years providing no fee was charged, but thereafter the therapist would secure any information from her family physician.

Despite her attitude toward therapy in directing it, restricting procedures, and establishing limits, she was readily accepted as a patient, since she presented an excellent opportunity for a combined experimental and clinical approach. When informed of this type of acceptance, she agreed readily.

The actual approach to her problem, in addition to being oriented to her demands, was based upon a combined experimental-clinical procedure utilizing in sequence subjectively condensed and expanded experiential time, employing the one to enhance the other. She proved to be an excellent subject, developing a profound somnambulistic trance within 10 minutes.

The first instruction given to her was that she was to accept no suggestion that was contrary to her wishes and to resist effectively any attempt to violate any of her instructions. Next she was told to execute fully all of those instructions given her in actual accord with her expressed desires. In this manner her full, responsive acquiescence was secured in relationship to both her resistances and her actual cooperation with possible therapeutic gains.

The therapeutic plan devised for her was relatively simple. The first procedure after the induction of a deep trance was to instruct her fully in the concepts of time expansion and time condensation. Then she was told that she was, without fail, to have a relatively severe migraine attack of not more than three hours' duration sometime within the next week. The severity of this attack and its termination within three hours were imperative for adequate therapeutic results.

The following week she was to have another and even more severe attack. It would differ, however, from the headache of the preceding week in that, while it would last in subjective or experiential time slightly more than three hours, it would last in solar time as measured by a stopwatch not more than five minutes. Both of these headaches were to develop with marked suddenness, and she was to go to bed immediately and await their termination. The patient was then awakened with an amnesia for her trance experiences and informed that she was to return in two weeks. Meanwhile she was not to be disturbed or distressed by any headaches she might have.

When the patient was seen two weeks later, she developed a trance readily upon entering the office. She reported that she had obeyed instructions fully and had experienced two headaches. The first persisted two hours and 50 minutes, and the second almost five minutes. Nevertheless the second headache seemed to be much longer than the first, and she had disbelieved her stopwatch until she had checked the actual clock time.

The first headache had developed at 10 A.M. and had terminated at 10 minutes of one o'clock. The other had begun sharply at 10 o'clock, and she had seized her stopwatch for some unknown reason and had proceeded to lie down on her bed. After what had seemed to be many hours, the headache had terminated as suddenly as it had begun. Her stopwatch gave the duration as exactly four minutes and 55 seconds. She felt this to be an error, since she was certain that the time must be somewhere near midafternoon. However, checking with the clocks in the house corrected this misapprehension.

With this account completed, the next procedure was to outline the course of her therapy for the next two weeks. To insure her full cooperation instead of her wary acquiescence she was instructed that she was first to scrutinize them carefully for their legitimacy and then to answer fully a number of questions. In this way she was led into affirming that 10 o'clock in the morning was a "good time to have a headache"; that Monday morning was the preferable day, but that any day of the week could be suitable if other matters so indicated; that on occasion it might be feasible to have headaches on successive days and thus "to meet personality needs" for a two-week period instead of "meeting them" on a weekly basis of one headache per week. It was also agreed that she would have to consider the feasibility of having a "spontaneous, unplanned" headache at rare intervals throughout the year. These however would probably be less than three solar hours in length. To all of this the patient agreed. Thereupon she was instructed to have headaches of less than five minutes each beginning at 10 o'clock on the next two Monday mornings. Again she was awakened with an amnesia and dismissed.

Upon her next visit the patient demanded an explanation of the events of the preceding two weeks. She explained that she had had two social engagements which she had canceled because of a premonition of a headache. In both instances her premonition had been correct. Both headaches were remarkable in her experience. Both were so severe that she had become disoriented in time. Both made her feel that several hours had passed in agonizing pain, but a stopwatch she had felt impelled to take to bed with her disclosed the headaches to be only a couple of minutes in duration.

She was answered by the statement that she was undergoing a combined experimental-clinical hypnotherapy that was developing adequately and that no further explanation could be offered as yet. She accepted this statement after some brief thought and then developed of her own accord a deep trance state. Immediately she was given adequate commendation for the excellence of her cooperation, but no further explanation was offered and no inquiries were made of her.

Further therapeutic work centered around teaching her a more adequate appreciation of subjective time values. This was done by having her, still in the trance state, determine with a stopwatch the actual length of time she could hold her breath. In this way it became possible to give her an effective subjective appreciation of the unendurable length of 60 seconds, to say nothing of 90 seconds.

Against this background of stopwatch experience she was given hypnotic suggestions to the effect that henceforth, whenever her "personality needs" so indicated, she could develop a headache. This headache could develop at any convenient time on any convenient day and would last a "long, long 60 whole seconds" or even an "unendurably long, painfully long, 90 seconds." It would quite probably be excruciatingly painful. When it was certain that the patient understood her instructions, she was dismissed.

She returned in two weeks to declare it was her last visit, since she expected therapy to be concluded. Thereupon she developed a profound somnambulistic trance. She was immediately told that the therapist wished to review with her the proceedings of the previous interviews and the resulting events. She replied, "That is all so unnecessary. I remember perfectly everything in my unconscious mind. I understand that I approve and I will cooperate fully. Is there anything new you wish to tell me?" She was reminded that it was possible that on rare occasions she might develop an "unexpected, unplanned, completely spontaneous headache."

She replied that she remembered and that if there were nothing more to be done, she wished to terminate the interview without delay. Upon the therapist's assent, she roused from the trance, thanked the therapist, and stated that a check would be sent in three months' time, at which time she would send also a preliminary report.

The reports received in the next two years and from her physician since then have all disclosed that the patient benefited extensively. She has on the average about three "unexpected headaches" a year, lasting from two to four hours. At no time has she required hospitalization, as had been the case previously.

However, once a week, with ritualistic care, usually at 10 o'clock on a Monday morning, she enters her bedroom, lies down on the bed, and has a headache, which she describes as "lasting for hours but the stopwatch always shows it only lasts from 50 to 80 seconds. It just seems for hours. And then I'm all over every bit of it for another week. Sometimes I even have those headaches on two successive days, and then I'm free for two weeks. Sometimes I even forget to have one and nothing happens."

CASE SUMMARY AND GENERAL COMMENT

This last case history illustrates a number of important considerations. It demonstrates effectively both the value of the experimental psychological approach in psychotherapy as contrasted to traditional methods, and the efficacy of an alleviation of a symptomatic manifestation when adequate allowance and provision is made for the unknown personality structure and its resistances to therapy. Also, it discloses clinical and experimental possibilities in the varied utilization of two distinct aspects of subjective time distortion.

However, of greater significance for the purposes of this book, this case history in conjunction with the material preceding it demonstrates the importance experimentally, clinically, and experientially of subjective time distortion whether as time expansion or as time condensation.

V. Research Problems

Few would deny that research is the sacred cow of the field of hypnosis. Perhaps that is the way it should be. The ability to replicate and validate our findings is the major means by which we assure ourselves that we are not falling back into the occultism from which hypnosis has only relatively recently emerged.

About how to approach and actually carry out such research, however, there are many points of view. Most of Erickson's papers on hypnosis, whatever their content, have an ambience of new discovery about them. He admits in informal discussions that most of his hypnotherapeutic work is actually of an exploratory and experimental nature. This attitude toward his clinical work may stem from his decades of intensive research exploring the basic issues of hypnosis in the laboratory. He insists, however, that subjects are so different that standardized techniques and rote methods can never do them justice. He believes an exploratory approach that centers about the subject's own unique frames of reference and individual differences is the only one that has any hope of evoking the relevant mental processes. This is as true in the laboratory as in the clinician's office.

From a practical point of view, however, Erickson does differentiate between "clinical" and "experimental" trance, with much greater demands placed on the latter. A basic issue that led him to make this differentiation is the inadequacy of the hypnotic trance he felt many investigators were using in their experimental work. He believes that the inability of these investigators to replicate each other's findings was due to the poor hypnotic training of their subjects and the researchers' unrealistic expectations about the amount of time, ingenuity, and effort that are actually required to secure valid trance states. Because of this the editor begins this section with a previously unpublished discussion wherein Erickson deals with this problem and suggests some approaches to securing valid trance states for experimental research.

Many of the issues discussed in these papers have been touched upon in his previous work, particularly his retrospective accounts of his earliest explorations of hypnotic somnambulism and the approaches to induction in Volume I. Throughout his career Erickson's results have been met with skepticism, and his innovative approaches have continually stirred controversy. The "field approach" to the investigation of hypnotic phenomena, which he often used to circumvent the hypnotic subjects' biases and tendency toward compliance, has never been a favorite with most scientific investigators in the United States, who prefer carefully controlled studies with statistically valid samples of subjects. While such carefully controlled research designs are certainly needed, and have been respected and much used by Erickson, he has felt that some investigators have been so beguiled by them that they miss the essence of hypnotic research for its mere manifestation. His experience has been that hypnotic phenomena are frequently so fragile and elusive that serendipity plays an important role in recognizing them. The very art of observing and purporting to control them can interfere with their natural development and expression.

This issue of "free" exploration versus careful control has always existed in the life sciences. Perhaps each investigator needs to find his own balance between them to enable his own particular genius to flower in making a contribution.

29. Clinical and Experimental Trance: Hypnotic Training and Time Required for their Development

Milton H. Erickson

My primary interest in this roundtable discussion today arises from a certain unhappy conclusion that has been forced upon me repeatedly after reading reports of hypnotic experiments, discussing the problems of hypnotic experimentation with various workers interested in the field, witnessing the hypnotic techniques employed by various students of the subject, and after recalling the innumerable errors, oversights, and serious mistakes committed by myself in the course of my own work. That unhappy conclusion, briefly stated, is that the whole field of hypnotic research is still so undeveloped that there is very little general understanding either of how to hypnotize a subject satisfactorily for experimental purposes, or of how to elicit the hypnotic phenomena which are to be studied after the subject has been satisfactorily hypnotized. From all that I have gathered, except in a few carefully made studies the general tendency is to carry on experimental work in hypnosis by employing a type of trance that is suitable primarily for the purpose of clinical demonstrations intended to give a general comprehensive survey of the types of behavior that may be elicited in the trance state, but actually unsuitable for the detailed experimental investigation of a specific form of behavior. In support of this one need only to recall the contradictory, unsatisfactory, and unreliable results usually obtained in specific studies of hypnotic manifestations.

The reason for such a confusion in experimental results is the typical utilization of a clinically satisfactory trance in experimental situations. The induction of a clinically satisfactory trance leads directly to the development of a peculiar psychic state of passive responsiveness in which the subject automatically accepts and acts upon any suggestion given as a purely responsive form of behavior. This type of hypnotic response I regard as satisfactory for clinical work only. A further and much more difficult step lies in the utilization of the subject's passive responsiveness to secure a spontaneous development of a pattern of

Unpublished discussion, circa 1960.

behavior merely initiated by the suggestions given; I regard this type of response as experimentally satisfactory.

To state this more explicitly, in the clinically satisfactory trance the subjects perform as instructed in accord with their understandings of what the hypnotist wants. Thus the hypnotist not only suggests the behavior but also, though perhaps only indirectly, governs and controls the course and the extent of its development, thereby eliciting behavioral responses oriented primarily about the hypnotist. In the experimentally satisfactory trance the entire orientation of hypnotic responses is totally different. Suggestions given are accepted passively but are utilized only as initiating stimuli for the desired pattern of behavior, the development of which then occurs independently of the hypnotist and is in entire accord with the subjects' general reaction trends and their understanding of the behavior suggested. Thus their responses are oriented not about the hypnotist but about the behavior as a thing complete in itself, thereby rendering the behavior itself the primary issue and not the behavior situation.

To illustrate these various points material may be cited from various experiments. In one instance an unpleasant artificial complex was suggested to a subject, who responded to it with every clinical evidence of having accepted it fully. However, when tested by a modified Luria technique for objective experimental evidence of the acceptance of the complex, the findings indicated that the complex simply had not been accepted and that it had not been a valid psychic experience. Investigation disclosed that, in giving the suggested complex, the subject had unwittingly been forced by the hypnotist's instructions to mail an unfortunate letter around which the complex centered in the *"mailbox on the street corner,"* when the mailbox habitually used by the subject and the only oneactually available to him in the suggested experience was located in the middle of the block. By thus limiting and restricting the subject to a performance of what the hypnotist wanted done and thereby precluding the subject's own natural, self-determined development of the suggestions given, there resulted only a clinically satisfactory acceptance of the complex, but an acceptance not experimentally demonstrable. Correction of the error to a mailing of the letter in the *"regular"* mailbox permitted an acceptance of the complex experimentally demonstrable through disturbances on the word-association test, involuntary motor responses, and respiratory changes. This is not an isolated instance, but it is a finding that has been made many times not only by myself but by others working on complex implantation.

Another type of example concerns the processes involved in inducing the reliving of an actual past experience. In one instance, later verified as to its accuracy, the subject was reliving his experience of driving a team of horses along the road. Quite unaccountably he suddenly stopped the team, and no explanation could be obtained except that he was "waiting." Impatience with the delay led to the giving of repeated, insistent suggestions that he drive on, but without effect. Indirect suggestions that the horses had started again were perceived by the subject not as hypnotic suggestions but as an impatient starting up by the horses themselves, and were responded to by a jerking on the imaginary reins and a shouting of "Whoa." Extensive inquiry finally disclosed the delay to be occasioned by a flock of geese impeding traffic, and not until the last one was safely out of the way would the subject proceed, regardless of the insistence of the hypnotist's suggestions. Thus the role of the hypnotist was limited strictly to the initiation of the process of reliving, and once started it continued in accord with the *actual experiential patterns of response individual to the subject*. Even when the hypnotist succeeded in intruding into the situation by his attempt to direct and control the course of developments, this was reacted to in a way appropriate only to the immediate psychic situation of the subject. This was an experimentally satisfactory trance.

Still another example may be cited to illustrate the integrity of the subject's own spontaneous development of the suggestions given in the experimentally satisfactory trance. In this instance the subject was known to be planning to attend for a second time a movie in which he was greatly interested. Accordingly hypnotic suggestions were given to the effect that he was actually doing so in the company of the hypnotist and that he was describing the movie fully as he watched it. After this process had been initiated and a sufficient account of the movie had been obtained, repeated attempts were made to interrupt his performance. The subject, however, announced firmly his intention not only of sitting through the entire show but of attending the second show also, and all suggestions to the contrary were rejected until resort was made to the not uncommon experience of having the film break and the show interrupted. Suggestions to this effect permitted the initiation of another behavioral process entirely in accord with the subject's experiential past and leading to the desired goal. An essentially identical experience occurred on another occasion with a different subject, and the same type of behavior has been obtained from many subjects and in relation to a great variety of hypnotic manifestations. Yet in all of these subjects it was possible at any time to elicit the same type of behavior but at a purely responsive level, subject to the control and direction of the hypnotist as is typical of the clinically satisfactory trance but lacking in that peculiar quality of subjective, experiential validity that obtains in the experimentally satisfactory trance.

Now the points I have raised so far serve to emphasize that *hypnosis can be employed to elicit purely responsive behavior*, which apparently constitutes a remarkable and vivid portrayal of memories, experiences, and understandings in a fashion adequate to permit a general comprehensive survey of the various forms of hypnotic behavior, or that it may be employed to initiate by suggestion spontaneously developed forms of behavior comparable to those evoked by outer realities. It is my belief that the former type of hypnotic behavior serves best to demonstrate clinical possibilities, while the latter type offers an opportunity for the experimental investigation of specific forms of behavior.

However, if I have given the impression that the hypnotic trance in a given subject is always one or the other of these two forms, I wish to correct that misapprehension immediately. Because of the individual peculiarities of subjects one always finds admixtures of the types of hypnotic responses I have characterized. In a total of approximately 500 individual subjects I have not found one who was simon-pure in either regard, but it is my experience that the majority of subjects can be trained to develop the more experimentally satisfactory trances.

Now that I have presented some views upon what constitutes a satisfactory experimental trance, I might summarize my remarks by an attempt at a definition of that trance state: *An adequate experimental trance state is one in which the passive responsiveness of the subject is utilized only to control and direct the selection of the general type of behavior desired, with the entire course of the development of the behavior once initiated dependent upon the individual reaction patterns of the subject.*

The next consideration for discussion concerns the problem of the proper technique for experimental hypnotic work. This includes not only the technique of trance induction but the techniques of suggestion requisite after the trance state has been induced. However, I have nothing to add to the general understanding of how to induce a trance except to stress the importance of making full provision for all individual differences and peculiarities of the subject and the highly personal character of the hypnotic relationship. I also want to emphasize the absolute importance of the element of time itself in securing hypnotic phenomena. This consideration has been sadly neglected despite the general recognition of the fact that time itself constitutes an absolute function of all forms of behavior and that the more complicated the form of behavior, the more significant is the time element. Hence I will limit my discussion to a consideration of this item.

To present this point I will give material illustrative of the general attitude and the common practices prevalent in hypnotic work which ignore the importance of the time element, and which consequently lead to a misdirection, misinterpretation, and an inadequacy of experimental work. This general attitude and the attendant practices derive from an unrecognized tendency to look upon hypnosis as a miracle producer, a tendency that probably arises from the startling phenomenal character of hypnotic manifestations. Because of this tendency we find many experimental investigations based upon techniques better adapted to the evocation of miracles than to the eliciting of hypnotic manifestations. Because of the oversight or neglect of the element of time, there is a marked confusion of the significance of the suggestions given with the processes of response and the actual behavior invoked. To illustrate, we find quantitative studies made of hypnotic phenomena by controlling the suggestions given by use of a certain phonograph record as if such a measure could control the nature and extent of the development of the response processes so aroused in different subjects; we find studies of amnesia accomplished by means of a simple direct command to forget chosen material followed by proper testing for evidence of amnesia; we find studies on dissociation based on the assignment of two tasks followed by a strict injunction that they are to be performed simultaneously but independently of one another; we find experiments on regression conducted by the simple measure of telling a 30-year-old subject that he is now 10 years old and promptly administering an intelligence test to secure evidence of the regression; we find experiments on hypnotic anaesthesia performed by direct suggestion of it and a direct testing for it; in brief we find, despite our knowledge that behavior constitutes an end-product of a long process of complicated reactions, that in hypnotic work the assumption is made repeatedly that the process of hearing and understanding instructions is identical with the process of the development of the behavior the instructions are supposed to elicit.

Another type of illustration which typifies an observation I have made repeatedly is the general belief that the induction of a sound hypnotic trance requires only a relatively brief period of minutes. Thus one worker, representative of many I know, assured me most earnestly that it was never necessary, even with naive subjects, to spend more than 15 to 20 minutes in inducing profound trances and that the average length of time for him was five to 10 minutes. Also he assured me, as have many others, that once the subject was hypnotized, the induction of any specific type of complicated behavior was simply a matter of giving appropriate suggestions. While I am ready to concede that trances can be induced and experiments conducted by such techniques, I doubt if the trances are ever more than the type I have described as clinically satisfactory only; the experimental results are therefore nothing more than evidence of passive responsiveness oriented about the suggestions given.

Now the question arises, what is the proper length of time that should be spent in inducing an experimentally satisfactory trance or in eliciting hypnotic behavior adequate for experimental investigation? No definitive answer can be given, not only because of individual differences between subjects but also because of differences within the subject in relation to various types of behavior. Hence the only safe procedure is to give suggestions in such fashion and sufficiently slowly that subjects have an opportunity not only to respond in a passively responsive fashion in accord with the hypnotist's suggestions, but also an opportunity to respond in accord with their own understandings of the behavior desired and to develop their responses in accord with their own reaction patterns. Only the latter type of behavior is to be accepted as evidence of an experimentally satisfactory trance. This implies the need for extensive experience to enable the scientific investigator to discriminate between the types of the behavioral responses obtained, but I know of no easier way until sufficient experimental work has been done to discriminate more satisfactorily between clinical and experimentally satisfactory trances.

Returning to the question of the actual length of time required, I can speak only from my own experience, which is supported by that of certain other workers, chiefly psychiatrists, interested in establishing in their subjects valid experiential processes by hypnotic techniques. My finding has been that on the average a total of three to eight hours, usually in interrupted sittings, should be spent in training a good unsophisticated subject to develop a sound hypnotic trance before there can be any experimentally valid attempt to elicit the various forms of hypnotic behavior. Once the subject has been trained adequately to develop a satisfactory trance, a period of at least 20 minutes should be spent in inducing each new trance intended for experimental work, although this period can gradually be shortened to five or 10 minutes.

Next is the question of how much time is required to elicit any specific form of behavior after a sound trance has been induced. For example, when it is desired to develop an amnesia for a series of nonsense syllables just learned, it is necessary to give the subject a period of 20 to 30 minutes and even longer to permit the development of an easily demonstrable amnesia, as shown by a relearning of the amnesic material in the waking state. Or, if it is desired to have the hypnotized subject develop a psychic blindness, a period of 20 to 30 minutes must elapse after the suggestion has been given before any attempt should be made to secure and test that behavior. That period of waiting is best spent in casual conversation, unrelated activities, with an occasional reiteration of the suggestion that sooner or later the subject will experience the desired effect. Even the giving of a complicated, attention-compelling task to subjects to keep them busy will not militate against the development of the desired behavior. The essential consideration seems to be the provision of a sufficient period of time to permit the development of a mental set conducive to the behavior. Unless this period of time is allowed, the subject's response, while in accord with the suggestions given, will be marked to the critical observer by inhibitions, denials, avoidances, and blockings not in keeping with a valid experiential response. The following example will serve to clarify this point.

Recently I suggested hypnotic blindness for two persons in the room. After a 20-minute wait I gave the same suggestions to two other persons and then proceeded to test the responses of all four subjects. The original two subjects demonstrated an entirely satisfactory blindness, but for the second two the psychic blindness was marked by avoidances, inhibitions, conflict reactions, and blockings which persisted for half an hour. After this time the psychic blindness for the second group became satisfactory. When we realize the importance of time in the evolution of behavior in the ordinary life situation, its importance in hypnotic behavior can be more fully appreciated.

I will close with the statement that I believe hypnotic experimentation constitutes one of the richest fields for research; it warrants every bit of time given to it; and, that as one's experience grows, the amount of time required for specific investigative procedures diminishes.

30. Laboratory and Clinical Hypnosis: The Same or Different Phenomena?

Milton H. Erickson

In late 1924 and in the spring of 1925 two similar isolated but most interesting events occurred. Subjects H and W, who had worked extensively as hypnotic subjects for the author but who were unknown to each other, were both on University of Wisconsin athletic teams. In the fall of 1924, at practice for a coming meet, Subject H, during practice jumping, caught his tongue between his teeth and cut through completely one side of his tongue except for a narrow marginal edge. He was rushed to the hospital for surgical care. Upon being told that his tongue would require suturing, that he would be placed on a liquid diet, and that he would be disqualified for the coming athletic competition the next weekend, his reaction was most obstreperous. He rejected all medical help and advice and promptly sought out the author for hypnotic aid. He could not talk understandably because of the swelling of his tongue; he had to write an account of his mishap; and the author was then too naive about medical problems and too eager to experiment to exercise reasonable caution in a medical situation.

Within four hours H was free of swelling, pain, and handicap. He was not seen again for three weeks. Then he came rushing into the laboratory at an hour he knew the author would be there. He explained:

> You remember that bitten tongue of mine about three weeks ago? First you hypnotized me and removed the pain. After I awakened from the trance, I did a lot of studying here in the lab, and you kept looking at my tongue every little while until the swelling went down and I could talk normally. Well, something else happened. On the way to my room [rooming house] from the lab that evening I developed an amnesia for the whole thing, and the memory of it just came back to me this afternoon, so I thought I had better tell you. It was a Saturday, three weeks ago, and the fraternity was having a special steak dinner that Sunday. I remember eating my share, but there was no pain or trouble with my tongue. At the next practice meet with the team some of the fellows asked me how my mouth was, and I didn't know what they

Reprinted with permission from *The American Journal of Clinical Hypnosis*, January 1967, *9*, 166–170.

were talking about, so I just said it was as big as usual. Then this afternoon I asked several of the fellows in my rooming house if they knew about my biting my tongue. They didn't, and wouldn't believe me about it. They just said that there was never anything wrong with my mouth except that I used it too much. Then I went to Dr. S. [the physician who took care of injuries for the Athletic Department] and he said he was "still too disgusted" with me to talk to me. I asked him if I had bitten my tongue. He just looked me up and down and said, "You not only bit it, but you acted like a damn fool when I wanted to give you proper medical attention and put you in the infirmary. But I suppose you thought you could get better medical treatment by going downtown for it. I should have kicked you off the team." To this the patient added. "But I did all right in the meet that weekend—one first place and one third place."

Since his interest was psychology (he later became a professor of psychology) a discussion ensued of all that had really occurred hypnotically. There finally resulted his spontaneous observation:

What you did for me is exactly like what we have done in the laboratory except that it is different. In the laboratory I accept suggestions and carry them out thoroughly. I've experienced anaesthesia before. It was just as good as the anaesthesia you produced in my tongue. But laboratory anaesthesia, no matter how real, belongs to the laboratory. It is a part of a scientific study. What you did for me was just as real as any hypnotic anesthesia I ever had in the lab. But it was also different, since the hypnosis you did about my tongue belonged to me. It was mine, all mine—not even you could have a part in it—it was mine. Maybe I can say it this way. I am a student. I am a member of the student body. The physical identity is the same. The meanings are different. Lab hypnosis and personal hypnosis may give you similar results. But they are different to the person.

Concerning his amnesia he could offer no explanation, but he did suggest that he might find out if he were to be hypnotized and questioned. This was done and the simple answer received was, "I just didn't want the memory of biting my tongue to enter my head during the meet. After that it wasn't important. But this afternoon I was studying on memory processes so I just quit having an amnesia."

The author and H discussed all of this material but without reaching any definite conclusions.

The next spring Subject W sprained his ankle during athletic practice and came to the author that evening hobbling on crutches prescribed by the athletic department physician after an examination had disclosed "only a severe sprain."

He gave an account of his accident, the coming athletic contest, his present severe pain, and then he asked if all the hypnotic work he had done in the laboratory could be employed to meet his present personal needs.

As with H, the problem was accepted, a hypnotic trance was induced, removal of pain and pain reactions was effected, and then regression was induced to effect a reestablishment of physical relationships as much as possible as they were before his accident. A final measure employed was temporary time displacement so that he could think about his sprained ankle as if it had occurred a year or so previously.

W (who later became a physician) won a place in two contests in the racing meet that weekend, and on the succeeding Sunday sought out the author because the temporary time displacement had been spontaneously corrected. He was given a full recollection of events, and his resulting discussion, less extensive than that of H, was essentially identical in significance. The pertinent points were:

> The anaesthesia of the sprain was as perfect as anything I ever did in the lab but I still have the anaesthesia for pain. That putting of the accident into the past messed up the thinking of my teammates, but I was completely clear in my own mind and I wasn't troubled about their confusion about a sprained ankle I knew I had had a year or so ago. As I look over all the hypnosis you did for my ankle, it's just as good and real as any of the lab experiments. But it is different in a peculiar way. Hypnosis in the lab belonged to you, to me, to the psychology department to science. The hypnosis for my sprain, all of the hypnosis you used for the pain, in some way belonged just to me. The best way I can put it is to say: Just like the ankle sprain was all mine, so was the hypnosis. That, too, was all mine. Lab hypnosis and personal hypnosis can give the same results, but they are different in their personal meanings. Do you suppose these new ideas of mine will interfere with the work you have planned for me in the lab? I'd sure hate to miss it.'' (In no way did his new understandings interfere with his work as a subject.)

Quite contrary to the above accounts is another kind of finding. Over the years many excellent laboratory subjects who demonstrated the phenomena of hypnosis exceedingly well and who withstood seemingly searching tests were found to be either unwilling, actually unable, or perhaps only partially able to use hypnosis when it involved personal needs. For example, one college student used in the laboratory to demonstrate anaesthesia could undergo obviously painful test measures with no evidence that there was any pain experienced. Yet when this same subject suffered an accidental and actually minor injury requiring three sutures, in no way could hypnosis be induced to lessen the distress of his injury. Some nurses who have proved to be excellent demonstration subjects have been found to be completely unresponsive to hypnosis when suffering from even minor as well as major physical discomforts. For example, a nurse who satisfied a group of physicians that she could develop a profound anaesthesia was unable to develop any anaesthesia when she suffered a fall and bruised herself, even though medical examination of her injury pronounced it to be painful but not serious in any way. In other instances excellent demonstration subjects at times of their own need have not been able to develop more than light trances. Apparently this question of personal needs is one that is interpreted by individuals in their own way.

Another experimental subject, a music lover, was being used to test the possibility of hallucinated experience forming a part of a conditioned response complex. One of the things she did in this experiment was to hallucinate the rendition of her favorite musical compositions. However, this subject always demanded payment for laboratory work in a remarkable manner. For all participation in any kind of experimentation she insisted that payment had to be made by letting her hallucinate some music while the author was busy at some other experiment and thus not sharing anything more than time and space with her. She explained that music hallucinated for experimental purposes was identical with the music she hallucinated for herself. There was only a personal significance which she did not want to share and could not explain.

In the years since then occasionally the author has encountered or dealt with persons who have had both laboratory hypnotic experience and medical or dental hypnotic experience. Of these, the more thoughtful have explained that laboratory hypnosis is one order of phenomena, that hypnosis involving significant physical needs of the self is another order of phenomena. An informative nurse told the author:

> You taught me a hypnotic saddle block at the medical society meeting the only time I was ever hypnotized. Later I got married and went to live in a isolated rural community. Neither a doctor nor a nurse was available when I went into labor about three weeks earlier than I expected to. I took the saddle block you taught me and changed it into mine. I'm sure your saddle block would have worked, but it was my baby, my first one, so I made the saddle block my own. My husband was away, caught by a forest fire, and the only person to help me was a newly married girl. But I was trained in obstetrics so I had no worries. The saddle block was just the same as yours, and then all at once it became different. It was personal. What that means maybe you can understand.

This nurse had been used as one of a volunteer demonstration group for the medical society. It was by mere chance that she was again met. Following her initial remarks she was questioned rather extensively. She was asked to describe more fully what had happened during the birth of her first child. She explained,

Being an obstetrical nurse, I knew I should have an episiotomy, but I knew that was impossible. But I remembered what you said about relaxation in your lecture so I relaxed my perineum. I don't really know how I did this, but I just relaxed it, but I kept all the feeling of movement because I knew I should know when the baby was born and when the placenta was passed. My friend helped me with the things that I couldn't do myself. When my husband got home three days later, he was very much surprised and had to go to get a doctor, since the telephone lines were still down. The doctor said everything was all right.

Since then I have had four more children. The next two I had in the hospital under "proper medical observation." The following two I had at home with a doctor in attendance. I have never had any medication or any anaesthesia for childbirth. The hospital doctor was very displeased because he did not like the way I developed my own saddle block. Neither did the general practitioner serving my community approve of my use of hypnosis. All doctors agree, however, that my pelvis is entirely normal. I don't know how to explain to you how I changed the saddle block you taught me into *my saddle block*, which I used for all five of my children. I would like to have you suggest a saddle block to me now, with me wide awake from the waist up, so I can discuss it with you, and after we have discussed it I will change it into *my saddle block*.

Her wishes were met. Her explanations can be summarized by the simple statement that:

They are both the same and yet they are different. The saddle block that I just produced seems to be a reliving of my saddle blocks during childbirth. The saddle block you induced, while it removed all feeling from the waist down just like mine did, seemed to be totally different but just as effective. I really wish I could give you more information. It just seemed to be a real experiencing of the saddle block you gave me in front of the doctors. In fact, I looked around almost expecting to see them.

Another finding, much more rare, has been encountered by this author and confirmed unexpectedly by several colleagues. It is that some persons who responded well to hypnosis directed toward their personal needs could not enter into the hypnotic state for either experimental or demonstration purposes. Yet they could do so readily for questioning about their possible personal needs, even in the presence of other, even lay, persons. Yet laborious effort and seemingly full cooperation on the person's part would not result in trance development. Also, after securing permission from such persons, a trance induced to inquire about personal needs would terminate when a shift was made toward experimental work. Yet these same persons would cooperate in experimental work in the waking state.

The above instances have been cited because of the clarity with which the hypnotic subjects (patients) gave their accounts. There have been, relatively speaking, many occasions on which there appeared to be a marked conflict between laboratory hypnotic findings and those encountered clinically. For example careful, well-controlled laboratory experiments may find hypnotic anaesthesia to be questionable and even of a most dubious character. Yet the clinician reports instances in which ordinarily extensive chemoanaesthesia would be required but in which hypnoanaesthesia was successfully employed without any medication. Hence there arise the questions: Was the laboratory experiment on hypnoanaesthesia a reliable test of hypnotic anaesthesia, and was the surgical patient merely complaisantly cooperative? Are hypnotic subjects merely self-deluded in both laboratory and clinical (including even major surgery) settings? Can there be a reliable comparison of laboratory findings with clinical findings? Are they of the same order of phenomena? Does not the frequent contradiction between laboratory and clinical hypnotic findings imply other significant factors as signified by the above accounts? In what way can definitive laboratory experiments on hypnosis and clinical utilization of hypnosis be tested on the same scientific basis, or is this impossible with the present state of understandings? What are the determining factors in each procedure so far as the person involved is concerned? Should not personality factors and personal motivation be regarded as vital to both laboratory and clinical studies? Are laboratory hypnotic states and clinical hypnotic states *sometimes* identical, perhaps differing only in the subjects' recognition of them? These are only a few of the questions that need to be answered, if such answering can be achieved.

Most thought-provoking in relation to the findings reported above, as well as to the controversy about the use of hypnosis for antisocial purposes, are the informative and outstanding reports on human behavior published by Milgram (1963, 1964, 1965). These are studies that should be read most thoughtfully by whomever undertakes either laboratory or clinical hypnosis, since they are indicative of the stresses a person in the waking state will endure and thereby, by inference, indicating that situations, motivations, obedience, and personality factors are highly significant in human behavior and response in a manner not yet understood in the waking state of a subject, much less in hypnotic states or other states of altered awareness.

31. Explorations in Hypnosis Research

Milton H. Erickson

I would like to present two concepts of different types of thinking: unconscious or subconscious thinking and conscious thinking. If I were to ask you to look at my watch and to continue seeing it right there, you would all know immediately, not being in a trance state, that I lowered my watch. In hypnotic response you would see the watch but it would be the psychical watch, and since I told you that you would see it right there, you would continue to see it right there and not in the moved position. You would substitute immediately the visual memory of that watch because there is an interchangeable use of reality stimuli and remembered experiences, visual memories, auditory memories, kinesthetic memories, etc. It is out of the use of these understandings, learnings, and memories in the mind that hypnotic subjects develop their behavior. In this state of special awareness, or special consciousness, the operator (the hypnotist) plays a role in communicating ideas to the subjects, of orienting the subjects in that unique, individual hypnotic situation which each particular subject finds himself.

The subjects need not necessarily accept anything the operator suggests. The subjects tend to respond in accord with patterns unique to each. In the hypnotic state the subjects are willing to accept ideas; to accept any idea that is offered. The subjects then take a second step: They examine the idea for its inherent value to themselves. That is one of the reasons for the time lag in hypnotic behavior. Time is needed for the examination of ideas, thoughts, and understandings. It is a very careful examination. That is why you have literalness in your subjects' understandings when you ask them this or that particular question. After having examined those ideas, there is the tendency to respond.

The subjects accept those ideas in terms of their own frames of reference and a lifetime of experiential learning. These experiential learnings may be unusual and quite unexpected. For example, there was a veteran who had leapt downstairs, fallen on the floor, picked himself up, and then walked back and forth to college every day for a week. Finally he came in to the Veterans Administration hospital to be examined because his foot was very swollen and because it made a noise when he walked. I happened to be the consultant on duty, and when I heard him walk across the floor, I winced. The X-ray showed a com-

Presented at the Seventh Annual University of Kansas Institute for Research in Clinical Psychology in Hypnosis and Clinical Psychology, May, 1960, at Lawrence, Kansas.

minuted fracture of all the bones in the ankle. When I showed this veteran the X-ray, he said, "But I thought broken bones hurt." That's what he honestly thought. He had an hysterical anaesthesia extending almost up to the knee, with anaesthesia for deep pressure and vibration. How did he ever acquire such an anaesthesia except through some kind of experience, through some kind of learning? Our unawareness of stimulations, and our unawareness of pressure on muscles are body learnings which come from actual experience.

Let me illustrate another type of body learning. The postman hands a box to the college student. He takes it to his room and opens it—homemade fudge. He eats it and enjoys it. Two weeks later he is sitting, studying, and happens to look out the window and sees the postman coming down the street. Immediately he starts drooling, not because the postman looks appetizing, but because in a one trial learning situation (and a stimulation that did not lead to complete satisfaction until quite some time later, when he had unwrapped that unknown package) there was a linking of the postman's uniform with the salivation process. I stress this example because the laboratory learning of conditioned responses usually involves so many repetitions of stimuli before you finally achieve the desired conditioned response. Here a particular situation set up a conditioned response so that the very next time the student saw that postman, he drooled. Laboratory learning is suggestive, but far from identical with, the learning which real life experience makes possible.

If I were to ask any of you to elevate your blood pressure, how would you do it? If I were to ask you to change the rhythm or tempo of your smooth muscle function, or to alter the circulation of your blood in any one part of your body, you would wonder how to do it. Yet your body has considerable experience in vascular dilation and contraction. When I was a medical school student, I clearly remember when our class would enter the lecture room of a certain professor. There would be a generally happy mood, and then the professor would snarl and say: "There will be a written examination!" My classmates would divide into two groups: (a) the diuretic group, and (b) the peristaltic group. There would be an almost instantaneous alteration of circulation and smooth muscle activity throughout the entire body, involving physiological, psychological, and neurological functioning. These alterations derived from the real-life experiences each one of us had had, time and again, in the past whenever we suddenly experienced altered patterns of body behavior, physiological behavior, somatic conditions, etc.

Let me cite still another instance of human behavior change. A little three-month-old baby boy is taken to a pediatrician. The baby doesn't pay much attention to the pediatrician clad in white. While at the pediatrician's he gets stabbed with a needle. Three months later, when the baby returns to the pediatrician's examination room, he begins to yell immediately. How did the baby get conditioned to understand all of that behavior, to alter all his physiological behavior? What kind of a memory does a three-month-old baby have of being stabbed in the bottom with a needle?

Throughout life there are various conditions of learning for individuals that involve their total functioning as organic creatures, where blood circulation, neural and muscle behavior, and other organ systems participate most actively. Whenever you set up the right kind of stimuli, you can elicit some of these experientially conditioned behaviors. It is possible to use hypnosis as a method by which you can secure patients' complete attention. It is then possible to focus their attention and to create a state of receptivity by such stimulation so that they function in accordance with those relevant past learnings.

I would like to stress that to be in a trance state does not mean that individuals are unconscious or that they cannot function with their conscious mind. I can think of a parallel with the sleep state. A man may wake up in the morning with the realization that he has not completed a dream. He is aware that he is in bed, but would like to go back to complete the dream. He proceeds to do so, knowing that he is dreaming, that he is completing the dream of a delightful plane ride or a pleasant picnic with a dual awareness of operating in two spheres. I recall a physician who underwent surgery and who felt very sorry for the surgeon because the surgeon didn't believe in hypnosis. The physician-patient wondered if the surgeon were distressed or worried, if the surgeon was beginning to come around to some belief in hypnosis as an anaesthetic agent. He also wondered about the nurses who were watching the operation. Simultaneously this physician-patient was on a "fishing trip" in Canyon Lake, delighted to find how well the fish were biting, and pulling them out of Canyon Lake one after another—all the while enjoying a delightful fishing trip. This physician-patient functioned with a dual awareness: He was aware he was in the operating room where he had an hypnotic anaesthesia which was necessary for his own surgery, and at the same time he was also participating in a fishing trip. When the tray of instruments fell on the floor, there was a "simultaneous" jump of a big fish out of the water, accompanied by a big splash and noise as the fish fell back in. The physician-patient wondered whether he was merely reinterpreting the stimulation of the fallen tray and translating into the jumping of the big fish even while the event was happening. He demonstrated excellent dual functioning at two different levels of psychological awareness.

I regard hypnotic techniques as essentially no more than a means of asking your subjects (or patients) to pay attention to you so that you can offer them some idea which can initiate them into an activation of their own capacities to behave. The best way to illustrate this point is by way of a clinical example. Barbara was a 14-year-old girl who had been failing in her adjustments at school and had developed serious behavior manifestations. She said her feet were too big, so she was not going to go to school, church, or out of the house. She was not going to talk to anybody. Her mother, who was my patient and a good hypnotic subject, consulted me about her daughter's problem. The mother described how Barbara's behavior had been going on this way for two long weeks, that Barbara had been secluding herself in the home, not talking, and was most unresponsive. I told the mother I would make a house call, and that she was to go along with whatever I said. She was not to discuss the visit beforehand with her daughter.

When I arrived at the home, I took out my stethoscope and said to the mother, "I think that the first thing I ought to do is examine your chest. So will you please take off your blouse and bra, but call your daughter in here to act as a chaperone and have her bring a towel." The girl of course could not refuse to come in; she had to come in to act as a chaperone. That was the first thing that I got the girl to do for me. It seemed to be so innocent, so appropriate, so right, but I was getting a response from her. I carefully examined the mother's chest, all the while with Barbara standing there beside the bed in her bare feet, with a sullen look on her face. Finally I got up from where I had been sitting, stepped backward, and brought my heel forcefully down on Barbara's toes so that she let out a yell of pain. I turned to her, seemingly very irate, and said: "If you had only grown those damn feet big enough for a man to see, you wouldn't get them stepped on." *If you could grow those damn feet big enough for a man to see, they wouldn't get stepped on.* Barbara looked at me, first in a frightened way, and then all of a sudden the smuggest smile I ever saw came over her face. She turned and walked out of the room. On the way out she said, "Mother, can I go to the show?" Barbara went to the show that day, she went to Sunday school the next day, and returned to school the next Monday. It was the end of her symptomotology.

What had I done? I had asked Barbara to respond. I also made her respond by stepping on her toes. I did it in a totally unexpected way. Then I took the idea that her feet were so big, that she was ashamed to be seen in public, and in a horribly impolite fashion I convinced her that I honestly felt that her feet were very small, and that she was remiss in not having grown them larger. Could I have ever told Barbara that her feet were of normal size, of a good size by just pointing it out to her, by measuring her feet, by showing her that she had feet no larger than her classmates? Barbara needed therapy, she needed to stop secluding herself. It was to get Barbara in some way from within herself to make response-behavior that would be corrective of her situation and her condition that I proceeded as I did. *Hypnosis is essentially that sort of concept, i.e., a way to offer stimuli of various kinds that will enable patients in response to those stimuli to utilize their own experiential learning.* I helped Barbara reorient to the size of her feet rather than to *ideas* about the size of her feet. Hypnosis facilitates exceedingly effective learnings that would be impossible otherwise except by prolonged effort and therapy.

HYPNOTIC ANAESTHESIA

Let me give you another example. A little three-year-old girl had to have an adenoidectomy, and hypnosis was used. After the adenoids were taken out, the doctor said, "Now, you're such a nice little girl and that didn't hurt at all, did it?'' The little girl looked at him and said, "Your pupid [stupid]. It did too hurt but I didn't mind it.'' I questioned this little girl about her hypnotic experience, as I have a number of other children. They do not all necessarily say that. Some say that they didn't feel anything at all. What took place? In some way that three-year-old girl altered her perception of pain and made it less meaningful for herself. She restructured it in some fashion just as the businessman with purely imaginary worries restructures those worries into a gastric ulcer. How does the businessman create this ulcer out of his body learnings, his experiential conditioning, etc.? The research approach in hypnosis ought to seek out the means by which hypnosis facilitates the utilization of body learnings, tissue learnings, physiological learnings. What were the learnings, understandings, and the body conditionings that the three-year-old girl had achieved that resulted in her statement, "I didn't mind it.''

I think that cancer pain is a very severe pain experience. If you can get your patients' attention in some way so that they can be induced to use their learnings, you can abolish the pain. It doesn't matter whether you keep them awake, or keep them asleep, or keep them in a state of dual awareness. In some way you need to communicate to patients the desirability of doing something about their pain, just as the businessman does something about his worries and converts them into a painful ulcer with tissue destruction. Before I begin to induce hypnosis in cancer patients, I explain to them that pain isn't a simple, pure thing. There is hard pain, there is soft pain, burning pain, cold pain, stabbing, cutting, heavy pain. I think of all the possible adjectives that I can to describe the pain so that my patient will listen to me. Then I point out to the patient, "You know, pain in some part of your body doesn't hurt you half as much as it does in another part of your body." I know from psychiatric practice that people can displace sensations. I also know that patients with cancer pain are worried about the metasteses in their body, in their liver, in their spine. The pain that they have in their trunk is the thing that they know or believe is going to kill them, and they know that I know it. Thus sometimes I tell the cancer patient, "Suppose you had all that body pain right here in your left hand. You are not going to worry about that. It isn't going to hurt half as much as the pain in your body." I get them to "displace" a share of that pain into their hand. I don't know what the mechanism of displacement is, but I do know that human beings make use of that mechanism. I know that cancer patients can suddenly find that they have pain in their left hand which they don't mind, and the pain in their body is considerably decreased.

Is anaesthesia a state of unconsciousness? I don't know, but I don't think so. I think at times that anaesthesia is primarily a matter of amnesia. I know that I can teach a cancer patient, "It's all right for you to have pain, but why have pain for very long?" And why ever remember pain?'' To one patient I explained, "You know, pain for you is made up of three things: anticipation of pain to come, memory of pain you have experienced, and the current experience of pain. Let's just not remember the past pain. Let's have an amnesia for past pain and for future pain.'' I call it ''amnesia for future pain,'' an unawareness that pain can be anticipated. Then you have cut down the pain complex by one-third. Similarly you can shorten it by time distortion; by applying time distortion to the particular current pain, and reduce it greatly.

There is another mechanism that you can employ by hypnosis, and that is a reinterpretation of pain. The illustration I give to cancer patients is: Suppose you were alone in a house, 10 miles from any other habitation, and that you are absolutely alone. You are sitting with your back next to a curtain and you are reading a tremendously exciting suspense story. In that suspense story a hand came through the curtain and stabbed the victim in the neck. Just at that moment, as you read that line, a tiny little bug steps off your collar onto your neck, and as a result you hit the ceiling, not because that little bug tramped so hard on you but because of the general psychological situation. There had taken place a reinterpretation of the stimulus, a magnification and intensification of a minor stimulus.'' And so I ask my patients, ''This short, cutting, stabbing, blinding pain of yours, could you make that into a dull, heavy pain?'' In the hypnotic state subjects are open to ideas. *They like to examine ideas in terms of their memories, their learnings, their conditionings and all of the various experiential learnings of life*. They take your suggestion and translate that into their own body learnings. There was a cancer patient who had transformed the sharp stabbing, blinding pain into dull, heavy pain, and I then suggested that he take the dull, heavy pain and transform that into a feeling of relaxation and weakness. In other words his attention was redirected again, but this time into heaviness, weakness, and relaxation. I think that a great deal of research remains to be done on the matter of pain, on its transformations into nonpain or decreased pain situations, so that we can better offer suggestions and frames of reference which patients can utilize in terms of their own body experiences.

In the control of cancer pain I teach my patients to listen carefully to my words and to follow my train of suggestions closely. I can direct their attention to the shoes on their feet, the glasses on their face, the collar around their neck, and the way their hand is on their thigh, or to sounds outside the room, etc. As they follow my train of suggestions, it is not long before they forget about the shoes on their feet and the cloth around their neck, etc. *In their effort to constantly redirect their attention from one idea to another, there is a more rapid slipping away of earlier suggestions*. I explain to the cancer patient: ''While you're thinking about this or that particular happy thing, you won't have enough energy left over with which to feel the pain of your cancer, because all of your energy is going to go into this matter of thinking over all the nice things that you ought to say to your wife, your grandchildren, or something of that sort.'' I get their attention focused.

What does focusing of attention mean? I know that you can get certain types of physical behavior and certain types of psychological behavior after you have induced the *hypnotic state, which is a state of special awareness and special responsiveness*. Cancer patients have much activity going on within them. But you know that they also have a lifetime of body learnings that are available within them for therapeutic application.

CATALEPSY

Then there is the phenomenon of catalepsy which also occurs within the patient. Did you ever try to hold yourself completely still in the ordinary state of conscious awareness? Soon your nose, your ear, or some other part of you begins to itch, especially if you know that you should not move. The urge to move becomes stronger and stronger and more and more fatiguing. How can the hypnotic subject maintain a state of rigidity with utter comfort and satisfaction and ease? The catatonic can do it. I have posed a catatonic patient against a wall with lights to outline his shadow, and drawn the outline of his shadow on the wall even though he was standing on one foot, with one arm out in one direction and the other arm in another, his head bent. That was 8 A.M. in the morning. At 12 noon I had someone else go out and outline the shadow; at 4:00 P.M. a third person went out to pencil mark around the shadow. There was practically no shift from the hour of 8 A.M. until 4 in the afternoon. How could he do it? Certainly there are significant differences between the catatonic patient and the normal person in the appreciation of fatigue. I have posed a cataleptic hypnotic subject, but of course have not presumed to do it for as long as a patient for many reasons, not the least of which is that I like to have my subjects remain my friends. I have posed them for an hour without any particular distress. I believe catalepsy is a phenomenon that is at the frontiers of our understanding of body learning. We ought to experiment with, test, and examine what constitutes it. I can recognize it in the way that I can recognize a number of other hypnotic phenomena, but I do not know what it is.

RAPPORT AND DISSOCIATION

Let us now consider the phenomenon of rapport. An obstetrical patient comes into the delivery ward: She hears her physician, she hears the nursing personnel, but she doesn't hear the screams of other women in labor. She doesn't even know that there are other women in labor. I hadn't specifically told her that either. There has occurred a redirection of her attention, and we say that she is in rapport with, and is responding to, only a certain number of persons, events, and things. What is this narrowing of the field of awareness, the narrowing and shrinking of the field of consciousness? Can you deliberately shrink the field of conscious awareness so that it excludes the pain of an injured foot, the pain of a badly burned foot? One way anaesthesia can be developed in a case with burned feet is to ask patients to forget their feet and then lose their sense of body continuity. I have inflicted painful stimuli upon a foot after such a thought had been accepted without the subjects reporting stress, because they had forgotten their feet. Why shouldn't they feel the painful stimuli on their feet, even though they had forgotten their feet? They were naive subjects and they didn't know that I was going to pinch their feet or inflict pain or distress on them, but they had forgotten their feet. What does that actually mean? What is an amnesia? What is dissociation?

My daughter had said that under no circumstances would she ever, ever, permit anaesthesia. I know my daughter's interest in hypnosis and her interest in psychology, but she was only a grade-school child at the time. I had promised her that I would not offer her any suggestions regarding anaesthesia. Once, in a medical setting where I was demonstrating hypnosis, I asked my daughter to see herself sitting "over there" on the other side of the room. She was very interested in hallucinating herself "over there." Then I asked her to feel herself on the other side of the room, really to feel herself sitting there, to experience herself sitting over there. Then one of the doctors, over to one side, came up and pinched her very thoroughly, tested her for pain. He was very certain that my daughter, experiencing herself "over there," did not show any pain reactions. The dissociation, the hallucination of herself "over there," was quite complete. How could she be pinched "over here" when she was "over there"? How could she feel pain "over here" when she was "over there."

We have the analog of this experience in another type of behavior. I haven't been able to recall the names of my psychology friends of many years past because I am no so busy in psychiatry and hypnosis. I had a delightful ride from Kansas City last night. My driver was working for his doctorate degree in psychology. After talking with him for a while, I began to call to mind name after name of psychologists that I had known back in 1929 and 1930, with vivid recollection. Why? I had never met this graduate student who was driving me before that evening, but he was a psychologist, and I knew that he was studying for his doctorate degree. It was a relaxed, friendly social situation in which conversation came easily. It brought back to me memories of a time when I was much closer to his present age. There was an awareness on my part that I was going to address a meeting where there would be many psychologists in attendance. These many factors provided a setting which facilitated the coming forth of all those forgotten memories. This was not hypnosis. However, if I wanted somebody to call forth memories of past events, past experiences, and past learning, I know that I could suggest to him that he be back in Worcester State Hospital talking to Dave Shakow or Paul Huston or somebody like that, and that he could begin to recall the names of the patients who had been on the ward when he had been there, and we would find a similar facilitation of recall.

My daughter "over there" could associate to the feelings that she would have "over there." She wouldn't have any feelings "over here." I later let her find out about anaesthesia. She said that she was very interested in this because she did not think that it was right for someone to suggest to another person, "Now, you can't feel anything." That was the first time I really understood why she objected to anaesthesia, even though she was quite willing to learn many other possible hypnotic responses.

It is difficult to tell somebody who is sitting in a chair in the middle of a room, "Now just feel yourself to be sitting in a chair behind me." No one can really do that in the waking state. In hypnosis, however, individuals are more open to ideas, and they more readily consent to examine them. If I were sitting in a chair behind the speaker, I would be facing in the opposite direction from that in which I am facing now. What would I see? I would be seeing an audience. The individual would permit himself to build up association by association until his thoughts would become more and more filled with an understanding of what an audience looks like, how it behaves. Soon it would become more and more possible to construct with these memories a feeling and image of yourself sitting in a chair behind someone and seeing that someone's back and then sitting in that chair. The individual would be able to take all of those past learnings and fit them together, and then he would feel himself in the chair behind me, looking at the audience.

In the ordinary state of conscious awareness, however, we are constantly orienting ourselves to the concrete reality around us. We do this as a matter of biological preservation. None of you would forget that there are people to the right and to the left of you, behind you and in front of you, in this audience. You remain well aware of these facts, and from moment to moment you reinforce this orientation to reality. In the hypnotic state subjects take one look at the hypnotic situation and they have established their orientation. They do not need to keep returning, verifying and reverifying their reality situation. They know the situation, and they are aware that, should any change in that reality orientation occur, they would be able to make the modifications. Thus they are perfectly willing to make these adaptations when the occasion arises, but they do not have to keep verifying that they are in this particular room, that there are lights in the ceiling, etc.

HYPNOTIC AMNESIA

What is hypnotic amnesia? I know that there are amnesias which occur in hypnosis. I also know that every hypnotic phenomenon can be found in everyday life, but only in a minor and disconnected way, and only at certain times. My favorite way of inducing amnesia is by a rather simple technique. When the patient with whom I know I am going to use an amnesia comes into my office, I may say: "You know, it was very pleasant driving to the office. Today is such a nice day in Phoenix. Were there many cars on North Central Avenue?" Perfectly casual conversation. The patient answers, and then, in response to a posthypnotic cue she develops a trance, and we proceed with the therapeutic work. However, on this occasion I want her to have an amnesia, so when she awakens I say, "How was the traffic on the corner of Camelback and North

Central?'' I'm right back into the conversation that preceded the therapeutic interview. I have thus reestablished and made dominant the trend of thought that preceded the therapy. In other words I have gone clear around and back to the beginning of the interview, until the patient walks out of the office, thinking about the traffic and the nice day in Phoenix and the number of cars on Camelback and North Central roads, and proceeds about her business with a total amnesia of the therapeutic work. Why shouldn't she have a total amnesia? By a simple asking of questions, casual thoughts have been used to emphasize a train of thought, a train of association in her mind, to bypass the conscious memories of the therapeutic interview.

A patient comes to you about a migraine headache. You sense that the patient is going to be very resistant about hypnosis and about therapy in general. You inquire sympathetically about the migraine headache. In one such interview I learned that there was a history of right-sided migraine headaches that had been going on for 11 years—always right-sided migraine headaches. I asked, ''Is the headache present at this moment?'' The patient said that it was. Then I asked, in absolute earnestness, ''Will you please describe—you say it's an 11-year-old migraine headache—will you please describe . . . you did say 11 years, will you please describe the exact sensation you have right there,'' and I pointed to a place at the left side of her head. The patient wondered what I meant and why I pointed to this specific spot. As she tried to answer that question, I interposed, ''Will you compare it with the same feeling on this side, and do you notice that you're beginning to have a pain over there similar to this one?'' The patient began to examine that, for she had had plenty of experience with pain. Pain is something that you experience, pain is something that you remember, pain is something that you learn, and you can have it in all parts of your body. Pain is a learned experience. I just asked her to learn about pain ''right there.''

She accepted that idea and started to examine this area for pain, and she discovered pain. *I call this a hypnotic technique. I have offered a suggestion, and the subject accepted it.* She then made use of memories of pain and learnings about pain, and when I suggested to her that the pain was growing, the patient discovered that the pain was growing, and suddenly she had a left-sided migraine headache. What happened to the right-sided migraine headache? I had not asked it to disappear; I had not offered any therapeutic suggestion. On the contrary, I offered the suggestion that she have a left-sided migraine headache all at once, and she obliged me. However, she relinquished the right-sided headache. Now, if I can give her a left-sided headache, then I ought to be able to take it away. She has had 11 years of right-sided migraine headaches only, and suddenly she lost that for a left-sided migraine. It should be much easier to deal with a migraine of such recent occurrence acquired under these particular circumstances.

Hypnosis is a state of awareness in which you offer communication with understandings and ideas to a patient and then you let them use those ideas and understandings in accord with their own unique repertory of body learnings, their physiological learnings. Once you get them started, they can then proceed to utilize a wealth of other experiences. I do not know how that patient got rid of a migraine headache that she had on the right side repeatedly over a period of 11 years, but she did lose it right there in the office. She proceeded to develop a left-sided migraine headache, which I was able to hypnotically suggest away. The left-sided migraine, as the right-sided one, was willingly given up by some utilization of body learnings. I don't know what they were. I don't know if she dissociated from her headache, or whether she just displaced the headache, or reinterpreted the headache, or just forgot the headache, or whether she suppressed the pain impulse that gave her a perception of headache. I know only that I presented ideas intended to stimulate the patient to behave in accord with actual body learnings over a long period of time.

ISOLATION (DISSOCIATION)

What are the implications of the hypnotic experiences which I call "isolation phenomena"? For example, instructing a patient to forget his foot, and then painfully stimulating the foot without disturbance to the patient. I use an isolation technique with highly resistant subjects who generally want to go into a trance. I tell a patient, "You know, in hypnosis you can really be so objective that you can look upon yourself, think about yourself in a nonsubjective fashion, with tremendous objectivity. Now take your hand, look at it, it's a nice hand. I wonder whose it is? That is an interesting hand, I wonder whose it is? Is that little finger going to move?" You and your patient look at that hand, and there is no sense of ownership, no sense of personal identity with that hand. You have just isolated it in an objective fashion. You're both looking at that hand. Not so long ago, when I was doing that with a patient, I reached over and squeezed on the phalanx in order to get joint pain. My subject watched what I did and said, "You know, that ought to hurt that hand." I have personally experienced polio, and I know something about the things that can happen to a person who has had polio. You can forget your body, you can lose your awareness of the various parts of your body. You can lose it to such an extent that you have to open your eyes to see if you are looking at the sheet or looking at the ceiling, because you really don't know whether you are lying on your back or on your stomach. You don't know where your feet are. You remember that you have feet, you remember that you have hands, but you don't remember what the feelings are like when your hands are closed and when they are open.

With subjects in an hypnotic trance you can bring about an isolation of the hand so that they can regard that hand as someone else's. You can cover up the hand and you can manipulate it. These subjects are very surprised when they find that the hand position is changed, because they didn't see it change its position. They didn't feel it change its position, nor do they feel pain. I have discovered that in working with polio patients who have forgotten physical movements you can do a great deal for them by asking them to remember their kinesthetic memories. I explain that word "kinesthetic" to the child and to the young adult so that they understand it. I tell them that if they can remember the taste of something and if they can remember the smell of something, then they can remember the feel of a movement. Thus with some of those patients who still have muscles, even though these muscles are inadequate, incompetent to use, you can get them to remember kinesthetic memories and kinesthetic images, so that they actually do it. In hand levitation, for example, sometimes your subjects will respond to you very adequately when told to lift their hand higher and higher, and the hand is lifting, is lifting, lifting. At other times when you say, "Your right hand is lifting way up in the air," you sit there and you watch that hand remaining exactly where it was. Finally you tell these patients, "Take your left hand and put it on top of your right hand." They put it on top of their right hand, and because they have substituted an actual arm movement for kinesthetic memories, the right arm begins to lift. Joint sensation and kinesthetic memories are as valid as any other kinds of memories. You can substitute them and modify them. I think there is need for a great deal of research on the characteristics of these different types of learnings and memories, the conditions for change, and the way in which they undergo spontaneous alterations during life.

REGRESSION

How valid is regression as a phenomenon? How far can you regress? I recall a paper that was submitted to me as editor of *The American Journal of Clinical Hypnosis* in which a doctor used regression with a nine-year-old boy suffering from overwhelming acrophobia. He couldn't ride in a car in a high place, on a hill, or a mountain. He would cower on the floor of the car and sob. It was an agonizing experience for him to go to any high place. The physician regressed this nine-year-old boy and explained very carefully that he could go "way back" until the very beginning of his fear of high places. The doctor wrote that he did not know how far back the boy was going to go, so he told him, "And take your voice along with you, your nine-year-old voice with you, so that you can tell me." The patient said, "I am three months old and I am riding in a plane." (This was done in the presence of the mother.) "I am awful scared being way up high here." The mother shook her head vigorously in denial: "That's all wrong, all wrong." The boy came out of the trance state and showed no signs of fear. He seemed perfectly willing to go look out of a window which he had previously shunned, and to look down and things of that sort. The mother took the doctor aside and said, "He didn't go in a plane, he's never been in a plane." It was a week or so later that the mother returned anxiously to the doctor's office and said, "You know, I'm completely mistaken about that. I took him on a trip just that once when he was three months old. I checked with my husband. He did ride in a plane at that time. I didn't want to take him, but I had to take him,'' showing some of her own reasons for forgetting the incident. How do you take the boy's voice and nine-year-old vocabulary back with him when he is regressed to the age of three months? How do you recover a memory of that sort, when the mother had forgotten it and the father had almost forgotten about it? How did that three-month-old infant know that he was three months old, and how did the nine-year-old boy take back with him a voice that could identify the age of that baby? Perhaps to the unconscious mind the primary problem is the intrinsic meaning of the idea or the communication which has been received, and then use is made of such capabilities and potentialities as are available to respond to and interpret this communication. I think age regression—whether partial, selective, or whatever aspect you focus on—can be investigated.

I know that everyone is capable of having perfectly wonderful dreams. I personally enjoy dreaming about things when I was a boy at home on the farm, about how nice it was in the early spring to feel the bare ground on your bare feet. Now and then I can have a very pleasing dream experience that enables me to answer a lot of questions or to give some understanding to my patients or to my little children about what farm life was really like, particularly my children. Sometimes it opens up for me the possibility of empathizing with my patients in terms of feelings, thoughts, memories, relating to their age by a dream memory, a dream revivification or perhaps a dream regression. How much of regression is revivification and how much of revivification is regression I am not able to answer at this time.

In summary, I earnestly believe that the different kinds of behavior that you can elicit in the trance state are at least as worthy of investigation as are the learning and the forgetting of nonsense syllables, the recognition of negative afterimages, and similar samplings of behavior which have been considered valuable for the exploration of the principles of human behavior. I do not think that hypnosis should be or can be investigated as a total phenomenon (whatever is implied by that global term). I think that hypnosis can best be investigated by a careful searching of the great varieties of human behavior which can be modified or changed or influenced by the hypnotic state. Learning, forgetting, sleeping, dreaming are but a few of the areas in which research on hypnosis needs to be done. I think research should focus on the various manifestations of hypnosis rather than a total hypnotic state. As for research on hypnotic techniques, one should never forget that these are only a means of attracting the subject's attention, and we should not lose sight of the purpose of these techniques because of fascination with the variations which can be employed.

DISCUSSION

Dr. Henry Guze: Many years ago a paper by Dr. Erickson dealt with the posthypnotic state. In view of what he said about hypnosis in his presentation, I would appreciate some clarification on what he considers to be the posthypnotic state.

Suppose he has treated a patient for pain in the manner that he has described. Does this patient go away and return to a posthypnotic trance to relieve pain at a later date? Is this another hypnotic state? If the pain is not experienced, are we to assume that the pain is not responded to? Is this patient constantly living in something of an hallucinatory state? The patient has perhaps put his body on the other side of the room, indulging in behavior which might, under a little pressure, be regarded as topological.

Dr. Erickson has stressed the verbal aspects in introducing ideas, concepts, attitudes, particularly that kind of attitude or idea, as it might be called, which creates a kind of refocusing of concentration of a certain kind. What about the patients who cannot speak? Can we hypnotize a deaf mute? Can we make a person who cannot speak go into a so-called hypnotic trance? I have been very interested in the problem of nonverbal communication. I would add, also, that I have maintained for some time the conviction that there is a continuity in terms of hypnotic phenomena phylogenetically from the lower animals up to man. If there are such things as hypnotic phenomena, it is quite reasonable that there should be such a continuity. Investigation of what we might call comparative hypnosis might reveal that many behaviors of other animal forms might be explained on the basis of an hypnoticlike state.

What is the relationship, if any, in terms of continuity? It is difficult for me to conceive that animals, if they do go into a hypnotic state, are able to go off into the realm of hallucinatory experience or imagery, which seems to be a basic constituent of hypnosis stressed in the presentation of Dr. Erickson. Finally, to what extent do you consider the hypnotic state and the psychotic state to be psychodynamically similar, related, or identical? Your emphasis on hallucinatory experiences, dissociation, and the like make me wonder about your thinking on this issue.

Dr. M. Erickson: Let me deal first with the matter as to whether the hypnotic state is similar or identical to the psychotic state. I think that hypnotic behavior is a normal, controlled, directed behavior useful to the individual. On the basis of my knowledge of psychiatry, psychotic behavior is disturbed, uncontrolled, and misdirected behavior which the individual has limited ability to change, modify, or understand. It is in some ways a misuse of a capacity to behave. A pansy in a tomato bed is a weed, just as a tomato in a pansy bed is a weed. A tomato in a tomato patch is a very desirable thing, as is a pansy in a pansy bed. In psychosis there is the wrong behavior, in the wrong place, usually at the wrong time. In hypnosis you have the right behavior, in the right place, doing the right thing, at the right time.

Now about this matter of the hallucinatory state of hypnosis. I do not like this formulation, unless Dr. Guze is ready to describe all memories as manifestations of hallucinations. I wonder how many of you ever had chilblains and then forgot about them for years and years. Then circumstances bring you back to Wisconsin in mid-winter and you are suddenly amazed to discover that even without getting cold, you've got a very good tissue memory of chilblains. Or is it tissue memory? I don't know exactly what it is. But your feet do itch frightfully. Why? You study it for a while, you're amused by it, and then you forget about it.

In my experience I have known people who never went into hypnosis, but who went to a movie because they had a severe headache, forgot their headache during the course of an interesting movie which had involved them, and perhaps didn't remember the headache until the next day. I don't know where the headache went in the movie situation, but I do know that they lost it sometime during the viewing of that movie, and that they did not necessarily have to have another headache to make up for it. I don't know what becomes of that headache that gets lost in the middle of a suspense movie, or a toothache that disappears on the way to the dentist, but it does disappear. There are many such things which disappear and are not accounted for.

In carrying out a posthypnotic act there is most likely a revival of the original trance, perhaps for a moment, perhaps for longer. It then passes on, just as you can have thoughts come into your mind that tense your muscles or alter your blood pressure, your blood circulation, and then the thought is succeeded by other thoughts with or without other physiological alterations throughout one's body. It's been a passing experience. The thought may have brought about an unpleasant memory, recalled an unpleasant set to the muscles, but then these disappear and may remain away indefinitely. There is no basis for considering that the original trance has to continue indefinitely for the posthypnotic suggestion to remain effective.

Can you hypnotize a deaf mute? That question came up in Caracas, at the maternity hospital in Venezuela. I was there lecturing to the staff, and one of the psychologists was very interested about the application of hypnosis. He found out that my Spanish vocabulary was limited to a fluent use of *si, manana*, and *hasta la vista*. They asked me if I could induce hypnosis in someone who could not speak English. I felt that was not only feasible, but also not too difficult. One of the physicians went into the maternity ward and spoke to one of the patients. He told her that, "The North American doctor is interested in obstetrics and is interested in you." This was all that was told to her.

The woman came in, sat down, and looked me over. I looked her over. After a few moments I reached over, took hold of her hand, and elevated it up in the air. I looked at it there, then let loose of her hand. I looked at my hand, pinched the back of my hand, and grimaced. Then I pinched the back of her hand, and she grimaced. I pinched hers hard enough that she was justified in grimacing. Then I lifted my hand, stroked the back of it, and smiled and looked happy. I pinched the back of my hand and looked happy and as surprised as I knew how. She looked at me with a puzzled look on her face. I took her hand, brushed it, and gave the happiest look that I could give her, then pinched the back of her hand again. She looked very surprised, and said in Spanish, "It doesn't hurt." Communication can be verbal, but it is also quite obvious that there is a great deal of nonverbal communication. Communication can be an angry look, a lovely look—all kinds of looks and all kinds of gestures.

Dr. Fritz Heider may or may not recall a conversation which I had with him many years ago about how deaf mutes swear in sign language. It is a very charming sign language, beautiful swearing, and it is meaningful, too. I think that you can hypnotize a deaf mute. I have asked blind people, blind from birth, to go into a trance and to hallucinate visually. The ideas which they have of what eyesight is, and how one would employ visual memory, are quite interesting and tend to be a composite of description of tactual, pressure, and kinesthetic memories.

Dr. Roy Dorcus: Dr. Erickson is a master of his art and he has given us a wonderful description of how he therapeutically creates in the individual the things that he wishes to bring about with respect to changes in behavior that the individual needs. I don't think that his discussion was primarily oriented to how these matters are related to the induction process, or really as to what hypnosis itself was.

He raised the question about catalepsy, how far this could be extended. I might indicate that in one instance we kept an individual in a cataleptic position for approximately 13 weeks. This was done for surgical purposes. The individual maintained this position, of course, during sleep. It was necessary because of a skin transplant, in which the transplant was made from the abdomen to the wrist and then from the wrist to the jaw. There were some real counterindications against placing the arm in a plaster cast for this length of time. It was not necessary to use this method because of the effectiveness of the hypnotic catalepsy. I do have a question with regard to Dr. Erickson's report of the case of a child with fears of height. I believe that this is closely related to another report presented to this Institute about the young woman who needed dental work. Even though the recalled memory made possible therapeutic management of the dental situation, there was found to be complete fabrication with regard to causality of the so-called memory of the traumatic situation. I have some serious doubts about this physician's report about the three-month-old child as to how this three-month-old child would know whether he was up in an airplane or on the ground and whether, by having the child report that he went back to this traumatic experience, that we are justified in concluding that this "recalled memory" was related to the particular problem which was being experienced. This is not to question whether the nine-year-old did not experience therapeutic relief, but it is my impression that it is very likely that you have have some projections and possibly some fabrication in this particular situation.

I can also affirm that it is possible to hypnotize deaf mutes. I had a patient referred for a particular reason. She happened to be a Czechoslovak who couldn't speak English, but the woman could read sign language from her daughter. I made one very foolish mistake in working with this woman because I started out with a visual technique, transmitting the signs through the daughter who could speak with her mother. I could not speak with her. I got her eyes closed and, of course, lost communication with her. At that point I had to take a hold of her eyelids and open them up until we could give her some signals again, and go back and start over.

I am in basic agreement with Dr. Erickson with regard to his general tenet—that is, the less stress and strain put on the subject (or patient) with regard to projecting himself into situations in which you wish to bring about some changes of behavior, (the better). If you can specify the situations for your patients, if you know something about their own background, then it is much easier to bring about the changes in behavior. If you happen to use some situation that is unfavorable for them—for example, in the situation where you might ask an individual to project himself into a very relaxed situation on the beach, you will find that occasionally you run into an individual who, because of sensitivity to sunlight, won't tolerate this sort of a projection. So if you either allow them to select the situation that is going to be appropriate for them, or if you can suggest one that is appropriate for them, the chances of getting the behavior one desires are greatly multiplied.

Dr. T. Sarbin: I would like to accent Dr. Dorcus' doubts about the case of the person reporting a memory of being in an airplane at the age of three months. This is so reminiscent of the Bridey Murphy phenomenon which, as you all remember, created such a stir a few years ago. It is the sort of thing that is very easy to induce in most subjects. In fact it is not difficult to have a hypnotized person report an experience during fetal life. We have to be very skeptical in accepting such reports as valid, even though such reports may be very important in therapeutic analysis.

I am very much interested and I approve heartily of Dr. Erickson's beginning analysis of hypnosis as an attention phenomenon, and some of his illustrations would seem to indicate that hypnosis is a matter of redeploying attention from one stimulus object to another. Redeployment of attention is a concept that is employed to account for changes in behavior in other social psychological situations than hypnosis, e.g., faith healing, conversion reactions, pain-free birth, etc. But when Dr. Erickson moves from attention concepts into a definition of hypnosis as behavior *within the person* that has to do with an altered state of awareness, then I have some questions.

Awareness is a term that is in common parlance. But when we introduce a definition of one unknown, e.g., "hypnosis," we don't want to use a word the referents for which are also unknown, or a word that has multiple referents. Ordinarily when you ask a patient, "What is awareness?" the subject uses the word "conscious" or its opposite, "unconscious." About 1941 Dr. James G. Miller wrote logical analysis of the multiple meanings attached to the word "consciousness." His study yielded, I believe, 17 major meanings and a number of subsidiary meanings. The same analysis could be applied to the term "awareness." Changes in "awareness," or changes of some kind that have to do with inner dynamics, as it were, are something that can only be inferred *from conduct*. The therapist, the hypnotist, and the analyst are limited to observations of conduct, to things that the patient says or does. They are free, of course, to take the sayings or doings and reconstruct them in any way that they wish. If we go back to the 18th century, we find that the sayings or doings were interpreted as a mysterious force, as animal magnetism. In the mid-19th century, the sayings or doings of the patient which came about as the result of hypnotic induction procedures were interpreted as disorders of the central nervous system. More recently these sayings and doings have been interpreted as learning phenomena. The ultimate test of what usefulness our inferences have about the behaviors that we call hypnosis can only be realized through observation and experiment.

Dr. Erickson was generous in his comment that such things as the analysis of the learning and forgetting of nonsense syllables have a place, but it seems to me that there was hidden in these remarks a criticism of such kinds of research, that this type of research would not really get us into the inner life of the person, which is the core of hypnosis.

Dr. Erickson's report presented us with a number of clinical anecdotes. The techniques that he uses in his clinical practice are imaginative, original, and I'm sure influence the patient in the direction of removal of symptoms, perhaps toward a change in character structure, or whatever the goals of the therapeutic endeavor are. But we must always bear in mind that individuals change their conduct in a number of settings. The settings certainly can be analyzed the same way that hypnotic influence can be analyzed. Dr. Watkins made the point in his report that we have to analyze variations contributed by the therapist, by the subject, by the interaction, etc. The procedures that we use in basic experimental design are no different. Whenever controlled experimentation has been done, invariably we find that the kinds of change, the kinds of influence that are produced under hypnotic conditions, can also be produced under nonhypnotic conditions.

My theme is that we are not moving forward if we look upon hypnosis as some kind of force or process that goes on exclusively within the individual, a force or process that demands explanatory concepts that are different from explanatory concepts that we use for the analysis of everyday behavior. In this respect I would urge the next generation of scientists to focus on the special social relations between hypnotist and client that influence action.

Dr. M. Erickson: When that three-month-old baby was taken to see a pediatrician, he did not know that the adult was a pediatrician. The baby did not even have a concept of a medical office, but that three-month-old baby was able to, and did, receive certain sensory impressions, visual impressions of whiteness, visual impressions of the pediatrician's shape and manner, as well as the cutaneous sensory impression of the hypodermic needle. Three months later, six months later, when the baby was taken back to the pediatrician's office, he was still unable to identify the pediatrician by name, or give the color of white, or recognize the hypodermic needle, but he was able to, and did, show a conditioned response of fear, anxiety, and distress. He can keep right on with that learning. I think the boy did have a plane ride at the age of three months, that perhaps, as he was carried up the ramp into the plane, he had the visual impression of a distance which was disturbing, and only later on put a name to this experience. I mentioned that he took the nine-year-old voice along with him in that regression, which meant that he took his nine-year-old understanding of height. He named the plane. I don't know where he got the memory of the plane, but it was verified that he had a plane ride. Most people have had the experience of seeing a strange, unfamiliar object and wondered and wondered what it was. And then one, two, or more years later it will suddenly dawn on them what it was that they had seen and didn't recognize at the time.

I would like to respond to Dr. Sarbin's comments about an altered state of awareness. If I wanted Dr. Sarbin to say a large number of very pleasant things, I think I would introduce him into a setting where there was soft music and flowers and sufficient other attractions which would induce in him the desire to say a number of nice soft words. However, if I introduced him into a situation where I was tormenting a dog, I expect I could induce him to say a great many unpleasant things. You alter a person's state of awareness by the conditions associated with, and the character of, the stimulation which you offer along with the inner behavior of potentials in that person. I do not think that I am in error to give the general term "state of awareness" to the memories, ideas, and emotions characterizing a person at a given time, nor do I consider this a "mystical appellation." I also do not feel that it is mocking the learning and forgetting experiments using nonsense syllables to say that just-as-serious scientific attention should be given to the study of hypnotic learning, hypnotic forgetting, and other hypnotic manifestations.

Dr. T. X. Barber: I was impressed with Dr. Erickson's statements concerning the technique of hypnosis. He said that it consists basically in asking the subject to pay attention. I can generally agree with this, and I believe most of the other people on the panel would also generally agree with it. Of course the problem remains, what do we mean by attention? In a general way this is probably the essential element of the hypnotic induction. Dr. Erickson emphasized this many times, but then shifted over into something different.

It seemed to me that half of Dr. Erickson's presentation was from the position of a natural scientist, psychologist, and psychiatrist trying to understand what hypnosis is; the other half of the time the presentation seemed to be from the position of someone of many years ago who really thought hypnosis was a mysterious, magical thing.

Dr. Erickson's main point seemed to be that what we're doing is trying to get the patient to use previous learnings. He put this in various ways, but always saying the same thing—experiential learning, bodily learning, conditioning processes. It was my impression that he was affirming that we have learned many things in our life, most likely due to some kind of conditioning process. The learning is present; the problem is, how are we going to bring it out? We do that by hypnosis: First we get the subject's attention, then (according to Dr. Erickson) the subject goes into a trance, and when he is in a trance, magiclike things happen. It is implied that a kind of mysterious thing happens because of trance. An example was a case of amnesia that Dr. Erickson presented. Before therapy began the therapist was talking about the traffic on the street; then, immediately after termination of the hypnotic therapy session, the therapist begins talking once more about the traffic on the street, and supposedly because the patient had been in trance, she immediately had an amnesia for all that went on during the "trance." She didn't remember anything else, supposedly because the therapist had reoriented her and he was again speaking to her in the same way he spoke to her originally (before the hypnotic induction). Why does the patient have the amnesia? The answer given by Dr. Erickson was that she was in a trance and the therapist reoriented her thought processes.

Let's ask a simple question: How do we get a person not to remember what has occurred during trance by simply talking to her again about what we were talking about before trance? The answer, as I believe Dr. Erickson said, was "I don't know." I would also say, "I don't know," but I would also say that it is not simply because we have indirectly given her a suggestion for amnesia. This is not magic nor are we back in the 18th century.

There is something more in this, and this is what I believe is happening. In all the studies of hypnotic amnesia that I have done, I have always found that the subject *in some very purposive, deliberate way* wants to do what I tell him. He wants to comply. This might be on an unconscious level, if you want to use that term. This is quite obvious, and we can pick it out all the time. If he is not a good, motivated, hypnotic subject, then he is not going to show amnesia. Suppose we tell the subject, "You won't remember something," or perhaps we suggest amnesia in another way. For instance, we may start talking about something that was occurring before the hypnotic induction and thus give the subject the indirect suggestion that he should not remember. What happens then? Suppose he says, "I don't remember what occurred," which shows amnesia. Then we ask him, "Why don't you remember?" What will the subject say? I wonder if Dr. Erickson has ever questioned the subjects. It appeared that Dr. Erickson just took the amnesia for granted. He starts talking about the traffic again, and the subject "doesn't remember." Did Dr. Erickson ask her, "Why don't you remember—what's happened?"

Everytime I have asked my subjects that, they all say something like this, and I'll try to quote them: "I don't remember because . . . well, I can't." "Why can't you?" "There is a block there." But if you really get around it another way and have somebody else question the subject, the answer comes

out, something like this: "I don't remember even though I know I can remember . . . but I can't let myself remember. I could remember if I tried . . . but
I won't try." Why is the subject not remembering? The subject is not remembering because in some way he is not letting himself verbalize what occurred;
he is *not letting* himself remember. What does that mean? What he is doing is
something like the following: "I will think about certain things, but I will not
let myself think about certain other things." A good hypnotic subject, when he
gets his cue that he is not to remember, will not let himself verbalize these
things to himself. They are there, he can remember all right. All that he has to
do is just let himself verbalize, but he doesn't let himself do it. Amnesia takes
purpose, effort, striving; it is a deliberate kind of thing. It is not something that
just happens magically just by giving the stimulus. I am bothered by Dr. Erickson's formulations because I get the impression that there is magic being attributed here that does not promote scientific understanding or investigation.

Let me cite a second example. Dr. Erickson reported about an age regression
back to three months. Both Dr. Sarbin and Dr. Dorcus commented on this. This
might very well be. Nobody can absolutely say that we cannot remember or that
it is impossible to remember what occurred at three months of age. It might be
possible even though I don't think that it is at all probable. That, however, is
not the question here. The question is that a subject was reporting this, and the
report was taken so uncritically and so readily accepted without asking a whole
series of questions. First of all let us suppose this boy actually took the plane
ride at three months of age. How do we know that this was not discussed at
some later time, that it didn't come up in some way later? How do we know
that at four, six, or more years of age the subject did not hear that at three
months old he took this plane ride. Dr. Erickson did not report if these questions
were asked. He seemed so ready to accept this report at face value that he gave
the impression that there was magic at work. There is the connotation of a real
mystery here that I just cannot accept. The evidence from psychoanalysis has
been critically reviewed so that we have reasonable doubt about the historical
accuracy of reported memories.

I believe that Dr. Erickson was on the right track when he was talking in
terms of attention. This is a word which we can use, although it is quite hazy.
I believe that he was on the right track when he was talking about conditioning,
learning, and how we have learned many more things than we utilize. But I
believe he goes off in some way when he is ready to uncritically accept evidence
about age regression.

It was said that a hypnotic subject was made cataleptic. All that means is that
the subject kept his body rigid and he sat there for one hour. Should we do
research on this? The implication was that this was an amazing phenomenon.
Motivate a person, or pay him some money; pay him enough to sit there for an
hour. If he is motivated, he will do it. That is all the research we need to do on
that. It is not amazing or mysterious if somebody can sit still for an hour. The
only research we need to do on "catalepsy" is to show that it can readily be

duplicated by a motivated person, and hypnotic subjects are usually very motivated.

Dr. M. Erickson: I believe that the hypnotic subject can do in a trance state the same sort of things he can do in the waking state. I might introduce someone to a dozen other people. At the end of that time, by virtue of having directed this person's attention first to Mr. Jones then to Mr. Green, to Mr. Brown, etc., and after I had finished the 15th or 16th introduction, I could ask him, "Tell me, what was the name of the first man, the second man, the third, the fourth, the fifth?" We would readily appreciate how rapidly a person can forget something, especially when his attention is constantly redirected. There would be no problem to prove that this person had really forgotten the names. Even when we have people who are strongly motivated to remember the names which have just been presented to them, we find that they forget easily. I don't think that this forgetting is a function of mesmerism or magic. I think it is ordinary normal behavior.

I believe that the hypnotic subject can, in the trance state, do something besides please Dr. Barber. I think he can use his own behavior for his own purposes, and do it in his own way. He doesn't lose his capacity to behave to please himself. I think he can also do things to please Dr. Barber as well as do things to displease Dr. Barber.

As for this Bridey Murphy mystical thing, I said that I think you can condition a three-month-old baby and that you can condition him in various sensory modalities. Later an interpretation can be placed upon that conditioned response. I also said that the boy took his nine-year-old voice into the situation with him. Is that magic? I don't know what else was taken along, but I looked upon it as a partial regression, and I don't think that this was a matter of gullibility. All we know is that these were the things done and that certain therapeutic results were obtained. I think that the therapeutic result was a valid occurrence, a valid experience for the boy. What is the explanation? Let us not call the explanation Bridey Murphy. Let's not call it any names at all. It is more productive scientifically to wonder what the processes are that constituted that experience. I fully recognize that you and I cannot apply the most useful concepts nor give the right terms as yet. We haven't examined the items of behavior most meaningfully, perhaps not defined these items of behavior in the most useful language.

Dr. Andre Weitzenhoffer: I feel that I must concur with the previous discussant and express my doubts as to the likelihood of a three-month-old child being capable of a conception of distance which the reported paper seems to have implied. Even if the infant had a conception of distance, I would question how he would come to fear distance unless he had been dropped. It is possible that he had been dropped by his father. I remember hearing about a father regularly lifting his child up and then letting him fall saying, "He's got to learn the hard way that he can't trust people." These are assumptions. I am only raising this question. I do not mean to question the validity of the reported regression as a regression, or its therapeutic value. I do want to raise this question about whether the three-months-old baby could have this memory of depth and height and somehow could have learned to fear this.

The comments of Dr. Barber and Dr. Sarbin lead me to make the following points. It is true that we can find individuals whom we thought were actually "hypnotized" (but who said they were not), who could produce the phenomena which have been produced in hypnotized individuals (at least by the best of our criteria). But it is to the point that we can also find individuals who, under the ordinary conditions of not being hypnotized, cannot produce certain phenomena, but when they are "hypnotized," are able to produce these phenomena. I do not mean anything transcendental, nor do I mean anything magical. You can take an individual and show that he cannot produce a certain type of hallucination. Then you hypnotize him by means of some ritual (I don't care what method you use), and then show that under these conditions the individual can produce hallucinations. I think then we do have a basis for saying there is a state which we can call "hypnosis." It seems to me that it is not enough to say that we can find nonhypnotized individuals who can produce the same phenomenon that these people who are hypnotized can produce. I am sure we can. I don't believe that under any condition we can produce phenomena which transcend the potentialities of the individual. We all have our potentialities. We can't go beyond this. I do think, however, that under normal conditions many individuals cannot make use of all their potentialities. In a sense I agree with Dr. Erickson that most individuals have potentialities that are not being actualized but which, under hypnosis, come closer to actualization.

Dr. Orne has been doing a lot of work with simulators. I know he has been concerned with these same problems, but from a different angle. He has asked himself the question: Is there some one single test which can be given to two groups of individuals (one group composed of good hypnotic subjects, and the other a group with simulators, i.e., people who have been instructed to simulate, to pretend, people who have been instructed to simulate to do their best, to behave like a hypnotized person), and which only non simulators can pass. He says that if he can find such a test, and if he can find that individuals can pass it only if they have been hypnotized by means of a ritual, then he will be in a position to say that we can speak of hypnosis as a state, as a condition.

Dr. Henry Guze: I, too, cannot accept the validity of a three-month-old memory of that kind. However, we should maintain an awareness of very early affects in development which in some way may leave some kind of state that later may be associated with an experience. We should not neglect the aspect of imprinting from animal behavior, and also the data which we have gathered on early-deprivation states, both in human beings and in the lower animals. As a comparative psychologist I have done work on very early deprivation, preweaning nursing deprivation in mammals, and we have definitely and distinctly demonstrated permanent effects, permanent changes. It is very difficult to draw the analogy, but I think that we should keep an open mind about the possibility.

The second point which Dr. Weitzenhoffer so very aptly brought forth is the problem of equivalent behavior. We are missing a very vital problem by forgetting that we can very often, in many states, elicit the same phenomenon by different means. For example, sugar and sachharine are both sweet, but this does not mean that because they both give us very similar sensations of sweetness that therefore the two chemical compounds are the same. Similarly we can find types of behavior, all along the various biological levels, which appear to be the same type of behavior on the surface but which are elicited really by different means. Therefore I don't think that we invalidate hypnotic phenomena by the fact that certain hypnotic phenomena may appear in some people during the waking state. I would be extremely cautious about this.

32. Expectancy and Minimal Sensory Cues in Hypnosis

Milton H. Erickson

The significance and effectiveness of minimal cues in eliciting and altering responsive behavior is frequently overlooked, even disregarded, in hypnotic work, not to mention other forms of endeavor employing interpersonal communication. As a measure of impressing this upon medical students and candidates for doctoral degrees in clinical psychology, the following teaching procedure was devised and carried out over a period of years, with succeeding classes divided into small groups, each handled in a separate fashion.

Well-trained somnambulistic subjects capable of manifesting readily all of the usual phenomena of deep hypnosis were employed. At every opportunity new subjects were employed; they were kept unaware if possible of the work to be done; and whenever they were used with different groups, the actual group task was varied if possible. Subject sophistication as to the nature of the work done was found to occur frequently, but this was early discovered to be an additional valuable experimental finding and also an experimental control. It was not, however, deliberately employed.

Pairs of study groups were formed composed of one to six students each. At first an effort was made to select homogenous groups, but this was found to be most uncertain, a fact that proved experimentally advantageous.

The experimental procedure was relatively simple. The subject, in a profound hypnotic trance, was told that he was to be a teaching subject for students. He was to develop a trance state slowly in response to whatever induction technique was employed, taking from five to 10 minutes before he entered the somnambulistic state. This he would manifest to the students by some specified cue such as a deep sigh, of which the students would be apprised in their preliminary instruction. Then, and not until then, would the students offer suggestions for specific phenomena. These suggestions were to be "listened to attentively and understandingly." They were "to be executed in exact, precise accord, and only in accord with their actual, their real meaning as given." Their response was "to be made unquestioningly," that "nothing more, nothing less than that actually expected" was to mark their responses to the suggestions given to them, that they were to respond adequately and well to the "real, the exact meaning

---

Incomplete report written in the 1960s.

of the suggestions as you hear them.''

To summarize—and it is necessary to summarize at this point to keep the nature and purposes of the experimental study in mind:

Somnambulistic subjects were told to accept ''in their exact, their precise meaning'' suggestions for specific hypnotic phenomena offered to them by students. They were earnestly instructed to respond with behavior that was no more and no less than the *actually expected responses*, and they were to listen attentively, well, and understandingly to the suggestions given.

The instructions to the students were given separately to each of the various groups. These instructions followed the same general pattern, but their content varied from group to group. For example Group A was told emphatically that Subject X was a remarkably fine somnambulistic subject and could develop all of the phenomena of the deep trance with the one exception of anaesthesia. A casual explanation was offered of individual variation of subjects, and it was pointed out to them that some subjects who seemingly could not develop certain phenomena would do so with the right operator.

Group B was given the same instruction about Subject X but told that, despite adequate ability in all other regards, X could not develop auditory hallucinations. Group C was told that Subject X could do anything except visual hallucinations, and Group D was instructed that Subject X could manifest everything except posthypnotic amnesia.

Each group was given the same total list of phenomena to elicit and the same set of token suggestions by which specific phenomena could be elicited. For example, in securing anaesthesia of the hands, the pattern of suggestions followed a noticing of the feeling in the hand, its warmth, its weight, its beginning feeling of coolness, of coldness, of slowly developing numbness, of final absence of feeling.

For visual hallucinations the pattern of suggestion included feeling oneself staring into distance, of vision getting blurred and indistinct, of fogginess and haziness developing, of finally seeing nothing but a meaningless haze in which would develop lines and shadows and curves and shadings and blurred forms that would become more and more clear and visible until they saw some chosen visual hallucination removed from the experimental situation such as a movie, a wedding party, etc.

For each of the deep hypnotic phenomena comparable sets of detailed, rather amateurish sets of instructions were made up and presented to each student group for careful study and use during this work with the subject.

Editor's Note: While this incomplete report ends here, Erickson has noted to the editor and others in workshop discussions that the results of this experimental paradigm were very similar with many classes over the years of his teaching career. The students in Group A who did not really *expect* their hypnotic subjects to experience anaesthesia consistently found in fact that they did not, although they were competent with other hypnotic phenomena. Likewise Groups B, C, and D, who did not expect their subjects to manifest auditory hallucinations, visual hallucinations, or posthypnotic amnesia, respectively, each found that they did not. Erickson explains these results as illustrating the importance of the operator's expectancy betrayed by minimal sensory cues in the hypnotic situation. Each group of students involuntarily and unknowingly betrayed their expectations via minimal sensory cues (voice dynamics, nonverbal behavior, etc.) to their hypnotic subjects, who had been previously instructed by Erickson "to respond with behavior that was no more and no less than that *actually expected*" by the student operators.

Although this report is incomplete, it contains enough of the experimental paradigm that may be of value to other teachers, clinicians, and researchers who may wish to replicate it.

33. Basic Psychological Problems in Hypnotic Research

Milton H. Erickson

Research in hypnosis and the presentation of ideas about hypnosis too frequently parallel the arguments that the seven blind men offered about the elephant. They argued first with much intensity and finally they did research. One got hold of the tusk and another of the tail, another felt the flank, another, the ear; the fifth examined the trunk, etc. Then, after each had done his complete examination of his particular part of the elephant, their arguments became intensified.

So it is with hypnosis. Everybody has a particular point of view, and it is necessarily a limited point of view, just as mine is. I am going to ask a critical question, therefore, of my colleagues: Why should anyone assume that hypnosis is of necessity a matter of distorting reality? Certainly such a forthright assumption is far beyond the call of any scientific duty. One could equally well and perhaps more rightly and informatively say that hypnosis is a state of readiness to utilize learnings. Why should it be viewed as a distortion of reality instead of some kind of readiness to use abilities normally? It has also been said that "Hypnosis is an alteration in perception," as if this were an abnormal process, an indictment of hypnosis. But is it not a part of our learning experience in life, and does it make hypnosis a distortion of reality?

I have been credited with using hypnosis to maintain the "strength of the ego" in deep hypnosis. The ego, so far as I know, is a helpful and convenient concept, but that is all that it is. "Ego" is a verbalization to permit better communication of abstractions employed in conceptualizing. Then to speak of "strength" as a reality attribute of an abstraction serves only to lead scientific thinking further afield.

It is also stated that hypnosis is a state where one person takes responsibility for another. I think that is on a par with the supposedly explicit and specific statements that hypnosis involves an interpersonal relationship in which one person, the operator, restructures the perceptions and conceptions of another person, the subject. Let us examine this statement to see if it is equally applicable in other fields. Anaesthesiology is a relationship wherein one person takes the

Reprinted with permission from G. Estabrooks (Ed.), *Hypnosis: Current Problems*. New York: Harper & Row, 1962, 207-223.

responsibility for another. Education involves an interpersonal relationship in which one person, the teacher, restructures the perceptions and conceptions of another, the student. Eating involves an interpersonal relationship in which one person, the waitress, restructures the perceptions and conceptions of another person, the diner. In other words these presumably specific scientific statements intended to describe hypnosis are so generally applicable as to be descriptive of the teacher, the lover, the bus driver, and so on. One does not describe hypnosis scientifically by offering with an air of profundity vague generalities that can be paraphrased in a wealth of ways. Science is the method by which we endeavor to achieve more and more explicit and specific understandings of phenomena, expressed in terms applicable to the phenomena themselves and not to other unrelated things.

The question has often been raised of universal hypnotizability and its bearing upon health and sickness. It is almost universal for us to be born with two feet and two hands, but what bearing does it have upon the question of health or sickness? So far as I know, hypnosis as a form of human behavior has been in existence since the beginning of the human race. Then why should hypnosis necessarily be singled out from the entire variety of human behaviors and designated as something that is highly specific or even slightly specific in relationship to mental health or mental sickness, emotional health or emotional sickness? Yet there is much thinking along that line because so many people believe unthinkingly that hypnosis is an abnormal state. Furthermore we may ask, Are not the manifestations that are developed in the hypnotic trance the behaviors learned in an ordinary waking state? One could parallel this type of thinking by the statement that the circulation of the blood is highly specific to mental, emotional, and physical health, and that such circulation varies according to sleeping, waking, and activity states. All of this is true, but it neither discloses nor constitutes any specific understanding of health or of blood circulation until it is refined in relationship to highly specific items of special reference.

In illustration of some points I wish to make I will cite the instance of a paralyzed man bedridden for 15 years. I saw him when he was in his 80s. He had pneumonia, was dying, and was delirious. The thing that astonished me was what that man was doing in his delirium. His history was this. His mother had been a very religious woman who compelled her children, from the age of four, to listen to her give a daily prolonged reading of the Bible. Year after year, every day, this was done without fail so that she repeatedly read through the Bible. Before his mother died this man had had six years of that daily listening to the Bible. His reaction to her death and to that Bible reading had been one of utter bitterness and resentment. At his mother's death he was placed in a foster home where there was no Bible reading, no church attendance, and no going to Sunday school.

He grew to manhood with these foster-home attitudes, married, never allowed his wife or children to go to church, and declared the Bible and all religion to be unacceptable. In his early 70's he suffered the paralyzing cerebrovascular accident that rendered him permanently bedridden. Then he developed pneumonia, became delirious, and in that delirious state he *recited the Bible*, chapter by chapter, hour after hour. Using a Bible to check his recitation, I found that he was reciting it correctly. To everybody's knowledge in the community he had not even looked at a Bible since the age of 10 years. I encounter people in the psychology laboratory and in the field of psychiatry and medicine who say in all seriousness, "Hypermnesia and those regressive phenomena attributed to hypnotic subjects are dubious, questionable, open to question," and they work out all manner of experiments to prove that hypermnesia and regressive phenomena are impossibilities and, what is worse, they believe their inadequate findings. That dying old man proved that regression to childhood memories is an actual phenomenon. Yet there are any number of attitudes taken to disprove the legitimacy of hypnotic experiments and the concepts that one deals with in hypnosis despite their occurrence in the ordinary course of human events. If that aged, sick, delirious, brain-damaged man could recover childhood memories, is it not reasonable to assume that comparable behavior can be achieved by the young and healthy?

Another example I wish to cite is that of a hysterical patient who sat in a wheelchair for nine years, presumably totally unable to walk—"paralyzed." Once her child, who was on the other side of the room when the housekeeper went out, started the electric motor that ran the wringer on the washing machine and got his hand caught in the wringer. The patient, who was in a wheelchair on the far side of the room, jumped up, rushed across the room, rescued the child, and never thereafter showed any ability to walk. Of course hysteria can be called a functional thing: yet that hysterical paralysis was sufficiently real to govern most significantly that woman's life. What did that woman say about this rescuing of her child? She said she did not do it, she did not and could not get up out of her chair, that the child had just looked at the washer. Nevertheless the occurrence had been observed in its entirety. That woman was not deliberately or even unconsciously lying. Two orders or categories of behavior were manifested, one which occurred in reality and another which constituted a reality of understanding for her. Yet research workers will propose methods of study to determine the "validity" of such behavior despite its actual occurrence and overlook the far more important need to devise methods and procedures to elicit such manifestations for study as such. So often the experimenter blindly contrues experimental negative results to signify nonexistence of phenomena instead of incompetency of procedure.

Somewhat comparable is the case of Jimmy. For 30 years he had been a deteriorated patient in a state hospital, sitting around on a bench, drooling, untidy, filthy, just about as "deteriorated" as a patient can be. His record disclosed his condition to have been at a constant low level since admission. He was simply and obviously an old, hopelessly deteriorated schizophrenic patient. Then one day a fire broke out in the hospital, and the attendants in that ward became frightened and panicky. Jimmy got up, walked over to the first attendant, said, "Listen, you take your keys and go to that end of the hall and you stand by the door." He went to the other attendant and he said, "Now you get all the patients and you march them over there." Then to the second attendant Jimmy said, "Give me your keys," and Jimmy himself systematically searched each room thoroughly, and when he had made certain that there was no frightened patient concealed in any part of the room, he locked the door and moved on to the next room. This done, he left the ward, locking the door behind him so that no patients could run back into the ward. He then walked over to make certain that the two attendants had marched all the patients outside and were handling them adequately out in the yard. This done, he said, "Here are the keys," and lapsed into his old "deteriorated schizophrenic self" again, a seemingly total loss. Now this instance may be quite different from that of the hysterical patient—or is it different? When you produce in hypnosis tremendous alterations in the subject's behavior, is it not possible that processes comparable to those which sometimes occur under ordinary or pathological conditions are set into action in a limited, but controlled and instructive fashion?

Another thing I want to mention is the matter of conditioning. Everybody knows that you can get conditioned responses in the psychology laboratory. You ring a bell, you flash a light, do this and that. You do it a sufficient number of times and you can get a conditioned response that governs the subject, and you can do a number of things in relation to that conditioned response. I think of Ann, who walked into a dentist's office when she was eight years old. She was a frightened little girl, and she was squalling and yelling because her parents were the type of people whose children would cry when they went to see the dentist. The dentist believed in the wet-towel method of handling crying children. He slapped her face with a wet towel, picked her up and put her in the chair, slapped her face again, and told her, "Shut up and be a good girl." So she was! At age 21 Ann walked into another dental office and said to the receptionist, "I want to talk to the dentist. Tell him I'll be out in the hallway." The receptionist told the dentist about it as he went out in the hallway where Ann was standing fearfully. "You won't slap me, will you?" she asked pitifully. Ann was a college graduate, an intelligent girl, but such was her uncontrollable fear that she had to make absolutely certain that she would not be slapped. It was impossible for her to believe otherwise at first, and the dentist had much work teaching Ann that brutality was not a part of dentistry. Ann had never been to a dentist since that childhood experience—she had been thoroughly conditioned in one single experience. The dentist had to be most laborious in his deconditioning of the girl, who now wears complete dentures as a result of that original experience.

Why should not one assume that if such a massive thing can happen in one little instance of everyday life, massive phenomena comparable in intensity and effectiveness can be secured by hypnosis in a directed and controlled fashion? Why not assume that the same forces that condition people in ordinary life can be as effective in hypnosis? The people are the same, they still possess their innate abilities, and we all know that a single starry-eyed look can initiate generations of events. Why assume that hypnosis negates the possibility of sudden effective conditioning?

I recall a little girl about seven years old to whom in jest, pointing to the empty air, I said, "You know, that's an awfully nice doggie there. He's black, isn't he?" And the little girl stepped over and petted the dog. She fed him cake. She had a delightful time playing with that dog, and I had a delightful time following up the results of that simple jest, because the little girl was so very pleased with that dog. When visitors would come, she would ask them, "Please walk around the dog. He's sleeping in the hallway." For many months she played extensively with the hallucinatory dog.

The girl is now grown up, a mother of children, and she hopes that every one of her children will have as nice a dog as she had when she was a little girl, though she recognizes that it was some kind of visual image or hallucination, but nevertheless a very real experience and memory, and a good and happy one. She found that dog as real to her in ordinary, everyday, waking life as are the figures in a nighttime dream during physiological sleep, and such dreams can be decidedly vivid and happy. And what about the imaginary playmates that children have? I knew a little girl who had a playmate named Booboo. Full respect had to be accorded Booboo in every possible way. I have encountered many people who have had imaginary playmates that were a normal part of their lives as children. Comparably, why should not one expect a subject in the hypnotic state to manifest the same sort of normal behavior with similar realism? Why should not the highly intelligent child grown older experience again a past reality as competently as when a child? Why assume that visual images are willful confabulations in adults and experiential realities spontaneously developed in children? Scientific study of such possibilities is needed, not dogmatic negation.

There is the matter of a phantom limb discussed in Dr. Wright's chapter. You can encounter people in ordinary, everyday life who will discuss their phantom limb as a reality. The reality of the phantom limb as an experiential phenomenon cannot be questioned. From whence comes the learnings that produce a phantom limb? What are the processes that enter into it?

The phantom limb is a phenomenon that occurs both in the uninformed *and in those having advanced academic and professional degrees* in both psychology and medicine. In a way it is a parallel of the phenomenon of partial body dissociation that can be produced hypnotically. Perhaps the same or similar mental processes are involved. The matters of dissociation, association, and reassociation are still a virgin field for hypnotic exploration, and much more can be accomplished by research than by the fervent presentation, without cognizance of the actual phenomena, of personal theories of role-playing and simulation. It is satisfying personally to offer theories and hypotheses, but it would be so much better to investigate actual phenomena. Research should be centered around phenomena, not around achieving fame by placing in the literature a well-argued theory intended to "explain" some unexamined manifestation. Profound studies of hypnotic phenomena themselves are needed rather than idle, though earnest, speculations and pronouncements. This constitutes the real need in scientific advancement.

In a related area, what are the forces, the sensations, the experiential learnings that enter into what we call the body image? The body image is an extremely important thing to all of us. When we lose a limb, or have a hand or foot amputated, it is important to remember that experientially we still have a body image in our total unrecognized understandings of ourselves which did not undergo an amputation. That vital sense of the "beingness" of the self is often overlooked, and this feeling of the integrity of the bodyself offers another point of departure in understanding what constitutes self-realization. Why should not the person in a hypnotic trance be able to develop upon suggestions manifestations conducive to a study of the nature of dissociation, depersonalization, and related phenomena? These are areas of research vital to both medicine and psychology.

Now I wish to consider another misconception about hypnosis. It is often asked whether or not some hypnotic phenomenon is real. Is the hypnotic trance a valid phenomenon? For instance, a question is asked that indicates that failure to close the eyelids or failure to be able to open the eyelids is definitive of the light state of hypnosis. To use eyelid closure to define hypnotic states even in part seems to be as absurd as defining mobile life as the ability to move in a *northerly* direction, as if the direction were pertinent. The minimum of experience in hypnosis discloses that hypnotized subjects can open or close, or keep closed, the eyelids, as is also the case in the waking state. Why then, in various books on hypnosis, in various experimental studies, is there such effort to define hypnosis in terms of the presence of absence of little bits of isolated behavior, not even necessarily related to hypnosis? There are whole classifications devised to show that in the light trance you find phenomena "A" and "B" and "C," that in the medium trance there occur "D," "E," and "F," and in the deep trance there develop phenomena "G," "H," and "I," as if that were absolute law, as if human behavior followed rigid sequences and rigid relationships.

There are people who try to define hypnosis in terms of sequences of behavior, of selected situations, or of the interpersonal relationship (as if a tall, blue-eyed subject and short, brown-eyed operator were important in effecting a special form of hypnosis). There are also efforts to define it in special descriptive terms to be applied to both operator and subject.

Hypnosis is also falsely defined in terms of the purposes to be achieved, as if you could have "medical" hypnosis and "dental" hypnosis and "psychological" hypnosis. This is on a par with describing anaesthesia in surgery as "right kidney anaesthesia," "left kidney anaesthesia" and "gastric resection anaesthesia." Hypnosis should not be defined in terms of the operators and their interests nor in terms of special points of view. This statement is but introductory to another point of interest, and that is the discounting of hypnosis if certain phenomena are not consistently present. For example, it is dogmatically asserted that if catalepsy is not consistently present, hypnosis is to be doubted, that if posthypnotic phenomena are not consistently present, hypnosis is doubtful. In other words the assertion is too frequently made that there is good reason to doubt hypnosis unless all of certain arbitrarily chosen hypnotic phenomena are present. Comparably, it might be declared with equal credibility that since vision, hearing, and limbs are universally present in human beings, congenital absence of one or more of these would raise serious doubts in a "scientific" mind about identifying such a person as a human creature.

There is the tendency to test hypnotic phenomena with nonspecific tests to determine specific results, with consequent negative findings and hence false negative conclusions. For example, the testing of anaesthesia with a psychogalvanometer may prove the presence of tissue responses and of neural behavior, but this is not necessarily pain. Yet because the psychogalvanometer may show fluctuations, the conclusion may be reached that there is no hypnotic anaesthesia, that the subject is fabricating or simulating or role-playing. The obvious possibility that the psychogalvanometer may also indicate sensations and reactions other than pain can be easily overlooked. A painful stimulus is not necessarily a pure stimulus, and other responses than those occluded by anaesthesia may register. The mere devising of a test, however thoughtfully done, does not mean that it is applicable or meaningful. It too must first be subject to rigorous testing. For example, even questionnaires and other similar studies, based upon carefully sought opinions, do not serve to define hypnotic phenomena, however well they may summarize more or less informed opinions.

I know clinically that there is such a phenomenon as psychological anaesthesia. I recall the instance of a World War II combat veteran with an excellent war record who, while attending college, leaped downstairs, sprawled on the floor, picked himself up, and walked home. The next day his foot and ankle were so badly swollen that he had to wear a bedroom slipper to class. Sometime later, since the swelling continued unabated, he came into the Veterans Administration hospital, where I examined him. As he walked across the room, the sound of crepitus was definitely audible. The X-ray film showed extensive comminuted fractures of the bones of the ankle and foot. When so informed, the patient astonishedly remarked, "But I thought broken bones hurt!"

Medical examination showed an apparent profound loss of all sensations—tactile, pressure, warmth, cold, and vibration—for the entire lower leg up to within three inches of the level of the lower end of the patella. Above this level sensations were normal. Obviously the patient, who disclaimed any pain experience with his injured ankle, had developed, apparently at the moment of injury, a profound, uncontrolled, hysterical anaesthesia that was nevertheless physically clearly delineated. Just as this sort of manifestation can occur as a spontaneous development in a person with an excellent "normal" record, a comparable hypnotic phenomenon of equal effectiveness can be developed for scientific study. The simple fact that analogous conditions can develop both in everyday life and in hypnotic states should be ample warrant to accept those of the hypnotic state as sufficiently valid to justify scientific examination.

Hypnosis is a state of awareness, a very definite state of awareness with special types of awareness. Hypnotic subjects are not unconscious in any sense of the word. Rather they are exceedingly aware of a great number of things and yet able to be unaware of an equally great number of things. They can direct and redirect their attention in remarkable ways ordinarily not possible in the waking state but possible in the nighttime dream state, which is a form of cerebration. They can do the same sort of things that they do in the ordinary waking state, but often in a more intentional, controlled, and directed manner. For example, consider all the things that are being overlooked in your present state of conscious awareness. Have you forgotten the shoes on your feet, the collar around your neck, and the glasses on your face? Certainly you have, and you will forget them again and again, but not consciously upon request. You can be sitting with a newly-made friend whose name you know when suddenly another train of thought comes along, and you find that you have forgotten his name, an easy thing to do unintentionally in the waking state, but also easy to do upon simple request in the hypnotic state. Quite probably the same mental processes are involved. Much research is needed to define these manifestations.

There is also the problem of pain. Hypnosis has been used repeatedly and successfully to alleviate or even to abolish pain in severe chronic cases and with startlingly successful results in some cases of terminal painful malignant disease. The clinical reality of the pain relief is unquestioned, but the scientific understanding of what is done, and how, leaves much to be desired. The clinical demands of the situation require that every presumably efficacious suggestion be employed, while a "scientific" approach demands that a "controlled and systematic" approach be used. However, the situation is one involving human life and suffering, and advancement of objective scientific knowledge is not the primary goal. This fact should not exclude from acceptance the finding that pain can be abolished or alleviated, nor should the results be dismissed as "simulation" or "role-playing," because "controlled study of individual items" was not done. The problem is this: Can the laboratory worker devise an experimental study or analysis that will permit an understanding of the validity of the clinical results achieved instead of dismissing the results as attributable to unknown and unknowable factors? The true task of scientific research is to adapt itself to existent problems, not just to form hypotheses for examination.

The pain of cancer is an experiential reality. Too often the uncritical assumption is made that pain is a pure and simple sensation and therefore should be so tested in the laboratory. As a clinician I find that patients use a wealth of adjectives to describe pain—burning, surging, cutting, throbbing, dull, heavy, stabbing—and therefore as a clinician I offer suggestions directed not only to the pain but to the presumed aspects or attributes of that pain. The assumption is that if an aspect of the pain can be altered, then the entire pain experience can be changed. Clinically this is so. The job of laboratory research is to discover what does happen rather than to discount the validity of the patient's experience. Then, too, pain is not simply an experience of immediate reality, but is something that is interpreted in terms of past experiences as well as future expectations. The clinician knows that the patient with a painful terminal disease suffers from the pain of the immediate moment, to which is added the memory of past pain and the anticipation of future pain. Hence the clinician using hypnosis for pain relief knows the importance of suggesting amnesia for the memory of past pain as a means of reducing current pain. Equally important are suggestion to prevent the anticipation of future pain.

How does one examine the "frames of reference" within which the patient views and experiences pain in the laboratory, where pain is regarded as the response of a specific type of nerve to a noxious stimulus? The clinician has to formulate a general approach, and the laboratory worker who wishes to contribute to an understanding of human behavior and experience in relation to pain needs to devise experimental procedures to measure these matters.

Additionally, while alleviation or abolition of pain, especially by drugs, are the traditional methods of treatment, the spontaneous, natural way of dealing with pain involves a multitude of behavioral reactions such as distraction of attention from the pain, amnesia, dissociation, displacement, the development of analgesia or of anaesthesia, and a reinterpretation of the sensations. Clinically, and through our own daily experience, we know many varieties of behaviors can occur. In the use of hypnosis clinically it is our obligation to be aware of these possibilities and to utilize them. In the scientific psychological laboratory the obligation is to study as a phenomenon the reinterpretation, let us say, of pain as a worthy scientific phenomenon in itself.

Hypnosis, by permitting the individual to call upon and utilize singly or collectively the great multitude of bodily learnings accumulated in a fragmentary fashion over the years, offers endless opportunity for the laboratory scientist to single out and examine individual manifestations. In this way hypnosis offers a means of reaching an eventual understanding of the processes entering into the development of various behavioral phenomena. This will not be achieved, however, if scientists formulate a hypothesis of what things should be and then look for those items that fit the hypothesis and discard those that do not, as is the case with those who say that hypnosis is role-playing and consider any contrary hypnotic phenomena as invalid, or those who say that hypnosis is a regressive phenomenon and ignore the great wealth of obviously nonregressive hypnotic phenomena.

Perhaps the most important thing to be said in the matter of hypnotic research is that there is a phenomenon of behavior and experience best termed in our present state of understanding as "hypnosis." Nothing is gained by saying that there is no such thing as hypnosis, that hypnosis is not hypnosis but merely something else; just as nothing was gained by the emphatic and long "proved" declarations that iron, being heavier than water, would sink in water and that machines heavier than air could not fly through the air.

One needs to assume that certain forms of behavior and experience which differ from ordinary conscious awareness can, with common consent, be called hypnosis. With this achieved, there can then be a systematic study of the various individual items of manifestation. This would be far more fruitful than formulating an all-comprehensive definition of a set of phenomena occurring in a human being, especially since these phenomena are little understood and manifested by a human personality infinitely less understood.

I wish to discuss two other matters pertaining to areas for research in hypnosis, both of which have been touched upon repeatedly more or less indirectly.

Foremost is the matter of how one should scientifically study hypnosis. It is not sufficient just to devise careful tests, measures, and procedures, and then apply them to phenomena to secure results. That is but a beginning, a means of discovering if a test may be useful. The testing of the specific gravity of iron against the specific gravity of water yielded no informative results in the matter of shipbuilding until the shape of the piece of iron became an essential part of the inquiry. And so it is with hypnosis. What are the tenuous shapes, forms, variations, and seemingly abstract considerations that will make possible concrete realizations? The readiness to accept, not to discard, to examine, not to disparage, each item of behavior that seems related to hypnosis is most important. We need to take the attitude that there are things we do not know or understand, and because we do not understand them, we ought not attempt to offer comprehensive formulations of hypnosis as a total phenomenon, but rather endeavor to identify manifestations as such and examine their relation to each other.

Finally there is another area of vital importance for research both in the clinic and the laboratory. This is the matter of induction of hypnosis. Throughout the ages there has been a dependence upon, and an adherence to, formalized, ritualized, traditional methods of trance induction, as if hypnosis were a phenomenon dependent upon the utterance of certain words in a certain order while the subject sits in a certain position and physically performs certain designated acts. Too often it is completely overlooked that hypnosis, like physiological sleep, is a process of behavior that can occur under a great variety of circumstances. Physiological sleep is likely to occur most easily when lying in bed, but it can occur in a lecture room, while driving a car, or when helplessly angry with another person. It is what actually occurs during physiological sleep that is important, not the externalities, even though externalities of all kinds can be significant. So it is with hypnosis. Induction procedures are of service, but the question remains, "What is it that does occur when hypnosis develops?" The induction procedure provides a setting, and only a setting, in which hypnosis may develop; it offers a period of time during which it develops; it offers various distractions to absorb the attention of the subject while hypnosis occurs; but the question is, "What is it that actually takes place within the subject while the operator busies himself with a ritualistic recitation of a learned formula of procedure?"

This is an area of research that is of tremendous importance in determining the scientific nature and character of hypnosis itself. However, all attempts to study hypnosis in relation to eye fixation or body relaxation are simply confusing; they are like attempting to study physiological sleep in terms of (1) a hospital bed, (2) a studio chair, etc.

Hypnosis itself, what processes occur within the subject, in what manner the body alters its usual functioning, and out of what experiential learnings of the past the body so learned to function, all constitute a part of the exceedingly rich field for research in hypnosis.

In brief, we need to look upon research in hypnosis not in terms of what we can think and devise and hypothesize, but in terms of what we can, by actual observation and notation, discover about the unique, varying, and fascinating kind of behavior that we can recognize as a state of awareness that can be directed and utilized in accord with inherent but unknown laws.

34. The Experience of Interviewing in the Presence of Observers

Milton H. Erickson

The experience of interviewing two psychiatric patients in the presence of observers and of attempting to induce hypnotic trances in them with the knowledge at the time that my efforts were being filmed for subsequent critical analysis by highly qualified persons constituted an interesting project for me. The primary consideration for me was the execution of the proposed task as adequately as possible. My own personal emotions were considered neither important nor relevant.

The emotional reactions of my patients, however, in relation to me, to the interview, to the hypnosis, to the surroundings, to the attendant circumstances, or deriving from their own psychiatric condition, were all considered to be a proper part of the proposed study. Therefore it would be a part of my responsibilities to be as aware as possible of the patients' various emotional states, to direct and to utilize them in such fashion that the patients' attention and interest would be directed to me rather than elsewhere.

The proposed experimental procedure definitely interested me. It offered an opportunity to deal with a patient in an entirely new kind of situation that could be recorded most effectively for future and for independent study. It was also a situation that the patient presumably could comprehend to a considerable extent and to which he could quite conceivably react in a variety of interesting ways. Also, the proposed procedure gave rise in my mind to recurrent, curious questions of what manner of affective, sympathetic, and empathic responses the observers, immediate and subsequent, would make which were comparable or related to those I would experience in the actual work situation with the patient. As it later developed, now and then when I experienced one or another reaction to my patient, there would recur, momentarily only and not as a distraction, the curious question of what, if anything, the observer could possibly sense of a comparable character.

My mental set in approaching the task was that of discovering what I could understand of the patient's behavior and what I could do about it or with it. The fact that I was under observation was of no concern to me, however primary

---

Reprinted with permission from L. A. Gottschalk and A. H. Auerback, *Methods of Research in Psychotherapy*. New York: Appleton-Century-Crofts, 1966, pp. 61-63.

that fact might be to the observers. My task was that of observing the patient and working with him, not speculating about the possible activities of others.

To begin, my first procedure was to make a visual and auditory survey of the interview situation. I wanted to know what my patient could see and hear and how a shift of his gaze or a change of his position would change the object content of his visual field. I was also interested in the various sounds, probable, possible, and inclusive of street noises, that could intrude upon the situation. I inquired about the age, height, weight, and sex of my patient, and I tested various possible seating arrangements to check relative physical comfort, the possibilities of adequate recording, and the predominant content of the patient's general field of vision. I also inquired about any special accommodations to be made to meet the requirements of the recording apparatus. As a measure of more adequately understanding my patient's possible reactions to the observers, I made special inquiries about their positioning. Since one observer (Dr. G.) was there by special request, I felt he should be placed so that he would have the least possible effect upon the others present.

Upon the arrival of my patient I immediately became intensely absorbed in the task confronting me. Occasionally I would feel momentarily oppressed by a sense of having only a limited time, followed by a strong need not to let my patient sense that hurried feeling. Now and then I became aware that I had been so attentive to my patient that I had forgotten where I was, but I would comfortably and instantly reorient myself. On at least three occasions I became momentarily puzzled by a pair of glasses on the side of the room toward which I was facing. Each time I was astonished to discover them on a face and then to recognize the face as that of Dr. G.

Now and then I felt an urgent need to give some brief recognition to the immediate environment in some casual way so that my patient would not be given the impression of an intentional avoidance. One other intense emotional reaction on my part concerned the use of my cane at a moment when I moved it rather ostentatiously. My purpose was to force the patient to give his attention to the cane and thereby to effect a displacement of his hostility from me to the cane. As this was being done, the thought flashed into my mind that perhaps the observers would not understand the purposefulness of the maneuver. There was an immediate feeling of strong dismay that this irrelevant thinking might have altered adversely the manner in which the cane was being moved. This emotional concern vanished upon noting that the patient was responding adequately.

At the close of the first interview I felt no particular fatigue and I was as interested in seeing the next patient as I had been in seeing the first. At the close of the second interview I had an immediate sensation of great fatigue, physical and mental, but this passed promptly. It was followed by a distressing feeling that I might have worked my patients too hard, but this was replaced by a feeling that I had completed a much longer and much more difficult task than I had realized at the outset. I then felt highly pleased that an experimental approach with adequate recording was being made to the difficult subjective, intuitive, interpersonal relationship that exists in the clinical interview. As I completed this thought, a sudden wave of recollections surged through my mind. Throughout both interviews, as I noted each item of behavior, each fleeting change of expressions on my patients' faces, I had comforted myself by thinking, "But I can have a second look at that." This was later mentioned to Dr. G. in discussing the experimental project.

I consider this sound-film recording of a physician-patient interview to be a most valuable research procedure for investigating what constitutes an interpersonal relationship. It offers an opportunity to secure a fixed and reliable record of the actual occurrences, both pertinent and incidental, that record being in no way itself subject to alterations by mood, memory, bias, or any other behavioral force. Furthermore this record is impartial in its treatment of both the interviewer and the interviewed, and there can be no weighting or shading of the evidence in the record itself. It also permits a sharp and informative contrast with data obtained from the same situation by trained observers, and it should reveal much concerning the nature and character of human error.

Of exceeding value is the sound-film in recording those qualitative variables of interpersonal communication such as facial expressions, gestures, intonations, inflections, mispronunciations, changes of tempo, and all the other minimal but effective modifications of speech that carry significant meanings. A sound-film is of particular value since it permits at any time a review, again and again, of any minimal manifestations, which is what I meant when, during the interviews, I comforted myself by the thought, "But I can have a second look." In the actual clinical situation responses are often made in minimal fashion and similarly sensed; often the entire process of communication is unconscious, and a sudden irruption into the conscious mind may complete a long process of unrecognized communication. Also of great significance is the fact that the sound-film permits the participant to discover many things which he did unwittingly, unconsciously, and even perhaps with no realization that he could manifest that manner or kind of behavior. I know that in the situation of dealing with patients I often wish I knew exactly what I was doing and why, instead of feeling, as I know I did with both patients, that I was acting blindly and intuitively to elicit an as yet undetermined response with which, whatever it was, I would deal.

In brief, this method of recording the interactions between selected people in a chosen setting offers a rich potential for understandings of extensive value for both therapist and patient.

REFERENCES

Ackerly, S. Instinctive, emotional and mental changes following prefrontal lobe extirpation. *American Journal of Psychiatry*, 1935, *92*, 717-729.

Barnett, L. *The universe and Dr. Einstein*. New York: William Sloane Associates, 1950.

Brickner, R. *The intellectual functions of the frontal lobes—a study based upon observation of a man after partial bilateral lobectomy*. New York: Macmillan, 1936.

Brickner, R. An aspect of the physiology of intellect, illustrated by Jacksonian seizures. *Bulletin of the Neurological Institute of New York*, 1938, *7*, 245-259.

Brickner, R. Conscious inability to synthesize thought in a case of right frontal tumor and lobectomy. *Archives of Neurology and Psychiatry*, 1939, *41*, 1166-1179. (a)

Brickner, R. Factors in the neural bases of intellect and emotion. *Yale Journal of Biological Medicine*, 1939, *11*, 547-556. (b)

Brickner, R. A human cortical area producing repetitive phenomena when stimulated. *Journal of Neurophysiology*, 1940, *3*, 128-130.

Brickner, R., Rosner, A., and Munro, R. Physiological aspects of the obsessive state. *Psychosomatic Medicine*, 1940, *2*, 369-383.

Cooper, L. Time distortion in hypnosis: I. *Bulletin of the Georgetown University Medical Center*, 1948, *1*, 214-221.

Cooper, L. Time distortion in hypnosis, with a semantic interpretation of the mechanism of certain hypnotically induced phenomena. *Journal of Psychology*, 1952, *34*, 257-284.

Cooper, L., and Erickson, M. Time distortion in hypnosis: II. *Bulletin of the Georgetown University Medical Center*, 1950, *4*, 50-68.

Cooper, L., and Erickson, M. *Time Distortion in hypnosis*. Baltimore: Williams & Wilkins, 1959.

Cooper, L., and Rodgin, D. Time distortion in hypnosis and nonmotor learning. *Science*, 1952, *115*, 500-502.

Cooper, L., and Tuthill, C. Time distortion in hypnosis and motor learning. *Journal of Psychology*, 1952, *34*, 67-76.

Erickson, M. The investigation of a specific amnesia. *British Journal of Medical Psychology*, 1933, *13*, 143-150.

Erickson, M. A study of an experimental neurosis hypnotically induced in a case of ejaculatio praecox. *British Journal of Medical Psychology*, 1935, *15*, 34-50.

Erickson, M. Development of apparent unconsciousness during hypnotic reliving of a traumatic experience. *Archives of Neurology and Psychiatry*, 1937, *38*, 1282-1288.

Erickson, M. A study of clinical and experimental findings on hypnotic deafness: I. Clinical experimentation and findings. *Journal of General Psychology*, 1938, *19*, 127-150. (a)

Erickson, M. A study of clinical and experimental findings on hypnotic deafness: II. Experimental findings with a conditioned response technique. *Journal of General Psychology*, 1938, *19*, 151-167. (b)

Erickson, M. An experimental study of regression. Address delivered before the American Psychiatric Association in Chicago, 1939. (a)

Erickson, M. Demonstration of mental mechanisms by hypnosis. *Archives of Neurology and Psychiatry*, 1939, *42*, 367-370. (b)

Erickson, M. Experimental demonstration of the psychopathology of everyday life. *Psychoanalytic Quarterly*, 1939, *8*, 338-353. (c)

Erickson, M. The induction of color blindness by a technique of hypnotic suggestion. *Journal of General Psychology*, 1939, *20*, 61-89. (d)

Erickson, M. The appearance in three generations of an atypical pattern of the sneezing reflex. *Journal of Genetic Psychology*, 1940, *56*, 455-459.

Erickson, M. The development of an acute limited obsessional hysterical state in a normal hypnotic subject. Address delivered before the Central Neuropsychiatric Association in Ann Arbor, 1941.

Erickson, M. A controlled experimental use of hypnotic regression in the therapy of an acquired food intolerance. *Psychosomatic Medicine*, 1943, *5*, 67-70. (a)

Erickson, M. Experimentally elicited salivary and related responses to hypnotic visual hallucinations confirmed by personality reactions. *Psychosomatic Medicine*, 1943, *5*, 185-187. (b)

Erickson, M. Hypnotic investigation of psychosomatic phenomena: Psychosomatic interrelationships studied by experimental hypnosis. *Psychosomatic Medicine*, 1943, *5*, 51-58. (c)

Erickson, M. Hypnosis in medicine. *Medical Clinics of North America*, 1944, *28*, 639-652.

Erickson, M. Hypnosis in painful terminal illness. *The American Journal of Clinical Hypnosis,* 1959, *1*, 117-121.

Erickson, M. The interspersal hypnotic technique for symptom correction and pain control. *American Journal of Clinical Hypnosis*, 1966, *8*, 189-209.

Erickson, M., and Brickner, R. The development of aphasia-like reactions from hypnotically induced amnesias: experimental observations and a detailed case report. *Psychosomatic Medicine*, 1942, *4*, 59-66.

Erickson, M., and Erickson, E. The hypnotic induction of hallucinatory color vision followed by pseudo negative afterimages. *Journal of Experimental Psychology*, 1938, *22*, 581-588.

Erickson, M., and Erickson, E. Concerning the nature and character of post-hypnotic behavior. *Journal of General Psychology*, 1941, *24*, 95-133.

Erickson, M., and Kubie, L. The permanent relief of an obsessional phobia by means of communications with an unsuspected dual personality. *Psychoanalytic Quarterly*, 1939, *8*, 471-509.

Erickson, M., and Kubie, L. The successful treatment of a case of acute hysterical depression by a return under hypnosis to a critical phase of childhood. *Psychoanalytic Quarterly*, 1941, *10*, 583-609.

Foerster, O. Das operative Vorgehen bei Tumoren der Vierhügelgegend. Wien. klin. Woch., 41: 986, 1928.

Freeman, W., and Watts, J. *Psychosurgery*. Springfield, Ill.: Charles C.Thomas, 1942.

Hibler, F. An experimental investigation of negative after-images of hallucinated colors in hypnosis. *Journal of Experimental Psychology*, 1940, *27*, 45-57.

Huston, P., Shakow, D., and Erickson, M. A study of hypnotically induced complexes by means of the Luria technique. *Journal of General Psychology*, 1934, *11*, 65-97.

Inglis, N. Interview.

Landis, C., and Hunt, W. *The startle pattern*. New York: Farrar & Rinehart, 1939.

Milgram, S. Behavioral study of obedience. *Journal of Abnormal and Social Psychology*, 1963, *67*, 371-378.

Milgram, S. Issues in the study of obedience: A reply to Baumrind. *American Psychologist*, 1964, *19*, 848-852.

Milgram, S. Some conditions of obedience and disobedience to authority. *Human Relations*, 1965, *18*, 57-76.

Rhine, J. Interview.

Sawyer, W. *Mathematician's delight*. Middlesex, England: Penguin, 1943.

Schilder, P. Psychopathology of time. *Journal of Nervous and Mental Diseases*, 1936, *83*, 530-546.

Welch, L. The space and time of induced hypnotic dreams. *Journal of Psychology*, 1935-1936, *1*, 171-178.

SUBJECT INDEX

NAME INDEX